'Stephen Glover writes so well ... This book is a good read if ever there was one' – Peregrine Worsthorne in the *Evening Standard*

'An oddly moving, sad and occasionally savage book ... what comes out here builds up into an absorbing story of hurt and betrayal' – Magnus Linklater in the *Scotsman*

'*Paper Dreams* is stylishly written and often entertaining' – J. W. M. Thompson in *The Times*

'Beautifully, even exquisitely written. Glover is a master of comic timing' – Lynn Barber in the *Literary Review*

'Stephen Glover has written a vivid and exhilarating account' – Nicholas Coleridge in the *Independent on Sunday*

'*Paper Dreams* will become a classic of its genre' – Frank Johnson in the *Daily Telegraph*

Stephen Glover became a freelance journalist after leaving Oxford, and travelled widely in Africa. In 1978 he joined the *Daily Telegraph*, where he worked for seven years as a leader and feature writer, parliamentary sketch writer and book reviewer, before leaving to help found the *Independent*. He is now associate editor of the *Evening Standard*.

He is married to the actress Celia Montague. They have two sons and live in Oxford.

STEPHEN GLOVER

─────────────

PAPER DREAMS

PENGUIN BOOKS

PENGUIN BOOKS

Published by the Penguin Group
Penguin Books Ltd, 27 Wrights Lane, London W8 5TZ, England
Penguin Books USA Inc., 375 Hudson Street, New York, New York 10014, USA
Penguin Books Australia Ltd, Ringwood, Victoria, Australia
Penguin Books Canada Ltd, 10 Alcorn Avenue, Toronto, Ontario, Canada M4V 3B2
Penguin Books (NZ) Ltd, 182–190 Wairau Road, Auckland 10, New Zealand

Penguin Books Ltd, Registered Offices: Harmondsworth, Middlesex, England

First published by Jonathan Cape 1993
This revised edition published in Penguin Books 1994
1 3 5 7 9 10 8 6 4 2

Printed in England by Clays Ltd, St Ives plc

For Celia

For Celia

Contents

Contents

Preface to the Penguin Edition

Since *Paper Dreams* was first published in May 1993, a great deal has happened to the Independent newspaper and the Independent on Sunday. Though the outlines of impending doom might be discerned in the original edition, what could not be foreseen was the astonishing speed with which the edifice would collapse.

The book as it first appeared was a drama without a final act. I have now added a twelfth chapter which concentrates on the calamitous events of the last twelve months. This replaces the short postscript to the first edition. I was conscious, as I wrote the new chapter, that I was necessarily adopting a somewhat different style to that which I had employed in the preceding eleven chapters. *Paper Dreams* as it was written was inevitably a personal account by someone who had been intimately concerned with the founding and development of both Independent titles. The addendum is written more from the outside, though I have drawn on the help and advice of many friends and contacts still working for the papers.

For the first edition I drew on my own recollections, on personal notes and on many papers in my possession. Wherever conversations are recounted, they are as close as the author can recall to the precise words used. Because of the nature of the story I have not, as a rule, used other people's reminiscences, save where they accord with my own, but I did, in search of greater understanding, speak with many former colleagues at the Independent and the Independent on Sunday, as well as with others.

So many people have helped me in so many different ways to get to this point, and I am grateful to all of them. The list which follows is not exhaustive: Sebastian Faulks, Nicholas Garland, Jonathan Fenby, Stephen Fay, Mark Lawson, Alexander Chancellor, Christopher Gilbert, Patrick Marnham, Henry Porter, Andrew Brown, James Fergusson, Mike Stent, Francis Wheen, Michael Sheridan, John Carlin, Bibi Mowlam (Beazley), Kirstie Steele, David Lipsey, John Morrison, Jan Thompson, Christopher Huhne, Steve Conaway, Stephen Rose, Tom Attwood, Roy Greenslade, Alexander Games and Hilary Gibbs.

I was also grateful to Andreas Whittam Smith and Matthew Symonds for agreeing to talk to me about the early days of the Independent; to Bruce Fireman for helping me with several definitions of financial terms; to Justin Arundale, the Independent's librarian, for his unfailing and courteous help; to Geoff Smith and his staff at The British Newspaper Library at Colindale; and to Jane Bown, for digging out an old photograph of the three founders of the Independent. I would also like to thank Andrew Caldecott for his wise advice.

I am particularly grateful to Andrew Gimson, for making so many enlightening points about the book when it was in manuscript form, to David Godwin, my editor at Jonathan Cape, to Tony Lacey at Penguin, and to my agent, Gillon Aitken, for his support and belief. Above all, I owe thanks without number to my wife Celia for her many brilliant editing suggestions and creative ideas.

Prologue

The Prime Minister Visits the
Second Eleven

On Wednesday March 20th 1991, John Major lunched with a small group of journalists at the Independent on Sunday. Such a visit was unprecedented at either the Independent or its young sister paper. Almost since its first issue in October 1986, the Independent had been lobbing grenades in the direction of Margaret Thatcher, and it was not likely that she would want to come and break bread with those whom she regarded as being among her persecutors. Mr Major, who had been Prime Minister for four months, had no cause for such sentiments, and he quickly accepted an invitation which Don Macintyre, our political editor, had sent on my behalf.

His visit was to be a watershed in the relations between the two newspapers, but he nearly did not turn up. On Monday the 18th Mr Major announced via his press secretary, Gus O'Donnell, that he would not be coming to lunch because he objected to an article which had appeared on the front page of the previous day's issue of the Independent on Sunday. This piece, written by Don Macintyre, had reported that when the Prime Minister arrived in Bermuda for an Anglo-American summit he 'looked tired enough to draw concerned enquiries from President Bush'. It quoted Mr Bush asking 'How's the weary traveller?' and 'Are you wiped out?' According to Mr O'Donnell, Mr Major did not think that the report was untrue, merely that it highlighted a trivial exchange. Mr O'Donnell suggested that if I, as editor of the Independent on Sunday, were to say that we were sorry, Mr Major might agree to come. I said that I could hardly apologise if there had been no error of fact, but I very much hoped that we would see him on Wednesday. Late on Tuesday afternoon Mr O'Donnell rang me again to say that the Prime Minister had decided to come after all, 'though you may find that he is not his usual jolly self.'

Each twist and turn in this odd little mating dance I related to Andreas Whittam Smith, editor of the Independent and chief executive of Newspaper Publishing plc, the parent company of both titles. He seemed much amused. Andreas had known about the impending lunch for a couple of weeks, but I had decided not to ask him, nor anyone else from the Independent.

It was an agreeable and informative lunch, though at first Mr Major was touchy. When he arrived in the dining room I conducted him to the window which has a commanding view of the City of London.

'What a dull view,' he commented.

'And there,' I said, pointing down nine floors to the cemetery which is overlooked by our building, 'is Bunhill Fields.'

'Oh, yes?'

'Yes. It's where people like William Blake and Daniel Defoe and John Bunyan and the hymn writer Isaac Watts are buried. . . . It used to be a graveyard for nonconformists.'

'I think I would have guessed that,' he said sharply.

After this, things began to improve, though there was a temporary relapse when Mr Major raised what he described as 'that malicious piece'.

'It wasn't malicious,' I said.

'Yes it was. It was pure malice.'

'Well, it might have been mischievous,' I conceded, and we settled for that. Mr Major appeared then to forget the offending article, and spoke candidly and fluently about the poll tax, the effects of the Gulf war, his cordial relations with the German Chancellor, Helmut Kohl, and his more workaday dealings with President Mitterrand. He had formed a very low view of Boris Yeltsin. Andrew Gimson, our political columnist, referred to 'Mrs Thatcher's last interview'. 'Can you assure me it was her last?' Mr Major quickly interjected. He described Sir Alan Walters, her economics guru, as 'a very good third world transport economist'.

Later that evening Alexander Chancellor, editor of the Independent Magazine, came into my room and helped himself to a whisky. He was in a jolly mood.

'Well, the talk on the Independent is only about the Prime Minister's visit.'

'Is it?'

'Yes, I suppose it's quite funny really. Poor Peter Jenkins is hopping mad. He said that he could not believe that no one from the Independent had been asked, and that it was more or less an insult to Andreas not to ask him. He told Andreas that.'

'But he must have known that Andreas knew all about the lunch. I've even given him an account of it.'

'Did Andreas know? Peter didn't seem to have grasped that. He kept saying I can't understand Stephen. And then he said: the Prime Minister has come all this way to meet the Second Eleven when he could have met the First.'

'I see,' I said. This seemed a little bit rough. The Independent was selling just a fraction over 400,000 and the Independent on Sunday, a little over a year old, was selling just under.

'Do you think I should have invited Andreas or Peter?' I asked Alexander.

'I don't know,' he replied. 'I suppose you might have done if you had felt able to.'

Why had I not? Mr Major had accepted an invitation from the Independent on Sunday and would probably not have expected to meet journalists from its sister paper with whom he could lunch separately if he so wished. Even so, I might have asked Andreas or Matthew Symonds, the Independent's deputy editor, or Peter Jenkins if I had felt that they would have added something to the occasion. I had observed at other lunches that Andreas and Peter tended to dominate the proceedings, which can impede a politician from talking frankly and openly, as is the purpose of such occasions. On one occasion at lunch Matthew had told Michael Howard, secretary of state for employment, that he felt insulted by the minister's views on training.

Some of my friends criticised me later for not asking one or more of my Independent colleagues, but the truth is that I had simply not wanted them there. Some journalists on the Independent thought that the lunch was an open flaunting of the Sunday paper's separateness, but this was not so. Many got the impression that Andreas had not even known about the lunch.

One evening a few days later I had a drink with Matthew Symonds in his room. He told me that following the Prime Minister's visit Andreas was 'in a strange mood' and was complaining to him that he wanted to become more involved with the Sunday newspaper. I replied that I always took Andreas's advice very seriously. Matthew said that Andreas wanted 'to take some meetings' on the Sunday paper. This was an old demand which I had previously resisted. It seemed to me that an editor should be allowed to edit unless he were not thought to be up to the job, in which case he should be sacked.

'Even Rupert Murdoch doesn't try to edit his papers,' I told Matthew, 'and Andreas doesn't own this company.' His shareholding was about 9 per cent.

'You're a hopeless romantic!' Matthew exclaimed. 'You've got such an old-fashioned notion of editorship. Because of the nature of this company you have less power as an editor but you have more as a director.' Matthew reminded me that at the beginning of its life I had edited the Independent Magazine before handing over to Alexander Chancellor.

'Yes, but the difference is that I told Alexander that I would leave after six weeks and that's exactly what happened, whereas Andreas would never leave.'

'He would lose interest after a time.'

My reluctance to let Andreas take editorial meetings at the Independent on Sunday did not arise simply from what Matthew regarded as my romantic notion of editorship. It had much to do with my view of Andreas, which had changed a great deal since 1985, when Matthew and I had joined him to plan the launch of the Independent. Though Andreas had played almost no editorial part in the genesis and development of the Independent on Sunday, he was apparently proposing that he should be allowed to run it at a time when most observers thought that the newspaper was good and getting better.

I did not believe that he had any magic key to boosting its circulation.

We talked for about half an hour. Matthew kept on repeating 'I think you are making a big mistake.'

As I left, he said, 'Good luck, anyway.'

This sounded ominous.

1

Escaping From the Mist Man

I see Andreas Whittam Smith, back in the old days of Fleet Street that have faded almost into pre-history, moving between the Daily Telegraph and his own office by St Paul's Cathedral where he presided as the newspaper's City editor. He appeared to glide down Fleet Street with the dignity of a great old battle-ship, as though his unbending legs were being propelled along the surface of water by some hidden motor. Once, with a sudden graceful movement calculated not to undermine the impression of a stately progress, he rose an inch or two on to the platform of a slowly moving bus.

Everyone at the Daily Telegraph was interested in Andreas Whittam Smith, since he was by common consent the man most likely to be the next editor of the newspaper. In those days – I am speaking of 1978 – there was a recurring topic of discussion among Telegraph journalists gathered in El Vino, a wine bar patronised by hacks and lawyers, or the King and Keys, a hellish pub where few, save Telegraph printers and hardy journalists, dared to venture. The talk was of how long Bill Deedes, the editor, would survive *in situ*. In the event he lasted another eight years, and Andreas Whittam Smith never became editor.

Most afternoons I encountered Andreas at closer quarters when he and other senior newspaper executives poured out of the editor's room to make way for a motley crew of leader writers lounging in the outer office, of whom I was one.

Andreas seemed almost permanently swathed in a long dark grey overcoat. He looked like an old-fashioned bishop, or possibly archdeacon, the more so, as Sue Davy, Bill Deedes's secretary, pointed out, because of his ruddy, port drinker's complexion. He is, in fact, the son of a canon. Many years later I learnt that his appearance owes nothing to alcohol, which he takes sparingly, and I became something of an expert on the changing hues – not only red, but magenta and a kind of chalky grey – which mark his shifting moods.

Out of shyness or mutual indifference we did not speak to each other in those days. I was a young man in my middle twenties and Andreas was a well-established journalist in his early forties. Until he asked me seven years later to join him and Matthew Symonds in planning a new quality daily newspaper, we didn't exchange more than a couple of hundred words. Occasionally we would mumble hello to each other, rather than merely nod, as he levitated his way through the editor's outer office. Once, possibly thinking I might be a rising star, he asked me to lunch at his City headquarters where, sitting in his tiny room, his guests grappled with pre-cooked chicken. Another time, after I had written a series of articles about Africa, Andreas hovered for a moment in the outer office to compliment me.

The first proper conversation I had with him took place in the drawing room of his Kensington house in June 1985. Matthew Symonds, a colleague on the Telegraph who had arranged the meeting, was also there. Andreas's domestic appearance was surprising: the clerical garb had been jettisoned in favour of an open-neck shirt and pullover. He had not lost his episcopal dignity, a sense that every action and gesture was somehow deliberative, but he seemed a little nervous, perhaps because he was about to appear in the role of a conspirator in front of someone who was, after all, an employee of the Daily Telegraph, as was he himself. He gave me a whisky in an antique glass and bade me sit down and, with an almost sheepish grin, began to speak.

'Matthew tells me that he has already told you about our progress.'

'Yes. We had lunch . . .'

'Well, we think, as Matthew will have indicated, that there is a market gap for a new quality newspaper.'

Andreas's description of the as yet unnamed newspaper was sketchy and in some respects bore no resemblance to what appeared on the news stands sixteen months later. His vision was of a paper competing with the Daily Telegraph, hovering between the quality and tabloid markets, with many pages of colour. He said that newspapers had not fully adapted to the fact that most people got their news from television, and so the new newspaper would carry news summaries and lots of longer analytical pieces which would explain, as television usually didn't, what lay behind the news. The paper would not be aligned to any political party and it would carry several pages of arts and television listings, which were believed to be of particular appeal to younger readers.

'Well, tell me Stephen, what do you think?' asked Andreas.

The answer was that I thought there was a dreamlike quality to his account, as if he were reeling off lists of things in which he did not wholly believe. I also thought that Matthew was one of the world's most unlikely budding press magnates. This was not a hasty judgment. I had known him since we were both at Oxford some ten years earlier.

'I think it all sounds very interesting.'

Every journalist dreams of starting a newspaper and most talk about it. How many brave young Northcliffes, inspired in El Vino, have discussed their plans to transform the British newspaper industry. I looked at Andreas in his drawing room and wondered whether he was the stuff of greatness, whether he even looked like a potential newspaper editor. I compared him in my mind with Bill Deedes, the only editor whom I knew well, and I thought how direct, how innocent almost, Andreas seemed.

His idea to launch a newspaper, as I learnt not that night in his drawing room but soon afterwards, had its genesis three months previously. An American magazine journalist had telephoned him to ask whether he thought Eddie Shah's planned newspaper Today would succeed. Almost without thinking, Andreas said that it wouldn't, but when he put down the receiver he thought again. Why shouldn't Shah prosper if he could take full advantage of the significantly lower costs of new technology and reduced manning levels? And if Shah could successfully launch a paper into the middle market why couldn't someone do the same in the quality market? He went to see a friend called Graham Walsh, head of corporate finance at Morgan Grenfell, to ask him whether in principle it would be possible to raise money for such a venture. The answer was yes. He then rang the advertising tycoon Maurice Saatchi, whom he knew slightly, and received some encouragement. Saatchi referred him to one of his senior executives, John Perriss, with whom Andreas and Matthew spent several hours talking about the new newspaper. They developed with Perriss the notion of a 'gap in the market' consisting of young, affluent, politically uncommitted people.

That night in Andreas's house we scarcely discussed new ideas. Andreas asked me about how a new newspaper might handle books (at that time I reviewed novels for the Telegraph) and foreign coverage, about which he might vaguely have considered me an expert. I said that, except in the most important countries, one could save a lot of money by relying on news agencies such as Reuters rather than one's own correspondents. Nor, where it was important to have correspondents, was there any need to lavish money on their offices. I had in mind the Telegraph's elegant bureau in Paris, in the *premier arrondissement* just by the Hotel Meurice, where there were two correspondents, an office manager, a man who made the tea, a woman who cut and filed the newspapers and a ravishing girl who operated the telex machine.

Andreas sat bolt upright, legs crossed, with a reporter's notebook perched on one knee, into which he assiduously wrote much of what I said, as though he was in the presence of a newspaper genius rather than an extemporising journalist. 'Yes, yes,' he would say at each new point, nodding his head vigorously. I said that one-sentence paragraphs in news stories should be avoided, and he solemnly wrote down what I had said.

Before Matthew and I left, it was agreed that I should think further about how best to cover books and foreign news in the newspaper. Matthew would produce a paper about home news coverage and sport and Andreas would consider the financial pages. We would meet again quite soon. Then, as we reached the bottom of the stairs, Andreas turned to me and said shyly, 'It's a lot less lonely with three than two.' And so the three of us became partners.

*

I was baffled as to why, after so slight an acquaintance and with so little personal knowledge, Andreas chose me. Equally perplexing was his choice of Matthew.

Matthew had become a leader writer on the Daily Telegraph in 1981. He later wrote a fortnightly economics column on Andreas's City pages, and the two of them struck up something of a friendship. They talked of what they might do to improve the Telegraph if Andreas became editor. (Matthew would naturally be his deputy. He told me later that he had 'hitched his wagon to Andreas'.) They also discussed a way of rescuing the Telegraph from impending insolvency by raising extra capital through inviting readers to buy shares in the newspaper. As late as May 1985, Andreas put this promising idea to Lord Hartwell, the proprietor of the Daily Telegraph, who consulted his financial advisers and turned it down. Seven months later Hartwell lost control of the Telegraph to a Canadian tycoon called Conrad Black.

At the time of our first meeting in June, Andreas and Matthew were still pursuing what Matthew, with his love of military metaphor, particularly with a nuclear resonance, later called a 'twin-track policy'. One track led to Andreas being editor, and Matthew deputy editor, of the Daily Telegraph. The other track led to the same relationship on a new paper.

I had met Matthew at Oxford, though we didn't become friends then. He was an outsider, often to be found in the college rooms of James Fergusson, who later became obituaries editor of the Independent. I also encountered him occasionally in the offices of Isis, the university magazine. Much of his life at Oxford revolved around his car, a sporty red French coupé, which he drove with extraordinary abandon. He was an unusual creature, with carefully coiffured, bouffant hair and Cuban heels, whose purpose was to boost his perfectly average height. He frequently wore dark glasses. At Oxford, and for a long time afterwards, he had a bad stammer. When this was at its worst he would go into a kind of spasm as he wrestled the words out of his mouth. As he has grown in success and confidence his stammer has virtually disappeared, but at an awkward moment it can momentarily return and the wrestling resume.

After Oxford I did not see much of Matthew but afterwards, at intervals of between six months and a year, he would ring up and propose lunch or dinner. As time went on, these became for me increasingly gloomy affairs. One evening he came to my flat in London in a particularly dejected mood.

'God, Stephen. I feel so depressed,' he said, as he came through the door, wearing his winter plumage of a dark blue overcoat and carrying as usual a Samsonite briefcase and black rolled umbrella.

Matthew had a job working for the syndication department of the Financial Times which involved churning out articles for foreign clients which were generally not published in his own newspaper. He felt, I am sure rightly, that this somewhat unglamorous job did not do justice to his talents, and he asked me whether there were any vacancies at the Telegraph. For the first time I experienced the enjoyment of exerting patronage, albeit at one remove. There was, if not a job at least an opening, and subtle lobbying of Bill Deedes by my friend and colleague Peter Utley (whom Matthew also knew) did the trick. So Matthew became economics leader writer of the Daily Telegraph, and his ascent began.

*

Not long after I joined the Daily Telegraph an old hand called Rod Junor told me a story which I half believed, and even now do not wholly discount. According to him, there was a personage called the Mist Man. Naturally the Mist Man had a deputy for holidays and days off, of which there would have been many. Every evening, between bouts of drinking at the King and Keys, the Mist Man would go up to the sixth floor of the Daily Telegraph and survey the shining world beneath. If he could discern so much as a pocket of mist loitering in some forgotten glade he would inform the appropriate father of the chapel who would 'call out' the drivers until management, anxious lest the paper should not be distributed, paid over mist money.

This story, if not true in fact, has a kind of symbolic truth. The Telegraph of those days was a monument to laziness and general shirking. If, for example, you ordered a new bulb for your anglepoise light you would expect to wait two or three weeks. A couple of burly men in blue overalls would eventually come into your office, carrying a large step ladder. They would gaze at the defunct electric light bulb as though it contained a dollop of nuclear waste and then, with much admonitory muttering, they would gingerly remove the dangerous article, only to discover that they had forgotten to bring a new bulb. Naturally it would cause a strike if you bought a bulb yourself and simply inserted it, so you waited until the same burly men returned with their ladder, and possibly a bulb.

Many Telegraph journalists, though they had cause for complaint about overmanning and inefficiencies, were themselves spoilt children in this *laissez-faire* world. When I was taken on by Bill Deedes as a leader writer I discovered that I was one of a team of eight who between them were expected to produce three short editorials a day, each of about 330 words. That made 17 editorials a week (there being only two on Saturday) or an average of fractionally over two editorials per leader writer per week – slightly more if you account for holidays and other prolonged absences. One or two leader writers occasionally exceeded this testing average, and so it was possible to write only one or even no editorials in a week.

The skill of 'dodging' an unlooked for editorial had been honed to a fine art by some of the leader writers at their conference which had been thoughtfully fixed by Bill Deedes at 3.45 pm, allowing them to spend the morning at home before enjoying an unhurried lunch with a politician, fellow journalist or girlfriend.

'Well,' Bill would say after half an hour's enjoyable discussion about the American presidential elections, directing his comments at Michael Hilton, one of the foreign affairs leader writers, 'what about a leader?' Michael would screw up his face as though someone had pricked him on a tender spot. 'Nah, I don't think so,' he would reply. 'We wrote about the US last week.' Discussion might then turn to domestic politics and after a while Bill would repeat the same tack. 'Peter, would you like to have a go?' This comment was directed at the venerable blind journalist T. E. Utley, known always as Peter. 'Delighted to,' he would reply, 'but I don't know whether I am the best equipped to write on this particular subject.' It was, however, a point of honour in this game never actually to suggest an alternative leader writer by name.

The Telegraph offered a kind of intellectual idyll. There might not be very much work, but everywhere there was talk, and at the fountainhead stood Peter Utley. I had met him the day I joined the Telegraph and he greeted me like a long-lost friend. He was not very far short of sixty, a wise and practised journalist, a monument to high Toryism. I was young and ignorant, yet still he treated me as an equal. He helped many young journalists by exposing them to an intellectual rigour which few had encountered at university. There was no obligation to subscribe to his politics. He taught young people better to understand and express their own thoughts, and gave them constant encouragement tempered by elegant criticism. 'Dear boy! *Beautiful* article,' he might say, 'though I'm not sure you used the word "refute" absolutely correctly.'

The younger leader writers would gather in Peter's room for tea after the leader conference. Here we might discuss the future of the paper or Lord Hartwell or Bill Deedes. For a period we became quite obsessed with some silly word game until Peter's questions were judged too obscure. On other occasions we would improve, under Peter's guidance, the argument for an as yet unwritten editorial, which the conference had left suspended in mid-air. Sometimes Peregrine Worsthorne, then a columnist on the Sunday Telegraph, later its editor, would come into Peter's room to seek his advice for his column. Peter would stand there, blind, oracular, magnificent, applying his abiding political precepts to the problems of the day. Perry, a brilliant star in his own firmament, was in Peter's galaxy a satellite to his glorious sun.

Presiding over the idyll was the puckish figure of Bill Deedes. Bill had been a Conservative member of parliament, and, briefly, a cabinet minister, but for all that he was one of the most unassuming men I had ever met. The Deedes family fortune had fallen somewhat from its glorious apogee. As a politician, Bill had witnessed first-hand the breathtaking decline of British power after the second world war. Both these factors seemed to have persuaded him that everything was bound to decline, and the Telegraph, with its rapacious unions, weak management and constant strikes must have been for him a perfect paradigm of his world view. He saw his task as creating a little pool of tranquillity for himself and his personal staff – the leader writers – insulated from these destructive forces, and for a time he succeeded. He was not much interested in the exercise of power: indeed, his editorial control over most of the newspaper was slight. Once, when I was trying to goad him into action, he said to me almost tartly: 'Stephen, I have never given an order on this newspaper, and I'm not going to start now.'

Lord Hartwell, referred to by Bill as 'the proprietor' or, in softer mood, as 'Lord H', was not really one for giving orders either. He was the second son of a self-made man, William Berry, the first Viscount Camrose, but he appeared and acted as though his family had been paternalistic grandees since before the Norman Conquest. If this tendency had been an affectation of youth, age had rendered the performance utterly sincere. Lord Hartwell was what he seemed: gracious, kind and reserved to the point of extreme shyness. An encounter in the lift was a tribulation for both parties. He probably knew who you were – once every year or so he would ask you to a bewilderingly embarrassing lunch on the fifth floor, where he had rooms decked out like a gentleman's club – and of course you would recognise this unique character anywhere. His tailor had contrived to lose him in a 1930s' time-warp, and with a stiffened collar and narrow tie, Lord H had added a couple of authentic touches of his own. If your eyes should by unhappy accident catch his as the lift creaked heavenwards, he would mumble apologetically and you would mumble back. Both parties understood that to avoid such exchanges it was advisable to assume a kind of zombie-like trance.

Although Lord Hartwell was at most a 'wet' Tory with alleged leanings towards the SDP, so far as the editorial line of his newspaper was concerned he was, as in so many other matters, the prisoner of his employees – here the leader writers. Peter Utley, though not an unstinting admirer of the 'Manchester Liberalism' of Mrs Thatcher, naturally came to the support of the Conservative government, save when it had in his view blundered in Northern Ireland, in which case he was a sophisticated and fervent upholder of the unionist interest. Charles Moore, a leader writer before he went to the Spectator magazine where he soon became editor, was also disposed to take the party line. The most Thatcherite, as opposed to Conservative, of the leader writers were Frank Johnson, John O'Sullivan, and Colin Welch, the deputy editor. Being somewhat iconoclastic by nature, these three were eager to lash ministers who appeared to deviate from the true path. Another leader writer, Jock Bruce-Gardyne, actually became for a time a middle-ranking treasury minister during part of Mrs Thatcher's first administration.

Whenever the government had got itself into an obvious pickle, so long as it had done wrong while trying to do right, the leader writers would sit around in Bill Deedes's room, brows furrowed, sucking their pencils, wondering how they would get Mrs Thatcher or Sir Geoffrey Howe or whoever off the hook. Matthew and I were regarded by some of our colleagues as being politically suspect. Matthew was a pretty overt supporter of the SDP, and for a time had an SDP sticker in the rear window of his car. I had Tory sympathies but no affection for the Conservative party. For all that, one was regarded by many strangers as being politically deviant for working for the Daily Telegraph. At dinner parties disclosure that one was employed by the newspaper would draw the same frosty looks as an openly admitted association with the Ku-Klux-Klan.

The greatest absurdity was that the paper which clamoured in its editorials for trade union reform had a management which was overborne by its own unions to the point where the unions themselves did much of the hiring. Our editorials urged governments to follow the ways of fiscal rectitude and yet money was spent within the Telegraph with little or no accountability.

It could not last for ever. Lord Hartwell and his managers were making a fatal noose for themselves – or perhaps his managers were making a fatal noose for Lord Hartwell. They had decided to build two new printing plants, one in London's dockland development, the other in Manchester, at a cost of over £100 million. They proposed also to introduce new technology which would involve redundancies costing nearly £40 million. The trouble was that no bank would lend them all this money, and what they couldn't obtain from the banks they were unable to raise entirely through a share placement. That was when, having brushed aside Andreas's proposal to sell shares to readers, they found themselves negotiating with Conrad Black. He agreed to invest £10 million but insisted on pre-emptive rights in the event of the issue of further shares. Seven months later, in December 1985, the Telegraph needed more money and Black got control. The old regime was finished.

To look back at the Telegraph is to describe a vanished world which existed only yesterday. I loved it but, like Andreas and Matthew and no doubt most journalists on the newspaper, grew increasingly exasperated by the strikes, the palpable inefficiencies and the errors of management. The Independent was born out of the disintegration of the Telegraph, and if Lord Hartwell could miraculously have stopped this disintegration, or even merely stemmed it, the new paper might not have been born at all. Yet the story seems to have had the unstoppable momentum of tragedy.

The Independent was the child of the Telegraph – but a child which did not wish to repeat the mistakes of its parent. Where the Telegraph had a powerless editor, the Independent was supposed to have a strong one;* where the Telegraph had no financial control, our paper would be run on tight budgets; where the Telegraph was printed on old presses in London by recalcitrant, overpaid printers, the Independent was going to be produced on new presses by sweet-tempered contract printers in the provinces. At the Independent everyone was expected to work, and nearly everyone did. Andreas, Matthew and myself were also determined that the new paper should not be shackled to any political party as the Telegraph had been to the Conservatives.

---

* I describe the paper as the Independent for the sake of convenience. It did not acquire its name until January 1986.

After Conrad Black acquired the Telegraph, it moved from 135 Fleet Street to the Isle of Dogs, and with the advantages of lower manning levels and new technology gradually became efficient and very profitable. Its building in Fleet Street, which looks rather like an Italian railway station raised in honour of Mussolini, was bought by Goldman Sachs, the American Bank. The Independent occupies a late 'fifties office block on the northern fringes of the City. There are no newspapers left in Fleet Street and its pubs no longer echo to journalists' voices.

★

After that meeting at Andreas's house, I felt that the new newspaper was probably a pipe dream. I said so to my wife, Celia, who urged me not to come to a hasty conclusion. I also spoke about the newspaper with my friend Nick Garland, the cartoonist on the Daily Telegraph, who attended editorial conferences and was therefore a kind of honorary leader writer. Indeed, when I had joined the Daily Telegraph I had assumed for several weeks that he was a real one. He would sit at the back of the room, sketching away, very occasionally throwing out a comment, and in the comic and disorderly setting of editorial conferences he had at first appeared to me merely as one of the more work-shy and eccentric of the leader writers.

Though he was good enough not to say that the idea was completely batty, Nick was clearly sceptical. We both knew that there had not been a new quality daily newspaper launched in Britain for as long as anyone could remember. And quite apart from the general implausibility of the idea, there was the question of Matthew. Though I felt some affection for him, it was the affection of the *cognoscenti*. I realised that traits which outsiders might find off-putting concealed a more endearing insecurity. Then there was the matter of secrecy. If the existence of our nascent triumvirate were to get out, the reaction on the part of the Telegraph bosses would not be one of unalloyed joy. Probably most of our colleagues would be struck with disbelief, even hilarity, but once that had subsided it would hardly be possible for us to stay at 135 Fleet Street.

But although I was tempted to let Andreas and Matthew get on with it by themselves, some deeper instinct took me back to

Andreas's house a week or two later. I had felt the first intimations of excitement.

Until early September Andreas and I were to some degree borne along by Matthew's enthusiasm. I had joined later. I did not find the editorial ideas particularly impressive. Andreas still had half an eye on the editorship of the Daily Telegraph since, to the extent that it was not yet certain that Conrad Black would acquire the paper, he remained the existing regime's most likely heir apparent. I did not think that that the new newspaper would happen if Andreas stayed at the Telegraph; the money could not be raised without his contacts and his knowledge of the City, which were possibly unrivalled among journalists. I wondered whether he would ever be capable of jumping into the dark. He was forty-eight and had a solid if unglamorous job paying him £40,000 a year plus car which he might not wish to give up even if the editorship of the Daily Telegraph eluded him. He had never, so far as I was aware, shown a flicker of entrepreneurial vigour. (I was wrong about this. He later told Celia that he had tried, and failed, to start two businesses.) Though on the surface he seemed confident enough, I detected in him as many reservations as I felt myself.

Matthew was different. He scurried hither and thither like some indefatigable terrier. His apparent lack of doubt was not bluster. Somehow he had risen above his own inner anxieties and was more of a true believer than either Andreas or myself. He was responsible for several of the early editorial ideas. It was Matthew, more often than not, who suggested an early date for our next meeting, and when the meeting came showed the greatest confidence, bravado almost, in discussing problems which lay ahead. It was Matthew who brought in Douglas Long, the former chief executive of Mirror Group Newspapers, to give us invaluable help – and later Lord Sieff who became our chairman. In these very early months Matthew played Octavius to Andreas's Mark Antony. I believe with something approaching certainty that without him the enterprise would have guttered and blown out in its infancy.

Our most important task throughout that summer was to work out whether our newspaper could make any money. If it could not, there would be no prospect of raising the necessary finance. The meetings we had during late June and July were largely about figures. We would meet in the evenings at Andreas's house, occasionally at Matthew's which was near Richmond, and try to work out how many copies we would have to sell. It was at this point that we realised how little we knew about the costs of newspaper production. Even Andreas, a City editor who had been a financial journalist for twenty-five years, knew practically nothing. He might have known about ICI's balance sheet or even the government's money supply figures, but he did not know what it cost to produce the Daily Telegraph, either because no one had told him (management and journalists being two separate breeds) or because he had not cared.

Matthew and I were even less informed, and the three of us might have remained becalmed in our ignorance had it not been for Matthew's wife, Alison, and Douglas Long. Alison was some sort of financial executive on the Financial Times and knew about editorial budgets. Andreas, Matthew and I slowly worked out how many journalists we required and Alison advised us as to how much money we needed to pay their salaries and employer's national insurance contributions, and provide them with offices, expenses, cars if applicable, and so forth. She also knew how much foreign correspondents cost the Financial Times. I assumed that ours would cost half as much, or less.

Douglas helped us in estimating production, distribution and paper costs. He had decided to retire from the Daily Mirror after Robert Maxwell bought the paper in 1984, though Maxwell had offered him the job of deputy chairman having sacked him as chief executive. He was in many ways a classic Fleet Street manager: wary of journalists (he had been one himself), apparently tough and hard-boiled, and inclined to a certain breeziness with detailed figures. But he was also a romantic at heart and, from the moment he was contacted by Matthew, Douglas smiled on the enterprise, even though he must privately have thought us a bunch of amateurs. Our idea was that he would be chairman of the new paper.

He had several ex-Daily Mirror connections: a former colleague called Ronald Cotton helped him with distribution costs. Douglas would produce bits of paper on which were scrawled rough costings, and with Alison's help we would try to build them into a general picture. I can see us sitting around Matthew's kitchen table in early July 1985. There is a bottle of whisky on the the table. Alison and Andreas are working with their pocket calculators; Andreas is upright, serious – concentrating as though this is as important as any work he has ever done. Matthew and I are looking on with some detachment, trying to predict the outcome of their calculations. Douglas is beaming on the proceedings, a little bored, a little sceptical. One hand is tapping gently on the table, the other is holding a tumbler of whisky. When he speaks it is in long rambling sentences that forget how they began and trail off before they end.

After several such meetings we concluded at a meeting in Andreas's house on August 8th that the breakeven of the newspaper – the point at which it would become profitable – was a little under 300,000 copies a day. Could we sell as many? None of us seemed to think that it was a fantastically high figure set alongside other quality papers. Over the previous six months The Times had sold an average of 479,000 copies a day, the Guardian an average of 487,000 copies and the Telegraph 1,221,000 copies. A circulation of 300,000 did not seem implausible. I was beginning to think that we might be able to do it.

*

Andreas went away on holiday to France in the middle of August and did not return until the beginning of September. Celia and I went off to our cottage in Shropshire. For a moment the project was suspended. This was its last chance to die without a struggle. Andreas must have spent much of his holiday thinking about the new newspaper. When he returned a change had come over him. His doubts were no longer obvious. He had decided to take the gamble.

What forces had moved him to make this decision? Some time after the launch of the Independent I asked Andreas's wife, Valerie, whether she had been surprised that the paper had succeeded. She appeared almost offended by the question.

'Of course I knew it would succeed. I never had any doubts.'

'Not even at the beginning?'

'Not even at the beginning. Did you?'

'Well . . .'

Perhaps it was Valerie who, on that holiday in France, stood like a Valkyrie by her husband's side and drove him on. Or perhaps he heard deeper voices of his own.

At forty-eight Andreas was quite old to be an entrepreneur. By this stage he could reasonably have assumed that he was destined to play no more than an important part in somebody else's drama. Apart from doing a two-year spell with the merchant bank N.M. Rothschild upon leaving Oxford, he had spent his entire career as a financial journalist in increasingly important positions on every quality newspaper in Fleet Street, and then as editor of the Investor's Chronicle. Andy Smith, turned down for officer training during National Service because he supposedly did not have leadership qualities, was gradually transmogrified into the dignified and aloof personage of Andreas Whittam Smith. In the early 'seventies he was laid low for several weeks by a serious and mysterious illness which was never diagnosed. He lost some weight and became a keen jogger. He had become City editor of the Daily Telegraph in 1977. This was a good job, but at that time, in the circles Andreas moved in, the Telegraph was about as unfashionable as it was possible for a paper to be. Its readers were thought to be excessively right-wing, and intellectually and socially below the salt.

For twenty-five years he had watched and written about other people making money without making an enormous amount of it himself. He had a pleasant terraced house in Kensington, which Matthew informed me with an almost proprietorial swagger was worth £400,000, acquired through careful management of his salary, occasional modest playing of the market and, I believe, a small legacy. But that was about it. He had spent his life writing about people not always obviously more intelligent or more knowledgeable about business, sometimes less so. And I think this must have rankled, as it would for many of us.

Part of him must have yearned for recognition outside those

people in the City who respected him as a good journalist. This was demonstrated by his subsequent behaviour when he embraced the famous and not quite so famous people into whose orbit he came as editor of the Independent. Not long after the launch of the paper, he mentioned how he had met and spoken with four cabinet ministers at a single party. He said this with such innocent and boyish glee that it was difficult to reproach him.

On Thursday September 11th 1985 I picked up Andreas at 8 o'clock in the morning at his home in Brunswick Gardens, and drove him in my car to Tamworth in Staffordshire to see Ron Cotton, Douglas Long's friend from Daily Mirror days. We discussed in the car how the new paper might satisfy the demands of an emerging group of people, as had the Daily Telegraph during the 1930s when that paper had increased its circulation tenfold. Eventually we arrived and found Ron in a sort of small warehouse on a windswept industrial estate, where he proceeded to unfold the wonders of newspaper distribution.

'Basically, the system has changed very little since 1911,' Ron informed us.

'Ah,' we said, having very little idea as to what system he was talking about.

Even when we left we did not really understand what the system was. It relied in those days on trains 'fanning out' from London and Manchester, where national newspapers were printed. This phrase of Ron's – 'fanning out' – was borrowed by Andreas and employed with professional insouciance at our first money-raising meetings two months later. Once the fanning out had gone according to plan, the papers were then picked up by some 400 wholesalers who in turn distributed them to some 40,000 retailers. I remained a little confused as to the distinction between a wholesaler and a retailer but thought it best not to press Ron on this point.

In those days the three of us were very much equals, even though Andreas was the senior journalist, and this was in part because Matthew, so often the driving force, could hardly be condescended to by Andreas. This must be a very typical human pattern: there is often a rough equality on the edge of any perilous journey; only arriving makes things different.

Twelve days after the visit to Tamworth, the three of us drove to Bradford in Andreas's Ford Granada Estate to see Hew Stephenson, then managing director of Westminster Press's printing plant. I had been ringing printers to ask whether they would be prepared to print our newspaper. Mr Stephenson had responded to my telephone call as though I was a renowned newspaper proprietor rather than one of three journalists without any money who were dreaming of starting a newspaper. The three of us were still working at the Daily Telegraph, and so that Matthew and I might arrive at work on time for our editorial conference in the afternoon we had to be at Bradford by 10.30. Matthew suggested that he and I stay the night at Andreas's house so as to make an early start. This was a plan born as much from his desire that we should feel enmeshed in the skeins of confederacy than from any practical consideration.

Timing turned out not to be a problem: Matthew was at the wheel. As we roared up a hill just short of Bradford a quarter of an hour early, we joked about how our newspaper delivery lorries might slither about in the snow blowing off the Pennines. Just over twelve months later, the Independent was being printed in Bradford.

Mr Stephenson welcomed us and showed us around his sparkling new plant. None of us knew anything about printing, but we were learning to nod in the right places. Then we adjourned to Mr Stephenson's office, where he managed to maintain the impression that he was well used to meeting journalists who were about to launch a new national newspaper.

'Tell me,' he said after Andreas had given him a potted version of our plans, 'which of you is going to be editor of this new newspaper?'

There was a silence. We all looked down. Of course the three of us knew perfectly well that Andreas was going to be editor and there wasn't the faintest dispute on the matter. However, Andreas was behaving like a boy on his first day at a new school.

'Well,' he said shyly after at least half a minute had passed. 'I suppose it's going to be me.'

And so we returned, this happy band, to London, Matthew and I to write editorials, and Andreas the lead story on the front page of the Daily Telegraph.

2

An Important Meeting in the
Tottenham Court Road

The first whiff of money came in the unlikely form of Tom
Attwood. He was small, softly spoken and gave the impression
of being permanently slightly stunned, as though he had just
been pulled through a hedge backwards and was still trying to
recover his composure. He would stretch out the bottom part of
his jaw as if to release his neck from some sort of restriction.
Tom worked for a small and relatively unknown City firm
called Stephen Rose and Partners which raised 'venture capital'
for 'start-ups'.

Tom was an old friend of Andreas's PA at the Telegraph,
Linda Tanner, and from time to time they met for lunch. At one
such lunch in August Linda asked him how one would set about
trying to raise £20 million. Even in the mid-'eighties this must
have been an unusual thing for a secretary to ask. Tom and
Andreas met on September 10th.

Stephen Rose and Partners turned out to be an inspired little
company but, because it was small, it had no side, no sense of its
own importance. Our deliberations around Andreas's and
Matthew's kitchen tables had produced only a few pages of
figures which, to use a word beloved of Matthew, were 'broad-
brush'. These 'financials' had not been wrung through a
computer model and would thus be almost worthless in City
eyes. Moreover, some of the assumptions behind the financials
were – another favourite word of Matthew's – 'flakey'.

Though like almost everyone else initially disbelieving, Tom did take us seriously. At first not everything ran smoothly. Matthew invited Tom and myself to dinner at his house, and Tom, emboldened a little by drink, suggested that Stephen Rose and Partners might be given a small share in the equity of the newspaper in part payment for their services. In due course they were, as was perfectly natural, but at this moment the suggestion drew forth an overbearing lecture from Matthew.

Tom told us that we would need some sort of selling document to raise the money. He had been playing about with his IBM and he seemed to like the figures that came out of it. One week he was a sceptic, the next an agnostic, the third a convert. He went to work on his colleagues, and one by one they fell, though Stephen Rose himself held out for a couple of weeks. Tom began to oversee the preparation of proper figures – a projection of profits and cash flow based on our estimated costs and hoped for revenues. By the last weekend in September, which we spent in Stephen Rose's small office in the City, we were close to having some respectable 'financials'.

The document we had in mind would incorporate a great deal more than a set of figures. It would also describe the newspaper's character and it would have to establish through research that the new paper would be read by enough readers for it to make a profit and attract the right sort of lucrative advertising. For this we needed more expert help, and the obvious people were to be found at Saatchi and Saatchi, where Andreas and Matthew had already talked with John Perriss.

He was the first proper advertising man I came across. His title was executive media director, though so far as I was concerned he might as well have been called panjandrum-in-chief. In early August the three of us met him at Saatchi's surprisingly humble headquarters, a low 'sixties building tucked away in Charlotte Street. Much of what he said I found difficult to follow, and I scarcely said a word. Matthew was most at home, talking gaily about ABC1 adults and 'media behaviour'. The drift of Perriss's thesis was that there were many 'affluent' young people who did not read newspapers regularly. Many of them were also relatively 'light' – i.e. infrequent – viewers of television. However, being quite wealthy, as well as young, they bought a lot of things. If you could attract such readers to a new newspaper, and 'deliver' them to advertisers, you would be in clover.

These desirable readers became known as 'the missing readership' and it was going to be our job to find them.

It was easy to poke fun at the jargon in Perriss's reasoning, but the fact is that the Independent did attract a higher proportion of affluent young readers than any other quality newspaper. And it is certain that without an argument of this sort we would not have convinced a single institution in the City to invest. Investors liked the notion of a gap or a missing readership, and supporting figures to prove it. The key word in the City was 'comfort'. The City loves comfort, by which is meant assurances made by a respectable set of people backed up with plausible looking figures. The idea was that if the investment went wrong investors could say to their superiors – because they had been given 'comfort' – that Saatchi and Saatchi, no less, had produced a business plan with persuasive original research.

We began to hope that Saatchi's would provide its services to us on tick for several months until we raised the money. Naturally we would have to convince the company that there was some prospect that it would one day be paid. Saatchi's had much to gain if the new newspaper succeeded. In the first place, it would have the glory of being associated with a new media venture from its infancy. In the second, it could expect to handle the paper's launch promotion for which it would receive a handsome cut.

Andreas gave me an elaborate explanation of how Saatchi's was run. At the top were two field marshals, Charles and Maurice Saatchi. Actually one of these field marshals, Charles, did not like to be seen very much, which was not very field marshalish of him. Beneath these two were a fair number of generals who tended to be called managing directors. Then there were the major-generals – John Perriss would be one – who were still men of huge power. Below them came the brigadiers. We would have a brigadier in charge of our 'team' if one of the generals gave the go-ahead.

Andreas, Matthew, Douglas Long and myself went one morning in mid-September to Charlotte Street to attempt to persuade Roy Warman, a general with the official title of joint managing director, that Saatchi's should help us. He was said to be tough, not given to idealistic flights of fancy, and we were nervous. We gathered in a little windowless room and in he came – an unsentimental looking creature with the kind of ironic confidence you would expect to find in a person of his rank. I sat at his right hand. John Perriss sat to his left, deferring as was proper to the senior officer, hoping silently that he would grant us our request. As Andreas gave his talk, not very different from what he had said to me some three months earlier, to which had been added our financial figures, I began absent-mindedly to play with a box of matches. At some point – Andreas had got on to listings and their attraction to younger readers – the box unaccountably came apart, which is not something boxes of matches generally do, and dozens of matches were scattered. Some went over my arm, others on the floor, one or two in my hair, and a few brave, reckless matches came to rest on the table in front of the folded hands of Mr Roy Warman. Incredibly, he seemed not to have noticed the mishap, so absorbed was he by Andreas's monologue, and I began gradually to pick up the matches and restore them to their ruined box. It was when I had got to those heroic few that lay in front of the great man that our eyes met. His were as cold as steel. They said to me that a person did not pick up matches. Not a person who is trying to start a newspaper and asking for Saatchi and Saatchi's help. Very slowly, I withdrew my offending hand and placed the torn box back in my pocket, and my eyes said back to his, quite right, it is a very good principle in life to leave matches lying on a table.

Roy Warman gave his agreement, and vanished from our lives. I never saw him again. If he had turned us down, we would have found it difficult to find another advertising agency prepared to devote the same resources as Saatchi's. John Perriss was a great supporter, and his enthusiasm must have been a strong factor in making up Warman's mind.

The agreement was that a team would be put at our disposal for a couple of months to help us prepare a business plan to raise money in the City. If we succeeded in getting the money we would pay Saatchi's for the work it had done at the rate of £25,000 a month. If we didn't get the money, there would be nothing to pay. The brigadier in charge of our team was called Mike Ainsworth, whom we met a few days later.

Mike didn't look much like a brigadier, unless perhaps in the Dutch army. He had longish curly hair, which looked as if it received the careful attentions of an electric hair-dryer, framing a cherubic face which in my mind's eye seems always to have been bronzed. He appeared to be almost permanently amused, not in the sense of laughing at some private joke, but as though he found life one huge joke in which he expected us all to share. His enthusiasm for the project was immediate and apparently unquestioning. To start with, I found it even more difficult to understand his jargon than I had that of John Perriss, but I was beginning to realise that this arose not so much from my own stupidity as from the propensity of any self-enclosed group to expect others to understand its terms. If Andreas, Matthew or I had had little to do with advertising men, Mike Ainsworth didn't know a lot about our world.

Mike was military in some respects. For one thing, he naturally appreciated our desire for secrecy and, with a *jeu d'esprit* not wholly to my taste, he and his 'team' codenamed the newspaper 'the Daily Arthur' after the character Arthur Daley in the television programme *Minder*, thereby implying that the enterprise was rather rackety. Then there was his unremitting sense of urgency which we stoked up cheerfully. All our meetings were held as though we had seven hours to erect a Bailey bridge but were short of the most vital parts. We wanted to leave our jobs at the Telegraph but felt unable to do so until we had raised some money, and that could not happen until we had produced a business plan. For a period of two or three weeks we met practically every morning, earlier and earlier, until Mike would be forced to arrive with wet hair, and we would eat croissants and drink coffee as we discussed our business plan.

Our first task was to carry out some market research termed a 'newspaper satisfaction study', and our early meetings were spent dreaming up questions, at which Matthew was particularly adroit. The research took place over the weekend of September 21st to 22nd, a little more than a week after our first meeting with the Ainsworth team. Its purpose was to establish that not everyone was happy with their existing newspapers – to define and identify the 'missing readership'. The sample of a little over 1,000 people included readers of tabloid newspapers as well as all the qualities, on the principle that the wider you trawled the more you might discover. About 20 per cent of the sample did not read newspapers.

The results of the research threw us into temporary gloom. We were beginning to believe our own propaganda and we half expected all respondents to say how much they loathed their existing newspapers. Unfortunately, among those questioned 84 per cent of quality newspaper readers were 'completely satisfied with their existing daily newspaper'. But you could look at it another way. The 14 per cent who were not completely satisfied with their papers could represent nearly a million readers.* Two per cent of respondents were not sure.

There was also enthusiasm for a wide number of general propositions, some of which now seem either fatuous or meaningless. For example, 42 per cent of quality newspaper readers and non-readers of daily newspapers believed that 'it would be nice to have a daily newspaper with a really modern approach to news' and the same proportion thought that 'information in a national newspaper should be presented in a more interesting way'. More tellingly, 47 per cent of the same 'base sample' agreed that 'nowadays daily national newspapers should complement the TV and radio news by offering more commentary and interpretation than they do'. Eighty-one per cent of readers said they would prefer a paper with no loyalty to a political party and nearly half thought that 'national newspapers ought to contain regional news and events'.

These propositions, some of questionable value, were put together in the business plan to give the general impression there were plenty of people who wanted lots of things which their newspapers were not giving them. The research did not conclusively prove that there would be a market for the Independent – the only way to do that was to 'test market' an actual dummy paper, which we did in September 1986 shortly before the launch of the newspaper – but it did provide vital

---

* I learnt for the first time the distinction between 'buyers' and 'readers'. Every newspaper has one buyer, but usually between two and three readers. Advertisers tend to be more interested in the number of readers, as well as their 'buying power' and social class.

'comfort' to future investors. That was true of the entire business plan, which was presented in a green plastic clip-folder whose pages were irritatingly difficult to turn. It spoke of 'young, upmarket consumers' and 'young career orientated ABC1s' – the famous missing readership – and asserted that 'there is a high wastage in current quality press against our specific target group'. This meant that some advertisers were promoting in newspapers many of whose readers were unlikely to buy their products.

Our research may have been inconclusive, and the jargon displeasing, but the plan did contain a persuasive argument. There appeared to be a surprisingly large number of people, many of them young and with money to spend, who read quality newspapers infrequently or not at all. These people seemed to show some sort of interest in a new newspaper which was 'modern' (whatever that meant), eschewed political bias and was upmarket but not overly serious. If you could attract such readers in reasonable numbers then – and here Saatchi's knew what it was talking about – you would also attract advertisers because of the 'wastage factor' already referred to. Moreover, new technology greatly reduced the costs of production. If Saatchi's advertising projections were correct (and coming from such a source they offered a great deal of comfort), and if we had calculated the labour and overheads reasonably accurately, breakeven was about 300,000. The business plan foresaw the Independent moving quickly into profit. By 'Year Five' the circulation would rise to 480,000 and annual profits to £16.1 million. Time would show these projections to be wildly optimistic, but these were the sunlit uplands which would beckon to investors.

By early October we had our business plan but we still hadn't approached any would-be investors. Stephen Rose and Partners introduced us to the stockbrokers de Zoete and Bevan (subsequently part of Barclays de Zoete Wedd) who had enormous money-raising power. On October 8th we went to their offices situated in the ugly skyscraper in the City which houses the stock exchange. Their leading man was David Porter, a thin, bald, worried creature who seemed more like a churchwarden than a corporate finance director of one of the largest stockbrokers. More appropriate to his role in life was a swell called

Johnny Townsend, a senior partner in sales, who, cigar in hand, looked as though he had walked out of his tailor's in Savile Row five minutes before. There were various rather superior young men, all of whom I supposed to be earning at least £100,000 a year each.

Their reaction to our presentation was a bit sniffy. We had thought that our business plan might provide the basis for raising money but David Porter said that there would have to be a proper City prospectus, which would take three or four months to prepare. Three or four months! How then could we launch the new paper the following October, as we had planned? We had been hoping to leave the Telegraph in a few weeks.

To our surprise, de Zoete and Bevan said that they would help us, so long as we found a merchant bank to oversee the preparation of a prospectus. This would have to contain detailed and 'verifiable' financial information. Appointments were made for us at Kleinwort Benson, Barclays Merchant Bank and Charterhouse Japhet. Kleinworts, the grandest of the three, a sort of continuation of Eton by another means, turned us down, as did Barclays. If we had got Kleinworts we might have been home and dry, since it didn't like failing to raise money once it had started. Instead we got Charterhouse Japhet. This, in its way, turned out to be another piece of luck.

*

Our competence to launch a newspaper was never openly questioned by Saatchi's or any of our financial advisers. They simply took on trust that we could do it. Investors were equally credulous when we started our first presentations in November. They would sometimes try to tear our figures apart, or express reservations about the validity of some piece of research, but they were as quiet as mice as to our suitability as journalistic founders. They may, of course, have made their own private enquiries, but if so they never revealed what they had been told.

Questions could have been asked merely on the basis of the business plan. There, tucked away a little apologetically at the back, were several 'editorial working papers' knocked out by Matthew and myself. These were unexceptional as far as they went, but much was left out. There was nothing on business and City coverage (Andreas had omitted to produce his paper) or home news (the most important element in a quality newspaper) or arts coverage. There was an adequate paper on foreign news written by myself and a slightly less than adequate piece about books coverage, which I had also dashed off. Matthew had tackled the sports pages with a plausible air of expertise, not forgetting the interests of the Grand Prix fan. He had also written a paper about leaders and features in which he set forth the notion that the new newspaper would espouse 'a philosophy which mixes the politics of the 'extreme centre' with a preference for 'free market solutions to economic problems and a responsible liberalism on social issues'.

Our advisers or investors may have expressed no doubts about our expertise, but I certainly had my own private reservations. My experience as a writer was quite varied but I had none as an editor, yet here I was being wheeled out in front of investors as a foreign editor-in-waiting of a national newspaper. A similar *caveat* could be entered for Matthew, and he had arguably thrown his net less widely as a journalist than I had. Andreas's case was somewhat different. No one could dispute his considerable experience as a writer and editor of financial news, but the snag was that he had never done anything else. It was very unusual for a journalist whose background was entirely in financial journalism to become the editor of a national newspaper. Andreas's grasp of politics was very plainly not the equal of Matthew's. He also knew very little about foreign affairs. His lack of knowledge was to turn into an advantage, since as editor Andreas was able, like the child who sees the emperor has no clothes, to ask questions which experts often forget to ask.

The truth is that the world will nearly always take you at your own apparent estimation of yourself. Here we were, three seemingly confident journalists, saying that we knew enough about journalism to produce a good newspaper. Who were our advisers and potential investors to say otherwise? They cared about newspapers, and as readers knew something about them, but they were not inclined to challenge us on our own ground. We were engaged in a glorious bluff, not consciously or cynically but having, as must be necessary in all such cases, somehow bluffed ourselves as well. Quite a lot of our ideas about the new paper turned out to be wrong, and had in due course to be amended or even ditched, but more important than this was our conviction that we were right, even when we were not.

And Andreas could have been a Nobel laureate in conviction. It was he, above all, who sold the proposition to a gathering band of advisers and then to investors. He spoke slowly and softly, his eyes flicking between his notebook and his audience. He seemed engagingly shy, his nose and its surrounding territory turning red rather than magenta, which betrayed to my increasingly expert eye a high but still controlled level of nervousness. He would never make exaggerated claims, and everything he said was firmly authoritative, calmly hedged with phrases like 'I think that' or 'My own belief is' or 'My feeling is'. In contrast, I would dread interventions by Matthew or Douglas. If a question were raised after Andreas had spoken, Matthew would sometimes jump in before Andreas could reply. Sometimes they would both begin to answer at once and it was anyone's guess as to who would capitulate first. Matthew's contributions generally gave the impression that we had completely mastered the problem under discussion. Occasionally, possibly undermined by some inner qualm, he would go into a spasm which might last twenty seconds, during which time the audience of five or six would sit politely and attentively without daring to interrupt.

Douglas could be a different sort of liability. There was no saying where he would enter the proceedings. He might do so when distribution was being discussed, about which he knew more than the rest of us, or he might essay some observation about foreign coverage, about which on the whole he knew rather less. In either event, he would speak as if he were having a shot at the world speed-speaking record, never pausing for breath, until he would quite suddenly desist, as though he had no air left in him. Despite the somewhat random nature of these interjections, he gave off a sense of authority which I think came from an inner sense of his own standing. He had, after all, recently been chief executive of a large newspaper group, and that fact alone must have inspired some confidence in investors. On the other hand, he was unmistakably an artefact of the old Fleet Street rather than a harbinger of new things. At our first meeting at de Zoete and Bevan, Douglas began talking rather stylishly about guineas instead of pounds.

He was present at meetings as non-executive chairman-designate of the new company. This would be an important, though not critical role. Andreas was supposed to be chief executive – i.e. he, rather than Douglas, would run the company – as well as editor. Matthew would be a director as well as deputy editor. I would be foreign editor though it was not proposed that I should be a director. Indeed, Matthew had implied that he would rather that I were not one. Before the three of us had met in June he had agreed with Andreas that he should be a director, and I think he felt that this was a trophy to which he was exclusively entitled on account of his earlier involvement with the enterprise. For some time I went along with this, reluctant to push myself forward. In any case, this was an entirely theoretical distinction, since we did not yet have a company of which any of us could be directors. But I began to think that I should be a director, though I was far from clear as to the responsibilities involved. If I were not a director I might be under the sway of Matthew, which would be unthinkable.

One evening in late October I telephoned Andreas to say that I would like to arrive a quarter of an hour early for an evening meeting which had been arranged at his house. I was held up by traffic, and got there only five minutes before the meeting was due to begin.

'Andreas,' I said. 'There was something I wanted to raise before Matthew arrives.' I was standing by one of the windows in Andreas's first-floor drawing room, looking out for Matthew's car. He was due in about two minutes.

'I was wondering', I continued, 'whether it might not make sense for me to be a director of our company. After all, I now seem to be doing as much as anyone else.'

'Yes. I think it would be a good idea,' Andreas replied. As he spoke the front door bell rang. It was Matthew.

Towards the end of our meeting, Andreas made a great show of reviewing our 'structure'.

'Well, perhaps we should just consider who will sit on our board.' Andreas consulted his notebook solemnly.

'Yes,' Matthew and I both said.

'Douglas is obviously a director, and of course I am, and you are Matthew. Then we are going to have to have a finance director, an advertising director and maybe a marketing director. Would he sit on the board, Matthew?'

'No,' said Matthew.

'I'm not sure,' said I.

'And then,' continued Andreas, 'there is Stephen. Do you think the foreign editor should sit on the board, Stephen?'

'Well,' I said, 'obviously I should be very happy . . .'

'What do you think, Matthew?' Andreas asked.

Matthew was cornered, but I do not think that he really minded. After all, the three of us worked together as partners and my elevation, if that is what it was, cannot have seemed unnatural to him. Two months previously Matthew had been doing a lot more legwork than me, and a little more than Andreas, but it was no longer so.

Not long afterwards the three of us met again to discuss the question of founders' shares. It was beginning to dawn on us that we might make some money out of the newspaper. Tom Attwood explained that it was usual in start-up companies for the founders to be given shares at an advantageous price at the expense of other shareholders. This is supposed to be a reward for having an idea which is financible. Founders may also have options or convertible shares ('sweat equity') which only become of value if the company performs well, in which case they can make a lot of money. In City jargon, they are 'incentivised'. No one had yet worked out exactly how such a scheme might operate in our case, but the notion was growing that there would be a number of ordinary shares and convertible shares which the founders would have to divide among themselves. There would also be share options awarded to staff when they joined the newspaper.

After a morning meeting with Saatchi's, Andreas suggested that the three of us should have a cup of coffee. We found a little coffee shop in the Tottenham Court Road. Andreas opened the batting skilfully.

'Well, Stephen,' asked Andreas. 'How do you think we should deal with these shares?'

'Um,' I said, not having the slightest idea. Andreas put the same question to Matthew who was equally flummoxed.

Andreas, on the other hand, had prepared himself for this meeting. He was a City editor, after all, and knew about shares. He produced his reporter's notebook and made a proposal with great swiftness. It was that he should have 60 per cent of the founders' shares, and Matthew and myself 12 per cent each. Douglas would have rather fewer, and the rest would be shared between our as yet unappointed finance, advertising, and marketing directors.

'Well, Stephen, what do you think?' asked Andreas.

'It seems fine,' I said.

In fact I was rather surprised, but nothing would have induced me to barter about money. My surprise was that Andreas's proposed division did not seem to me to reflect the work that the three of us had done or the rough equality which apparently existed between us. It seemed particularly unfair to Matthew, without whose terrier-like qualities the project would probably have collapsed a couple of months earlier. On the other hand, it was indisputable that the newspaper was Andreas's idea. Had it not been for him we would not be standing in this coffee shop.

We left with the figures still hanging inconclusively in the air. Andreas went off to his City office, Matthew and I to the Telegraph building in Fleet Street. As we walked to Matthew's car, I asked him what he thought about Andreas's proposal. He said that he had been a little taken aback, but that it had, after all, been Andreas's idea in the first place. 'I expect,' he joked, 'that we shall all end up fighting over the money as in *Dallas*.'

Andreas was soon persuaded by our financial advisers that he should have fewer shares and others, particularly Douglas, rather more. There was never any acrimony over the matter, and the final arrangements seemed to me perfectly fair. But Andreas's manner in the coffee shop had thrown a shaft of light into his mind, the significance of which one had missed, as a reader may rush past an early clue in a detective story.

★

It was a time of bluff and counter-bluff, of moving between lives and roles with alarming speed. In the morning there were printers, architects, computer experts and estate agents to deal with. They knew we hadn't raised the money and that we were still working journalists, if that is not an extravagant term for anyone then on the staff of the Daily Telegraph, but to these people one had to show a brave and confident face. There were mornings closeted with Matthew, Douglas and a Dutch architect called Aart Verbeek who advised us to have expensive raised floors in our building (which we had not yet found) to accommodate computer cabling. I can see Douglas looking at the ceiling, his eyes rolling in despair, murmuring 'Christ'. There were mornings with Bill Wrightson, a computer expert of Napoleonic stature and confidence, who told me that by his mathematical calculations we needed only forty journalists, though we planned to have about two hundred. There were mornings spent looking at computers, mornings trudging around innumerable buildings, mornings at Charterhouse Japhet or at Stephen Rose and Partners. And in this whirling, dizzying life the one thing you could not do was say stop, I don't know about that, I am not qualified to make that decision. That is the essence of the entrepreneur. Put aside humility, there is nobody else but you, no time to dither and wonder, the decision must be made.

Our financial advisers told us that we would not be able to raise any money unless we had a financial director, an advertising director and a marketing director. If investors took our editorial expertise on trust, they certainly would not believe that we could run a company without such people. John Perriss recommended as the advertising director Adrian O'Neill, who did a similar job for TV Times, and had previously worked for the Observer.

On December 5th I met Adrian for lunch. Tom Attwood and Andreas, who had already met Adrian and approved of him, were also there. Adrian struck me as one of the most self-possessed people I had ever met. He was only thirty-four, but his manner was that of a much older man. What impressed me even more was what I took to be his wig. Or was it? As he spoke, I observed that his head was covered with slightly curly black hair whose density equalled that of a high quality Axminster. As hard as I peered, I could not catch a glimpse of scalp. Either he had the most amazing head of hair or a wig which was fitted by a true master.

A few days later I shared my dilemma with Matthew who, while granting that two men might reasonably hold opposing opinions on this matter, was firmly inclined to believe that the hair was all Adrian's. I suppose that I gradually came around to the same view, and the wig controversy slumbered until miraculously it was re-opened five years later by Carlo Caracciolo and his colleagues from La Repubblica when they invested in the Independent. For a time they were as spellbound by the controversy as I had once been, even asking Alexander Chancellor for his view on the matter, which was that no one wishing to obtain a wig would buy one like whatever Adrian had. This was accepted by the Italians.

Adrian introduced a second controversy which to this day has not been settled. Until he appeared, almost everyone we met pronounced Andreas's name with a long stress on the first 'a' and a short stress on the 'ea'. Adrian pronounced the name with a long stress on the second syllable to make it sound like 'André-arse,' and many have chosen to follow this usage. Perhaps they hope to invest the name with extra dignity. Or perhaps they are paying obeisance to what they believe is the exotically correct rendering of a Greek Christian name. Andreas is in fact a little village in the Isle of Man, and it was there in 1936 that Canon and Mrs J.E. Smith spent their holidays, with a happy result.

At lunch Adrian helped us make what turned out to be a wrong decision.

'I am conscious,' he said, in his deliberative, slow delivery, 'that it is your intention to separate the roles of advertising and marketing.'

Andreas agreed that it was.

'Have you thought at all of combining the roles?'

We had not, but now we did. Adrian said that he was 'confident' that he could do both jobs. Andreas quickly acceded.

There were two possible finance directors, found for us by the headhunters Korn Ferry, whose costs were met by its chairman, Walter Goldsmith. He suggested that we pay him later in the form of shares. The stronger candidate was Christopher Barton, finance director of Portsmouth and Sunderland Newspapers, a large regional group. Andreas, Matthew and myself interviewed him at Andreas's house. He was a short, tubby man, as nervous as Adrian O'Neill seemed imperious, who appeared to agree with everything we said before expressing a subtly different point of view. His eyes darted alarmingly from one to another of us, irrespective of who was speaking, giving the impression that he was frightened of being made to divulge some awful secret. Tom Attwood, who met him on other occasions, believed that he was very shrewd, and that his experience would suit us well. Christopher agreed to join us if we raised the money.

During the afternoons we were still working at the Telegraph. Incredibly, Lord Hartwell and Bill Deedes and our colleagues knew nothing of what we were up to. Perhaps they were too preoccupied with their own predicament. As the paper slipped minute by minute into the abyss, they must have assumed that we were all roped pretty tightly to them.

We didn't resign because we were not yet sure that we would raise the money. There was no question of our not earning our keep. During this period I wrote as many leaders and book reviews for the Telegraph as ever I had. Yet I felt uncomfortable. We were, after all, planning to launch a newspaper which we foresaw as the Daily Telegraph's main competitor. On the other hand, our old paper was literally falling apart, and our staying could not prevent that fall.

David Porter's belief that we would need three or four months before we could raise the money had been endorsed by Charterhouse Japhet, where we were dealing with a senior director called Bruce Fireman. Bruce's view, and that of his colleague Tom Bartlam, was that it would take that long to write a prospectus. Our business plan would not satisfy the demanding criteria of City investors. It seemed an incredible length of time to us, but we were not in a position to quarrel. Charterhouse had not yet agreed unequivocally to raise the money which we needed. Bruce and his colleagues were engaged in a process called 'due diligence' which was referred to as though it were some sort of sacred ceremony. It involved

Charterhouse confirming to its own satisfaction every statement we had made. Could the newspaper be printed? Could it be distributed? Was the quality newspaper market capable of expansion? Would it attract advertising? Until these questions were satisfactorily answered, Bruce would not even look at an investor. However, it was agreed that Tom Attwood and his colleagues could try to raise £2 million of 'seedcorn' capital from venture capitalists on the basis of our existing plan, though even this would be conditional upon successful completion of the due diligence. If investors would agree in principle to invest, and if Bruce then told them that the due diligence was all right, we could leave our jobs, put down a deposit on computer equipment and the rental of a building – and be on schedule for launching the new paper in October 1986. In late November we began to see investors.

A kind of Bayeux tapestry of the Independent might depict the newspaper's history as a series of parties. The launch party. The anniversary party. The party for another launch. The party commemorating a hundred issues. A thousand issues. Always, looking back, we seem to have been drinking champagne. Andreas, in particular, loved an excuse for a party, which was fine in him. The first in this endless succession took place in his drawing room to celebrate the raising of £400,000 from Newmarket Venture Capital Limited. I do not suppose that the Independent ever made me so happy again. Suddenly, after all the talk, here was real money. I remember looking out of the window on to the quiet Kensington street and thinking, this is it, we are really going to do it. Then I noticed a Porsche pulling up by Andreas's front door. It was some unknown general from Saatchi and Saatchi who had come to bestow his blessing on us.

Within three weeks it was clear that we were going to raise the £2 million 'seedcorn capital' which we needed. Newmarket induced slight panic in us when their non-executive directors appeared to have second thoughts, but we trotted back to see them and all was well. The money-raising was not as difficult as we had expected, partly because Tom Attwood and Stephen Rose warmed up the venture capitalists before our meetings, and partly because during those meetings our 'team', particularly Andreas, performed well. The venture capitalists were naturally more inclined towards a punt than most City institutions, though they didn't chew gum or smoke cigars or in any way live up to their name. I think the kind of newspaper which we described was the kind of paper that many of them wanted to read. Only one potential investor turned us down. We had approached East Midland Allied Press (Emap) to ask whether they would print our paper. They said they would. They also expressed some interest in making an investment, so we made our presentation, unsuccessfully as it happened, to Sir Frank Rogers, chairman of Emap, and his colleagues. Sir Frank was the next day appointed a non-executive director of the Daily Telegraph.

By the middle of December we had the money.* There was however the problem of Bruce, of whom we were all rather frightened. I had interviewed ministers and the odd prime minister, and felt at home in the company of politicians, and especially of journalists, but I felt absurdly intimidated by this banker, as apparently did Andreas and Matthew. He used terms like 'working capital' and 'internal rate of return' and 'loan stock' whose meaning was quite beyond me as, I suspected, it was also beyond Matthew. However, when you are trying to raise many millions of pounds you cannot interrupt the proceedings and say, 'excuse me Bruce, could you remind me exactly what you mean by "internal rate of return".' Andreas, with his financial background, apparently found it all easy going, though a calculation concerning internal rate of return seemed to fox him.†

Bruce would not be hurried. He was one of nature's sceptics and, quite apart from the intrinsic merits of his 'due diligence', he loved the sense of drama which the long, drawn-out process offered him. For one thing, it gave him the opportunity to

---

* The six original investors were Newmarket Venture Capital Ltd, T.R. Technology Ltd, Witan Investment Company plc, Murray Ventures plc, Charterhouse Development Ltd and Framlington Capital Trust.

† Working capital is the difference between current assets and current liabilities, i.e. the capital for use in the day to day running of the company which is not locked up in fixed assets such as plant and premises. Loan stock is a fixed interest security. Internal rate of return is the annual rate of growth in the value of an investment.

cross-question us as though he were Perry Mason; he gave Mike Ainsworth a thorough going-over on Saatchi's advertising projections. I think he knew that he was very likely to give the go-ahead but he was not to be rushed. The ripeness was all. Below the extremely competent adversarial manner there was, though I did not yet know it, a romantic journalist manqué who could hardly believe his luck. Later, when Bruce had long ceased to be an intimidating figure for me, he told me that when he was seventeen he sold newspapers on the streets of Paris in the hope that if ever he became a press tycoon people would say, well, it all began when he was seventeen and was selling the International Herald Tribune in Paris. He was in his early forties when we met him, and I think he had begun to accept that destiny had not marked him down for the role he had craved as a young man. But he had been given a freakish chance to help launch a newspaper and he was going to give it his best. He would get there in his own time.

As Christmas approached, we had the money yet we didn't have it until Bruce decided that the due diligence was complete. If and when that moment arrived we would leave the Telegraph, and Charterhouse would begin to raise the many extra millions of pounds which would be needed. Even though by this time dozens of people knew about the newspaper – now called 'the Nation', a name thought up by Andreas or his elder son – it was still a secret in Fleet Street.

On December 16th there was a lunch at the Skinner's Hall in the City, at which Andreas was the host, to award prizes to the winners of the Daily Telegraph Share Race. I found myself sitting next to a stockbroker called Lord Faringdon who worked for Cazenove. We chatted away, and over the port he leant confidentially towards me.

'I hear that some chappies are trying to get some money together in the City to launch a new paper.'

'Oh, really?' I said, as if launching new papers was dull stuff.

'Yes. I don't expect they'll get very far.'

'No, nor do I.'

It could not be a secret for much longer.

There was still the question of founders' shares. We discussed the matter at a meeting at Charterhouse a few days before

Christmas. Bruce believed that Andreas had too many shares under existing plans, and told him so in a characteristically blunt manner. He thought that Douglas should have some more – at least as many as Matthew or myself. Matthew thought that his wife Alison should have some shares in recognition of the work she had done back in July and August. Bruce doubted that this was possible. Then there was the question of how many shares our proposed advertising director, Adrian O' Neill, and finance director, Christopher Barton should have. There was also Linda Tanner, Andreas's secretary. Andreas was determined that she should have some founders' shares. The debate promised to go on all afternoon.*

We had an appointment with an architect called Peter Tuffrey, who was supplanting Aart Verbeek in our affections, at a building we had found in City Road, a little to the north of Moorgate. As the hour approached, I leant across to Andreas and suggested that we should leave.

'You had better go,' he said. 'I'll stay here.' Matthew was at that point locked in battle with Bruce over the shares he wanted his wife to have, and he did not have the look of a man who wanted to meet with architects. So I left them discussing our future wealth, and took a taxi to City Road.

When Tuffrey had received his instructions and gone, I remained behind. It was getting dark, and I sat down on the floor of the huge office which would become our newsroom. I was completely alone. I knew that this was going to be our building and this was where our newspaper would be.

---

* The final apportionment of shares between 'the founders', which I learnt about the next day, was as follows:

	Ordinary Shares	Convertible Shares
A. Whittam Smith	407,800	1,224,000
A.D. Long	136,000	408,000
M.J. Symonds	136,000	408,000
S.C.M. Glover	120,000	360,000
A.R. O'Neill	64,000	252,000
C.S. Barton	64,000	252,000
L.M. Tanner	32,000	96,000
	959,800	3,000,000

3

Johnny Townsend Calls in a Few Old Favours

On the morning of Friday December 27th 1985 there was a story on the front page of the Financial Times under the headline 'New quality daily planned'.

A quality national daily newspaper produced on new electronic technology and printed by contract outside Fleet Street is planned for next autumn.

Detailed plans for the newspaper, a broadsheet, are to be announced in the New Year. It has been in the planning stage for six months.

The project provides further evidence that the national newspaper business is in the throes of a transformation led by Mr Eddie Shah's new technology national newspaper due to be launched in early March.

The broadsheet's founders are led by Mr Andreas Whittam Smith, City editor of the Daily Telegraph, and Mr Douglas Long, who was deputy chairman and chief executive of Mirror Group Newspapers until Mr Robert Maxwell bought the group last year. Among others involved are Mr Matthew Symonds and Mr Stephen Glover, both senior journalists on the Telegraph . . .

The article was remarkably accurate. Almost everyone who has been written about in the press knows how common are errors of fact, which arise mainly from the propensity of journalists to rely on a single source who may have incorrect or incomplete information. The writer of this piece had a source who knew virtually everything. Apart from a slight tendency to overplay Douglas's role, and a couple of figures which were not spot-on, the article was flawless. Who had leaked it? A possible suspect was Matthew. He was so bursting with pleasure at the whole venture that the wonder was that he had not blown the gaff before. Another suspect was Westminster Press (owned by the same group as the Financial Times) a number of whose employees we had met earlier. Some time later we discovered that the unnamed writer of the Financial Times piece had obtained his information in the City.

After this piece we could hardly stay on at the Telegraph even though (and of this the article was unaware) we had not actually raised the money. We had pledges which would become irrevocable only if Bruce Fireman declared that the due diligence had been satisfactorily completed.

Andreas, Matthew and I met at the office of Stephen Rose in London Wall on the morning that the article appeared. The City, in recess for Christmas, was deserted. I wrote a statement for the Press Association, the national news agency, confirming that the three of us were leaving the Telegraph to start a new national newspaper, and telephoned it over. 'Could you spell Whittam Smith?' asked the man at the other end. 'Is that with or without a hyphen?' 'Without,' I said.

We agreed that Andreas would go and see Lord Hartwell and that Matthew and I would tender our resignations to Bill Deedes. I had a strange dread that Bill, not knowing quite what to do, might insist that we stay on at the Telegraph for a limited period.

It was not to be. When we saw him the next day, Bill was peremptory. This was perversely hurtful.

'Yes, well,' he said, speaking in a disjointed, nervy sort of way, which indicated that he did not propose to have a discussion on the matter. 'I don't think you can stay here.'

'When would you like us to leave?' I asked, half hoping, against my self-interest, that he would implore us to remain until he had found replacements.

'Oh, I think you had better be off immediately – after this afternoon's editorial conference,' he replied. 'No point in hanging about now.' Thus ended nearly eight years of life at Fleet Street's most eccentric newspaper.

Andreas had a different experience with Lord Hartwell, whom he saw a couple of days later. The old proprietor, whose newspaper, founded by his father, was slipping from him, showed the patience of a saint.

'What do you think you should do?' he asked Andreas.

'I think my position has become untenable,' came the reply.

'Well, good luck.'

Throughout that Friday we were inundated with calls from the press, most of which were answered by Andreas. He gave no hint of the fact that we had not raised the money beyond peradventure. He spoke calmly, softly, and as usual everyone seemed to believe him.

'We've completed the first round of financing,' he would say. 'That is about £2 million. Total financing will be something under £20 million with perhaps £6 million or £7 million in equity and the rest in loan capital. Our readers will be in the ABC1 category between twenty and forty-five years old . . .'

Bruce Fireman, however, took a different line with us. He was not going to rush his jumps merely on account of a leak. This opened up the not very amusing possibility that we might find ourselves having resigned to start a newspaper only to announce a few days later that we had not raised the money after all. I mentioned this to Matthew who exploded into manic, hilarious laughter.

'Could you give us some guidance, Bruce, as to whether you will go ahead and try to raise the rest of the money?' asked Andreas meekly at a meeting at the beginning of the following week.

'We'll have to wait and see,' replied Bruce.

I came close to disliking Bruce during those few days.

During this time of limbo, I arranged to have a drink in the new El Vino by Blackfriars bridge with my former Telegraph colleague Frank Johnson. He was now working for The Times, which had been 'going downmarket' under the editorship of Charlie Wilson. Frank spent most of his life – when not pursuing an arduous, self-imposed programme of reading books or listening to classical music records – thinking, talking and gossiping about newspapers. And plotting.

As I walked into the wine bar, I encountered a number of Telegraph journalists, among them a couple of sub-editors who a few days before had been in the habit of sneering good-naturedly at one's 'copy'. I half expected these old cynics to sneer now but they came forward shyly and congratulated me, as though I were some sort of hero whom they had not seen for an age.

Frank was less reverent. 'The trouble is,' he said, 'that no one has ever heard of this Whittam Smith.' But he was also quite excited.

'Look, son,' he said, addressing me in his usual bizarre mode. 'It could work but only if you make the Nation into a kind of British Le Monde.' By this he meant that one should aim to produce an unashamedly elitist newspaper.

'Well, I would like to,' I replied 'but it can't be done.' I explained that the concept, which seemed to have been confirmed by research, was for a kind of yuppy Daily Telegraph. The moneymen would not believe that an austere upmarket paper would fill the gap we had described to them. Frank did not evince much respect for research or moneymen's views as to what would constitute a successful newspaper.

'Le Monde, that's what you should do. Le Monde. That's what this country needs, son. What an opportunity!'

Within a week of the publication of the Financial Times scoop, Bruce had at last to concede that he was satisfied. The due diligence was complete. The £2 million was released and Charterhouse undertook to help raise the rest of the money with the assistance of de Zoete and Bevan and Stephen Rose and Partners.

On Tuesday January 7th 1986 we had our first board meeting at Charterhouse. Our company, which had been given the off-the-shelf name of Watling (127) plc, became Newspaper Publishing plc. (This name had been thought up by Andreas.) Andreas, Douglas, Matthew, Adrian O'Neill, Christopher Barton (absent through skiing) and myself were made directors.

There was then a ceremony. The investors came into the boardroom, bearing their cheques. They had the air of anxious parents depositing their loved ones at a new school whose head-master has a notorious reputation as a sadist. They asked a number of nervous questions which we dealt with as well as we could. Then came a question about new technology. Bill Wrightson, our Napoleonic computer boffin, had been placed in a corner, well away from the boardroom table. He now rose to his feet with the confidence of an expert witness who is about to reveal a crushing and incontrovertible piece of evidence. He explained how the newspaper would be produced on Xenotron page make-up terminals and Atex sub-editing terminals. He spoke in a manner so detailed and complex that it was unlikely that anyone present understood a word of what he said. When he sat down there was a discernible sigh of relief. He had just administered an unexpectedly large dollop of comfort.

*

Now that we had our seedcorn capital we could write letters of intent to computer suppliers, negotiate contracts with printers with a reasonable amount of plausibility and put down a deposit for the lease on the lower four floors and basement of 40 City Road. We could pay ourselves salaries. Matthew wanted us to order cars, but Andreas persuaded him that investors might re-gard this as jumping the gun. Though we couldn't engage anyone until we had raised all the money, we could also start re-cruiting. Our intention was to line up 20 or 30 journalists.

Though I had later fleeting doubts, after January 7th I believed that we would publish a newspaper, even though we had only raised £2 million of the £18 million we needed. I wasn't yet sure that it would be a very good newspaper, but I was pretty certain that at the beginning of October it would be there on the news stalls.

But I was worried that the three of us were not journal-istically up to the task we had set ourselves. For one thing, neither Andreas nor Matthew knew much about 'good writing'. They didn't think for a moment that it was unimportant in a quality newspaper, but they admitted that they were not practi-tioners of the craft. The question was whether they could recognise the elements of good writing. On January 11th Peregrine Worsthorne wrote dismissively of the planned news-paper in a diary item in the Spectator, saying that 'based on a knowledge of the writing of the three journalists concerned' his opinion was that 'only one of them is much good'. The three of us felt the blow of this early criticism. Matthew and Andreas owned up to being the two journalists in Mr Worsthorne's bad books.

My main thoughts were that we should try to attract the best writers in Fleet Street and get the journalistic establishment at least sympathetic to our cause. We were none of us very well-known journalists. I thought of Sir James Goldsmith's Now magazine and the theory of Frank Johnson, who had worked for it. He argued that the magazine had flopped because influential journalists on Private Eye and elsewhere had induced in the 'chattering classes' a mood of withering contempt. This mood had influenced the advertising agencies, ever sensitive to what the chattering classes were supposed to be thinking, and less advertising was directed towards Now.

As soon as the Financial Times article appeared, journalists of a certain sort had begun to come to our small temporary offices in London Wall which Philippa Rose, daughter of Stephen, lent to us. One of the first was John Torode from the Guardian, a celebrated malcontent on that newspaper, who was welcomed by us with open arms. John, whom I had never met before, has the charming habit of prefacing or finishing most statements with the word 'sorry'. He explained to us how the editorship of the Guardian was now probably beyond his grasp; he did not find his colleagues to be as congenial as once he had; he was greatly attracted to what he supposed to be the political ethos of the Nation.

'Of course,' he said, gesturing towards the three of us, 'you would obviously be one, two, three.' Obvious though this statement might be, we nodded eagerly in agreement. 'Forgive me, but I don't think it would be absolutely absurd for me to hope to be number four, if you see what I mean. Sorry.' Again we nodded sympathetically.

Andreas asked John whether he was a member of the SDP. John replied that he was indeed a founder member of that organisation.

'Would you be prepared to resign your membership?' asked Andreas.

'Ye-es, I *think* I would,' said John cautiously. 'If others in a similar position did as well.'

Matthew was keen that we should appoint Torode as features editor-in-waiting, and may have half offered him this position over a vinous lunch a week or two later. I had my reservations because John was more of a writer than an editor. Besides, another and in my view much stronger candidate soon emerged in the shape of Alexander Chancellor, assistant editor of the Sunday Telegraph.

Alexander was the creator of the modern Spectator, which he edited from 1975 until 1984, when he was unexpectedly sacked by the magazine's proprietor, Algy Cluff. Shortly after leaving Oxford I had gone around to the Spectator's new offices in Bloomsbury with an introduction from my friend Tina Brown to meet Alexander, newly installed as editor. He was almost the first journalist I had ever met, and struck me as a very agreeable and worldly sort of old Etonian. He was keen to discover whether I had a private income. On learning that my father was a clergyman, he commissioned me to write an article about the 'call to the nation' which had been made by the Archbishop of Canterbury, Dr Donald Coggan. He said that his father had advised him to enter the Church on the basis that he would certainly become a bishop, the clergy being generally so stupid, and thereby inhabit an episcopal palace. When I told him that there were only about five such palaces left in England he was a little cast down. Then eyeing me a little sternly he asked a question which was at odds with his jolly man-of-the-world exterior: 'You do realise that as a journalist you will be on the wrong side of the barricades?' I had not, but he was right.

Over the years I had come across Alexander from time to time but we did not become close. I suppose that he remained for me a slightly intimidating figure, frozen as in a bas-relief, proffering wise and avuncular advice to the young journalist setting off in the world. So when we bumped into each other in Fleet Street in the middle of January I reacted less as a would-be founder of a newspaper than as someone encountering an old mentor. Alexander, on the other hand, was full of a new respect, tempered a little by unconcealed surprise. He invited me to have lunch with him a few days later at the Gay Hussar. This went well enough, though we did not discuss the possibility that he might work for the Nation.

Apart from Alexander, I cultivated Alan Watkins, political columnist on the Observer. He would not give up that position for the vagaries of a new newspaper but he was keen to write a weekly column on Rugby Union, and I quickly agreed. I drank cups of tea with Miriam Gross and talked about how the Nation might cover books and the arts. I had lunch with Sebastian Faulks, who worked for the Sunday Telegraph. I tried to persuade Frank Johnson that he should leave The Times, and I asked the writer and journalist Patrick Marnham to come and eat sandwiches in our little London Wall office. I was in almost daily communication with Nick Garland, the cartoonist on the Telegraph, whose elaborate, on-off flirtation with the Independent is amusingly chronicled in his book *Not Many Dead*. With Nick I had dinner with the poet and journalist James Fenton, whom I began to think of as one of our new breed of foreign correspondents, distinguished above all for their qualities as writers. All these people, apart from Frank, were to work for the newspaper.

At the beginning there were no easy catches. Alexander flirted with us for a couple of weeks. When Peregrine Worsthorne was made editor of the Sunday Telegraph in late February (Max Hastings was at the same time made editor of the Daily Telegraph in place of Bill Deedes) Alexander's inclination was to come over to us, but Perry begged him to stay on as deputy editor. Alexander went to see Andrew Knight, installed by Conrad Black as the new chief executive of Telegraph newspapers, and was offered a salary increase of £15,000 a year, and a car. All this he related to Andreas, Matthew and myself in a wine bar close to our offices. Though he had announced that he would not be joining us, we drank champagne as though in celebration. Alexander left the impression that we might not be wasting our time if we contacted him again when we had raised all the money.

We were in a state of limbo. Many journalists wished us well but few were yet willing to jump. Some regarded the enterprise as doomed. At the Daily Telegraph, Peter Utley thought I had taken leave of my senses. 'Dear boy! What have you done?' he exclaimed. 'Don't worry, I will put in a good word for you when you need to return. It'll be all right.' He expected us to return, cap-in-hand, to our old employers in about six weeks.

Tony Howard, deputy editor of the Observer, gave us a little longer. He had the reputation of being a newspaperman's news-paperman, with a close understanding of the press, and my heart did not jump for joy when he uttered his verdict to me at a party in mid-February.

'How is it going?' he asked.

I gave him a brief account of our position.

'I don't know about Andreas. My worry would be that his experience has been entirely in business journalism.'

'So you don't think we'll make it?'

'I think you will raise the money, that'll be all right, but I don't see you getting all the readers from the Telegraph. I can't see you expanding the market.'

'How do you think we will do?' I asked.

'I think you will sell 150,000 and last until Christmas,' he replied.

★

On January 24th we had a shock. That day Rupert Murdoch removed his printing and editorial operations to Wapping. The unions, which had for years seemed invincible in Fleet Street, had apparently been routed by a daring manoeuvre. Mr Murdoch would henceforth produce all his national newspapers within his fortress on better equipment and with far fewer workers.

We had a scheduled meeting at Charterhouse at 10 am when it was already clear that something was afoot. Everybody looked a bit grim, especially David Porter, from de Zoete and Bevan, who asked for our reaction in a tone which suggested that he thought it was all over for us and he, for one, was not going to break his heart over it. We shared the gloom because our com-petitive cost advantage had been more or less wiped out. We had been presenting ourselves as the low-cost producer, and now Mr Murdoch and The Times had suddenly joined our ranks. The only argument, which Andreas now made, was that if the unions were embroiled in a fight with Rupert Murdoch they would have little time to wonder whether or not to oppose our plans to use comparatively cheap contract printers in the pro-vinces. This turned out to be the case.

Wapping was to give us another boost which we could not have predicted that morning. Although most journalists working for Mr Murdoch's papers were induced to go there, fortified by a well-judged bribe, many of them, particularly on The Times and the Sunday Times, were confirmed in their view that Mr Murdoch was not the kind of chap they really wanted to work for. When, in the middle of April, it was announced that we had raised all our money, and would be launching our paper in early October, there was a rush of applicants from these two newspapers. Mr Murdoch may have regarded these journalists as ideologically unsound, and he may have been overjoyed to be rid of them. But they included many of his best journalists, and their defection to us helped to create the feeling that our newspaper was the place to be.

This newspaper was just about to change its name. Andreas was the first to have doubts about calling it the Nation. He started to say that it sounded a bit right-wing, even though the New Statesman, the leftish weekly, had once been called the New Statesman and Nation. He said that if one were going to launch a fascist magazine one could do no better than call it the Nation. I saw his point, though I was less worried. The name made me think of Disraeli rather than skinheads swathed in Union Jacks.

Several people lay claim to having first thought of the Independent as a title. Nick Garland in his book awards the prize to his wife, Caroline. Whenever I have mentioned this to Matthew, he has snorted much as a Shakespearean scholar might if it is suggested that the Earl of Oxford wrote Hamlet. Matthew asserts without a shadow of a doubt that the idea was *his*. He does not deny that Caroline Garland *may* by some fluke have thought of the same name around the time that he did, but he says that it is inconceivable that her suggestion, even if it was ever conveyed to us by Nicholas Garland, would have carried any force at all.

Andreas also claims ownership, though more subtly. About a year after the launch of the newspaper I wandered into his office to find him bent over some hand-written pieces of paper. 'Come and look at these,' he said. He showed me some old notes which, he told me, he had made in March 1985, when the idea of launching a newspaper had first entered his head. 'I was rather surprised to see this,' he said, indicating with his forefinger two words amid a jumble of jottings. They read: 'the Independent?' 'So even then', continued Andreas in an easygoing sort of way, 'I was thinking of our eventual title. Interesting, don't you agree?'

Matthew regards Andreas's claim with no more indulgence than Caroline Garland's. I suppose that they must all three have had the same idea, but how it was introduced into our minds in January 1986 will forever remain a mystery. I make no claim whatsoever to authorship. My reaction to the suggestion that we might call the paper the Independent was pedantic. 'I'm a bit worried', I told Andreas, 'that it's not grammatical. It's an adjective and I'm not sure that you can call a newspaper by an adjective.' Andreas pondered this objection gloomily, then his face lit up. 'I see what you mean,' he said, 'but what about Charles the Bold, where the adjective has the force of a noun? People would see the paper as the Independent *one*.'

We asked Mike Ainsworth whether Saatchi and Saatchi could do some research. They came up with about a hundred possible names which were whittled down to six: Arena, the Examiner, the Nation, 24 Hours, the Chronicle and the Independent. A sample of 500 ABC1 people between the ages of twenty and forty-five were asked to rank the names. The Examiner came top with 105 votes, the Chronicle second with 102, and the Independent third with 101. Arena got 81 votes, the poor old Nation 78, and 24 Hours 59 votes.

The researchers had produced little pen-portraits of what respondents said about each title, though how many respondents had said exactly what was, as is usual with such research, decidedly murky. The Examiner and the Chronicle may have got the best ratings, but they carried for respondents the suggestion of being 'for older people', 'right-wing', 'upmarket' and 'masculine'. The Nation was seen as 'strongly right-wing; not open-minded; a bit downmarket; traditional more than modern outlook'. The Independent, by contrast, was seen as 'a young name; quite left-wing but not unbalanced; reasonably open-minded; no class bias; no bias to the professions or business; reasonable sex bias; good for both single and family people; very strong on modern outlook; low regional bias'.

At a meeting in our office Adrian O'Neill expressed his enthusiasm for the Examiner. It had, after all, come top, and

Adrian always took market research very seriously. He liked the Examiner's upmarket connotation, whereas the Independent's 'profile' as described by respondents seemed to him dangerously like the Guardian's. I said that the Examiner and the Chronicle sounded like a joke. Newspapers only had such names in nineteenth-century novels. I confessed that I still had a weakness for the Nation, though I agreed that the Independent had its attractions. Andreas and Matthew were strongly in favour of the Independent. Adrian clung stubbornly to the Examiner. Andreas finished the meeting by saying, 'Well, it *looks* like the Independent,' glancing nervously at Adrian.

Andreas spent more time than Matthew or I did with our financial advisers. He would interview journalists who came of their own accord or were brought in by Matthew or me, but he did not generally go hunting for them. To my slight dismay he had not heard of several well-known journalists whom I mentioned. When the name of the novelist Piers Paul Read cropped up in conversation Andreas asked me who he was. His ignorance was, I supposed, the consequence of having spent all his journalistic life cloistered in the City.

One journalist whom I invited to come and talk to Andreas was Peter Paterson, television critic of the Daily Mail and formerly a distinguished writer on trade union affairs. Peter had some ten years earlier tried without success to launch his own quality newspaper. His failure, far from turning him against a similar venture which seemed quite likely to succeed, drew him to us. Over lunch he had said to me that he would be interested in becoming our home affairs editor, i.e. the person in charge of domestic news. I thought very highly of him, and liked him a lot, but began to wonder how good he would be at running a large department. We also discussed the job of political editor, essentially a writing job despite the name, about which he was less keen. When he met Andreas he suggested that we should emphasise our independence by staying outside the lobby in the House of Commons. The system involves newspapers receiving unattributable briefings from senior government sources. 'I quite agree,' said Andreas enthusiastically, though I guessed that the idea was new to him. Within a few days, being outside the lobby was represented as one of the venerable pillars of our independence, and almost everyone soon forgot that Peter Paterson had ever thought of it.*

Until we got our cars in April, the three of us would occasionally share a taxi. In my experience Andreas would do almost anything to avoid sitting on one of those put-up, jump seats which London taxis have. My theory on getting into taxis was as follows. If you are a younger man in the company of a man of your own age and an older man, and if you get into the taxi first, you should in 50 per cent of cases elect to sit on one of the jump seats. In the other 50 per cent of cases you should sit on the bench, in the hope that the other younger man will cheerfully take his medicine and place his bottom on a jump seat.

If these conventions are obeyed, the older man will always be able to sit on the bench. However, if the other young man refuses to sit on the jump seat, unless he is forced to do so as the last one to get into the taxi, the older man is obliged to make a choice. He may, if he is of a philosophical turn of mind, accept the odd turn on a jump seat in the belief that where youth has erred, age must show the way. Or he may push himself forward so that he is invariably the first or the second person to enter the taxi, and proceed to plonk himself on the bench. This is what Andreas Whittam Smith chose to do. Nothing would induce him ever to sit on a jump seat.

Such was the evidence of my own eyes but it was not, after all, very damning. I chose also to ignore a story which Christopher Huhne, an old Oxford friend, told me at this time about Andreas and a former colleague who had announced that he never wanted to work on the same newspaper as Andreas again. It came after a drinks party which Celia and I had at our house in Greenwich on January 30th.

It had been a good party. Several people from the Telegraph came, including Bill Deedes, who was to be replaced as editor in a little over three weeks. He shot in and out in a few minutes as though he were a Soviet plenipotentiary paying a courtesy visit to a Siberian salt-mine. Andreas also came, and was the centre of

* The newspaper's eventual political editor, Tony Bevins, appears to have had the same idea independently, which he expressed in a paper written for Andreas dated April 20th 1986.

much interest. He stood surrounded by a circle of admirers, red-faced, pushing peanuts into his mouth at an alarming rate, explaining what kind of newspaper the Independent would be. I introduced him to Peter Stothard, deputy editor of The Times, whom I had known at Oxford – we are going to have to have this Oxford thing out before long. Peter shrank back as though he had been asked to shake hands with the headman of a leper colony. This was not because Andreas had ever done anything remotely unpleasant to him. Peter was a company man, commendably loyal to Rupert Murdoch, and even at this early stage he must have thought that it was safest to regard the future editor of the Independent as an official enemy.

After the party several of us went to a restaurant. Christopher Huhne seemed to feel that a judgment of some kind was called for. I had known Chris since he had stood by my bed when I had glandular fever at Oxford and badgered me into standing with him for the editorship of Isis magazine, in which endeavour we had eventually triumphed. He was now putting the world straight as an economics leader writer on the Guardian.

'My fear', he said, 'is that neither you nor Andreas nor Matthew has had much experience of news. You've done features and leaders and, in your case, book reviews but none of you has had real, hard news experience.'

'I'm not sure that's true,' I replied. 'After all, I've reported quite a lot from Africa, and Andreas must have written hundreds of news stories in his time.'

'Yes, but that's financial news. You've none of you had good hard *domestic* news experience.'

There came a time during any difference of opinion with Chris when it made for an easier life to say nothing.

*

Matthew and I would quite often accompany Andreas to Charterhouse where Bruce Fireman and his colleagues, assisted by lawyers, were preparing a prospectus or 'offer for subscription'. The plan was that in early March, armed with this document, the founders and their financial advisers would set off to visit sixty or seventy potential investors to raise £16 million. According to Tom Attwood, this, combined with the first round financing of £2 million, would represent the largest amount of money ever raised in the City for a start-up venture.

Bruce told Andreas that he could not be chief executive as well as editor. He said that investors would not believe that he had the experience to run a company as large as Newspaper Publishing was going to be. None of us, particularly Andreas, was overjoyed by this ruling, but there was little we could do to resist it. Bruce produced an alternative candidate whom we did not like. We then fell back on the device of installing Douglas Long, previously gazetted as chairman, who had a managerial track record which might sufficiently impress the City. Our idea was that Douglas would be managing director for a year or two, before making way for Andreas. 'I shall still be *primus inter pares*,' Andreas muttered when this had been fixed, as though to himself, but in fact quite audibly. Douglas's benign and somewhat detached presence suggested to us that during his short reign he would prove an easy-going colleague.

With Douglas as managing director (he was denied the grander sounding title of chief executive) we had to find a chairman before the presentations to investors began, as well as a couple of non-executive directors, in order to supply investors with the necessary comfort. Andreas and Bruce tried without success to tempt Sir John Sainsbury, chairman of the supermarket group. Matthew's father then suggested Lord Sieff, formerly chairman, now president, of Marks and Spencer. Matthew's godfather, Harold Lever, was set to work on his old friend Marcus Sieff, laying stress on the great contribution to 'the national life' which the Independent might make. Marcus, who was aged seventy-two and had certainly earned his position at the old family firm, was persuaded to associate himself with a group of people unknown to him who were launching a newspaper which might very well go ignominiously bust within a year of its launch – if it ever raised the money.

George Duncan, an accountant who was chairman of Lloyds Bowmaker Finance Limited and a director of Lloyds Bank plc, agreed to become a non-executive director. So did Ian Hay Davison, also an accountant by training, who between 1983 and 1986 had been deputy chairman and chief executive of Lloyds of London, in which role he had tried to flush out crooked insurance underwriters. Andreas told me that he had given Hay

Davison a ten-minute sketch of our affairs, whereupon Hay Davison had said, 'I'll do it!'

From the window of the boardroom at Charterhouse you can see the north side of St Paul's Cathedral. The bank is housed in an ugly early 'sixties building which had been put up in a space obligingly cleared by the Luftwaffe, where Canons had once lived. We would arrange ourselves around the coffin-shaped board-table; after a few meetings everyone had a fixed place to which he immediately went. Bruce asserted later, after the money had been raised, that there were two positions from which it was possible to dominate the table. One was at the centre, where he sat, his back to St Paul's and his eye on the clock. The other was at the far end, where Andreas took up residence. Bruce believed that Andreas had known instinctively where he should put himself, and was full of admiration.

I sat at a diagonal from Bruce, to his right, facing St Paul's. The meetings seemed always to have a two o'clock in the morning feel to them, even when it was midday: people sat shirt-sleeved and fortified themselves with coffee and mineral water. It was possible, without appearing unusually distracted, to get up from time to time and to gaze at St Paul's, to marvel at the closeness and distance of these two worlds. Sometimes I was irritated by the slowness of the proceedings, and would count the minutes to lunch. There was an addictive type of scampi to look forward to, and usually an agreeable Pouilly Fuissé, which most people did not drink. Bruce later assured me that Newspaper Publishing had paid for every scampi.

The writing of the prospectus was a collective enterprise. Someone would write a passage on 'The Market' or 'Advertising' which would then be torn to pieces by the assembled company and painfully re-constructed word by word. Sometimes we might argue for half an hour about a single phrase. Once we wrangled for twenty minutes about whether to say 'while' or 'whilst'.

When the prospectus had been largely written, it was subjected to a process called 'verification', a kind of austere first cousin to due diligence. It involved substantiating every statement in the prospectus. Since the directors were personally liable for misrepresentation, this was an undertaking which we were inclined to take rather seriously. However, it could not be pursued without challenging the meaning of words themselves. Matthew and I were required to substantiate the passages in the prospectus touching upon editorial matters. We were put in the hands of a junior colleague of Bruce's called Nigel Brooks, whose deconstructionist approach might have been imbibed at the feet of Derrida. Statement in Prospectus: 'A key aspect of the Independent's appeal will be the editorial team's commitment to balanced reporting and determination to eschew political bias or party labels.' Brooks/Son of Derrida: 'How can you say that it will be a *key* aspect?' MS/SG: 'Well, it's certainly our intention . . .' Derrida *Fils*: 'But it may not be the outcome. What do you mean by *balanced* reporting?' MS/SG: 'Well . . .' And so forth.

And yet, on another occasion a few weeks before this, I was ushered on arrival at Charterhouse into a different room. There was a turned-on personal computer sitting alone on a huge polished table. Standing by the computer was Dr Tony Armstrong, the bank's boffin. A little further away stood Bruce, Andreas and Matthew in troubled contemplation. 'The breakeven is too high,' Bruce was saying. 'We'll have to increase advertising revenues.' I got the impression that Tony would only have to lean forward and touch a button on the computer and everything would be fine again.

The forty-four page prospectus was completed at the end of February. It was known as a 'red-herring', which meant that all dates were missed out. The final prospectus, with dates filled in but otherwise identical, was only printed when it was plain that we had the money. It was a document far superior to the business plan which we had produced several months previously with Saatchi and Saatchi. Anyone wishing to raise money in the City from scratch should take a look at it. Its general tenor was that the Independent was going to be launched come what may. Computers had been ordered, premises taken, printers spoken to, dummies produced. (Actually this last statement made more of our primitive prototypes than was strictly warranted. It is amazing that Brooks had not seized upon it.) Here was an opportunity to climb aboard a bandwagon which was already rolling and would continue to roll whether you came aboard or not.

There were eight sections. The first dealt with the market and alleged dissatisfaction as revealed by the market research we had done in September 1985. The next section dealt with 'the product'. Here very little was vouchsafed for fear of alerting competitors. The third section dealt with 'the advertising market gap' (i.e. the old 'missing readership') and informed investors that national newspaper advertising had increased by 45 per cent between 1981 and 1984. It also carried a 'Christie Diagram' adapted from our earlier business plan. This consisted of four little squares forming a larger square – 'Older Upmarket', 'Older Downmarket', 'Younger Downmarket' and 'Upper Upmarket'. The first three were virtually empty but the fourth, 'Upper Upmarket' – wherein lay potential Independent readers, many of them of the 'missing' variety – miraculously contained every conceivable kind of wealthy consumer who might be attractive to advertisers: air travellers, mortgage holders, credit card holders, owners of new cars, etc.

The fourth section dealt with technical matters, the fifth with biographies of directors, and the sixth with the mechanics of the launch, scheduled 'for the first week of October, 1986'. The seventh section discussed the likely reaction of competing titles. The eighth contained financial information. There was an appendix running to fifteen pages with 'illustrative financial projections' and articles of association. When Andreas saw me pick up the finished prospectus, and begin to read it at the end, he was very impressed. 'In twenty-five years of financial journalism', he said, 'I have learnt that the most important information in a prospectus is to be found in the appendix.'

On the final page of the prospectus was an application form. Investors were invited to apply in units of £800. Each unit was divided between 350 ordinary shares at £1 per share and £450 loan unsecured stock at 15 per cent, 40 per cent of which was payable on application, 40 per cent on July 1st 1986, and 20 per cent on March 31st 1987. The purpose of the loan stock, which was principally Bruce's idea, was to give investors an early return on their investment as soon as the company started to 'generate cash'. It was assumed that it would be repaid by

September 30th 1989. The offer for subscription therefore consisted of 7,000,000 shares at £1 each and £9,000,000 of loan stock.*

The prospectus projected a circulation of 373,000 at the end of the first year of trading, rising to 471,000 by October 1990. On that basis, and relying on advertising revenues estimated by Adrian O'Neill, as well as standard inflation forecasts, the pre-tax profits in the year ending September 30th 1990 were projected at £13,786,000. Our accountants Arthur Andersen appended a letter to these 'illustrative financial projections' which employed masterly understatement. 'Since the company has no previous trading history,' ran the third paragraph, 'the projections are likely to be affected by unforeseen events and additionally, in view of the length of the period covered by the projections, it is unlikely that the assumptions on which they are based will remain valid throughout this period.'

None the less, the prospectus could not resist whetting the appetite of investors with 'projected returns'. 'On the assumption that the company then [on September 30th 1990] has a value of £85 million as a result of either flotation or sale (equivalent to 10 times its projected profit after taxation) and that there are 13,621,947 ordinary shares in issue . . . the value of £1 invested in an ordinary share would be £6.26.' Add in a couple of projected dividend payments, and the total possible return was £7.38 for every £1 invested.

The circulation projections were to prove optimistic, and the

---

* The capital structure of Newspaper Publishing was as follows:

Ordinary Shares in Issue

	After the offer	If projections achieved	Maximum conversion
Founders	1,000,000	3,030,947	4,000,000
First round investors	2,000,000	2,000,000	2,000,000
Second round investors	7,000,000	7,000,000	7,000,000
Staff option holders	—	1,000,000	1,000,000
Other option holders	—	346,000	346,000
Staff shareholders (max)	—	245,000	245,000
	10,000,000	13,621,947	14,591,000

'Other option holders' are Stephen Rose and Partners Ltd and Charterhouse Japhet plc to whom options were granted in addition to their fees.

profit ones wildly so; no dividend payments have been made to date. But the share price did at one point rise to £6.

*

As I write, I see the long shadows of Oxford. Several old Oxford friends came to work for the Independent, and others offered advice. Had I not met Matthew there, he would never have come to work for the Daily Telegraph, or hitched his wagon to Andreas, and he and I would not have joined the Independent. Perhaps there would have been no such newspaper.

It began at Isis magazine. I went around in my second term to the magazine's basement office in Keble Road. As I walked in, two young women stepped forward in what seemed a vaguely menacing way. Both were wearing smocks. One had dark hair, the other fair.

'Oh,' I said. 'I just wondered whether you needed some articles. I had this idea, you see, of two doing interviews side-by-side of Auberon Waugh and Lord Gowrie. You know how Waugh is always saying what an awful ass Gowrie is, well I just thought . . . put them together.'

'What a good idea,' said the fair-headed woman, whose name was Tina Brown. 'Have you fixed them up?'

'Er – yes,' I replied. This was half true. I had not yet telephoned Lord Gowrie, but I did not think he would be a difficult catch.

'We'd love a piece,' said the other girl, whose name was Sally Emerson. She was one of the two joint editors of Isis. Tina was features editor.

'If you want any help,' said Tina, 'I'd love to meet Auberon Waugh. Of course, I wouldn't expect to do the interview. But I'd love to come.'

A week or two later I drove Tina to Mr Waugh's house in Somerset. At first, he seemed perplexed by her presence, as though I had broken some private contract with him. 'I thought you were doing this interview?' he asked. 'Well,' I said, 'she wanted to come and I hoped you wouldn't mind.' But it didn't take long for he and Tina to develop a 'rapport'. By the time the formal interview began, it was becoming difficult for me to get a word in. So I sat back and watched a friendship bloom.

In the end Tina wrote up the Waugh interview. Well, she *had* asked the questions. I was left with Lord Gowrie. The two interviews appeared side by side.

The next time I saw Tina was in her room at St Anne's College. There was a young man with her whom she introduced as Simon Carr. He was dressed rather as a country gentleman and looked astonishingly like the young Evelyn Waugh, only taller. He wasn't very pleased to see me. In his hands was a small tin of dog-meat which he juggled about absentmindedly. After a few minutes he got up in a peremptory way and said that he would have to go and feed a dog – a beagle. An image arose of Simon Carr looking after his own private pack.

Isis was a centre of Oxford life where literary types with a worldly bent gathered – people who couldn't bear the union, though Simon Carr once brought the house down there. These Isis people were often going to write great novels – plays in Tina's case – and journalism was a means to an end, a journey to a more glamourous destination. Sally Emerson did write novels, and Simon Carr has written one too, which was very good, but in the end journalism sucked most of us in because it was more important, and stronger, than any of us had realised.

Sally and Tina were inseparable. I see them always in their smocks, blue or black, returning from the library lost in dreams of literature; later, when that other dream of Oxford began to end (Oh, my lost city!) waiting on the station platform, going up to London for that interview, a new future. Whenever they were apart they would spend hours sharing their deepest hopes, no secret spared, on the telephone. Sally had a boyfriend called Pete Stothard who was left-wing and went around still breathing the spirit of the 'sixties which had oozed softly into the next decade. He laughed a lot. After Oxford he got a job working for Shell's in-house magazine and married Sally. Later he became editor of The Times.

Sally and Tina were a year ahead of us and when they had shut themselves up in the library swotting for their finals it was our turn to run the magazine. Simon Carr, though also a year in front, hung on to become an editor of Isis, switching his allegiance from me at the last moment, and standing instead with a chap who could have been a rugger type, a man of business who did not want to be a novelist. When my turn came I dropped my running-mate, Tim Hely Hutchinson, and stood with the energetic and brainy Christopher Huhne. We won of course, but it didn't matter. Tim became editor the following term. Almost anyone who wanted to be editor became so in the end.

Matthew didn't, though perhaps he hadn't wanted to. I have a few memories of him in the Isis office, once bringing in a handwritten article which we did not publish. I had first met him in James Fergusson's rooms in St John's. James had already been editor of Isis, unusually without a running-mate, and had gone into a sort of early retirement. Matthew became his acolyte. Because James, who was urbane and already old for his years, put up with him, so others did. The two of them spent a lot of time drinking, sometimes in the afternoon, and on occasions I came in to find Matthew there.

I would not have said then that Matthew was destined for anything special, but I noticed how he had a higher opinion of himself than others did. He was not, in his own eyes, a peripheral figure. He was our equal with nothing to apologise for. He asked people to his mother's cottage near Oxford, and they came, muttering a little about Matthew under their breath, but slowly won round by easy jokes and wine and summer evenings into a world of his own making. Matthew knew Roy Jenkins and Enoch Powell; there was more to him than we had thought. Gradually he rose, and slowly James lost his power; and then they fell out.

As for Mr Toad, so for Matthew his motor car was a symbol of the person he would like to be. A ride in it was never to be forgotten. He would put on a pair of leather driving gloves and, if they were not already in place, his dark glasses. The engine was revved and the car leapt forward, as though released by a coiled spring. Prams were hurriedly pushed into shop doorways, dons skipped nimbly out of the way and old ladies crossed themselves as a red bullet passed down a normally tranquil Oxford street.

The car could be employed as an anti-social weapon when stationary. For a time at Oxford he went around with Benazir Bhutto, later prime minister of Pakistan, whose father was then president of that country. Once he brought Benazir to my flat in Walton Street, where he doubled-parked his car. Sipping his drink, he assumed an air of self-conscious nonchalance while a small traffic jam built up along the street. Benazir, casting anxious glances out of the window, grew gradually hysterical, demonstrating a sense of civic responsibility which did credit to a future prime minister.

'Mattypuffs,' she shrieked, using an intimate sobriquet which she had inherited from a previous girlfriend. 'The street is getting blocked!'

To my great shame, I once found myself in my own car racing Matthew's red coupé along a country road. At some point in the proceedings my car left the road and travelled some distance along a hedge which, I remember, was redolent with all the sweet smells of summer, before passing through a conveniently placed gap into a field. For many years afterwards, Matthew would regale companions with an elaborate account of this mishap, and, if he should ever pass the spot, he would point out how the gap in the hedge was now wreathed in barbed wire, leaving his passengers to speculate as to what might have happened if the accident had taken place a little later.

This was what was most attractive in Matthew – this sentimental attachment towards a shared past which he would lovingly reconstruct. Andreas, I was later to learn, has little sense of a shared past. For him, battles fought together, whether won or lost, might scarcely have been. Matthew had that rare ability, however abrasive or ruthless he might be in the present, however tormented by inner doubts which he could only overcome by an extraordinary act of will, to shroud the past in an almost magical light by making it seem peculiarly *felt*. Then he was mellow and at peace, quick to see the absurdity in others, sometimes even in himself.

*

Forty City Road was built in 1957 out of concrete and glass, a classically ugly building of the period. It is a T-shaped construction. The horizontal part of the T, which abuts City Road, comprises three long floors. The vertical, a shortened tail, has ten floors and a basement. We had taken a five-year lease on two of the long floors and, in the tail, the bottom four floors and the basement. This amounted to about 60 per cent of the building.

We moved in at the beginning of March. Andreas, Matthew, Douglas, Adrian and myself worked on the fourth floor while the rest of our space was being re-furbished under the supervision of Peter Tuffrey. Linda Tanner also worked near us. So did an old friend of hers called Brenda Beazley ('Bibi') who came to help us for a few days, when we were still at our offices in London Wall, and stayed for five years. At first telephonist and general dogsbody, Bibi after a few weeks became my PA. She was succeeded as telephonist by Wendy Pace who had worked for Andreas in the City office of the Daily Telegraph where he had correctly identified her as one of the world's outstanding telephonists. Wendy had nothing in common with her colleagues at 135 Fleet Street, the main Daily Telegraph office, whose policy was not to answer the switchboard in less than two minutes. Sometimes, if you were telephoning from darkest Africa with gunfire pip-popping in the distance, they would employ their occult powers to sense your desperation and leave you ringing that little bit longer. Wendy seemed for me in those early weeks at the Independent the incarnation of efficiency, good sense and politeness.

The building was ugly, yet it had at its feet one of the most enchanting parts of London, a beautiful old graveyard for non-conformists called Bunhill Fields. A thing of little consequence to John Major, this was a joy to me. It was as though one had stumbled upon the hanging gardens of Babylon in the middle of a motorway service station. Here, beneath old spreading trees, and among grassy mounds and ancient, cracked graves, are buried Daniel Defoe, William Blake, John Bunyan and Isaac Watts, the hymn writer – good people to be near. The graveyard is separated from the Independent's building by a wrought-iron fence which, by May, was draped with white clematis.

As you came through the door you saw an open-plan office. To your right were two desks occupied by Christopher and Adrian. If you advanced further, lifting your feet so as not to trip over the cables from Bibi's, later Wendy's, temporary switchboard which criss-crossed the carpet, you passed on your left Linda Tanner's desk, then mine, and then Andreas's and Matthew's, which stood at right angles to each other. On Matthew's desk sat his Amstrad computer which he had brought from home. To your left too, just before my desk, was a kettle on top of a cardboard box where Andreas and the rest of us made our own coffee. At the end of the office were a blue-green sofa and two chairs, one matching the sofa, the other a little darker, all of which looked as though they might have been purloined from a French brothel. Here we would interview people, or in the evening sit and chat, Matthew and myself often with a glass of whisky in our hands. Beyond were two half-glass partitioned rooms, in which more sensitive interviewing could take place.

During these weeks Matthew and I were often dealing with various practical matters. We went to a factory near Hatfield to choose a couple of hundred desks and chairs. Matthew insisted that a large red filing cabinet should be ordered for every journalist. We were also in charge of discovering whether the computer system which Bill Wrightson had recommended to us, and whose praises he had sung to our investors, was the best choice. About 150 Atex VDUs (Visual Display Units) had been ordered. These machines, which look much like personal computers, though costing much more, are linked to a mainframe computer. Atex, a subsidiary of the American multi-national Eastman-Kodak, was then the leading manufacturer of newspaper computers, and had been making similar machines for many years. There was no controversy about this part of the order.

But some doubt hung over the Xenotron page make-up terminals which Bill so fervently recommended. Each machine incorporated a large screen and a keyboard. We thought that we might need eight of these. The idea was that a journalist could design and make up four or five pages on one Xenotron terminal in a couple of hours. But though Bill was a passionate supporter, he let slip that there was a countervailing school of thought which did not hold the Xenotron page make-up terminal in such high esteem. These Jeremiahs pointed out that Xenotron, a small British company, had scarcely found a British client. They asserted the superior capabilities of Atex's own GT68 machine – an object of scorn for Bill – and said that the Xenotron terminals would not link-up successfully with the Atex VDUs we had already ordered. They gave the general impression that the Xenotron machine was not dissimilar to other British botch-ups – like one of those enormous whale-like aeroplanes our brilliant boffins were dreaming up while the chaps at Boeing were quietly going about the business of getting the first passenger jet to fly.

There can have been no two people less qualified to pick their way through the thickets of such arguments than Matthew or myself. Matthew had recently bought his Amstrad; I had done no more than tap a key of a computer in an electrical shop. Temperamentally, though, I was in favour of the Xenotron.

Matthew and I spent a couple of days at Xenotron's headquarters near Diss in Norfolk. We took with us a potential recruit called Nigel Lloyd, until lately managing editor of the Observer, whose ignorance of new technology seriously rivalled our own. In its own home the Xenotron machine looked quite impressive. Its manufacturers were not, however, the first people in the world to whom one would have turned for a straightforward account of its virtues and vices. We needed to talk to people who had actually used it – of whom, as has been said, there were practically none in this country. There were, however, several newspapers in Germany which had purchased the Xenotron.

So on March 18th Matthew and I flew to Cologne. We spent a couple of days racing around the West German autobahn system: to Frankfurt to see the Frankfurter Allgemeiner Zeitung, back up the autobahn to Essen. We had only a small car, an Opel Kadet, but Matthew could coax reserves out of its engines which would have made its manufacturers leap for joy. Large Mercedes were forced to give way in the outside lane as Matthew bore down upon them. It is odd how on such occasions one is reluctant to say the obvious thing, which is that one hopes to see one's wife and child again, and flick the dust of Blighty from one's shoes.

At dinner in Frankfurt Matthew was in a relaxed mood. The tensions of the autobahn were forgotten. Our visit to the Frankfurter Allgemeiner had had a deep effect on me. It seemed such a beautiful newspaper and the contrast with our own, as we had described it to investors, was painful. Possibly Matthew had been thinking similar thoughts.

'Have you ever wondered', I asked, 'whether the Independent should be more obviously a quality paper? I mean, the

Guardian is one thing, but with The Times going downmarket, and the Telegraph probably heading in the same direction under its new ownership, perhaps the right thing would be to launch a paper which was more upmarket.' This was what Frank Johnson had said at the beginning of January.

Matthew agreed. 'The same thought has occurred to me. I'm sure that's where the gap is. Of course we can't produce anything as austere as the Frankfurter Allgemeiner . . .'

'No . . .'

'We'd have to have pictures on the front. But it doesn't make any sense to go into direct competition with The Times just when it has vacated the higher ground. The market has changed.'

'I don't suppose', I said, 'that our financial advisers or Saatchi and Saatchi would be very pleased to hear that their paper with all its colour pages was going upmarket.'

'No. But we wouldn't necessarily tell them, or we wouldn't put it like that.'

'It would be much more fun . . .'

Though there was some commercial justification, we were both most swayed by our inner preferences. When we got back to London we mentioned our thinking to Andreas. He was not an immediate convert. 'Very interesting,' he said when we had finished our explanation. 'I'll consider what you say very seriously.' Presentations to the second round investors were under way, and I understood that he did not want to entertain an idea which was at odds with the newspaper he was selling.

The Independent which was launched on October 7th 1986 was much closer to the newspaper which Matthew and I had discussed in Frankfurt than it was to the Saatchi and Saatchi version. Who can say to what degree this can be attributed to us? From this moment Matthew and I had a different newspaper in our minds, and all the decisions we made were consequently affected.

The Independent was also pushed upmarket by the journalists who joined it. In particular, those who came from The Times and the Sunday Times, the Diaspora of Wapping, hoped that the Independent would restore the journalistic standards which they believed had been destroyed by Rupert Murdoch and his editors. Like most journalists, they were not interested in commercial considerations, though if pressed they might, like Matthew and I, have said that there was surely a market for a high quality newspaper. What really drove them was a belief that a paper of this sort had a *right* to exist.

*

Throughout March Andreas, Douglas, Adrian O'Neill and Christopher Barton visited about sixty-five potential investors in the company of one or other of our financial advisers. Matthew and I did not attend. Andreas said he did not want to 'crowd out' investors.

When later I met our investors, they would praise Andreas for his performance, which seems to have been an elaboration of what he had done so successfully during the first round financing. He was selling what was now almost a proper company with a highly regarded chairman and two non-executive directors who hadn't exactly been selling shop-soiled goods off the back of a lorry. In Charterhouse we had a well-regarded merchant bank, in de Zoete and Bevan a powerful stockbroker, and in Stephen Rose and Partners venture capitalists with many City contacts. These financial advisers identified potential investors – investment trusts, insurance companies, pension funds – showed them the prospectus, warmed them up before presentations, and afterwards coaxed and soothed them.

Above all, we had an irresistible idea, a new newspaper, which spoke to investors' hearts as well as their heads. I never believed what investors said later, which was that they were entirely persuaded by the potential returns on their investment. There had, of course, to be the strong possibility of such returns, but they were moved too by the idea of being associated with something which mattered, of which they could feel proud in twenty years when most of their other ventures had been forgotten.

Even so, we only just scraped home. With an issue of this sort the entire offer has to be subscribed. It is no good ending up with £13 million and saying, well, we'll take that, that will do very nicely. At first we rose quite smartly from £2 million to £4 million and then to £6 million. But around about £12 million things seemed to get stuck. Bruce Fireman would not admit this, and even started saying that we had 'done it', presumably believing that this was the best way to give heart to the troops for a final push. But the push took some time coming. Over Easter, Celia and I went to Shropshire, and on Easter day, March 30th, Andreas telephoned. 'I've added up all the pledges,' he said, 'and then I put in the likely ones, and I can't get the figure above £12 million or £13 million. I don't think that we're going to do it.' I could not challenge his arithmetic, but like Matthew, with whom I also spoke on the telephone, I just hoped that he was wrong.

The final push came. Johnny Townsend of de Zoete and Bevan 'called in a few old favours'. Up to this point we had been rather grumpy with de Zoete's, whose salesmen were more used to selling hundreds of millions of pounds of new shares in huge quoted companies rather than relatively small amounts in an un-quoted 'start-up'. Stephen Rose, with their greater experience of venture capital issues, had performed better. Townsend seemed to rescue de Zoete's honour.

Bruce had certainly twisted his and others' arms. While saying on the one hand that it was 'a done deal', on the other he was pushing and heaving everyone to the water's edge. I think – and this is a guess – Bruce would ring someone up and say, all we need is another million and we are there. Then he would ring up someone else and say the same thing. And then maybe one more. Thus £13 million edged upwards to £16 million.*

On April 17th, some days after the issue had been successfully closed, we had a dinner at Charterhouse, master-minded by Bruce. 'Well, now we'll see what sort of foreign editor you will make,' he said to me threateningly. The newspaper proprietor manqué, the ex-vendor who had sold the International Herald Tribune on the streets of Paris, had prepared the menu, and in so doing he had drawn extravagantly upon Evelyn Waugh's *Scoop*.

---

* The ten largest institutional investors in Newspaper Publishing plc were Touche Remnant, Charterhouse Japhet, Witan Investment, Lancashire and Yorks (of which no one seemed to have heard), Scottish Mutual, Standard Life, Newmarket, Framlington, Prudential and Foreign and Colonial. Andreas Whittam Smith was the ninth-largest shareholder.

We had *L'Hommard froid à mon oncle Théodore*, followed by *Filet de boeuf jardinière à la faon de milord Copper* with *les pommes Ishmaliennes*. Then there was *Scoop de sorbet de champagne avec les mangoes de Jacksonburg* accompanied by *Fraises Boot*. For those who could bear it, there was *Les Fromages Stitch* and *Café Pension Dressler*. Here was a *jeu d'esprit* which might have appealed to a real press baron. On that evening Bruce got closer than he ever had, or probably ever would again, to being what he had wanted to be. We could not have done it without him. For him the adventure was at an end; for us it was really just beginning.

4

It is. Are You?

Sebastian Faulks, the first literary editor of the Independent, once told me of the reaction of his father, a judge, to the news that he was leaving the Sunday Telegraph to help set up a new newspaper. Their conversation took place at the end of April 1986.

Mr Faulks: 'And when will it be published, your newspaper?'

Sebastian: 'The plan is to launch in the first week of October.'

Mr Faulks: 'First week of October! Goodness. And will it have book reviews?'

Sebastian: 'Yes.'

Mr Faulks: 'And arts pages?'

Sebastian: 'Yes.'

Murmurs of incredulity. Then, as though he had finally cornered his son: 'And will there be *foreign correspondents*?'

Sebastian: 'Yes – lots of them.'

Mr Faulks: 'Well, bless my soul.'

There were fewer than six months from the time we raised our money to the first issue of a *fully-formed* newspaper, not a provisional version which could be improved and developed at leisure. Yet in mid-April there wasn't any kind of blueprint. A designer with whom we were about to part company had done some rather unsatisfactory work for us. We had lots of theories and several possible innovations. And we had a number of excellent journalists waiting to join us. We had set up the infrastructure in which a newspaper could be born and prosper, but we didn't have a newspaper.

If we had had an idea for a motor car in the middle of April, could we have had the first model in the showroom, *not even a prototype*, at the beginning of October? No we could not. Almost everything takes more than six months from start to finish. The founders had no magic wand to wave. What happened was an extraordinary act of collective creativity.

Our plan was to appoint editorial and non-editorial heads of department as soon as possible, so that they in turn could get on with recruiting. Christopher Barton and Adrian O' Neill were given almost a free hand, with occasional reference to Douglas and Andreas, to take on their senior people. On the editorial side, Andreas, Matthew and myself shared the responsibility of finding heads of department for Home, City, Features, Business and Finance, Arts, Sports and so forth. As foreign editor, and a head of department myself, I also got on with hiring foreign staff. There were 189 editorial positions to fill, of which about twenty-five were in the foreign department.*

Before we had raised the money we had interviewed fifty or so journalists, in several cases offering them jobs conditional upon successful completion of the financing. One such person was Nigel Lloyd, who had accompanied Matthew and me to Diss to explore the wonders of the Xenotron page make-up machine. Nigel had been managing editor of the Observer where he was said to be choleric but also a first-class 'production man'. Tony Howard, a former colleague of Lloyd's, told me that he 'rated Nigel very highly', though conceding that his expertise lay in old, not new, technology.

Production men often have bad tempers. They spend so much of their time telling people to hurry up and mending the errors of less practical men. Over the years their simulated anger enters the soul, yet removed from the cause of their wrath they can revert to their former irenic selves. So it was at Diss, where Nigel, silver-haired, a little red in the face, resembled a kindly and slightly bumbling uncle who had spent the last twenty years

---

* There was a considerable 'overshoot' in recruiting, with 215 editorial staff being taken on by the time of launch.

farming blamelessly in the Australian outback. There was no evidence of his famed ability 'to go nuclear', when he was said to abandon the normal theoretical conventions of nuclear escalation – battle-field nuclear weapons, short-range missiles, intermediate rockets, etc. We hired Nigel, feeling that he had reserves of practicality which we lacked. He undertook, as the three of us had also done, to master the Xenotron machine. In the end we didn't order it; nor did any of us learn to use Atex's alternative GT68.

Another early recruit was Edward Steen, a recent friend of about my age. Edward had for some time been dissatisfied with his job as a feature writer on the Sunday Telegraph, and his pulse had not quickened when Peregrine Worsthorne was made editor. He was overtaken by a kind of manic enthusiasm for the Independent which, as a near neighbour in Greenwich, he had shared with me on a couple of occasions in March. At that time such enthusiasm was very precious. Sometimes he would push little notes through the letter box bearing his latest thoughts. Ed wanted to work in the foreign department as Eastern Europe editor, since he believed, quite rightly as it turned out, that things were hotting up in that part of the world, which he knew well. He regarded himself, if not as an Eastern European, then as an honorary citizen of *Mitteleuropa*. In another rush of excitement he once announced that he was exchanging his British passport for an Austrian one. I don't believe that he ever did.

As soon as we had the money, Ed signed on, declining an offer from The Times which had materialised at the same time. For a couple of weeks I drove him to work in the huge white Mercedes estate obtained for me, through the good offices of Matthew, as a temporary car. These morning rides with Ed proved surprisingly testing. From the moment we left Greenwich until we arrived at 40 City Road, a journey of about half an hour, he would not stop talking. A stream of advice poured out of him. Some possible recruits were elevated as geniuses, others plunged to the earth as dunderheads. I told Ed that Nick Garland, the political cartoonist on the Daily Telegraph, had decided after a lengthy and exhausting flirtation that he would not join the Independent after all.

'Ah, Garland's no good. He can't draw. Listen, boss ' – I felt that this form of address was part sophisticated insult, part real affection – 'you should try a friend of mine called Andrzej Krauze. He's Polish. I'll ask him to come and see us. When I was in Warsaw . . .' Ed had that strange ability to talk laterally, so that one name or image in his monologue would spawn another thought, and his conversation would spin further and further outwards until one tried to yank it back to its roots.

On another occasion during one of our morning drives, I mentioned some small disagreement which I was having with Andreas and Matthew.

'Tell bloody Matthew to shape up,' he said. 'Tell them to pull themselves together. They can't do that.'

I was beginning to feel that I was a helpless captive, and after two weeks I suggested that we should perhaps make our way to work separately. I said that I needed my time in the car to think. Ed looked at me a little reproachfully and said, 'OK, boss.' He took to his tiny motor scooter with good enough grace, buzzing to City Road like a demented wasp.

Ed was in fact full of good ideas. He encouraged several exceptional journalists to apply for jobs, most notably Rupert Cornwell, half-brother of John Le Carré, who became our first Moscow correspondent. His passionate conviction helped sway a few doubtful hearts. His judgment of people was either spot-on or completely off-beam. With Ed one knew either to take his advice or to reject it out of hand.

James Fenton, poet and journalist, was another early recruit to the foreign department. James had been an outstanding foreign correspondent for the New Statesman at the end of the Vietnam war. Later he worked for the Guardian in Berlin. He had recently been the lead book reviewer of The Times but, as a sensitive left-wing intellectual, he had had misgivings about taking the Murdoch shilling. I had met him in the company of his close friend Nick Garland over dinner at the Caprice at the end of January. He argued against making the Nation, as it was then still called, into an SDP cheerleader. I told James that we would like him to work for us in some capacity.

Over the following weeks the notion was developed, often via Nick Garland who served as a kind of middle-man, that James should become a foreign correspondent. He had a fancy for the Far East. I was keen on the idea, because I wanted foreign correspondents who were good writers. It seemed to me that much of what interested readers about foreign countries could not be strictly classified as news. Intelligent readers of foreign pages really wanted to know what a country was like, what was going on politically, culturally, and socially. This was a demand which could not be satisfied by a correspondent who knew only how to organise a news story.

One evening in the middle of April, James came to see me at City Road. He came up to the fourth floor. James looked as though he meant business. I suggested that we go into one of the two rooms at the end which were fenced off from the main office by half-glass partitions.

'Well, James, are you going to join us?'

'Yes, I think I'd like to,' he replied.

He was not a man of very many words. With him, the real conversation seemed to take place when you were not conversing. He regarded me with an unwavering scrutiny, sometimes taking fifteen or twenty seconds to answer a straightforward question. It was as though his own thoughts had to be checked and re-checked and passed by some rigorous inner censor before being allowed to proceed to his lips.

'And where would you like to go?'

Pause.

'What about the Philippines?' he asked.

'The Philippines?'

'Yup.'

We had not *planned* to have a correspondent but there was a lot going on there. Cory Aquino had just become president after the overthrow of Ferdinand Marcos, and her position seemed highly precarious.

'And would you cover other countries in the region?'

'Well,' – and here an advance-party smile played on his lips as the thought was being subjected to all the usual checks – 'I would like to draw a line, a sort of Papal Bull, and everything within it would be mine.'

'I see. Which countries do you want?'

'Well, I would like to go all the way up to Tokyo, but not including Japan, and then right down almost to Australia,

79

including Papua New Guinea. And I would like everything east of Hong Kong – Taiwan, Korea . . .'

'North and South?'

'Yup.'

'And Peking?'

'What about visiting rights?'

'Good idea . . . And would you prefer to be on staff or a super stringer?' This last term referred to a type of foreign-based journalist who works on a contract and not exclusively for one newspaper.

'What are you offering for a staff position?'

I mentioned a figure, hoping that he would accept. This time the pause was shorter.

'OK.'

'Well, that's marvellous.'

As we came out of our little room, we immediately bumped into Andreas. 'Andreas, James has agreed to be our staff correspondent in Manila.'

Andreas rose to the occasion splendidly. 'That's very good news.' Matthew, standing a little farther off, looked less elated. He told me later that he regarded James as 'a bit too left-wing'.

We left the building together and walked along the City Road towards Moorgate in a party mood. As we were walking, someone remarked that James, like Andreas, was the son of a clergyman.

Andreas let out a little pre-emptive cackle of laughter. 'There's nothing anyone can teach me about life in a vicarage. When I was thirteen I was arranging marriages, fixing funerals, taking fees. There was nothing I couldn't have done.'

We all laughed.

*

In a few weeks we received over a thousand applications for jobs which were sorted and put into three boxes – 'Yes', 'Maybe' and 'No'. 'Maybe' was usually only another form of 'No'. 'Yes' meant that the person would be called in for an interview. We did not, of course, rely exclusively on applications, and often made our own approaches.

Suddenly, in that late spring and early summer, the Independent became the place to work, and journalists streamed to City

Road, some in search of employment, others to look and flirt and merely behold the wonders of the place. Proprietorless, independent *and now with money*, the newspaper represented for many a journalistic ideal which in the age of Murdoch and Maxwell had seemed unattainable. In fact, of course, the Independent was merely a creature of a different sort of capitalism with different sorts of owners, but in those early days it was possible for journalists to believe that this was a kind of workers' co-operative, in some deep sense their own paper. Whereas in the companies from which they had escaped journalists were regarded by management as a regrettably necessary part of the process of producing a newspaper, here the management was dominated by journalists who encouraged everyone to attend meetings and express a view.

Share options for all staff helped to increase the feeling that this was a workers' co-operative. Though careful study of the prospectus would have revealed that they would never account for more than about 7 per cent of the share capital, these options promised an attractive return. Andreas had an effective little speech to potential recruits which I largely copied. 'If we achieve our projections' – and at this point, if he felt that his interlocutor had any financial nous, Andreas might open the prospectus and indicate a specific paragraph with his long forefinger – 'then after five years the value of each share will be £6.26 and your options will be worth roughly the same as your annual starting salary.' He had another speech, which I did not borrow. 'People work all their lives on a newspaper and all they get at the end of it is a gold watch. I want them to have some real wealth.'

The most important editorial job to fill was that of home editor. We had seen two candidates, neither of whom had impressed us very greatly. I thought of an acquaintance of mine called Jonathan Fenby. Andreas and Matthew looked at me quizzically when I mentioned him since Jonathan had had no experience of domestic news. He had been editor-in-chief of Reuters, the news agency specialising in foreign news, and a correspondent in Paris and Bonn.

I had met Jonathan a few years previously in the back streets of Marseilles. We were both following Gaston Deferre, a right-wing socialist who was mayor of that city, during regional elections. Jonathan and I fell in with each other, and on a later occasion had lunch in Paris. He was a restless, nervous man who looked as though he were in a perpetual hurry. I guessed that he was an outstanding journalist, and he was certainly very agreeable, so I naturally thought of him as a possible foreign correspondent. On April 4th I had had dinner with him and we discussed whether he might join the Independent. He telephoned me from Bonn on April 28th to say that if he were to remain abroad he might as well stay with The Economist. I told him that we were looking for a home editor and asked if he was interested. The next day he rang to say that he was. It was agreed that he should fly over from Bonn and see us on May 1st.

Jonathan arrived about two hours late looking as though he had spent the morning fully-clothed in a sauna. Even for a journalist he was a mess. The intrepid foreign correspondent explained that he had left his passport at home, and had dashed back from the airport to reclaim it. Then there had been a bomb scare on the tube from Heathrow. Andreas and Matthew were very polite, but I sensed at this stage that they felt my man was a bit of a chump, an opinion which I must say I partly shared. The three of us had to go off to lunch so we chatted with Jonathan only for a few minutes. Later we arranged to have lunch with him the next day.

Overnight Jonathan had recovered himself, and had drawn up a battle-plan for covering home news which stressed the need for strong coverage of the regions and Northern Ireland and on-the-day analysis of the news. This last idea echoed our original conception. After lunch Matthew announced that he thought that Fenby was the best candidate we had seen, and Andreas soon came round to the same view. We began to say to one another that Jonathan's ignorance of domestic news would turn out an advantage. He would look at Britain with fresh, child-like eyes and see things which we no longer saw.

Andreas telephoned him the next day to offer him the job of home editor. Jonathan had been brooding, or talking to his wife, and said that he needed some reassurance about the financial prospects of the newspaper. This was what Andreas had been waiting to hear. He flew to Bonn and, after his usual exegesis, got Jonathan to type his own letter of appointment. Over the next few weeks Andreas would repeat this exercise with several doubtful suitors, swinging into their homes, often with a letter of appointment in his hand, the master of financial projections which he would calmly and persuasively expound.

Four months earlier we had been employees of the Daily Telegraph and neither Matthew nor I could have hired anyone. Andreas could have, but on a much smaller scale. I felt the oddness of our position, as did Andreas. He said to me one day: 'It is strange to be employing people who in other circumstances might be employing us.'

It did not take us long to recruit most of the other editorial heads of department. Andreas more or less delivered in a plastic holdall David Brewerton, a former Telegraph colleague, as city editor, and Sarah Hogg, an old friend then on The Times, as business and finance editor. The separation of City from business was a notion of Andreas's; Sarah Hogg effectively ended up running both departments. She had eyes only for Andreas among the three journalistic founders and for a long time would hang on his every word. He told me that she had asked him to make her an assistant editor and that he had agreed. Andreas looked rather guilty because this was officially my exclusive title. I laughed it off as a triviality, though I felt in my heart that he should not have done it.

Charlie Burgess, deputy sports editor of the Guardian, became our sports editor. He was a big, lazy-looking man who shambled in and out of his interview with Matthew and myself as if he didn't care whether or not he got the job. We felt that he was shrewder than he seemed, and he was undeniably more experienced than the other candidate for the job, Simon Kelner, who became his deputy. As arts editor we appointed a young man called Tom Sutcliffe, who had been recommended by James Fenton. Tom was editor of the BBC radio arts programme *Kaleidoscope* where he had been kept on tight rations. Andreas told me that when he mentioned the salary on offer Tom had gaped at him.

Sebastian Faulks became literary editor after a photo-finish with Miriam Gross, who for a short time became Tom Sutcliffe's deputy. I had known Sebastian slightly on the Telegraph – he was a features writer and a colleague of Ed Steen's on the

Sunday – and we had had lunch at the beginning of February. He asked me about Matthew and I replied that there was more to him than met the eye. At the end of April I invited him to come to City Road. Sebastian sat on the brothel sofa and generally gave the impression of a man who knows he is going to be asked for the next dance by the most beautiful girl present. Andreas surprised him by asking for a written paper on books coverage, a ploy he used with several other people. 'Write a paper which will show how we can be better than any of our rivals.' When this was delivered a couple of days later it emerged that Sebastian and Andreas had had the same idea of running a daily book review in addition to the weekly books pages.

As features editor we appointed John Bryant, who held the same position on the Daily Mail. Bryant was a keen runner, and had made himself a little famous by acting as Zola Budd's 'minder' when his paper had brought her over to England. Having written to us, he came to his interview armed with a letter from his editor, Sir David English, which said he was God's gift to journalism. Matthew fell in love with the idea of Bryant, attributing to him numberless 'hands-on' gifts which he feared we lacked. Several weeks after we had hired him, he announced that he was going to The Times. With time running out, we recruited John Morrison, a friend of Sarah Hogg's, who had been editor of *Channel Four News*. Whereas Bryant had presented himself as possessing almost occult technical powers as a newspaperman, Morrison cheerfully admitted he knew nothing about 'print journalism'. This was suddenly accounted an advantage. As Jonathan Fenby, who knew nothing about Britain, would look at this country with a new eye, so John Morrison, ignorant of newspapers, would bring us new skills and insights.

So: we had an editor who had spent his life in financial journalism, and a deputy editor and foreign editor who had never edited. Count the business and finance editor into that elite corps as well, and the literary editor while we are about it. The home editor was a stranger in his own country and the features editor had never worked on a newspaper, which was also the case with the arts editor. Don't let anyone say that we weren't prepared to take imaginative risks.

The principle of importing new blood was applied elsewhere.

Matthew and I secured employment for our old friend Simon Carr, who became deputy listings editor to Elkan Allan. This was Simon's first journalistic experience since Isis. The same was true of James Fergusson, who was working in an antiquarian bookshop in Oxford. James had always been 'old for his age', and it seemed a natural, as well as a witty, idea to appoint him as obituaries editor. He invented the gazette page, one of the most distinguished and original parts of the newspaper.

*

Andreas, Matthew and I usually agreed about the people whom we saw. We were looking for the same qualities: intelligence and adventurousness were rated above experience. Andreas had a weakness for youth and for 'stars'. 'We should always ask ourselves the question,' said Andreas, 'is this person the very best there is?'

There were very occasional differences. Andreas once inexplicably took against someone whom I was thinking of hiring as our super stringer in Australia. Matthew blew a gasket when he learnt what salary I had offered Isabel Hilton, a brilliant and beautiful refugee from Wapping, as our Latin American editor. 'You could have got her for less,' he informed me. 'She is a leftie who couldn't bear Wapping.' Similarly, Matthew and I rather rounded on Andreas when we discovered that he had given Maggie Brown, our new media editor, one of a small number of precious parking-spaces at City Road. This was the first time that I had noticed in Andreas a tendency to be more indulgent to women than to men. I also discovered the supreme importance of parking-spaces: over the years no single issue caused more trouble. Douglas Long mentioned The Maggie Brown Affair at one of the daily 12 o'clock meetings which the directors had started to hold. 'All right,' said Andreas. 'I have sinned. I was wrong. *Mea culpa.* I shan't do it again.' Maggie was instead found a space in a nearby car-park at £8 a day.

Once departmental heads had joined us, they did most of the recruiting in their own departments. I spent more and more of my time thinking about foreign coverage and taking on foreign staff. Still, as late as July there were still some positions unfilled outside the foreign department where I felt I could help. We were still looking for a diarist. At the beginning of July Francis Wheen, whom I knew very slightly via Christopher Huhne, came to ask my advice about a publishing venture he was contemplating. It was a warm day, and without too slavish a regard for sartorial conventions Francis had put on a pair of shorts. What little I had previously seen of Francis I had liked. He was, according to legend, an Old Harrovian Trotskyist, a species by no means as common as might be popularly supposed. He worked intermittently for Private Eye, and for as long as man could remember had been writing a biography of the left-wing Labour MP Tom Driberg who ran the William Hickey gossip column in the Daily Express for many years. It seemed, as we talked at lunch, that Francis might have been reared for the job of diarist on the Independent, and after a meeting with Andreas he was duly appointed. His role at the Independent, and the Independent on Sunday, was to be an important one.

Around this time my relationship with Andreas started to change, as, in a different way, did that of Matthew. It was simply that Andreas was beginning to have a paper to edit, even though it was not being published. By the end of June over a hundred journalists had been hired, and all of them naturally looked to Andreas as their editor, as the crew of a ship will look to their captain. You cannot have three captains. This transformation, this re-alignment of power, was more irksome to Matthew than it was to me, since I had a department to create and run. Matthew was left at the centre, increasingly excluded from the decisions being made by departmental heads who would defer chiefly to Andreas. These were the glimmerings of a long period of unhappiness for Matthew during which Andreas showed little understanding of his predicament.

*

As a director I was in a strong position to obtain generous resources for the foreign department, though even so most correspondents were told that they would have to work at home to avoid the expense of an office. In defiance of the trend of recent years, I believed that we should devote more space to international coverage than other quality newspapers were doing. Andreas and Matthew agreed. Our readers would want to read about foreign news from correspondents who could write amusingly and engagingly about the world, and also with authority.

The allocation of editorial space was none the less an arbitrary affair. One afternoon Nigel Lloyd asked me how many columns I would like for foreign coverage. 'Oh, about nineteen,' I replied breezily. This was on the basis of a twenty-eight-page newspaper, which was implausibly slender, and as the paper grew to more realistic proportions so the foreign allocation increased commensurately until we had twice, sometimes even three times, as much foreign space as our rivals.

In May I appointed as deputy foreign editor Nick Ashford, a well-known foreign correspondent who had worked for The Times in South Africa and Washington, and was now that paper's diplomatic editor. He wrote me a letter expressing interest in becoming our stringer in Australia, and because of the comparatively unambitious nature of the request I did not immediately realise who had written it. Nick came to City Road. He was a handsome man of about medium height, prematurely bald, obviously tremendously fit and vigorous. I noticed from his c.v. that he had for a short time served as a regular soldier on leaving Haileybury. I told him that his wish to hop off to Australia seemed a bit bizarre. He replied that he had grown tired of The Times and wanted to leave. His wife could probably get a teaching job at an Australian university and both of them felt like a new start. He was toying with the idea of buying a fish-farm.

'Don't you feel that it might be a waste of your talents? I mean, you are a very senior journalist . . .'

'No, I don't think so.'

'Well, let me tell you how we intend to set up the foreign department.' I explained the system of area specialists – for Africa, Latin America, the Middle East, Asia, etc. These 'experts', based in London, would write about events whenever we did not have staff correspondents on the spot. We would also have our own writers in Washington (two of them), Moscow, Paris, South Africa, Bonn and the Philippines. There would be super stringers – this list was not quite fixed when I spoke to Nick – in Jerusalem, Cairo, Rome, Madrid, New Delhi, Brussels, Mexico and Tokyo. Elsewhere we would rely on stringers (correspondents who could work for several non-competing newspapers) who would be 'run' by the area specialists, and on news agencies such as Reuters and Associated Press.

I tried to persuade Nick that there was a more important role for him at the Independent than as a fish-farming stringer in Australia, and that the newspaper was going to be the most exciting place in the world to work. We talked about the jobs of Africa editor and deputy foreign editor. When he had gone, I asked Andreas for his view, and he replied that he would feel 'very reassured' if Nick were to become deputy foreign editor. He meant that by virtue of my age I was somewhat inexperienced. Nick became my deputy. I don't know whether the thought ever crossed his mind, but in truth he was better qualified than me to be foreign editor.

By early July we had nearly set up an impressive network of foreign correspondents. Rupert Cornwell had first been offered, and had accepted Paris, but then said that he wanted to go to Moscow, a wise choice in view of what was just about to happen in the Soviet Union. Tony Allen-Mills, a reporter on the Daily Telegraph, whom I had much admired for his fluency as a writer and quickness of reaction, had agreed to become our correspondent in South Africa. Then there were the super stringers, all of whom soon became fully-fledged correspondents. Tim McGirk from the Sunday Times was appointed as our Madrid correspondent and Michael Sheridan from ITN as our Rome correspondent. Patricia Clough from The Times went to Bonn. Robert Cottrell from the Financial Times was appointed in Hong Kong, where he would preside at the outer rim of James Fenton's Far Eastern empire. Charles Richards, also from the Financial Times, went off to Jerusalem. A beguiling adventurer called Bruce Palling, who heralded from Australia by way of Thailand, Vietnam and Rhodesia, began to pack his bags for Delhi. John Carlin, already in Mexico for The Times, was taken on by us there, and Andrew Horvat, Tokyo correspondent for the Los Angeles Times, switched his allegiance to us.

In June Alexander Chancellor agreed to become our Washington correspondent with the title of US editor, intended to emphasise his eminence. It was a brave decision on his part, and perhaps on ours, since he had not reported since his days as a Rome correspondent which had ended shortly before he became editor of the Spectator. He and I had a series of delightful meetings during which Alexander negotiated his remuneration package with remarkable aplomb and elegance.

In London we had three assistant foreign editors, Harvey Morris (from Reuters), Christopher Gilbert (The Times) and Pat Ferguson (the Observer), whose nickname, according to his former colleague Nigel Lloyd was 'ratty patty'. Ed Steen was the regional editor for Eastern Europe. John Lichfield, whom I had met when he was a stringer for the Telegraph in Brussels, became, with a helpful nudge from his friend Ed Steen, our West Europe editor. Our Middle Eastern editor was John Bulloch, a wise old war-horse also from the Daily Telegraph, who had given me help and advice for many a foreign leader I had written. Richard Dowden from The Times became Africa editor. The job of Asia editor was as yet unfilled. There were several sub-editors and two 'copytasters', journalists who sift and classify tens of thousands of words of incoming 'copy'.

After Rupert Cornwell's defection to the Soviet Union, we did not have a Paris correspondent. Alexander Chancellor suggested Patrick Marnham, whom I had consulted for general advice six months earlier. I admired him greatly as a writer, particularly about Africa; as a reporter he was admittedly an unknown quantity. Ten years previously, when he was working on Private Eye, he had commissioned me, before I legged it off to Africa as a freelance journalist, to write two 'Letters From'. He had also, though he could not have known this, had a profound effect on my eating habits as they related to veal. Some years before he had written in the Spectator a harrowing account of the mistreatment of young cattle, in Italy I think, as they were fattened to be converted into veal. Since that day no morsel of veal has passed my lips.

In mid-July the two of us had dinner in a small Italian restaurant in Hammersmith. Patrick had told Alexander that he was interested in the Paris job. Feeling that it was really just a matter of agreeing terms, I ordered some wine, and waited while

Patrick perused the menu. 'What will you have?' I asked. 'I'll have the veal,' he replied.

*

If Andreas, Matthew or myself had been asked on the first of May what the Independent would look like, we would have been unable to provide an answer. We knew as much about newspaper design as about the art of drawing. In this we were not unusual: over the next five years I learnt that most journalists have primitive feelings about newspaper design which they none the less sometimes articulate with an authority which can be mistaken for expertise. We had instinctively not liked the work done by the designer whom we had sacked, but it could not tell us how to describe what did not yet exist. We were drifting towards a crisis.

Designers are a different breed from journalists. Mutual suspicion and ignorance characterise the two species. For advice I telephoned Harold Evans, former editor of the Sunday Times and The Times, who was married to Tina Brown with whom he lived in New York. Harold suggested a couple of people. One was Edwin Taylor, a former colleague on the Sunday Times. The other was David Driver who worked on The Times.

A courtship with Mr Driver ensued. To begin with, I was the suitor. There were late-night telephone calls, one from a call-box by a dual carriageway in the pelting rain. He thought he would come but he wasn't sure. He needed a little more time. At this point I passed the baton to Andreas who tried to take the affair into Mr Driver's home. He would never say no; nor would he irrevocably say yes. After a time we finally had to accept that he could not bring himself to leave his existing employer.

Nigel Lloyd then suggested that we contact Ray Hawkey, with whom he had once worked on the Observer. In early May Hawkey agreed to help, and Tony Mullins, the art editor of the Observer, was seconded to assist him. They began to work on a dummy, the first part of which they presented on June 2nd.

At the same time a character called Michael Crozier swam into City Road. He had some executive position at The Times where he inhabited the murky world between journalism and design. He spoke in an extraordinarily soft and quiet voice; his unflagging thin half-smile gave one the impression that he thought he was talking to a fool. In an attempt to show his prowess as a designer he produced for me a putative features page which contained an imaginary article on religion. By way of illustration, he had drawn a huge crucifix around which the text of the article swerved and clung in a giddy manner. I may have known nothing about design but I knew that I did not like this very much.

None the less, Crozier was taken on as an executive without a position. Andreas promised that he would be found a portfolio as soon as possible. His reasoning was that Crozier had considerable technical skills and had mastered the Atex computer system at The Times which was similar to our own. As the weeks passed, Crozier showed an interest in the developing dummy, and made himself useful to Hawkey and Mullins. Nigel Lloyd, who had some experience of designers, was adamant that Crozier was not of their number. 'He's just like me, he's a journalist, not a designer.' Actually their likeness was not so marked. The two men differed in several respects, not least in their knowledge of computers.

Throughout June, Hawkey and Mullins toiled away at their dummy. They had been told by Andreas, Matthew and myself that the Independent was a newspaper particularly aimed at young people. It was supposed, with its short summaries and longer background pieces, to complement television news. We wanted it to look as though – to borrow a phrase from the SDP – it had broken the mould. The use of colour was encouraged.

By the end of the month the two designers had finished, and 500 copies of the dummy were printed, some for market research. What they had produced certainly looked different. It did not resemble any broadsheet paper which anyone had ever seen. To my uneducated eye, it appeared like a cross between the Sunday Times and the Daily Mail. They had chosen a squat, chunky sort of headline type called Gibraltar. The photograph on the front page, reproduced unusually large, showed a burning South African township, and in half the printed copies appeared in very creditable colour. I quite liked the dummy, and took a copy home. Celia said that she did not think much of it.

On July 7th there was a meeting to discuss this dummy to which heads of department and a few others came. One of the others was Alexander Chancellor. Another was Nick Garland who after telling me in March that he was not going to join us had re-opened negotiations in early June. Even so, he had been an agonisingly difficult catch, and Andreas had been forced to dive down like Superman into Nick's house in Hampstead, armed with a pocket calculator and sheaves of financial projections.

Had these two not been present at this meeting it is likely that the history of the Independent would have been different. Everyone except them, myself included, regarded the dummy with varying degrees of equanimity, and in no case with outright enmity. Andreas, with his love of judging things in percentages, announced that the dummy was '75 per cent there'. Others were less enthusiastic, but their criticisms were particular, of this graphic, of that picture, of this size of headline. Nicholas Garland, and Alexander when he joined the meeting halfway through, simply said that the dummy was no good at all. It was a dummy of the wrong sort of newspaper. When Nicholas complained about an enormous incomprehensible graphic spotted with nuclear installations, Alexander said, 'Yes, I found myself moronically counting them.' The dummy, he added, looked so downmarket that it was difficult to believe that a reader of The Times would be drawn to it. Alexander then made the revolutionary statement that the Independent need not look so self-consciously different from the other quality newspapers.

The meeting broke up unhappily. I said to Nick and Alexander that they could not have more effectively punctured the prevailing complacency if they had met for breakfast and rehearsed. (They had, they later told me, discussed the dummy together on at least two occasions.) Several people felt that it was a bit rich for these two johnny-come-latelies who had played no part in the dummy to pass judgment in such a way. But the two of them were not deterred. The next day Alexander telephoned me to propose that he and Nick should engage a designer to produce an alternative version. (This was his wife, Susie's, brainwave.) Feeling some misgivings now about the Hawkey-Mullins design, I said that I thought this was a good idea, and undertook to tell Andreas. The following day Alexander and Nick went to see a designer called Nicholas Thirkell, whom Alexander had met once at the Sunday Telegraph. It was agreed that he would produce a front page for all of us to see the following week.

The next Wednesday, the 16th, Andreas, Matthew and I met Thirkell, accompanied by Alexander, Nick and James Fenton, who had attached himself to the counter-revolutionary movement. Thirkell was a large, shy man with an almost perfectly spherical, bald head who, whenever spoken to, gave the impression that he felt that he had just been insulted. After a certain amount of preparatory talk, he nervously unveiled his prototype front page. Nothing could have been more different from the Hawkey-Mullins dummy. It looked, as Thirkell did not deny, indeed was eager to concede, not unlike The Times of ten years before. By the 'chiselled' masthead (these were terms which I learnt later) was an eagle sitting on some kind of nest, which Thirkell described as 'visual interest'. Beneath this, the headlines, in a classic typeface called Century, were restrained. The picture was quite small. There were seven or eight stories, arranged vertically and horizontally, a half-column of summaries and another half-column advertising imaginary features inside the newspaper. There were thick, horizontal 'Oxford rules' separating some of the stories from one another.

It was so obviously a thing of beauty, so undeniably superior to the existing dummy, that Andreas, Matthew and I could not withhold our grudging approval, even though this front page did not remotely correspond to the newspaper of the future that had been floating around our minds. It looked like part of the past, not of the future. Alexander, Nick and James, who had already seen it, looked as pleased as Punch. Thirkell began to sense that he might be riding the winning horse. Andreas and he agreed that he would produce pages two and three in the same style for the following week.

Anyone – perhaps I should say almost anyone – confronted today by this front page would say that it is unmistakably the progenitor of the Independent. Thirkell's chiselled masthead, though smaller, is very similar to the one in use today. He introduced Century, as the Independent's headline typeface, and Oxford rules, both of which the newspaper used until March 1993. Of course there are differences – Thirkell cannot claim authorship of the Independent's expansive use of photographs – but the crucial point is that he took us from one path, which had been marked the future, and plonked us down on another one, which was known as the past and classicism and restraint. After the launch many people said, in speaking of the Independent, that it was brilliant of its founders to produce a newspaper *which looked as though it had been there for a hundred years.* It was brilliant – but it was Thirkell's brilliance, and Alexander's and Nick's for leading us to him.

Nicholas Thirkell has never been credited by Andreas or Matthew with playing much more than a peripheral role in the design of the Independent, and Matthew attributes the major role to Michael Crozier, who casts himself in a similar light in his book *The Making of the Independent.* Crozier gives Thirkell a walk-on part, portraying him as a marginal figure whose insignificant contribution was soon decisively rejected. When discussing the eagle, Crozier fails to mention that it was Thirkell's idea, and gives himself the credit for finding a freelance artist to perfect it. The eagle was Thirkell's invention. Though on his first dummy it is an unattractive, crabby-looking bird, five weeks later he produced a flying version which is almost indistinguishable from the eagle which today soars by the Independent's masthead.

For the three weeks following the unveiling of Thirkell's prototype, skirmishes continued between the revisionists, led by Alexander and Nick, and the revolutionaries, comprising Mullins (Hawkey having slipped from the scene), Nigel Lloyd and Crozier. Andreas, Matthew and myself slowly edged towards the revisionist camp, though we still hoped that Mullins could be persuaded to incorporate Thirkell's ideas, and that the two of them might work together. Andreas was worried that Mullins might stomp off, and did not yet have enough confidence in Thirkell's alternative approach to wish to precipitate such an outcome. During nearly all the discussions about design he looked miserable. At one meeting he said, 'This is hopeless. Somebody says this is better, somebody else says that is better. It's meaningless – it's like discussing Bordeaux, saying that Château-this is better than Château-that. I shall just have to make a decision.' But he did not do so.

At the end of July I went to America with Alexander Chancellor for a few days, partly to interview candidates to serve as his deputy in Washington, and partly to try to find a house suitable for our US editor. There was a further reason. I had never been to the United States before, perhaps a unique distinction for a foreign editor. I had travelled widely in Africa, knew most of western Europe and some of eastern Europe well, but I had never visited America. This oversight caused Alexander much amusement, and as he reflected upon it, or told someone about it, he would break into joyous laughter, a sort of cross between a hissing and a gargling sound.

In Washington we met Peter Pringle, a former Sunday Times journalist who was now writing books about nuclear weapons and arms control while doing a little work for the Observer. He was a big, jolly man in his late forties who when he laughed, which was often, produced a sound startlingly similar to Alexander's laugh, though with a little more emphasis on the hissing, and a little less on the gargling. He had scarcely heard of the Independent but after the three of us had got drunk a couple of times, and Alexander and I had told him that it was going to be the most exciting newspaper in the history of the world, he agreed to become Washington correspondent, and Alexander's deputy.

Though our main business was in Washington, we managed to spend a couple of days in New York, which Alexander showed me around like a proud father. We had dinner with an acquaintance of Alexander's, a New York lawyer. Also present was Nick Von Hoffman, an American journalist who had written for the Spectator when Alexander was its editor. As dinner progressed, Alexander, assisted by the odd drink, became exuberant.

'So you're going to start a newspaper?' asked the American lawyer disbelievingly.

'Well, not exactly single-handedly,' replied Alexander. 'In fact it's really nothing at all to do with me. But Stephen, this dozy-looking creature here ' – here he pointed towards me, in case the lawyer was in some doubt as to whom he might be referring, 'is one of the founders and he can tell you all about it.'

'Is that so?' said the lawyer suspiciously.

'Yeah, and it's his first visit to New York – and to the United States of America.'

'You don't say?' The lawyer looked a little hostile.

Later he evinced signs of wishing to expand his knowledge about littl' ol' England.

'Say, Alexander, did you go to one of those public schools of yours? '

'Well, I did go to the only school which really matters, and that's called Eton. You can forget the rest.' Whereupon Alexander erupted into joyous laughter.

We returned on August 2nd and I prepared to throw myself back into the foreign department where there were still a couple of appointments to make. We had been unable to find a good Asia editor. I remembered Michael Fathers, an old Vietnam hand now working for Reuters in Nairobi, who had come to see me back in February. He had asked me penetrating questions in a café near our offices in London Wall. Now I telephoned him in Kenya. He flew to London and took the job.

The design controversy had not gone away. Mullins had rather unwillingly adopted some of Thirkell's ideas, though in a way which Nicholas Garland regarded as half-baked. Matthew, who thought that Nick was 'pretty barmy' and wildly overstated his case, believed that we had achieved a prudent compromise. Andreas, with the launch only two months away, felt that we could not risk losing Mullins. Nick had disappeared to France on holiday, and seemed to spend most of the time following events at City Road from a telephone kiosk. On the afternoon of August 4th he and I spoke on the 'phone. Nick complained that although we had approved of Thirkell's work we were still not letting the man oversee the design, and Mullins was firmly in charge.

Everything Nick said made sense. I formed a plan, which was to suggest to Andreas that we ask Nick to fly from Bordeaux to London. This dramatic gesture would appeal to Andreas. I felt that Nick was probably right, but on this matter I had neither his passionate conviction nor the expertise to argue the case as well as he. Even Alexander, increasingly preoccupied with his American posting, did not. Nick was needed as a kind of battering ram.

In still offering support to Mullins we were adhering to the earlier version of the newspaper that Matthew and I had rejected at dinner in Frankfurt. We were trying to produce a paper with colour which looked like the thing we had described months ago to investors. On one occasion Nick Garland said, 'I have nothing against colour. I am sure that in five years' time all quality newspapers will probably have it. It's just that the Independent should not have it now.'

On Wednesday August 6th we had a meeting in my tiny office in the corner of the foreign department at which Andreas, Matthew, Nick (just back from Bordeaux) Alexander and myself were present. Matthew, who clearly regarded the debate as a waste of valuable time, left after a few minutes. Nick argued that Thirkell should replace Mullins. I felt that Andreas would be unlikely to accept this, and when he asked for my view I suggested that Mullins should continue with his dummy, but that at the same time Thirkell be asked to produce a complete dummy of his own which we could then compare with Mullins's. Alexander agreed that this was the best plan, as did Andreas, who described it as his 'insurance'.

Nick Thirkell accepted the commission, and was briefed by Andreas, Matthew and myself on August 11th. Not for the last time he shot himself and his supporters in the foot, by announcing that he was committed to going on holiday on August 21st. Since we were running out of time, we thought that this imminent self-imposed deadline was a good thing. But in fact Thirkell had set himself an impossible task – to design an entire newspaper in ten days – and was forced to ask his two partners to help him. Thereby he sowed the seeds of his own downfall. For his part, Mullins threw up his hands and left.

On the evening of August 21st Thirkell and his two colleagues came to City Road to present their dummy. Nick Garland had gone back to France; Andreas, Matthew, Alexander and myself waited in benign and expectant mood. Also present, and much less benign, were Nigel Lloyd and Michael Crozier.

One of Thirkell's partners said that the three of them had been working night and day. Perhaps his tone was a little too plaintive, but no matter. Thirkell nervously produced the complete dummy newspaper. We had already seen the the first three pages, though Nigel Lloyd, who passionately believed that the Independent should look like a newspaper of the future, had not, and he took the opportunity to lob a couple of stun-grenades in poor Thirkell's direction. Thus far, however, Thirkell was on safe and familiar ground, and Andreas, Matthew, Alexander and I sat like proud parents waiting to see their favoured child take first prize for French translation.

It was when he got beyond page three that things began to go wrong. Far from looking like a development of Thirkell's previous work, the pages began to resemble a poor and inferior copy of Mullins's dummy. We were all dumbfounded. Lloyd, supported by well-aimed covering fire from Crozier, began to lay into Thirkell, and none of us felt able to do anything about it. Whoever had described Nigel Lloyd as 'going nuclear' had not been a close student of warfare. This was a controlled and deadly onslaught, a sort of undercover 'snatch' at the end of which two or three bodies are found expertly trussed.

'But you can't do that,' said Lloyd, in his curious rasping voice, pointing to a particularly catastrophic example of Thirkell's work. 'You can't end a column here, and then start it again right up there. No *journalist* would do that.'

Thirkell was gradually being beaten into submission. 'Well, perhaps you're right about that, we have had to work under tremendous pressure – I can't tell you how tremendous the pressure has been – but I can't accept that the dummy is as bad as you say.'

Throughout these exchanges Andreas had been heating up like a pressure cooker and now the lid blew off. His dreams must have seemed almost shattered. Mullins had gone, and now, only six weeks before launch, all he had was this miserable ragbag.

It was Andreas who went nuclear. 'This is nothing less than a fraud. I'm not going to pay you a single penny for this work unless you come back and get it right.' As he said this his whole body actually *quivered*.

Understandably, Thirkell and his partners were not used to being spoken to like this. They said that they would like to adjourn. When they returned they announced that they had never been treated in such a manner and had no intention of doing any more work. To get out of the door, they then had to run the gauntlet of the people they had come to please. Alexander and I looked embarrassed and helpless. Andreas's face flashed bright scarlet. Matthew spat out, 'Disgraceful. This is a rip-off.'

The next day Michael Crozier was asked to take over the design of the Independent.

*

Andreas had ordained that we should have a six-week programme of dummies. No one else would have dreamt of so long a period, but he was right. The dummies began on August 19th, two days before the catastrophic meeting with Thirkell, and ran most days until the launch. To start with they were primitive; the automatic typesetter (made, as it happens by our old friends at Xenotron) produced one page after another, work that with old technology had taken hundreds of men, and pages were then photocopied and stapled together. From Tuesday September 2nd we produced complete printed dummies.

The very early dummies, spotted with white spaces where stories and headlines should have been, were dreadful. Quite a few journalists had yet to join us – only a few foreign correspondents were in place – so we had a skeleton staff. The computer system kept playing up and many journalists, despite brief training courses, were cack-handed with the new technology. Most important of all, we didn't yet have a settled design, and so we didn't have a newspaper.

As I write, I have before me a few pages from the first dummies which are lightly annotated in Andreas's hand. God knows how they came into my possession. By the lead story on a home news page of Thursday August 21st, he writes: 'Very good material but requires editing.' In the same article he underlines 'believed to be' and in another piece on the sports page he circles 'no doubt' – in both cases displaying his dislike of the smallest degree of uncertainty or speculation in a news article. By another story on the same page he has written 'interesting', which he has underlined. These occasional judgments appear on pages which are about as ugly as it is possible to be, but he has made no marginal notes about the design or lay-out.

Though Thirkell had gone off on holiday, in his absence the dummies gradually became more and more like the beautiful design which he had produced for us in the middle of July. His chiselled masthead, with its eagle carrying a folded copy of a newspaper, was substituted for a variety of displeasing, black mastheads which had rolled out of the design department. Adrian O'Neill did not like Thirkell's masthead, and at the end of one of our 12 o'clock directors' meetings had a stand-off with Andreas, Matthew and myself, who now embraced it with open arms.

'I think it's too old fashioned,' said Adrian, who had perhaps been talking to Saatchi's, firm believers in the the need for the Independent to look as though it were firmly rooted in modernity. 'I believe that it would be better if the letters were filled in, just so.' And he produced an inked-in masthead which we studied judiciously.

'I think the chiselled one is better,' said Andreas, who could be remarkably doctrinaire for a man who boasted that he knew nothing about design.

'My view is that it looks . . . old fashioned,' said Adrian.

Andreas was beginning to simmer a bit. 'I don't agree.' He glared at Adrian – a sort of fairly friendly first cousin to the glare to which he had subjected the departing Thirkell. There was a pause.

'Well, I think that you are making a fatal mistake,' said Adrian.

The spirit of Thirkell still hovered over City Road. In the dummy of September 2nd, and all subsequent dummies, the Oxford rule re-appeared, though in thinner and more elegant form than in his July front page. Then, after a certain amount of experimentation with other headline typefaces such as Gibraltar and Clarendon, Thirkell's Century is re-introduced. The headlines, set left throughout September, are centred in the dummy of October 1st and until March 1993, as they had been in Thirkell's original dummy.

Powerful though the spirit of Thirkell may have been, it was not by itself responsible for all these changes. Crozier might now have got his hands on the levers, which is to say he understood and employed the Atex system with great expertise, but he could not damp down the ideas which Thirkell and his co-revisionists had introduced. Andreas in his heart sensed that many of these ideas were right. That was why, notwithstanding the row with Thirkell, he allowed himself to be persuaded by Nick Garland and myself to let him do some more work. On September 8th Thirkell came to City Road to help in the design department, though he left shortly afterwards. But still the pro-Thirkell camp, in which Andreas had at least half a foot, rooted for their troublesome hero. He came to City Road four more times, mostly to speak to Andreas, and kept a safe distance from Crozier; he sent at least two letters with recommendations, some of which were acted upon. Meanwhile, when he was not there, Nick Garland and I – Alexander was away for most of September – directly or through Andreas tried to push Crozier in the right direction.

Crozier, in his book, depicts himself as being very much in control of the design during this period, and makes no reference to Thirkell or his continuing influence at this time. Perhaps we can understand why he blows his own trumpet so loudly. What may appear more strange is that Andreas should have subsequently written Thirkell out of history. He did not understand that he had been saved, nor by whom. But that was the future.*

*

* At the end of March 1987, Thirkell wrote to Andreas complaining that Crozier was representing himself as having 'total responsibility' for the now widely-praised design whereas, in Thirkell's view, 'our role was architect, and Michael Crozier's was master builder'. He asked for Andreas's thoughts on the matter, and he got them in a curt reply dated April 6th 1987 which acknowledged only that he had had 'a definate [sic] influence on the final design of the Independent'.

The last six weeks. Now, looking back, I can impose a bogus sense of order – this happened, that happened, and then we decided to do such-and-such – but it was not like that at all. It was like driving through dense fog at a hundred miles an hour, trying to remember the thousand things yet to do, unsure of the controls, and overtaken by occasional waves of tiredness which became more and more powerful, more encompassing, less re-sistible, as the date of the launch approached.

I can see Douglas Long who has changed in the last few weeks, changed back to the bullying, grumpy, and yet still sometimes charming, chief executive he must have been before. As the launch day approaches, Douglas becomes angrier and angrier, chastising Steve Conaway, our director of operations, and his sidekick, Chris Hugh-Jones, for the continual problems with the computer system. I can see Douglas complaining about piles of potentially inflammable cardboard boxes in the base-ment, as though they have nothing to do with him, are not his responsibility. 'Christ! Why doesn't somebody bloody well re-move them!'

I can see myself, sometimes the last to leave the building, walking across the huge empty newsroom from my own depart-ment to the home department and on to sport at the far end, turning off every left-on computer (journalists are so careless . . .) after one went up in smoke last week, to which event Steve Conaway reacted with characteristic and infuriating insou-ciance, and then locking and re-locking every door, wondering, as I drive away, what will happen to us *if the whole bloody building burns down?*

I can see Ed Steen with a half-empty bottle of vodka on his desk. I can *hear* Nigel Lloyd grumbling about the eagle ('that bird') and Christopher Gilbert, one of the assistant foreign editors, saying that Century headline typeface makes the Independent 'look provincial', hear him cursing the computer system (which keeps on 'going down') as though this tech-nology has been installed for a hundred years and we should jolly well expect it to work by this time. I can see Sarah Hogg cornering the peripatetic Chris Hugh-Jones and telling him that she will not leave until he answers her questions about com-puters – and satisfactorily too, thank you very much. I can see Nick Ashford's shy and worried smile.

And I can see Andreas Whittam Smith, brow furrowed, red-faced, bogged down in endless vistas of perplexity, advised a hundred different ways, talking like some crazed general of 'crossing a thousand bridges', but throughout it all, brave and, because of that, reassuring, floating around the newsroom encouraging, a little touch of Harry in the night: we're glad he's there.

*

Painfully, slowly, dummy by dummy, the Independent began to emerge. The photocopied, stapled dummies of late August which had so little in common with the the final version gave way to the first printed dummies of early September, clear forerunners these, which, as the month advanced, edged towards their destiny. It is not possible to say on this or that day the Independent was born, but somewhere in the dummies of very early October it has found itself, though there were still small design flaws – fussy little drawings, embellishing the health, media and education pages.

The journalists worked for the newspaper which they saw developing day by day, and it was for most of them the paper which they wanted to work for; upmarket, serious, even earnest, its nature lay in their hearts as it lay on the increasingly elegant, stately pages; form and substance flowed together. Tom Sutcliffe, the arts editor, called the new paper 'classic with a twist'. Certainly the twist was there in several innovations such as the listings, calculated to appeal particularly to the young, but it was the classicism which struck readers most when the Independent appeared on October 7th, the sense that the Independent had always been there, part of our history, yet missing from our lives.

Neither Andreas nor anyone else ever sat down and said, this is the paper we want. It was not like that at all. Andreas compared editing with conducting an orchestra, bringing out the best in everyone, creating a harmony out of separateness. It was more like controlling and directing the passage of a turbulent stream. Later, Andreas began to believe in his own journalistic genius, the transforming power of his own editorial ideas. He had a genius of a sort, but it was an organising and planning and visionary sort of genius rather than a journalistic one. The ideas which flowed into this growing newspaper came not principally from Andreas or Matthew or myself but from the journalists who had joined us, who shared an idea, beyond any neat definition, of what they wanted the paper to be. The stroke of genius was to let this happen.

And, as is necessary at the genesis of all such enterprises, almost everyone excelled themselves. It was not simply a question of hard work, though we all worked harder than we ever had before, but also of inspiration – an inspiration built up by hope and conviction. The good were brilliant, the mediocre were good, the bad became mediocre. The very bad, of whom there were only one or two, were fired.

In September we had two power cuts. The first was caused by a gas explosion in the local National Westminster Bank; the second by an unfortunate building worker who put his drill through an electricity cable. The same boom that had given the City the confidence to invest in the Independent, the boom which would give new readers the money to buy the newspaper and the advertisers the scope to advertise in it – this same boom was washing up City Road, sweeping down inoffensive late Victorian buildings for new offices.

We did not have our own emergency generator, having been advised by the electricity board that we could expect a power cut every nine years. Our computers went down. On the first occasion, some shareholders who were visiting the building had to be shown around by candlelight. Though we then ordered a generator, it had not arrived when the next power cut happened. There was much cursing and gnashing of teeth from the likes of Chris Gilbert, as though this were an affront to be taken personally. The day wore on with no sign that electricity was going to be restored, and a few journalists began to grumble that it was a waste of time for us to hang around, since even if the electricity came on there would be no time to complete the day's dummy. It was getting dark now, and a spectral figure that could just be made out as Andreas glided into the newsroom, asked the journalists to gather around. Some of them thought, and not a few of them hoped, that he was going to say that everyone could now go home, see you tomorrow, take advantage of an early night.

'We have been in touch with the London Electricity Board,' he said, 'and they have told us that supplies may be restored in an hour or two ... I have heard that one or two people are suggesting that we should pack up for the night, but I insist, *I absolutely insist*, that we remain here, until midnight if necessary. In less than three weeks we shall be producing a real paper, and we might find ourselves in a similar predicament, so we must, absolutely must, stay here, so that if the electricity does come on we may be able to produce something.'

Patrick Marnham, just about to leave for Paris, was standing next to me in the shadows. 'He's completely right,' he murmured. 'Completely right.'

I said nothing in reply. But I thought to myself, this man is a leader.

*

The last two weeks: meetings of departmental heads and others every morning, picking over the day's dummy, reading out news lists as though this is already a real newspaper. Then, for me, a flurry of foreign department meetings, stories of correspondents being unable to file 'into the computer', of money transferred to foreign accounts gone astray; worried voices from 6,000 miles away wanting reassurance about the market research of dummies, which was encouraging, certainly for the foreign pages, though some found the paper a little humourless. Then, in the late afternoon, Andreas and the departmental heads gather again in the half-glass office at the far end of the newsroom, nicknamed (by Ed Steen?) 'the Wendy House', where we plan the front page of tomorrow's dummy; not much sign here of Andreas's later adventurousness. It is a kind of dream, all this work and still no real newspapers, only dummies which hardly anyone else sees (though our rivals cunningly contrive to), dummies which have no audience and are in truth dead, and aptly named.

Now there are advertisements on television. A young man is hit on the head repeatedly as we hear opinionated voices in the background. 'In our opinion.' Smack. 'But in *our* opinion.' Another smack. (Hang on. Isn't this a bit violent?) And then a smooth reassuring voice tells us about a wonderful new news-

105

paper which will escape the sins of the fallen world. 'From October 7th. The Independent. It is. Are you?'*

A few days to go and we have a gloomy visitation from John Perriss and Mike Ainsworth from Saatchi and Saatchi, arranged by Adrian O'Neill. John says that he has watched the development of the dummies with anxiety. The paper has in his view grown too upmarket, and in its present form is unlikely to sell much more than 250,000. He and Mike say that we are not advertising our wares sufficiently on the front page. To throw out a few crumbs of comfort to our old supporters, who still have some residual authority over us, we agree to a more prominent 'summary box' occupying the whole of column eight, down to the advertisement, on the front page. But I cannot believe that this odd little compromise is going to make any difference to our fortunes.

How tired we all are. A few days before the launch Andreas asks me to stay behind after an afternoon meeting in the Wendy House. He wonders how I feel.

' Fine,' I reply.

'Linda Tanner says you look incredibly tired. You must be easy with your self. We can't afford to lose you.' And as he says this, I must be tired, for absurdly I feel my eyes pricking with tears.

Will it happen? Can it be that we are really going to produce a new quality daily national newspaper – the first for a hundred and thirty one years, our car stickers proclaim – of which I will be foreign editor, and Andreas will be editor and Matthew his deputy, *a paper which you can go into a shop and buy this time next week?*

On Sunday October 5th Andreas, Matthew and I meet for lunch at the River Room in the Savoy – an idea of Matthew's, this, a sort of pre-emptive nostalgia. But it is not a happy lunch, for in that morning's Observer Andreas has been profiled unsympathetically by some anonymous hand in a piece headlined 'Andy Pandy comes out to play'. He is depicted as sometimes

---

* Little badges carrying this slogan were distributed to staff and friends. Some had the alternative message, 'I am. Are you?' which became something of a collector's piece for homosexuals.

ineffectual and a spectator on life's events. He is teased for his background and physical appearance. Matthew and I are outraged; Andreas seems stunned, ruminative, as though he has suddenly found himself alone on the centre of a stage and is for a moment struck with terror. Trying to introduce some levity into the occasion, I suggest that we all write down the circulation of the Independent in six months time – a bottle of champagne for the winner. The pieces of paper are entrusted to me.*

Monday October 6th, the last day. I feel calm. We've been doing this for a few weeks now. There are television cameras at the morning conference which so irritate Andreas (or is he putting on a show?) that he says they will have to go unless the TV crew stop chattering. *'We are trying to produce a newspaper.'* In the afternoon a bottle of champagne is delivered for Andreas, accompanied by a Daily Telegraph 'compliments slip'. It reads: 'With the compliments and best wishes of everybody at the Daily Telegraph who wish you luck before we set about buying you! Max Hastings, October 6th 1986.' Andreas's office is bedecked with flowers. Celia, who feels sorry for him on account of the Observer piece, has sent him a bouquet of white roses. How many people want the Independent to succeed!

The Tory party conference begins in Bournemouth tomorrow but today there is not much news about. Mark Urban, our defence correspondent, has a small scoop about a Soviet submarine which has sunk in the Atlantic Ocean. Sarah Hogg and Andrew Marr, political correspondent, co-operate on a story about the latest sterling crisis which *faute de mieux* becomes the 'splash'. For foreign, James Fenton has done a piece about cooking a goat for Muslim rebels in the Philippines (well, the market research did say more humour) and Patrick Marnham is with the Pope in southern France (his piece goes at the bottom of the front page, 'the basement'). Williams Rees-Mogg, the nearest thing we have to a political columnist, has a piece on the

---

* Andreas's bet, when opened, is 410,000, mine is 320,000 and Matthew's is 170,000. I was the closest, though I don't think I ever got any champagne. How did Matthew manage to get up in the morning?

centre pages about the BBC. ('Mogg', was wooed by Andreas and succumbed at his own hearth, Peter Jenkins of the Sunday Times and Hugo Young of the Guardian having proved resistant).

Nothing sensational, but it will do.

On page two, Andreas has written, with help from Matthew, a what-we-are-all-about piece, slightly plodding and jejeune, which is signed 'Andreas Whittam Smith – Editor'. 'We have deliberately eschewed difference for its own sake,' runs the second paragraph, 'for example by resisting the temptation of being the first 'quality tabloid' or by over-using editorial colour.' On independence Andreas writes: 'We will both praise and criticise without reference to a party line. Our campaigning will emerge from our rt-steve-usrting [this is a gremlin in the system, forever obliterating whatever campaigning intentions Andreas had] rather than the other way around.'

Nothing sensational but it'll be all right, it will do.

After the first edition, there is a party and champagne. Shortly after midnight, copies of the paper arrive from Sittingbourne, the nearest of our contract printers to London. It looks fine but there is nothing, other than the price – 25p – and Vol. 1, both below the masthead, to distinguish the paper from the dummies which have gone before. Could we have fallen victim to a case of collective manic delusion? Andreas makes a short speech, thanking everybody for their hard work, though he does not mention Matthew or me, as I had thought he might. He toasts the Independent, whereupon the crowd bellows enthusiastically and cheers and sings 'For he's a jolly good fellow.' Lots of people ask the founders and others to sign first editions. On Nick Garland's I write, 'To Nick: Who more than anyone is responsible for this design. Stephen.' Later I go down to the computer room and ask Brian Hutt, our circulation manager, how the printing is going. On the whole, not too badly. He says that he does not believe that the circulation will ever drop below 400,000.

We have done it; this much at least. How extraordinary it is; for many people, for me perhaps, this night may mark the most precious achievement of their careers. And yet I feel an edge of anti-climax. Matthew comes up and half embraces me. Later I congratulate Andreas. I tell him that his is a very great achievement. Throughout the entire party he has scarcely spoken to Matthew or myself. Matthew proposes to Andreas that the three of us should meet briefly, perhaps shake one another by the hand, but this has not happened, and he feels a little sad. Andreas is on a high of his own, from which in a sense he has never come down.

5

Matthew Symonds Falls Off a Motorcycle

The next morning there was a breakfast arranged by Stephen Rose for the directors and investors at a restaurant in Finsbury Circus. Driving in from Greenwich, I listened to a piece on the *Today* programme on Radio Four about the Independent. A reporter had gone down to Waterloo Station to ask some people what they thought of the new newspaper. One person said that he had been unable to get hold of a copy. Another said that he had seen the paper and quite liked what he saw. A third was of the opinion that it looked rather dull. There then followed a brief studio discussion involving several 'leading journalists'. The general view was that it was a good try but that there was nothing special about the newspaper. The political columnist Simon Jenkins thought that it looked worthy.

The news at City Road was that we had had a complete print run of 650,000 from our four plants, and although Sittingbourne had not finished printing until after five o'clock in the morning, by and large distribution had gone fairly well. Later on, there were reports of sell-outs.

That afternoon a wreath arrived for Andreas accompanied by a card which read 'With compliments from all at The Daily Telegraph.' As wreaths go it was attractive enough, composed of bright yellow and white flowers, white berries which looked as though they were made of polystyrene, and dark green leaves. Trying to make a joke of it, Andreas walked into the newsroom carrying this thing, but the effect was irresistibly melancholic. With its trailing black ribbon, the wreath was a bad, sad joke which we thought reflected not so much contempt at the first issue as a residual degree of bitterness which some at the Telegraph felt at our defection, as well as a competitive fear. Someone suggested that it be laid on John Bunyan's rectangular grave in Bunhill Fields, which it was. This process sanctified the wreath, or deprived it of its threatening quality, and it became an inoffensive part of our world.

The first weeks after the launch were exhilarating: we had a paper and it really wasn't at all bad. To see someone in the street carrying a copy of the Independent made the heart pound with joy. For all that, the newspaper was by no means an instant success. The Fleet Street view, which is to say the view one heard most of, was that the Independent was worthy and solid but dull. Day by day circulation fell, though we then had no immediate idea, as we did later, of exactly what we were selling. The figures, when they came through, were at first disappointing and then worrying. The average daily circulation for October was 332,957, for November 301,050 and for December 272,180. In January, a month during which the sales of newspapers generally rise after Christmas, the average was 256,923. In the wintry weather at the end of that month, when distribution was often impeded by snow, we dropped below even that figure. We did not fully realise exactly how low we had sunk and, by the time we did, there were the glimmerings of a gradual circulation increase.

As the figures continued to slide, with no one able to predict when they would 'bottom out,' several of the directors became jumpy. One or two of the non-executive directors* began to criticise what they called 'the product'. Lord Sieff reported that he kept on meeting people at parties who complained to him that some articles were inordinately long. All such comments were prefixed with 'I'm not an expert,' or 'Speaking as an ignoramus,' but they were intended none the less to reflect displeasure.

* By virtue of his contacts with our investors, Bruce Fireman had been invited to join the board as a non-executive director at the end of November. Tom Attwood had harboured hopes in the same direction – justifiable ones, since at the time of the moneyraising Andreas had sent him a letter in which he said he would try to secure Tom a place on the board.

Among the executives, Douglas Long had a gloomy and a grumpy air. He criticised the newspaper for being too serious and worthy – he had after all been a journalist himself – but he became less and less inclined to take suggestions about how the company should be run. In a sense it wasn't run by him at all, and each director simply got on with his responsibilities, but occasionally a problem would arise which needed some attention from the managing director. There was no certainty that it would get it. On one occasion at one of our midday directors' meetings I mentioned to Douglas the problem of the width of the copies produced by our Peterborough printers. Because of the 'web width' of the presses, newspapers printed there were at least an inch wider than those from our other printers, and therefore rather unwieldy. This was inconvenient for readers, and was also a costly waste of paper ('newsprint'). Douglas's reply to my grumble was, 'You do your job and I'll do mine.' But there was no sign that he was prepared even to think about this issue.

We were selling fewer copies than we had projected, which meant that circulation and advertising revenue were lower than they needed to be.* The question of whether we would need more finance began to be discussed by directors. During this time Andreas held his nerve. His habit of giving his calm and measured briefings to the editorial staff after board meetings inspired confidence, even though the news he brought was not particularly good. Journalists, who on their previous newspapers had not been told a single thing about the economic fortunes of the companies for which they worked, were grateful and astonished that they should be given any information at all. Andreas was almost universally liked and admired. He had a word for the junior sub-editor or young reporter as he floated around the newsroom, and once he was even spotted in the canteen.

There was gossip, of a sort inevitable among journalists when things are not going very well, about a takeover by Fairfax, an Australian newspaper group, or about successors to Andreas

* As a rough rule of thumb, quality papers derive about half their revenue from circulation and about half from advertising. Tabloid papers generally rely less on advertising revenue.

who were supposedly being groomed by the board. Robert Maxwell was also rumoured to be licking his lips. The previous July we had learnt that the publishing billionaire had covertly acquired 4.8 per cent of the company via nominees called Lancashire and Yorkshire. (He seems to have crept in when de Zoete and Bevan made its final push.) Our Articles of Association made it difficult, but in practice not impossible, for any one shareholder to own more than 10 per cent of the company. A takeover by Maxwell was regarded by staff as a kind of sick joke which could happen, as sick jokes sometimes do.

The most persistently anxious of the directors was Stephan Conaway who was in charge of all aspects of the production of the newspaper and, after a few months, its distribution. At one of our daily directors' meetings in January he informed us (Steve is highly numerate, and has among other qualifications, an MBA in Finance and Accounting from Ohio State University) that we were losing £20,000 a day. He was convinced that we would need more finance. His apocalyptic vision seemed overdone, for unlike the other executive directors, all of whom were classified as founders, he had virtually no shares to lose. Moreover, in the event of collapse he would probably by virtue of his skills be able to get a job in almost any country. He had previously worked at the International Herald Tribune in Paris, and had brought with him Chris Hugh-Jones and Hella Schrader, a German, as a kind of job lot.

Stephan W. Conaway, to give him his full title, was a member of that curious breed – the American expatriate. The question is why such a person, well-educated, experienced, apparently at the top of his profession, should choose not to work in his own land where, after all, salaries are usually larger. It was not as though Steve was particularly Anglophile; he seemed, so far as one could judge, to have made himself a capsule securely full of wholesome American artefacts plus American wife and children in Hampstead Garden Suburb, from which he peered quizzically at English ways. I naturally formed the theory that Steve was escaping from something – but what? His family had owned small weekly newspapers in the mid-West – Minnesota, I think – and as a younger man Steve had learnt the arts of setting type, and had even briefly been a sort of cub reporter. He gave the impression that the weekly papers were not thriving as once they had, or possibly not at all, and I developed the notion that in this connection there was some disappointment in the past, perhaps not his own past, but his parents' or grand-parents', which he had inherited as inescapably as his natural good manners. And although he was self-confessedly a man of science, occupying a rational world where all problems had potential solutions, even those consigned to his colleague Chris Hugh-Jones, this ancient disappointment, perhaps enriched by the innate gloom of Germanic or Nordic ancestors who had trudged across the snowy wastes of Minnesota, took the form of apparently rational pessimism.

Polite and generally conciliatory in person, Steve ran a tight and austere ship in the computer room. None of his staff was permitted to take a drop of alcohol in City Road, even at official parties. Steve had a tendency also to be doctrinaire about the way journalists should use the computer system which he had designed. If a journalist – this would include Andreas, Matthew or myself – expressed misgivings about a certain technical procedure, he would reel off an explanation, usually incompre-hensible because of its techno-jargon and American phraseology, which freely translated meant, this is the way it has to be and it ain't going to be changed.

One of Steve's bugbears in the weeks following the launch and for the rest of time was the lateness of deadlines. Every page was supposed to be finished by a given time so that it could be automatically typeset and then faxed to each of our printing plants. When pages were finished late, a regular occurrence in the first few weeks, there was a tendency for them 'to bunch' in the system, which meant that transmission to our plants was delayed. Whenever this happened the journalists involved blamed Steve's computer people who in turn blamed the jour-nalists. Steve's answer was that he had designed a foolproof system which could only go wrong with help from journalists. He would then tell us about the St Petersburg Times, a news-paper in Florida for which he had worked for several years, where editors who missed their deadlines were evidently strung up and given a spell in the local stocks.

It was well within the bounds of possibility that such a man would sooner or later clash with Matthew, who had already formed the view that Steve was 'crazy', a judgment which he applied to several people over the years with whom he could not 'relate'. The first bout came just before Christmas, and the morning after an office party. Steve sent a characteristically terse memorandum to Matthew complaining that for the third edition of December 22nd production had been stopped at all four printing plants to make a trivial change. He thought that there were 'better ways to spend time and money'.

Matthew's response was to send a memorandum to Andreas and me, only copied to Steve, which within the conventions of office politics amounted to an open declaration of war. He took 'the strongest possible exception' to Conaway's memo. He explained how 'at 10.40 last night' he was confronted with 'what was a breakdown of discipline on the editorial side which was moving through into operations'. There had been 'nobody in the newsroom' and 'the only way to make the point that the newspaper was still in production was to find a story which we should have been running, but had in fact missed'. Matthew admitted that 'the story was not of great importance', but Steve should jolly well have found out why he had acted as he did. 'I have not been as angry as this since the company was formed,' concluded Matthew.

Andreas called Matthew, Steve and myself together in the small meeting room at the end of his office. Steve defended, albeit in a more emollient form, the memorandum he had sent. While Steve was speaking, Matthew muttered in an audible stage whisper 'what an awful man he is' which we all pretended not to hear. The engagement was a stalemate, with Andreas playing the part of an embarrassed referee who has not quite got on top of the facts. Matthew and Steve settled into a relationship of cordial mutual dislike.

No doubt – to use that phrase detestable to Andreas – Steve's emotions were heightened by his consuming pessimism about the finances of the Independent. So far as Douglas Long was concerned, his case was a good deal worse. Some time towards the end of November, Douglas made an extraordinary proposition to Andreas which suggested to me at the time that he had gone a little mad. It may be that he wanted to precipitate a crisis.

There are possible clues in a memorandum on the subject of 'key-man insurance' for directors, sent by Douglas to the company secretary, Keith Parkinson, on October 24th, and included in November's board papers. There is a stubborn, almost rebellious tone to the note, and at the end a trace of melancholy, even resentment, in his awareness that he is not indispensable. He writes that he has cancelled his appointment 'for the medical examination now required' for the reason that it is 'faintly ridiculous to spend shareholder's money on the substantial annual premium which surely must be demanded to insure someone of my age for £1m.' Now that the paper was 'up and running' he could be 'replaced quite easily'.

One afternoon at the end of November Matthew rushed excitedly into my office, displacing a couple of blameless members of the foreign staff with whom I was chatting. He told me that Douglas had asked to see Andreas. Douglas had said (according to Andreas, who had told Matthew) that he did not like the way the company was being run. It lacked a sense of direction and purpose. Douglas had then reportedly said that he would only remain as managing director if there were a new management structure. Andreas, Christopher Barton, Adrian O'Neill and Steve Conaway would all report separately to Douglas. As for Matthew and Stephen, they would sit on an editorial board, along with Andreas, Sarah Hogg and perhaps Jonathan Fenby, and they would cease being directors. In short, the Independent would be run like a normal newspaper.

Neither Matthew nor I was over the moon to hear that Douglas wished us to give up our seats on the board. After hearing Andreas's account of Douglas's wishes as related by Matthew, I did not think it necessary to go and speak directly to Douglas myself. This was a mistake, if only for the reason that it is better in life to confront the person who is supposedly doing you down.

Andreas asked each director individually whether he wanted the new management structure. Clearly it suited no one, least of all Andreas who had no wish, after all he had achieved, to be answerable to Douglas. Douglas in the meantime had retreated to his commodious office on the fourth floor with its drinks cabinet and television, and made no attempt to put his case. A compromise might perhaps have been worked out, if Andreas had wished for one, but he did not. All the executive directors wanted Douglas to go and for Andreas to succeed him.

Douglas's last board meeting was on December 23rd. The board minutes, bland as ever, give no inkling of the painful nature of that occasion. Do not look to such official accounts to know the true life of a company. Douglas sat there like a wounded dog, immobile, silent except for one intervention, but dignified withal, patient for once, and unsurprised. We acted as though he was not there. Already he was becoming for Newspaper Publishing plc a non-person, someone referred to only with a dying chuckle and the shake of a head, unmourned, mocked and then forgotten.

At the February board meeting Andreas was confirmed as the company's new chief executive.

*

Though circulation was flagging, Andreas entered the new year in optimistic form. Even before Douglas's departure, he had already started to produce his own figures which monitored the health of the company. Late in the evening, when others were concerning themselves with the details of the front page, he could often be found at his desk, bent over a pocket calculator, which from time to time he prodded with his right forefinger, as he covered pages with figures in black ink. Sometimes at our midday directors' meetings (with Douglas gone these had moved from the boardroom to the little room off Andreas's office) he would proudly produce a sheet of figures, perhaps 'a four-week moving average' of circulation or the latest advertising yields.

A second television promotional campaign was due to start on January 12th, and editorial changes were set in train. Coverage of obituaries, law reports and letters was increased, and more space was also devoted to share price and unit trust lists. These improvements, made particularly with an eye to The Times, which was beginning to supplant the Daily Telegraph in our minds as our chief rival, were set out by Andreas in a memorandum to all editorial staff dated December 28th 1986. This shows his qualities as a planner and his liking for generalised exhortation: 'During the period of promotion, it is especially important that the paper sparkles with good writing. Editorial departments must take special steps to generate such work. In particular, editorial must be running stories and features that can gain coverage on TV and radio; this is very important. (department heads.)'

Andreas's technique of editing was on the whole remarkably disengaged. To a large extent the paper just happened, which is to say that departments ran their affairs with very little direction. Jonathan Fenby compared Andreas to the king of mediaeval France towards whom the various dukes and counts who actually ran France would pay obeisance (Jonathan saw himself as the duke of Burgundy) while maintaining their independence. This metaphor, amusing to Andreas, was not wholly accurate, since he enjoyed a degree of respect from his heads of department which would have made any mediaeval king of France jump for joy. But he was extraordinarily *dégagé*. This method of working was generally successful because most of the 'barons', as Jonathan called them, were imaginative and diligent editors. It was also agreeable to be able to run the foreign department with a virtually free hand.

However, it was not entirely a good system. It created a paper which was too plainly composed of parts which all subscribed to the same standards but interpreted them differently. And the parts were not all equally good. The features on the 'centre-spread' were rightly regarded as wooden and uninspired. John Morrison, our features editor who had no experience in newspaper journalism, would have been grateful for the guiding hand of a knowledgeable editor, but Andreas lacked the specific expertise to help him. Some of the 'feature packages' on the home pages were excessively worthy and long-winded.

Matthew and I had chivvied Andreas into agreeing to have weekly meetings with us – he was increasingly reluctant to place himself in a forum in which he might be subject to our influence – and we would complain, usually to no avail, about some pieces. Whatever he may have said in his memorandum about the virtues of a sparkling newspaper, Andreas had an amazingly high tolerance of earnest journalism, and could cheerfully wade through lengthy articles whose authors had never spared a thought for the arts of entertainment.

Andreas as editor was most in evidence at the main morning editorial conference, to which heads of department or their deputies and sundry others came. This was a 'post-mortem' during which Andreas would flick through the morning's paper and pass school-masterly judgments. 'Interesting piece by so-and-so.' 'I liked such-and-such's article.' After Justin Arundale became our librarian – this was much later, in November 1987 – he would be asked to read the paper before the meeting and to underline misprints ('literals') or other obvious howlers. If Andreas was in a bad mood he could get very upset about a literal. Once he held forth on the iniquities of the phrase 'of course', which he ranked in the same stylistic sewer as 'no doubt'. On these occasions, his manner of editing put me in mind of a first world war general inspecting the troops at the front and kicking up a fuss because someone's cap badge is not straight.

As time went on, and he grew more confident, Andreas began to leave more of a mark on these conferences. He was not an editor with an eye for detail – unless of a mundane sort, as when he swooped down on on the latest miscreant 'of course' – but he produced imaginative ideas. 'What about a satellite picture?' he asked an astonished Alun John, our picture editor, when the M25 'London orbital' motorway had been completed. He could be engagingly self-deprecatory when he came up with such ideas. 'Tell me if you think I've gone mad, what do you think, Jonathan, about this?' His lack of a rounded journalistic experience was here a positive advantage. In this respect – in contrast to his insatiable appetite for earnestness – Andreas was automatically on the side of the reader. Too many journalists, particularly specialists, are so close to their material that they have lost that necessary sense of wonder. Andreas, with his hard and energetic intelligence, looked at problems for the first time.

One morning some time later he announced at a morning conference that the previous evening he had sat at dinner next to the Soviet ambassador who had told him that the Soviet Union wished above all else to find a way of withdrawing from Afghanistan. The war, according to the ambassador, was costing too many lives and growing increasingly unpopular in the Soviet Union. Andreas suggested that Rupert Cornwell, our

Moscow correspondent, should try to find out whether what the ambassador said was true. After the conference, John Torode and I had a little chuckle. 'He just doesn't understand the Soviet psyche, does he, John?' I said. 'No, he does not,' replied Torode, in a conspiratorial, old hand's way. 'When he's been looking at the Soviets as long as we have he'll realise that you can't trust a word of what they say.' But Andreas was right.

*

The lowest point for circulation was January 1987. From the beginning of February sales began to rise quite sharply. Other than the better weather, and the tendency for newspaper circulation to be stronger in February than January, there was no obvious explanation. We had simply 'bottomed out'. John Perriss and Mike Ainsworth had told us how after a few months sales of successful new launches hit the bottom of a J-curve (described as 'the hockey-stick effect') and then miraculously begin to rise. This exhilarating experience seemed now to be happening to us. Sales improved from 256,923 in January to 278,981 in February and 290,955 in March. Even though we might still need more money, it seemed that the Independent had become that unusual phenomenon – a successfully launched newspaper

A degree of success meant that some old flirtations could be re-opened and some new ones started. Andreas again contacted Peter Jenkins. Most people thought – perhaps Peter did himself – that he was less impressive producing one long ruminative weekly piece for the Sunday Times than he had been doing more frequent shorter articles for the Guardian. Now that the Independent seemed here to stay, Peter was attracted by the idea of returning to a daily paper with which he was more in political sympathy than with the Sunday Times, and which was moreover prepared to pay him a considerable amount of money. He joined as associate editor, with some ill-defined suzerainty over the centre pages where his political column was to appear. I had met him once before, when we had sat opposite each other at a dinner during a Labour party conference at Blackpool several years before. On that occasion my existence had not impinged upon him; now he made quite a big fuss of me.

Another recruit was Miles Kington, who wrote a funny column called 'Moreover' for The Times. Influenced by the widespread view that the Independent was short on jokes, Andreas mounted a midnight raid and brought back Kington in one piece. But whereas Peter Jenkins quickly became a presence at City Road, where he was installed in an office that was soon impressively lined with Hansard and foreign policy magazines, Miles Kington wrote his column in Somerset, and ventured only very occasionally to lunches at the Independent, during which he looked pained and affected a complete ignorance of newspapers. He would tend to escape early to get the train for Bath, as though these departed with the regularity of the trans-Siberian express.

A third recruit was Andrew Gimson, deputy editor of the Spectator. I did not know him, though when I was still at the Telegraph he had once commissioned me to do a piece about South Africa for his magazine. When his old Cambridge friend Charles Moore had become editor of the Spectator he had been lifted from the obscurity of the Tory Research Department. Because of his extreme youth he was nicknamed 'Andrew Gimslip' by Private Eye, though the sobriquet was misplaced, unless irony were intended, for in attire Andrew did not recall either gyms or slips or indeed sportswear of any variety. He was one of the fathers of young fogeyism, and looked as though he had walked, or possibly bicycled, out of the Cambridge union *circa* 1952.

Matthew and I felt that the leader column had not flourished under the management of John Torode who, much to my irritation, was dignified with the absurd title of 'chief policy editor'. Surely, I had said to Andreas, the editor is the chief policy editor. In John's grandiose title I had detected a tendency towards empire building, but I could not have been more wrong. John's little empire fell apart remarkably quickly, hastened by his hiring as his deputy a female former colleague whose skills as a journalist excluded leader writing. As time went on, John managed sometimes to drive Matthew to distraction, an art he unconsciously honed to perfection. His *pièce de résistance* was the stream of consciousness leader which abandoned argument in favour of a series of random statements. He would trip into

Matthew's room, an innocent if slightly troubled expression on his face, uttering no more than the normal quota of apologies, and invite the deputy editor to inspect the offending editorial on his computer screen.

By March 1987 I thought, like Andreas and Matthew, that John needed help, and that an ideal candidate was the extremely competent Andrew Gimson, who had the added benefit of harbouring some Tory instincts of which I expected to approve. I asked Andrew to come and see Matthew and myself when Andreas happened to be away. He was very agreeable and seemed to understand what the Independent had achieved and what it could yet become. Matthew, enjoying the role of acting editor, was keen to appoint Andrew on the spot, believing that he had nine-tenths of Andreas's approval to do so. Andrew was circumspect. 'I would love to come and work for you,' he said, 'and it is very good indeed of you to ask me. But if you don't mind, I would like first to meet Andreas when he returns.' In this he showed his great natural courtesy and prudence. When Andreas came back he was very pleased to confirm the appointment, and regarded Andrew with an indulgence which might have been lacking if he had already been installed.

I had suggested to Andrew that he should have some sort of title, and he hit upon 'chief leader writer', which seemed to rival in importance John Torode's office of chief policy editor. Amid this confusion they became the best of colleagues.

*

On the afternoon of Sunday February 22nd Andreas rang me at home. He asked whether he could come and see me to discuss something of very great urgency. I said of course he could, though having just returned from Kathmandu, where I had delivered a speech under the terms of the Andreas Whittam Smith amendment,* I wondered why the matter could not wait until the next day. However, he was very keen to come.

* In December 1986 Andreas had been invited to go to Australia, all costs paid, to deliver a speech. He had accepted this invitation without considering it a contravention of the 'no freebies' policy which he vigorously enforced. Andreas justified it on the grounds that he was giving a speech. I called it 'the Andreas Whittam Smith amendment'.

He arrived at about 9 o'clock. It was only Andreas's second visit to our house and he looked around appraisingly. The drawing room was being re-decorated so I asked him to come up to my little study which overlooked Greenwich Park. 'Nice place you have here,' he said in an effort to soften what he must have recognised as a bizarre visitation. He mentioned the lunch two days earlier at which he had collected the 'What the Papers Say' award for Newspaper of the Year. I asked him to sit in an armchair, and sat on an upright chair with my back to my desk and the window. He looked solemn, at first sight, like a doctor about to unfold painful news, but he was flushed, and his lips seemed almost about to break into a strange grin. I sensed that deep down he was excited about something.

'Something rather terrible has happened while you have been away, and although I know what I think I am going to do, I thought that I would come and ask for your advice.'

'Fine,' I said, feeling the thrill of being on the verge of an untold story.

'A source has told me that a woman whom Matthew recommended as chief features sub-editor is, in fact, his . . . mistress.* I understand that he asked John Morrison to interview her, though she has no experience of journalism. She works in publishing as an editor – for Butterworths, I am told. Do you know about this?'

'Well, I'd heard that John Morrison was proposing to appoint someone, but I haven't met her.'

This was not entirely true. One evening several weeks earlier I had seen Matthew sitting in his car in the part of the car-park at City Road which is covered. When I had gone over to say goodnight to him I had discovered that he was next to an attractive woman whom I did not recognise. Matthew did not introduce her, and the two of us had had a short embarrassed conversation as though she were not there.

'Are you sure that she's his mistress?' I asked Andreas.

'Yes, I made enquiries. She can't take up the job, of course. John Morrison quite agrees with me. He had no idea of who she was.'

---

* Everyone used this archaic term, mainly because Matthew himself did.

'No.'

'I have also discovered that Matthew took his mistress to the SDP conference in Harrogate last autumn. I've asked Graham Luff for a copy of Matthew's expenses, and it seems that he charged the Independent for a double room so that he could have this woman with him. It cost an extra ten pounds.'

'I see.'

At this point Andreas moved into another gear. 'There are a lot of things I am prepared to put up with, but the one thing I will not tolerate is fiddling of expenses, defrauding the company. I suppose you could say that she was a qualified publishing editor who may be very good at her job. But I simply cannot stomach the expenses thing.'

'I can see that it was wrong of him,' I said, 'but it was only ten pounds. He should obviously be asked to pay it back and be read the riot act.'

'If Matthew can cheat us out of ten pounds he can cheat us out of ten thousand pounds! Don't you agree?'

'No, I don't think I do . . . What do you propose to do?'

'I think there is only one course of action open to us. I think that I will have to ask him to leave. I do not see how I can work with him again. There are simply some things I cannot bear . . . Do you think I am right?'

'Andreas, you can't do that to Matthew. Think what he's done for the company. Sometimes I've thought that if it hadn't been for him, back in 1985, we might have given up. You can't toss him out now for . . . for what is not much more than an unfortunate error of judgment.'

'I am afraid that I cannot see any other alternative,' said Andreas. 'I don't see how I could ever work with Matthew again. I would always be wondering about his motives.'

In springing to Matthew's defence I thought that he had been foolish but not in any sense venal. I was not moved just by a desire to defend someone I liked who had brought me together with Andreas in the first place. I did not think that Matthew's departure would be a calamity for the company, and a little demon in the back of my mind even whispered that with Matthew gone I would indisputably be Andreas's successor. I was simply unthinkingly moved by an elementary sense of justice which nine people out of ten would have felt.

'Andreas, if you sack Matthew now, he will be ruined for what, for a little stupidity over a job, for ten pounds which he may have felt was a little indulgence from a company for which he has done so much.'

And so it went on, with neither side giving any ground. Eventually Andreas said he would have to leave. 'I'll think about what you have said, though I'm afraid I have not changed my mind.' I was tempted to ask him why he had bothered to come.

The next day Kingsley Amis came to lunch with Andreas, Matthew, Sebastian Faulks, myself, Peter Kellner and our food correspondent, Jeremy Round. Matthew was particularly keen to air his views, pontificating about the Middle East in a kind of competitive double act with Peter Kellner, who had recently joined the paper to write about politics. Tolstoy himself could not have guessed that beneath Matthew's bravado hid a stricken soul. Mr Amis look increasingly downcast, his only friend a not very subtle claret. Andreas, apparently insensitive to the mood of his guest, said that what the Independent needed was a story which would add 50,000 to our circulation. Did Mr Amis have any ideas? Mr Amis did not. After lunch Sebastian took the great novelist off to a pub in an attempt to deaden his recollections with further draughts of alcohol, but to no avail. Mr Amis soon threw in the towel as one of our occasional book reviewers, confessing to Sebastian that it was 'that lunch which did for me'.

In the afternoon I had another meeting with Andreas. He seemed to have come around a little to my view of things, and spoke for the first time of the harm it might do the company if Matthew were forced to resign. In the meantime, however, he asked Graham Luff, the chief accountant, to comb through Matthew's expenses forms.

Matthew was shattered by Andreas's behaviour. Quite apart from the effect that the story would have on his wife and family if and when it became widely known, he was faced with the possibility of losing his job in the most miserable of circumstances. I gave him an account of what had passed between Andreas and myself, and he thanked me for my support. A further investigation of his expenses revealed no other mistress-associated costs. Andreas began to talk less about sacking Matthew, and then he desisted. It was as though he had awoken from a trance.

Matthew had been almost broken by this assault, and his immediate reaction was to find someone else to share his pain. When the following week Andreas went away for a few days, Matthew called in Andreas's super-efficient and attractive personal assistant, Melanie Ward. He believed, correctly, that it was Melanie who had spilled the beans to Andreas. It seems not to have occurred to him that she might have been acting honourably, defending what she regarded as the best interests of the newspaper. He laid into her, reducing her to tears. This much I discovered at the time; later I learnt that he had followed up this attack with further ones. Melanie kept a record of these encounters. Several weeks later she went to see Andreas and asked him to read it. He refused to do so, saying that what had passed between her and Matthew was none of his business. Shortly afterwards Melanie announced her resignation, and left the company a few months later.

Matthew has never forgiven Andreas. At the time he said to me: 'I shall work with Andreas as a colleague but I will never forgive him. One day he will need my help and he will turn to me and I will not be there.' Not long afterwards, when Andreas was away on holiday, Matthew moved out of the large office which they shared and had a new one constructed for himself.

Andreas's feelings could only be guessed at, since we did not discuss the matter again until Private Eye broke the story several months later. His attitude towards Matthew did not obviously change, though on one occasion they almost came to blows in my presence over a footling thing. Matthew had conceived the idea that he and Charlie Burgess, the sports editor, should pay a visit to the San Marino Grand Prix at the end of May, the justification being that Charlie did not know as much about motor racing as perhaps someone in his position should, and here was a splendid opportunity for Matthew to show him the ropes. Andreas instantly objected on the grounds that such a trip would have the look of a 'freebie', even though the company would be paying. Matthew persisted, repeating the argument that it would be useful for Charlie, and portraying himself in the role of a philanthropist whose only consideration was to nurture a more fully rounded sports editor. At this point Andreas blew up. 'Matthew, you must learn to do what you are told.' Matthew evidently did not appreciate being addressed in such a way by a fellow founder. His face went a chalky white, the skin tightened around his mouth, and for a glorious, hideous moment I thought that he was going to tell Andreas to bugger off. He just managed to keep control of himself.

Andreas's visit to my house in Greenwich marked the moment at which my view of him changed. What Matthew had done had not greatly surprised me, but what Andreas had said had shocked me. He had done things before which I had forgiven him as one forgives dozens of little faults in others and oneself. Now I was less disposed to do so, and I studied him more closely, so that his new faults cohered around this central image of him sitting in my study at Greenwich, attempting, as I saw it then, to destroy a man who accounted himself his friend. I knew too that what Andreas had contemplated doing to Matthew he could at any time do to me. In a mad way, this episode drew me closer to Matthew in the short-term, not because he remained especially grateful to me for what I had done, but because we were to some degree united in shock at Andreas's behaviour – a shared secret of which no one else was aware.

Even before Private Eye published the story nearly everybody at the Independent knew about it, and there was a widespread feeling that Matthew had been let off because he was one of the boss class. The poor bloody infantry did not believe that such indulgence would be vouchsafed to them. Some people believe that it was at this moment, the letting-off of Matthew, that a grain of corruption entered the soul of the Independent. I only know that this episode had a profound effect on the future of Newspaper Publishing, which is why I write about it now.

In July 1987 Private Eye got hold of the story which had been common knowledge at City Road for several months. In the first of three vivid instalments, the magazine related how Matthew had tried to get a job for his mistress. The magazine also described how Matthew had taken his mistress to America earlier in the year and introduced her to Alexander Chancellor as such. This was true, as was virtually everything Private Eye wrote about Matthew. There was also a description of Matthew crashing a BMW motorcycle, which had been loaned to the Independent for a road test, in the car-park at 40 City Road.

Matthew was on holiday when this piece appeared. Andreas, who had read it, was unaware of the American story or the motorcycle escapade. He wrote a note to Matthew, requesting 'the information to deal with accusations made about you in Private Eye inasmuch as they have a bearing upon your responsibilities as a director'. When he returned and read this note, Matthew let fly with a letter to Andreas which he rashly composed on his Atex computer. Within a few minutes of its completion it had been intercepted by an enterprising computer hacker and dispatched to Private Eye, which re-printed large chunks.

Matthew emerges in the letter as the fighter he is, defiant and unbowed, but in his robust defence of himself he also shows how slight is his understanding of the motivations behind his actions. It seems not to occur to him now or later that he has acted unwisely. Far from being a knowing participant in events, he is the victim of misunderstandings and smears. He admits that he took his mistress to America but it was only for the purpose of ending the affair – which is to say that an episode which might be interpreted unfavourably should, in fact, be represented as demonstrating how sensitive and thoughtful Matthew had been. The room he shared with his mistress at the Algonquin was 'the smallest and cheapest I have had during five stays at the hotel. In order to make absolutely sure there was no cost to the company, however, I waived my right to fly business class to Washington.' He describes the incident with the motorcycle in almost pathetic detail. 'When I said that I had not ridden a bike since I was 17 I was urged to mount one of the machines . . . As I came to a halt, not wishing to negotiate a tight corner, I was taken unawares by the bike's weight and let it drop to the ground.'

When this and more was re-printed in Private Eye, quite a few hearts leapt for joy at City Road, for Matthew was not much liked. Andreas seemed less disposed this time to drive him out of the company. I think he felt that this would amount to a public admission of wrong-doing which would harm the Independent, whose image then was one of almost boundless probity. But Marcus Sieff and some of the other non-executive directors were understandably dismayed by what they were reading in Private Eye. Andreas wrote Matthew a letter, copied to Marcus Sieff and the board, citing Matthew's misdemeanours and chiding him. I believe that Lord Sieff had a private talk with Matthew.

But Private Eye had not finished. In its issue of October 30th it promised in the next issue, 'Twenty things you never knew about Matthew Symonds.' Many of Matthew's friends and even some of his detractors felt that this was taking a good joke too far. Alexander Chancellor (whom Matthew secretly blamed for leaking the story of the mistress's visit to America) telephoned his friend Richard Ingrams, formerly Private Eye's editor, now its *eminence grise*, and asked him to call off his hounds. Charles Moore, editor of the Spectator, and an old colleague of Matthew's on the Telegraph but no great friend, also attempted to intervene. Ian Hislop, the editor of Private Eye, telephoned Andreas and read out some of the 'twenty things', many of which related to Matthew's time on the Independent. As Hislop read out each alleged fact, Andreas reportedly replied, 'Yes, well that's true. Yes, I can't quarrel with that.'

Matthew began to wonder whether some sort of legal action might not be possible to restrain the magazine, and he, Andreas and myself slogged through the traffic to visit our solicitors, Oswald Hickson & Co, just off Fleet Street. Paul Davies, a taciturn and wily Welsh lawyer who advised us on libel when we were on the receiving end of writs, thought that not much could be done. When Paul had finished speaking, there was a pause. Then Matthew spoke. 'I just feel so let down,' he said, 'so incredibly let down.'

Private Eye went ahead with publication on November 13th. Matthew swore that he would never read 'that magazine' again, and he searched for the person or persons who had been supplying it with information. Like others who have behaved badly, and been harshly treated, he began to look around for someone he could blame for what had happened to him, so that after a time he seemed almost to believe that his misfortunes had an exterior author quite outside his own actions. He bore Alexander Chancellor a grudge for having gossiped about his American fandango. For a while he thought that a features sub-editor called Sebastian O'Kelly was responsible for having intercepted his letter to Andreas. Later Matthew identified another culprit. Sebastian's time on the Independent was short-lived. He was dismissed after several warnings for having muddled a BMW 5 series car with a BMW 3 series in a headline.

Matthew's new suspect, the alleged author of his misfortunes, was Francis Wheen. Matthew believed that Francis had given the story to Private Eye, where it appeared in two vivid instalments in July 1987, and he still does. I confess that for a time I assumed that Francis was the culprit. There was, as they say, strong circumstantial evidence. Francis had just resigned from the Independent as its diarist. He was known to have had close connections with Private Eye, and to have contributed many stories to the 'Street of Shame' section where 'Twenty things you never knew about Matthew Symonds' had appeared.

But you should not convict a man on circumstantial evidence alone. Since my departure from the Independent on Sunday, Francis has told me that he did not give the story about Matthew to Private Eye. Even if I did not believe him, which of course I do, there is the letter which he wrote to me when he left the Independent at the beginning of June. It is almost a eulogy to the founders, including Matthew if not by name then by association. This is not the letter of a man about to 'dish the dirt' on Matthew.

Personal.

June 1987

Dear Stephen,

Thank you for your very kind note. Leaving here is a wrench. I am very grateful to you for having thought of me as a diarist and having mentioned me to Andreas last year. I've enjoyed myself enormously. The paper and its founders deserve all the praise and honours that are being showered on it (& them!). I told Andreas that I hope I can contribute as a freelance and he seemed sympathetic, which softens the blow slightly: I'd hate to think that I was cutting myself off from the paper altogether. Astonishing that one can feel such a powerful affection for such a new institution; but one does, which is yet more proof of your achievement.

Yours, Francis

Over the years Matthew has come to believe not only that Francis leaked the story (which would not, after all, have been the *most* heinous crime, considering that it was true) but that he somehow created it, and is therefore responsible for all the pain. As for myself, the fact that I had defended Matthew became a thing of much less consequence to him than my later association with Francis. At the time Matthew and I were drawn together by these events, but Matthew's certainty of Francis's involvement – phantom of his imagination though it was – was in the end decisive in casting us apart.

*

In the middle of April a sensational story came into Andreas's hands. It was the circulation booster which he had been yearning for when poor old Kingsley Amis came to lunch. Not a penny was paid for the story, which was unsolicited, yet its publication brought the Independent to the notice of people who had scarcely heard of it, and for many readers defined in a flash the kind of newspaper which the Independent was trying to be.

Phillip Knightley, an Australian investigative journalist who had once worked for the Sunday Times, came into the newsroom carrying a plastic bag which he handed over to Jonathan Fenby. Inside the bag was the manuscript of a book which Heinemann was intending to publish in Australia. Its name was *Spycatcher* and its author was Peter Wright. Jonathan took the manuscript home (via a dinner where one of the guests happened to be a Home Office official who said what an awful chap Wright was) and read it. He thought that it was remarkable. In coming to this view he may have been influenced by the attempt of the British government to block the publication of the book in Australia several months before.

The next day Jonathan went to see Andreas, whose first reaction was that the material was too hot to handle. He suspected that to publish it would be in contravention of the Official Secrets Act and, quite apart from a reluctance to be carted off to prison, he was worried about what might happen to the newspaper. For several days he remained cool about the idea of publication. Lawyers were consulted. Andreas then came up with the wheeze that we would not publish an excerpt from the manuscript but contrive to drop references into stories on other subjects. For example, he imagined that in an article on the Soviet bugging of the American embassy in Moscow some reference might be made to similar British shenanigans as described by Peter Wright. Jonathan, who was rather proprietorial about the manuscript, which he kept in his possession, said that this was not a very good idea. He suggested that he and our political editor, Tony Bevins, who had read the manuscript, should see what could be made of it in terms of news stories. They proceeded to fillet Mr Wright's manuscript, with help from a young reporter called Sarah Helm, and produced about twenty different pieces. When Andreas read these he suggested that they should instead produce one very long story which would be run on the front page with a couple of 'sidebars'.

I knew nothing of the affair until Thursday April 23rd when Matthew came into my room. He told me that Fenby had got hold of Peter Wright's memoirs and that Andreas was thinking of 'going big' on them. Matthew said the most interesting revelations had to do with MI5's attempts to prove that Wilson was a Soviet spy. I said that sounded a bit old hat. Matthew added there was an amusing story about MI5 bugging the French embassy which he and I agreed seemed a sound thing to do. He appeared less than euphoric about the manuscript, and I shared his reservations. In a way we were right. When eventually I acquired a copy of *Spycatcher* I had to keep pinching myself to remember how important the book was supposed to be. To a great extent it was the government's paranoid, secret-obsessed reaction to it which made it into a bestseller – and gave the Independent a superlative scoop.

Jonathan and his colleagues having finished their story, it was agreed that it would be published in the issue of Monday April 27th. I happened to be duty-editing the newspaper on the previous day, though Andreas came into the office during the afternoon. Christopher McKane, Jonathan's deputy, had laid out the front page, which was shown to Andreas. While Jonathan bustled about in his shirt sleeves, sitting down at a computer and pounding the keyboard as though going in for the world record for key-stroking, Andreas stood aloof, observing the proceedings. 'Well, Stephen,' he said to me almost shyly. 'You must tell me if you think I am doing the right thing.' Christ, I thought. It is a bit late in the day to be asking that. He telephoned as many non-executive directors as he could get hold of to tell them what he was proposing to publish, and then, shortly after 9 o'clock, he went home. Jonathan and his colleagues raided Andreas's fridge and drank the remains of a bottle of white wine to celebrate.

Andreas was not carted off to prison, although the next morning a secretary came into the main editorial conference to say that his presence was required at the Law Courts. He arose with the look of an early Christian whose time has come to meet a lion in the Coliseum. It turned out that the order came not from Her Majesty's Government but from Heinemann, upset that its copyright had been infringed without its say-so. Andreas gave an undertaking in Judges' Chambers that he would not publish any further material from *Spycatcher*, though this did not preclude picking over what had already appeared in that morning's newspaper.

The Independent's scoop dominated the national news throughout Monday, and did not die down for many days. Interest focused on the central allegation that thirty senior staff of MI5 had plotted to bring down Harold Wilson. A number of Labour MPs got quite steamed up. Andreas was interviewed several times and said what editors must always say on such occasions, which is that publication is in the national interest. On television he did not bear a cocky, catch-me-if-you-can expression. Speaking a little haltingly, he looked and sounded grave and earnest, but resolute too – a proper editor who had minutely weighed the public interest and declared it to be preponderant. The impression was one of *responsible independence,* and although a few readers wrote in to say that they were cancelling their subscriptions because we had broken the law, the reputation of the newspaper was generally enhanced.

As was perhaps natural, it was forgotten, or it was not mentioned, that Andreas had had qualms about publication. Jonathan Fenby's role drifted into the margins of the official account, and he was never thanked by his editor. Andreas became, in many minds, the sole champion, though there had been other people with him in that boat, at times with their hands more firmly on the tiller than his.

I marvelled a little at this, and I was also privately amused by Andreas's increasingly portentous references to the public interest. I knew that Andreas had been influenced in large measure by his need, intimated at the Kingsley Amis lunch, to find a circulation-boosting scoop. Publication of *Spycatcher* was not driven by the public interest pure and simple. The Independent's own precarious finances were also mixed up in the affair, and Andreas's role was as much that of dashing buccaneer as sober-minded editor. This did not seem reprehensible to me: newspapers, which fulfil an almost sacred role as the fourth estate, as guardians of liberty and enemies of arbitrary power, normally have to make money to survive. But this paradox did not detain Andreas. He admitted that publication had helped our circulation, and therefore our finances, but this was represented as an agreeable by-product rather than one of the overriding motives.*

Rather to our surprise, the government did not invoke the Official Secrets Act. Instead, it instituted proceedings under contempt of court, alleging that we had broken an injunction which had been placed on the Guardian and the Observer not to publish any material from *Spycatcher*. This became a protracted case, meandering from one court to another, attracting differing

---

* The effect of *Spycatcher* on the circulation of the Independent is difficult to calculate, but average sales rose sharply between April and May, from 291,259 to 311,268. June was better still, at 327,122, which must in large measure reflect the influence of the general election. *Spycatcher* was regarded by most employees as the turning point in the fortunes of Newspaper Publishing plc.

and sometimes conflicting judgments, until the Independent finally got off with paying a small amount of costs. There were unlimited opportunities during this process for Andreas to beat the public interest drum.

Several months later, one Saturday morning in early September, Andreas telephoned me at home to complain about Nicholas Ashford's weekly column which appeared that day on the foreign pages. He was in a bad mood.

'Stephen, I am very concerned by Nicholas Ashford's column this morning. 'Have you read it?

'Yes, I have. I'm not sure I agree with it but I thought it was rather good.'

Nick had got hold of an American copy of *Spycatcher* and formed the view that the government's wish to oppose its publication was, from its own point of view, both understandable and prudent. He had asked me whether I thought it was all right for him to write this in his column. I had replied that of course he could. It was his column. I had assumed that Andreas would welcome this show of independence, and relish it as an example of the diversity of opinion to be encountered in the Independent.

'Well, I am very unhappy with it,' said Andreas. 'I believe that he should never have been allowed to write it.'

'That is my responsibility. He asked me whether it was all right to write it and I said that of course it was.'

'I'm afraid I can't agree. Can't you see what the government's lawyers will make of the fact that the deputy foreign editor of the Independent believes that *Spycatcher* should have never been published – when this newspaper was the first to run an excerpt? They'll have a field day.'

'I should have thought that allows you to say that you encourage a diversity of opinion, that this is what independence is all about.'

'W . e . l . l,' Andreas drew out the word in a disapproving way. 'I am very sorry indeed that it was published. We'll have to see what happens. It's too late to do anything about it now.'

*

Our coverage of the June 1987 general election seemed to have as much effect on our reputation as the *Spycatcher* affair, and attracted as many new readers. Because it was a three-way election, Tories, Labour and Alliance, independence was a particularly effective flag to sail under. A poll around this time suggested astonishingly that our readers were split almost equally three ways between the three main parties.

In its leader column the paper resisted backing one political party, though careful reading might have revealed a buried predisposition against Labour and in favour of David Owen (as opposed to David Steel) and his vision of the 'social market', a fashionable buzz-word, of which Matthew was particularly enamoured. The paper's reporting was judged scrupulously even-handed, which could not always be said of The Times under the editorship of Charlie Wilson. To a large degree, election coverage was master-minded by Jonathan Fenby and the fearless Tony Bevins, who would sink his teeth into any politician's ankle regardless of party, or indeed of any other, consideration.

Notwithstanding the newspaper's independence, a straw-poll established that most of our journalists were Labour voters. This may confirm the worst fears of captains of industry and members of right-wing think-tanks. But left-wing journalists, provided that they are not doctrinaire, generally make better reporters, in so far as they are more likely to be sceptical and questioning. Whoever believes that all judges are fair, all policemen straight and all officials honest will not make a good journalist. Our straw-poll revealed – these figures even at the time were rough – that out of about one hundred journalists ninety-five proposed to vote Labour, two Alliance, while one was a 'don't know'. The two who said they voted Tory had to be hustled out of the building in fear of their lives.

During the campaign, circulation continued to climb sharply, which was no more than a newspaper should expect at such a time, but sales went on increasing throughout July and August, when a decline would have been normally expected. Circulation rose every month until December, when it hit the seasonal dip of Christmas, before resuming its upward trend in February 1988. The year 1987, which had begun gloomily, was the *annus mirabilis* of the Independent.

Ah, success! How it changes us in spite of ourselves. On the afternoons of Thursday June 18th and Friday June 19th the six executive directors did the rounds of some of London's leading and most flamboyantly named advertising agencies. The purpose was to choose a replacement for Saatchi and Saatchi which, as a result of taking over a smaller company, had inherited an account with News International, owners of our rival The Times, that was judged incompatible with our own. On Thursday we went to Bartle Bogle Hegarty, Deighton and Mullen and Gold Greenlees Trott, and on Friday to Davidson Pearce, Butterfield Day Devito Hockney and Slaymaker Cowley White/BDG. We were driven around London in a 'stretched' white Mercedes. 'Be careful,' Matthew shouts to the driver along the car from the far back seat where he is sitting with me. 'If you crash you may take the entire senior management of Newspaper Publishing with you.'

Everywhere in what Steve Conaway calls 'glitzland' we are told how marvellous we are. Of course we are not *perfect* – if we were, we would not need to be persuaded that advertising could improve our circulation. But we are a phenomenon. We are told we have 'badge value' – why, young people in the street carry the Independent as a kind of fashion accessory (this is true) and the newspaper can be sometimes spotted as a kind of free prop in television ads *because it says something about its readers*. A man at Gold Greenlees Trot, who says that he has been going up and down the country for the last few weeks doing research about the Independent, announces that before long we will be selling 400,000 copies. 'Are you sure?' I ask him, absurdly. 'Yes, I'm sure it's going to happen,' he replies. We work around the clock at City Road, scarcely going out, hardly seeing anybody apart from journalists, but in the world outside it seems that there are hundreds, maybe thousands, of people like these thinking about the Independent, judging us, liking us, wanting somehow to be part of us.

And so, listening to all this, drinking Perrier water, sipping coffee, munching designer sandwiches, it dawns on us more powerfully than ever before that we are a success. Sure these people want to flatter us, but you do not waste flattery on the weak. It is a sort of epiphany, a moment in our fortunes around which the drama turns. I felt it too a few days earlier in Steve Conaway's office, into which he has imported carved oak rococo sideboards and suchlike (shipped from the snowy wastes of Minnesota or bought in the Old Kent Road?) When I saw the technicians and their computers and most of all their sense of belonging, I felt that all this amounted to something, and possessed an almost irreducible permanence; a life of its own partly outside our wishes, acts and intentions. Which is what I feel sitting in glitzland.

When we had seen the last suitor, and agreed that Bartle Bogle Hegarty were probably the best, we drove in our white limo to the underground car-park where some of us had left our cars. Though Christopher Barton had seemed interested in sharing a ride, Andreas wanted to return home by himself. He is left sitting alone in the back of the Mercedes. Off he goes, like a man trying to ride a whale, enjoying alone the first intimations of tycoonery.

6

The Directors Change Their Cars

A day in the foreign department began with a meeting in my
tiny office at 10.30 am. I or Nick Ashford, or anyone else present would make a few remarks about that day's foreign pages.
Then one of the assistant foreign editors – Christopher Gilbert,
Harvey Morris or Pat Ferguson, according to that week's rota –
would read out a news list on which he had been working for a
couple of hours, to which Nick or I would make additions. At
that time of the day the list might contain a number of im-
ponderables such as 'Washington – Devs' (where Alexander
Chancellor and Peter Pringle were still asleep) or 'El Salvador –
Update' (where John Carlin was not only still in bed but possibly beyond our reach). There was also the opportunity for
jokes as in 'Paris: Finance Minister resigns. Marnham???' The
question marks reflected the view of 'the desk' that Patrick
Marnham, though undoubtedly brilliant, had his own firm
notions of what was and was not worth writing about, which
did not always correspond with its own.

After this came the main 11.15 conference. Andreas walked
through the newsroom, shouting 'Meeting,' and departmental
heads or their deputies followed after him like a shoal of fish
towards the conference room at the far end. Sometimes our own
deliberations ran on, and Andreas would send a plenipotentiary
all the length of the newsroom to my office to seek some representative of our department. In the early days I used to attend
on behalf of 'Foreign'. When Andreas and Matthew were away

I presided. But after a time I grew bored of these meetings, and Nick Ashford or one of the assistant foreign editors often went in my place. I felt that I had more useful things to do. It seemed to me that the post-mortem, an increasingly drawn-out overture to the business of reading out lists, was becoming too much influenced by what other papers had done. In the first months, little mention was made of them, unless a rival paper clearly had an outstanding story which we had missed, but after a while there was a tendency for Andreas, still more for Matthew if he were taking the conference, to judge our paper by the yardstick of the stories other papers had carried rather than by our own lights.

From time to time Andreas would have one of his 'red-mists'. For example, he might have a go at a foreign representative for missing or underplaying a story. His objections could be petty, concerning, say, the absence of a verb in a headline, about which he had strong and, in my view, sometimes misplaced feelings, or they could be more reasoned and substantial. In either event, it was probable that whoever was in attendance from the foreign department was wholly innocent of the charge, which could have been more justly levelled at the night assistant foreign editor, or at myself, who had overall responsibility. Nick Ashford generally met such attacks with politeness, and, when he thought them well-founded, concern. Harvey Morris absorbed the punches with equanimity. Christopher Gilbert stood up for himself hotly. Pat Ferguson would look grumpy, and return to the foreign department muttering and cursing to himself.

If I did not attend the conference I wrote letters to correspondents, fired off memoranda to the foreign department, possibly complaining about literals or grammatical errors in that morning's newspaper, or dealt with expenses. Though our foreign network was second in size only to that of the Financial Times, we had relatively little money, and I continually fought skirmishes with correspondents over their budgets.

While I was closeted in my office dictating letters and memos to Bibi, Nick Ashford, if he was not at the main conference, would be at his desk outside – or rather, if he was on the telephone, which he very often was, his legs might be on his desk and the rest of him some feet away, tipped backwards on a chair. If it were Thursday or Friday, he would probably be writing his column for Saturday's paper. On other days he might be listening patiently to a young, possibly female, free-lance journalist about to embark for Patagonia, in which case he would offer advice as though he had no other call on his time; or he might be attending to the complaints of a not particularly im-portant Afghani refugee about our coverage. Otherwise he would be talking on the telephone to one of our people abroad, explaining what had happened to yesterday's story. He under-stood better than anybody how, far from home, correspondents can feel isolated and unloved, how a word struck out thought-lessly in London can weigh heavy on their hearts. They liked him because everything he said and did showed he understood their difficulties, and his counsel carried force with them because he had done so well what they were trying to do. Alexander Chancellor may have sometimes been a little less fond of him, for most days at 12.40 pm sharp – 7.40 am standard eastern time – Nick woke him up with a telephone call to dis-cuss the outlook for American news.

After the directors' meeting at 12 o'clock, which took me away from the foreign department for half or three-quarters of an hour, and lunch, which generally took longer, there was at 2.45 the first of two afternoon meetings. The task was to decide which stories should be run on the first two or three foreign pages, and at what length and prominence. Invariably, because of the favourable time difference, the first of these pages carried Asian news.

'Anything from Bruce Palling in India?' I might ask Chris-topher Gilbert.

'Only stream-of-consciousness stuff, I'm afraid. I can't make head of tail of it. Read it and see what you think.'

'Did you manage to get hold of James Fenton about the latest attempted coup in the Philippines?'

'No luck, I am afraid,' Christopher replied. 'Bibi has been trying James all day without a squeak. Every time she gets through she gets the foreign chappie who doesn't speak any English. All he can say is 'Meester Fenton up country. Meester Fenton up country.'

'Ah,' I reply. 'We had better take agency.'

James was in the habit of disappearing for weeks at a time to pow-wow with guerrillas in the jungle, with whom he was supposed to have a degree of ideological sympathy, or else to visit the prawn farm he had started, on which, it was said, dozens of people depended for their livelihoods. He none the less wrote an 'Out of The East' column most weeks, long articles about Muslim or Marxist guerrillas which he amazingly contrived to make interesting, and more conventional pieces about Filipino politics. Sometimes he enjoyed travelling around the large part of Asia which he had carved out. He reported vividly from South Korea, where the violence, mayhem and possibility of an overthrow of an undemocratic regime appealed strongly to the man who had written about the fall of South Vietnam and the ransacking of the palace in Manila of Ferdinand Marcos.

Once I had an angry exchange with James. Shortly after the launch of the paper he had covered the Queen's visit to China. Sir Geoffrey Howe, the foreign secretary, was in tow. As the days passed James grew increasingly bored – there was no mayhem or revolution here – and his articles began to take on a skittish tone. He began one of them, which had been earmarked for the top of the front page, with the sentence 'Sir Geoffrey Howe is really very handsome when you see him close up.' I decided to cut this out. When James returned to the Philippines, and received his airmail copy of the Independent, he discovered what had happened, and rang me in a bate. 'If anyone cuts my articles again, I shall resign,' he said. 'Don't threaten me, James,' I replied. But I don't think we did interfere with his prose again, unless to cut it for reasons of space.

The second foreign afternoon conference, which took place at about 4.30, followed much the same pattern as the first, though with deadlines approaching there was a greater sense of urgency. 'I don't want to push but time is getting on,' Christopher Gilbert would say. I sat at my desk on which stood an Atex computer, my back to the window, facing down my narrow, rectangular office. I can read on my screen some of the stories which are being described to me, though much of the copy, particularly from the United States and Latin America, has not yet been filed. 'No, I don't like that.' 'For God's sake, get someone to re-write this first par.' To my left, on a brusque, red bench-seat sit Nick Ashford and the assistant foreign editor responsible for lay-out. To their left is a door which is so thin you could punch a hole through it. At the end of the office, which is to say about ten feet away, sits Gabriel Thompson, who has been laying out the foreign pages on the Atex GT68, clutching a sheaf of photographs. Christopher and a copytaster also sit facing me.

Outside, visible through the half-glass partitions, the foreign department toils away. The clocks above Nick Ashford's desk tell you what time it is in London, New York, Tokyo, Moscow and Delhi. Time is running out wherever you are. Sub-editors edit stories and write headlines to the length apportioned to them by the GT68. Specialists write background pieces or re-write articles sent in by stringers. Occasionally I ask a specialist to offer a judgment on a story which we have been discussing, or one of them puts his or her head around my door to plead the merits of a piece. Isabel Hilton comes in to say that John Carlin has filed a heart-rending story from El Salvador which should be considered for the front page. Richard Dowden says he has an incredible 'colour piece' from a stringer in Mozambique. Ed Steen pops his head around the door. 'Sorry to disturb you busy folks,' he says in a respectful tone of voice which none the less implies that we may not be making the same full creative use of our time as he is. 'Can I just say that I don't think you should forget Poland in your deliberations.' 'We won't, Ed. Don't worry.' 'OK, boss.'

At 5.30 the front-page conference took place in the conference room in the corner of the newsroom. Around the perimeter of the room were red bench-seats, larger and more comfortable than those in my office, on which various heads of the larger departments or their deputies lounged. At one end sat Andreas, usually bent forward, pencil in hand, poised over news lists which lay on the low table in front of him, ready to write down the 'offerings' of those around him. To his right, wedged at a corner of the bench, was Matthew, often sucking a ball point pen. On important occasions such as budget day Peter Jenkins would come along. Opposite Andreas, at the far end of the room, Charlie Burgess, the sports editor, would assume an almost recumbent position. He rarely had any news story to offer but cast himself as a man of the people whose self-confessedly vulgar instincts could help to bring a demotic touch to the front page.

Jonathan Fenby was usually asked by Andreas to commence the proceedings. It was a point of honour with him, as with John Price, his abrasive 'number three', whom he often brought with him, to make as many stories as possible sound like the scoop of the century. Then came my turn: I would normally propose two or three foreign stories for the front. Then the City and business representative – Sarah Hogg tended to eschew these meetings – might offer one or two stories. Finally Charlie Burgess, who was by this time practically lying on the floor, would shake his head in a bored sort of way when Andreas asked him whether he had anything to offer.

Whatever happened, there would never be a royal story on the front. Andreas had already made known his dislike of such pieces though he claimed not to be a republican, only an enemy of trivia. But the paper did not formally become an exclusion zone for royal stories until the birth of the Duchess of York's first child on August 8th 1988. As he was going home that evening, Jonathan Fenby remarked to a sub-editor called Jan Thompson that a birth was expected any moment. He didn't think that the story should go on the front page, and suggested a news-in-brief item on page two. The next morning the news of the birth was contained in a short single paragraph at the bottom of the column, much to Andreas's delight. Almost by accident a new tradition was established, and for a long time the Independent reported most stories involving members of the Royal Family in a similar manner, until it was forced four years later to bend with the times.

On a good day Andreas might be offered nine or ten stories, on a bad one only five or six. A front page could carry anything between four and six or even seven stories – roughly 2,500 words in all. Andreas often took a conventional approach, choosing, after canvassing opinions, the most obvious 'splash' – i.e. lead story – at seven or eight hundred words, and then other stories in descending order of importance. He was very keen to have a 'basement' every day – i.e. a 'funny story' of about 350 words at the bottom of the front page. Mike Stent, who became night editor after Nigel Lloyd had left, was expected to tot up the number of words. 'How many is that, Mike?' Andreas would ask. 'Four thousand two hundred.' 'We'll have to get rid of something.' Sometimes, particularly when there was not a strong 'news splash', Andreas would try to confect an arresting lead story ('agenda-setting'), often with considerable success. In January 1988 an apparently straightforward New York story about Aids was spotted by Andreas on the foreign list and, with a little helpful 'spin' from Oliver Gillie, the medical editor, transformed into a sensational splash under the headline, 'One in 61 New York babies born with Aids.'

There was a democratic tone to these conferences. Andreas would not normally come to a decision without weighing up carefully all the differing opinions which he had sought. Sometimes, though, he would relish going against the majority view which he normally respected. Particularly in his choice of pictures Andreas showed himself to be more daring, less hidebound by conventional wisdom, than almost anyone else. Photographers like Brian Harris and Jeremy Nicoll felt encouraged to take a certain sort of picture, 'atmospheric' studies rather than news pics, which they knew their editor favoured. Without Andreas's penchant for such photographs the Independent would not have won its reputation.

There were dangers to an excessively democratic approach to editing. On the afternoon of Thursday September 18th Nick Garland had drawn a cartoon which as usual he showed to Andreas, who liked it so much that he proposed to put it on the front page. It depicted Mrs Thatcher standing in a desolate urban wasteland. The caption read 'Si monumentum requiris, circumspice.' With fatherly pride, Andreas brought the cartoon along to the front-page conference. He was however a little worried about the Latin tag: would the readers understand it? Charlie Burgess, who did not number a knowledge of Latin among his accomplishments, believed they would not. Michael Crozier, no lover of Nick Garland after the Thirkell affair, suggested that there should be an English translation near to the Latin caption. Others such as Jonathan Fenby thought that most readers would understand. I said that it did not really matter too much whether they did or didn't. Those who understood it would feel enormously pleased that the newspaper was in the hands of educated people, and those who didn't understand would feel enormously flattered that they had been expected to.

Andreas was swayed by the barbarians. The cartoon appeared the next day above the caption 'If you want a monument, gaze around.' When Nicholas Garland saw this he had a turn. He rang Andreas at home at 8.30 in the morning to protest that no one had told him about this change to the cartoon which Andreas himself had approved. According to Nick's account, which he gave me on the telephone the following day, Andreas had not taken at all kindly to being criticised in this manner.* Andreas told Nick that he was 'wrong, completely wrong'. Forty per cent of the conference had thought that the caption should be changed. He had absolutely no regrets. 'Come down off your pedestal,' he said. What had happened had happened. 'You can be sure that it will happen again.'

Poor, sensitive, angry Nick never quite recovered from this exchange. Shortly afterwards he published in the Spectator the first of several excerpts from his diary about the founding of the Independent. He began to contemplate the publication of the whole diary which, much to Andreas's displeasure, came out in January 1990. Even before it appeared, that book sealed his fate at the Independent. He slowly became a non-person – the man who had dared to criticise aspects of the glorious history of the paper, and even to poke fun at some of them – and Andreas and Matthew found it increasingly difficult to talk to him. The divorce had begun the morning after the caption was changed.

*

In September 1987 John Morrison resigned as features editor to become editor of the BBC2 programme *Newsnight*, where his considerable talents as a television man found their natural

---

* Andreas's account to me of the telephone conversation was one almost of bravado and, although less detailed, did not conflict with Nick's version.

outlet. Everybody breathed a sigh of relief, not least John himself. For nearly a year he had done a more than passable impersonation of a man on one of those television shows who wants to have a go at someone's else's job – say an accountant trying to drive a crane – and discovers that it is infinitely more difficult than it looks. He went around looking permanently surprised, as if on-alert to be told at any moment about yet another aspect of his new job which he had overlooked. He had discovered that almost none of the techniques he had learnt as a television editor were a blind bit of use to him as a newspaper editor.

I had half a notion that Frank Johnson, still grazing unhappily on The Times, might make a good replacement, and I suggested that he should get in touch with Andreas. There may have been one or two other candidates. Before Frank had time to think about it, Matthew told me that he had suggested to Andreas that he should take the job himself, at least for a year. His proposal had been accepted. He had felt, he said, that Andreas had been trying to 'marginalise' him as deputy editor (which title he would retain) and here was a chance for him to run his own show as a departmental head. It was obvious to me that since their row over Matthew's mistress the two of them had worked more uneasily in harness than would have otherwise been the case. I guessed that Andreas would be relieved to feel that Matthew was not competing to share his job. Though I did not think that Matthew would be the best features editor in the world, there was no reason to believe that he would not make a decent go of it.

Matthew told me that he had been offered a job at the BBC a few weeks earlier. John Birt had quite recently taken over as deputy director-general, and the same new broom which swept John Morrison to Newsnight nearly took Matthew to a senior executive position at Broadcasting House. Matthew described it to me as 'number six' in the hierarchy. His gloom with the Independent was very great, and he was plainly tempted by the offer, but something held him back. He said it was partly the deep affection which he felt for the institution. With our rising fortunes, he also believed that it was possible that his shares in Newspaper Publishing would make him a rich man, which the

BBC could never do. This was a fair bet. One-pound shares were already being quoted at £1.70, and the faintest glimmer of profits suggested that the founders' convertible shares might one day be 'triggered'.

There was still was a vacuum at the centre of the newspaper where Andreas should have been, but he would not let anyone else occupy it. The paper was generally very good, but it was to a large extent being run by the departmental heads. Andreas could be a Catherine-wheel of good ideas and he remained a figure of towering importance for the staff. But he seemed unable or reluctant to concentrate for long on manifest deficiencies. Even with the advent of Andrew Gimson, our editorials remained weak for a newspaper which was supposedly challenging The Times. Although he was continually saying that he would devote more time to editorials, in practice Andreas hardly ever did so, and left them largely in Matthew's hands. Matthew had extremely well-informed opinions about domestic and international affairs, but he favoured a preachy tone while often being unwilling to come down on one side or the other. Whether Andreas could have made a great improvement is another matter.*

It was partly Andreas's duties as chief executive which prevented him devoting time to such things. But he also found it difficult to plug away for any length of time at managerial tasks. Our worst problem was classified advertising. Display advertising was another matter. By 1988 the newspaper averaged 25 per cent of the display market in volume terms, considerably more than its circulation market share of nearly 17 per cent. This was a great achievement. By contrast, our share of the classified market was very much below our circulation share, and remains so. Everyone accepted that it takes longer to crack the classified market, which has thousands of potential customers, than display, where there are a few dozen agencies with which to deal.

---

* Matthew, although he had experienced the discursive conversations at Telegraph leader conferences, liked to dictate a line. Sometimes he would produce his old cuttings file containing his Telegraph leaders, and give it to a leader writer who seemed in need of particular enlightenment. He was especially proud of the leaders which he had written during the Falklands war and he would declare, not without a trace of self-directed irony, that he had 'had a good war'.

All the same, several executive and non-executive directors recommended actions which Adrian O'Neill, most of whose experience had been in display rather than classified advertising, was disinclined to take. On several occasions Andreas seemed on the brink of telling him to do so, but then Adrian would convince him, with the aid of masses of figures and statistics, that he was doing the right thing. For a time Andreas would forget the problem until a non-executive director brought it up at a board meeting, whereupon the whole process would be gone through again.

The fun of being chief executive lay in looking outside for deals or new relationships with other companies. Already by the late summer of 1987 Andreas was dreaming of taking over another newspaper – first The Times, then the Observer. Some time in August, I walked into Andreas's little meeting room at the end of his larger office.

'Come in, Stephen. Have you heard my new idea?'

'No, I don't think I have.'

'Well, I think we should buy The Times. It can't be making money and it's obvious that Rupert Murdoch doesn't feel any affection for it. If we could get it, we would have a newspaper with a circulation of – what? – '

'Well, The Times is selling nearly 450,000, and we're selling not far short of 350,000. . .'

'Yes, that's right, you would lose some readers who are taking both papers, and others would just drop away, but I suppose that we could hope to sell, well, perhaps 650,000. What do you think, Stephen?'

'Well, I'm not sure.' I actually thought that Andreas had gone crackers. Notwithstanding our circulation successes we were still losing large sums of money and here he was talking about buying another newspaper. 'I suppose that lots of people would not thank the Independent for actually closing down another paper, whatever they might think of it.'

'Yes, there is always that to consider. Well, we'll have to think about it.'

After that the finance department may have produced some figures – the first of many such exercises – but Andreas's expansionist mood was momentarily checked by the board meeting on August 26th. At the beginning, Marcus Sieff announced that he wanted to say a few words. This usually meant that he wished to enter a mild complaint about an article we had run about Israel, of which country he could legitimately be described as a founder. Normally we listened politely to these lectures, which I felt he was delivering mostly out of a sense of duty, before Andreas left it to me, as foreign editor, to make a few waffley remarks which were designed (as Marcus well knew) to close the matter.

'I just want to say a few words,' said Marcus, emphasising each of them as though he were addressing a classroom of backward children, 'about cost control. We have an excellent product -'

'Here, here,' said Ian Hay Davison.

'- but we are still losing money and we need to get a very firm control on costs. I have seen a lot of companies go bust in my time, and I'm quite old now, and we need to keep a closer eye than we have on the number of employees and particularly on temporary and casual staff. I would like to ask management to take a careful look at all costs and to reduce them whenever they can. And it's very important indeed to explain to staff what you are doing.'

This did not seem on the face of it a very serious rebuke but allowance had to be made for Marcus's great natural courtesy and the cimcumlocutory language of board meetings. Andreas had gone from red to chalky white during the lecture, and as soon as Marcus had finished he agreed meekly to do everything that had been suggested. 'I take what the chairman says with the utmost seriousness.' I never saw Andreas at any board meeting so humbled and contrite. It was as though Marcus had said, which in a sense he had, that he was a very successful businessmen who had run Marks and Spencer and we were a bunch of amateurs who could not even grasp the first law of business, which is keep your costs as low as you can. Marcus certainly practised what he preached: when he came to board meetings he would turn off every electric light he could find, and our deliberations would sometimes take place in a half-gloom.

For several weeks after this there was an economy drive.

Budgets for the next financial year, which began on October 1st, were hacked back ruthlessly. Andreas told everybody that we had to tighten our belts: we would have to make a profit by the end of the year. The upshot was that at the next board meeting in September we managed to project a profit of £46,000 for the next financial year by stamping on costs to an unrealistic degree.* For a time there was no more talk of trying to buy The Times.

These wild swings between restraint and expansionism which characterise the history of the Independent derived largely from Andreas's cast of mind. Naturally cautious, even sometimes self-doubting, he assumed with the first pinpricks of success an almost mystical belief in his own powers. Yet his self-belief could sometimes be suddenly undermined, as it was by Marcus Sieff, making Andreas again for a moment the lovably unsure man who once could not bring himself to say that he was the likely editor of the Independent, before it swirled up again like some unquenchable monster and carried him onwards.

On January 20th 1988 Andreas walked into my office – his third visit of the day – and we discussed the main morning conference which I had taken in his absence. The previous evening Andreas had attended the Whitbread literary awards, of which he was a judge. He remarked to me how very much esteemed the Independent was by 'highly intelligent people'. I agreed that this was so, and said I thought that during the past few weeks journalists had seemed sharper and more energetic. The paper seemed to me to be a little better.

Andreas: 'Yes, I agree, and I think that it's entirely down to me.'

SG: [ironically] 'Oh, of course, as soon as you got back [he had been on holiday in France until a week before] it got much better.'

Andreas: [ignoring or missing the irony] 'No. I'm not so much thinking of the Christmas holiday. It's that since September I didn't spend enough time on editorial matters. Now I've changed all that.'

* In the event we lost £1,563,000 in the financial year ending October 1st 1988, less good than our projection, but creditable in only our second year of trading. In its first year of trading the company lost £9,466,000.

Nearly two weeks earlier, on January 8th, I had sent Andreas a long letter to await his return from holiday. The gist of it, politely phrased, was that notwithstanding our enormous success the paper was in some respects on auto-pilot. 'What we lack is a sense that we know where we should be going.' The newspaper was too much composed of 'separate publications' some of whose faults, such as 'literals' and grammatical errors, were 'perpetual and institutionalised'. The home pages 'gave off a kind of middle-brow high-mindedness rather than an intellectual raciness'. The problem was 'that as things are presently organised only you are at the centre and, if you are attending to other non-editorial matters, as often you must be, nothing is done . . . I believe we [i.e. Matthew and myself] could help you more at the centre, and that if we did, that would help the newspaper.'

What Andreas said to me that evening in my office was his answer to my letter, which, like a poker player keeping back an ace card, he had decided to play in a dramatic fashion. He was saying, in effect, that he was the greatest, and my criticisms, if not impertinent, were at least beside the point. On a re-reading, my letter does seem a shade negative in the context of our successes, and, if this is so, it was because like Matthew I felt excluded by Andreas and perhaps exaggerated the ill-effects of this exclusion on the Independent. But even allowing for this little vanity of my own, the letter does in some respects intimate enduring flaws in the Independent, then largely disguised by success, more evident now.

From January 27th Andreas, Matthew and myself started to have fortnightly lunches at the Garrick, Andreas's club, to discuss the problems of the newspaper. This was a consequence of my letter, though Andreas never mentioned it. Our weekly afternoon meetings had fallen into desuetude many months before because Andreas nearly always found other engagements more compelling than discussing the newspaper with Matthew and me. Though quite often cancelled by Andreas, lunch proved a more regular appointment. When it did take place, he assumed the air, alternately distracted and excitable, of a wealthy parent attempting to keep an avaricious elder son off the subject of money. On these occasions, if no other, he would display a fondness for reminiscence about the early days which Matthew, with his sentimental attachment to the heroic past, lapped up. Much time was usefully wasted in this manner.

★

The idea of a magazine had been first floated in the summer of 1987 in the vaguest sort of way. At the July board meeting Matthew mentioned that in contemplating a magazine we had been looking at the very successful supplements published by La Repubblica newspaper in Rome. The connection was La Repubblica's fervently Anglophile and monarchist correspondent in London, Count Paolo Filo della Torre.

I had met Paolo when I was still at the Telegraph. Shortly before the launch of the Independent, he had asked Andreas and me to the Foreign Press Association, of which he was a leading light, in Carlton House Terrace. The two of us had answered questions from foreign correspondents about how the foreign desk had been set up. Or rather Andreas had answered the questions, for I had found it difficult to get a word in. Paolo sat throughout the proceedings, and much of lunch afterwards, with his hands folded over his generous tummy, a benign smile spread unwaveringly across his inscrutable face. Metro-Goldwyn-Mayer central casting would have snapped him up for a film about the Medicis. Notwithstanding his gigantic enthusiasms – whatever he liked was 'brilliant' or '*bellissima*' – I suspected that beneath the bravura surface lurked a supple mind.

Grand though he may have been, Paolo's two main ambitions were comparatively humdrum. The first was to secure an office at 40 City Road. This was finally achieved, with some assistance from me, in September 1987. His second ambition grew out of the first. It was to have an Atex computer on his desk, as all the Independent's journalists did, connected with our databanks. This proved more difficult, owing mostly to a lack of enthusiasm on the part of Steve Conaway, who was not greatly in awe of Italian counts. In order to get what he wanted, Paolo was driven to manoeuvring the two newspapers closer together.

It was Adrian O'Neill who in January 1988 raised in a more serious way the notion that we might publish a magazine. He had been talking to some people in 'the advertising industry', particularly at Bartle, Bogle and Hegarty. The general view seemed to be that there would be a market for high quality colour advertising if we could 'deliver' the same readers who were taking the newspaper. The best day to publish such a magazine was agreed to be Saturday. The argument was that a magazine, and perhaps an expanded newspaper, could make Saturday into a more important publishing day. At that time, quality newspapers were much the same on a Saturday as during the rest of the week, though selling fewer copies. Adrian argued against Friday, the main alternative, saying that when the Daily Telegraph magazine had been published on that day there had been a tendency for commuters to leave their copies on the train, which had suggested to advertisers that it was probably not being read.

Andreas, Matthew and I agreed that Matthew should take charge of the new Saturday newspaper section which was also planned, and that I should be 'project manager' of the magazine. Off the top of my head I had pretty well no ideas about what sort of magazine we should produce, so I went to New York to learn. That city is supposed to be the melting-pot of most good ideas. Unfortunately, this turned out not to be the case so far as colour supplements were concerned. Apart from the New York Times colour magazine, which was scarcely the equal of the Sunday Times magazine in Britain, New York, indeed the whole of the United States, was a no-go area for imaginative newspaper colour supplements. But the New York-Trip has its advantages. It allows one to ask questions which one's rivals would not be anxious to answer in London. And it means that one has to learn everything in five days, since to stay longer would be interpreted as skiving by colleagues at home.

Leonard Doyle, our New York correspondent, arranged a number of interviews for me. He was a soft-spoken Irishman with a good nose for a story. After quite a few drinks his romantic Irish republicanism would get the better of his prudence (he had me down as a unionist) though it didn't extend to support of the IRA. Somewhat to my surprise, since he was kept on pretty tight rations, he had acquired a pleasant office above a leather goods boutique close to the Rockefeller Plaza.

The terms of his lease seemed remarkably favourable. Leonard's wife served in the boutique, and he himself was not above lending a hand. Partly out of guilt that we were paying him so little, I allowed him to sell me a leather bag. It fell apart after a few weeks.

Not all the interviews had been perfectly matched to the subject. When Michael Packenham, editorial page editor of the New York Daily News, took me out to lunch, he started off by saying: 'Well, the history of *classified advertising* in this town has its roots in the second world war.' Um, well yes. From those who did know about colour magazines, this is what I learnt. They were nearly all bad because they were largely vehicles for advertising, with no real editorial point. Largely because no one usually had much pride in them, they were produced with relatively low-quality paper. Most of them had absurdly long 'lead-times', which is to say that they were printed so far in advance of publication that they could not show any awareness of contemporary news. My conclusion, obvious though it may have been, was that the only way of producing a good magazine was first to have an idea – which might include current events, necessitating shorter lead-times – and the advertising would probably follow behind.

When in New York I had dinner with Alexander Chancellor, who flew up from Washington. I wanted to sound him out about editing our new magazine. This did not mean that he had been a disappointing US editor: after a slightly shaky few months, during which I had upbraided him for never leaving Washington, he had taken to the wide open spaces with a vengeance, producing some of the most distinguished foreign writing in the newspaper. He was my leading candidate simply because as editor of the Spectator he had produced the best serious magazine of the age. Andreas and Matthew, while conceding this, pointed out that the Spectator had always had a very low circulation, and worried that Alexander's talents might be too rarefied for our magazine.

I could not therefore offer Alexander the job at dinner, and as we fenced around the subject, and drank much more than we should have done, he began to be irritable. As always on the relatively rare occasions on which he became annoyed, his upper lip began to stiffen, as though he had suddenly acquired some sort of gum-shield.

'I'm not wholly, absolutely one hundred per cent clear whether you want me to do this job or not.'

'Well, I'm just sounding you out really. Trying to find out whether you would like to throw your cap in the ring. In which case it would be more firmly there than anyone else's.'

'Yea, more firmly there than anyone else's. That's all very well, but – I know I'm drunk, so you needn't take any notice of me if you don't want to – I do think that the three of you, this great and glorious triumvirate, should jolly well make up your minds. I can think of lots of reasons for not making me editor but this is a bit too much like a flirtation, and I confess that it's just a teeny-weeny bit annoying. Anyway, I'm drunk, so you mustn't take any notice of me.'

Alexander also asked me why I did not appoint myself editor of the new publication. I said that I felt I did not know enough about magazines.

On the afternoon of Saturday February 27th, the day after I returned from New York, fifteen senior Independent journalists gathered for a 'seminar' on the magazine at The Swan at Streatley in Berkshire. The venue had been suggested by Peter Jenkins, who had stayed at the hotel not long before and pronounced the food and wine acceptable. Before dinner on Saturday evening, Andreas confessed shyly that when he was at Oxford he had brought a girl here, to what was then a small inn by the Thames. Thirty years on, it had sprouted new extensions and presented itself as much as a conference centre as a riverside hotel.

Our main discussion took place on Sunday, with myself, five-day authority on colour supplements in the chair during the morning session. We had got hold of lots of old magazines, including copies of Picture Post, which were passed around the table. Patrick Marnham, who had come over from Paris, told us about French colour magazines, and Michael Sheridan about Italian ones. I described the American scene with an expert eye. Elkan Allan then put the case for a listings magazine, which was judged by most people to be too narrow in its appeal. Peter Jenkins proposed we should publish a mould-breaking consumer magazine, 'a cross between Time Out, a high-class mail order catalogue and Which?' This idea did not go down very well either, particularly with Suzy Menkes, our fashion editor, who said that such magazines had existed for ages.

The decisive contribution was made by Nicholas Garland. Nick was a dormant volcano. Since his eruption over the design of the newspaper he had gone quiet, save for a rumbling of molten lava when his Latin caption had been removed, and people wandered over his slopes without fear. It seemed incredible Andreas had once been frightened of him. Now, without warning or provocation, he erupted once more. The difference was that on this occasion there were no opponents ranged against him, no Michael Crozier or Nigel Lloyd. He simply had a benign and attentive audience.

So far as Nick was concerned, talk of listings or mail order magazines was beside the point. The Independent had succeeded because it had assumed the very best of its readers, who were often a lot more intelligent than we were. (Slight shifting of bottoms on seats at this point.) What was needed was a magazine which was serious, restrained, even sometimes intellectual – like the newspaper. It would not attempt to be glossy like other colour supplements. There would be pieces about heavy politics and culture. The emphasis was on *words*. The best equivalent he could think of was the Spectator, a magazine which carried proper articles which were *read*. He didn't want to be crude about it – but a Spectator with *some* pictures was a reasonable way of summing up what he had in mind.

Like a cricket captain who keeps his best bowler to the end, I had arranged matters so that Nick was the last to speak before Andreas's summing up. Not everyone had warmed to what he said. One or two people pointed out that the much-vaunted Spectator sold fewer than 30,000 copies a week, to which Nick's answer was that you couldn't make a comparison between a 'stand-alone' magazine with a high cover price and a magazine which came with your newspaper at an extra cost of five or ten pence. He had swung the argument. In his summing up, Andreas appeared to have taken his remarks on board, and dismissed the idea of a 'Repubblica style picture led magazine'. He spoke of the magazine being 'the Independent by another means', an evocative if imprecise catch-phrase. The editor, whoever he was, would be 'very much one of us'.

That editor, it now seemed clear to Andreas, Matthew and myself, should be Alexander. After a little bartering about terms and conditions, he accepted, writing in a letter to Andreas that he 'would wish to be responsible to you, and no one else, for the running of the magazine'. It was agreed that he would return from Washington at the beginning of May and be succeeded as US editor by Peter Pringle. That meant I needed to find a new Washington correspondent.

Because I wanted to maintain our tradition of having writers as foreign correspondents – the more so because James Fenton had announced his resignation in January – my candidate for this job was Sebastian Faulks, our books editor. Like James, Sebastian had plenty of reporting experience, and could wield a pen with considerable skill. He had published one novel, and nearly completed another. However, he did not resemble in looks or manner a book-worm who had spent his life in a garret. Tall, blue-eyed and with curly, fair hair, he was more than something of a matinée idol. Nearly half a lifetime of good lunches, and a regular intake of claret or beer, had scarcely taken their toll. He had a great calm, and whatever novelistic turbulence was making waves in his soul was kept far from public view. At one of our occasional lunches, I had asked him after we had both had a few drinks whether he believed in God. 'Oh, sure,' he said, in an absent sort of way, as though I had asked him whether he liked going out to restaurants. 'I just don't think about him very much.'

On Good Friday, which was also April Fool's Day, I had lunch with Sebastian in a pub in Southwark, and offered him the Washington job. He thanked me very much for thinking of him but said that he would prefer to remain in England.

'But, my dear boy, aren't you interested in spending a little time in the world's most important country?'

'Not really, no. I like visiting it, I like New York, but I just wouldn't want to live there.'

'Why not?'

'Well, to tell you the truth, I would miss my friends here. I would miss going to pubs and drinking beer, and I would miss playing cricket.'

I tried a desperate shot. 'I'm sure that there are expatriate cricket teams in Washington . . .' But it was no good. Sebastian would not leave our shores. This left him free for a greater adventure.

★

The spring and early summer of 1988 was a fine time for the Independent. We were planning to launch a magazine. The reputation of the newspaper was high, and had spread far beyond our shores: foreign journalists came to sit at our feet to discover whether our successes could be repeated by them; at a lunch in New York Arthur Schlesinger, once special assistant to President Kennedy, told me that the Independent was an adornment to the English-speaking world – and something which could not have happened in America. Almost everyone seemed to love us. The economy was bounding along in those happy days of Thatcherism, and most months, except the dog-days of summer, we were making a profit. Andreas and Matthew started to speak of creating 'a billion-pound company'. It was time for the directors to replace their motor cars.

It was not as though our existing cars were obviously deficient. But Matthew had set his heart on a Jaguar. A pretext for replacement was found in the financial collapse of the leasing company which had supplied our cars. Matthew whispered in Andreas's ear that a man in his position needed a driver, and a young man who worked in the post-room was commandeered. But could Andreas be expected to hunch in the back of his small, if potent, BMW? No, he could not. A Jaguar was produced for his inspection, and he succumbed. With this as a precedent, the other directors followed. Matthew got his Jaguar. Adrian O'Neill chose a more sporty model from the same manufacturer. Steve Conaway plumped for one of the cheaper Porsches. I got a largish Mercedes. Christopher Barton was not at all pleased to get a slightly smaller one. Finding that his Jaguar spent much of its time in a garage, Andreas followed suit after a few months. His black Mercedes, with black leather seats and a blind in the rear window, looked like the car of a rather sinister African dictator.

On March 22nd, before this had happened, when Andreas's Jaguar was new and trusted, he was driven off to a grand Air

Force dinner near Stanmore, on the outskirts of London. The Duke of Edinburgh was present, along with the Air Chief Marshal and several marshals of the RAF. Alas, they waited in vain for the editor of the Independent.

At about 10 o'clock an anxious, not to say panic-stricken, Jonathan Fenby telephoned me. He was duty-editing the paper, and had just been rung by a squadron leader at Stanmore who said that Andreas had still not shown up. According to the squadron leader, they had received a telephone call from Andreas's car at about 8.30 informing them that Andreas was just about to arrive. But he had not materialised. Jonathan had then asked a reporter to ring the local police station at Stanmore to enquire as to whether there were any reports of accidents in the area. There were not.

'Could he have broken down?' I asked Jonathan.

'Surely he would have telephoned the RAF, or asked us to tell them.'

'Yes, I suppose he would.'

'I realise it's a bit far-fetched,' said Jonathan, chuckling nervously. 'But it seems so odd – after all, he set off at 7.15, nearly three hours ago – that I can't help wondering whether he might not have been kidnapped.'

'It is odd, I know. But who would want to kidnap him?'

'Well, that's true. All the same, what can have happened to him?'

It was a good question. I telephoned Matthew, who shared my amusement in the kidnapping theory. We discussed whether or not we would pay the ransom. Matthew thought that on the whole we shouldn't. It would subvert the rule of law. There was only one way to deal with kidnappers, regrettable though the consequences might be.

I spoke to Jonathan a couple more times. He had been trying without success to discover the number of Andreas's newly installed car telephone.

At about 11 o'clock he rang again.

'It's all right. Andreas has been found. He's at home.'

'At home!'

'Yes, he arrived back about twenty minutes ago. Never got to the dinner. I couldn't get much out of him. He muttered something about the traffic and then said he felt tired.'

'No other explanation?'

'None.'

'I suppose he must have felt a bit of an ass.'

The next day Matthew tried to tease some sort of explanation out of Andreas, but nothing would induce him to bend and talk about his escapade.

7

The $500 Million Dollar Man

My duties as 'project manager' of the magazine were not very taxing. I was responsible to the board for making sure that it would be launched smoothly and on time – the date of September 10th 1988 had been chosen. My job was largely to make sure that everyone knew what everyone else was doing. There were also some strategic decisions which did not fall neatly into other people's areas of responsibility. One was magazine paper, about which I became something of a minor expert. I wanted to use high quality paper in order to convey that our magazine was not just another colour supplement. Adrian agreed, and said that with superior paper we could in the long run get better advertising rates. Though Steve Conaway argued that we might as well burn dollar bills, we ended up with a high quality heavy matt paper.

I might have been expected to be of use to Alexander on the editorial side, but on the whole I was not. He did not particularly seek my advice and I did not foist it upon him. My greatest achievement was to secure him a car-parking space, after prolonged and tricky negotiations with Jan Newton, our administration manager. From the beginning of May he started to hire staff. Occasionally, though not often, he asked what I thought about someone. I suggested that he should consider Simon Carr as his deputy editor, and Alexander went through the motions of weighing up Simon's candidacy before rejecting him. There were doubtless perfectly sound reasons for this, not least his lack of experience. I felt too that Alexander was partly resisting the idea because Simon was so close a friend of mine. In the end he chose Paul Barker, who had for many years been editor of New Society magazine.

The first dummy was produced on June 18th. Since it contained only Latin text, not much could be made of it. The point was partly to prove that a magazine could be produced and printed. It was also an exercise in design. No one much liked the typography, but the cover picture of Francis Bacon was striking.

A couple of days later I went off to Israel for a week. Before leaving I had gone to see Marcus Sieff. His large office in the Marks and Spencer headquarters in Baker Street was filled with clocks which on the hour and half hour would rise up in competitive chimes. As a liberal Zionist who believed that most newspapers, including the Independent, gave Israel a hard time, Marcus was anxious that I should see examples of Arab-Israeli co-operation. He suggested that I should visit a factory, which supplied Marks and Spencer with underpants, where Arabs and Jews evidently worked in blissful harmony, and Neve Shalom, an Arab-Israeli 'village of peace'. He had urged me on previous occasions to send Charles Richards, our Jerusalem correspondent, to these Utopian settlements, but Charles, whether through stubbornness or absent-mindedness, had not ventured there. I said that I would try to go, but I had to make do with breakfast with the managing director of the underpants concern at the King David Hotel in Jerusalem. When on my return I told Marcus that I had been unable to visit the factory or Neve Shalom he looked at me with large reproachful eyes.

While I was in Israel I learnt that Peter Utley, my greatest friend at the Daily Telegraph, had died at the age of sixty-seven. For a couple of years he had been working without much inspiration as obituaries editor of The Times. He had rather taken against the new regime at the Telegraph and did not think much of the new editor, Max Hastings, whose views he regarded as dangerously liberal, especially on the subject of Ulster, about which Peter, in his final days on his old paper, was scarcely permitted to write. He also had little time for Conrad Black, the new Canadian proprietor of the Telegraph, who had run rings around poor Lord Hartwell. Mr Black was devoted to Napoleon whom Peter regarded as a Godless, Corsican upstart who had tried to destroy the old order in Europe, and half succeeded. Peter thought that Mr Black had for his part destroyed the old order at the Telegraph, which was a not much smaller sin, and instituted his own revolutionary practices. He did not have it in his heart to adapt, though our old editor, Bill Deedes, ennobled by Mrs Thatcher, had converted himself with almost shocking ease into a Telegraph leader writer and columnist.

The first proper magazine dummy, produced on August 20th, did not seem very good. The black-and-white cover showed, just discernible in the shadows, a middle-aged man with a moustache sitting with piles of money in front of him. (He was supposed to be a gambler.) There were two or three perfectly respectable articles but nothing unusual. The point size of the text verged on the minuscule, and several pages carried nothing but words – thousands of them crammed together forbiddingly with no thought of relief for the reader. Pieces by Geoffrey Wheatcroft and Nicholas Von Hoffman, two old Spectator stalwarts, had a familiar tang to them.

There were three weeks to go to the launch, and only two more dummies were planned. Forgetting how rotten the early dummies of the newspaper had been, we panicked – or rather Matthew and I did, since Andreas was away for a week. The panic was the greater because Alexander appeared to have only a few articles in his bottom drawer, some of which needed photographs which had not yet been arranged.

When Andreas returned to the office on Monday August 22nd Matthew and I told him how awful the dummy was. He accepted our judgment immediately. We suggested that I help Alexander launch the magazine, and Andreas readily agreed. Alexander, when called in by Andreas later, responded warmly. 'Oh, good,' he said. 'I think that is a marvellous idea.' His reaction seemed sincere. For one thing, he had probably got to the stage where he wanted some help, and may have thought that I, as a director, could offer him some extra useful firepower in his continual skirmishes with Steve Conaway. He also knew that I did not want his job. The next morning I told him that my plan was to stay on the magazine not a day over six weeks before returning to the foreign desk.

Now, at Andreas's suggestion, 'publisher' of the magazine, I moved into a little office next to Alexander's on the third floor. One of my first visitors was Derek Birdsall. He had been appointed by Alexander as art editor, and was the designer of the unloved dummy, including its cover. He was a Yorkshire-man, the bluffest of his breed, with an accent to match, and as big as a barn. (He had been lured away from his native land and lived like a pasha in Islington.) Derek played the part of the brass-tacks man of business out of J.B. Priestley to my wet-behind-the-ears young master out of early George Eliot. This was not a role in which I wished to be cast for long. We clashed first about the point size of the text which I found unreadable. Derek finally capitulated, though not without implying that I did not know what I was talking about. As if to acknowledge that the outcome of this squabble had changed our relationship, that he was less man of business than put-upon tenant farmer, he said, 'I've come to see you because I believe this is where the power is around here.' This prepared us for a greater battle over the headline typeface. Derek had an almost mystical reverence for a face called Baskerville, which to my eye seemed weedy. I thought 'Bodoni book' stronger and more elegant, and it be-came the headline face in the magazine. When this decision was made Derek resigned and went off to the pub. Alexander coaxed him back in a few days.

Before what was known at 'the crisis on the magazine' Andreas had arranged a dinner for Wednesday August 24th for some senior journalists on the newspaper and the entire maga-zine staff. He had chosen the Savoy Hotel, which was becoming for him a regular watering-hole. What had been intended as a jovial get-together, involving fraternal greetings and mutual self-congratulation between newspaper and magazine staff under the benign gaze of their great helmsman, turned out to be a delicate occasion. The table in the Pinafore room was in the form of an E, though without the middle prong. Andreas sat centrally at the top, and I was a couple of places to his left. A careless secretary drawing up the table plan had contrived to position Alexander so that he sat where the left prong met the main table, facing away from Andreas. He was unsure whether this was a deliberate slight, and chuckled merrily as he tried to grow accustomed to his placement.

Andreas made an impressively balanced speech, praising Alexander, who was finding it hard not to giggle, as the absolutely perfect man for the editorship while saying that the newspaper, having been through its own difficult birth, could help the magazine, whose first dummy was frankly disappointing. After the dinner Alexander compared Andreas's remarks to an official Kremlin statement in which the enemy of the Politburo is extravagantly praised before being eliminated, or the speech of a godfather at a Mafia reunion during which adulation is heaped on a dear friend seconds before a couple of gunmen emerge from a huge cake and shoot him dead.

Alexander hated meetings, and preferred to deal with people in ones or twos in *ad hoc* huddles. I didn't much like them either, but I felt that at the launch of a magazine everybody should know what everybody else was doing. There were, for example, all kinds of production problems. I also thought that meetings might help us produce ideas for articles which were in dangerously short supply. Subscribing in part to Andreas's notion that the newspaper could help the magazine, I invited several journalists on the newspaper to attend. One of these was Mark Lawson, a Promethean writer of extreme youth. He would sit cross-legged on the floor in the magazine's meeting-room and rattle off ideas for interviews – Michael Frayn, Dukakis, David Edgar – and for other pieces with amazing speed. Then he would disappear, bouncing back in a few days with a 3,000-word article, having risen at the crack of dawn to knock off a television review for the Independent. Mark, who was then aged twenty-five or twenty-six, was devoted to the newspaper and everything which he thought it stood for. Being drafted on to the magazine was all in the course of duty.

Alexander and I got on well, though I could see that my presence was rather painful to him. He was a secretive person who did not share his deepest thoughts easily; foolish people might imagine that such thoughts were not there. The happy-go-lucky air, the witty running down of himself and others, enveloped a serious and even quite ambitious person. To his own staff he cleverly played the role of man of the people; I was part of 'management', a race apart, whose most hard-nosed representative was Steve Conaway. Steve did some justice to this casting.

He had decided that the magazine was going to be produced without colour proofs and could not be persuaded otherwise, even by me as 'publisher'. During these weeks, if the magazine could be compared to a military unit in post-revolutionary Russia, Alexander was regarded by his staff as the easy-going, vodka-swilling commanding officer, while I was perhaps seen – not a role I cherished – as the tight-lipped Bolshevik commissar in whom power ultimately resided.

At our midday directors' meeting on September 9th, Adrian O'Neill told us that he had been given a 'preview' of the market research of the three dummies of the magazine which would be unveiled to staff that afternoon. He said that the findings were remarkably favourable. 'In that case,' said Andreas, 'we had better ask the market research people to play down the good points a bit.' This research was the first clue that Alexander's magazine was conceptually a good deal more attractive than most of us had realised. Or, to put it another way, he had followed his brief of producing a magazine *to be read* more successfully than had been appreciated. In its determination not to be like any other colour supplement known to man, the much maligned dummy was plainly the forerunner of the existing Independent magazine. Its structure, almost entirely devised by Alexander, has hardly changed.

The first issues of the magazine were full of articles which would not have been there had it not been for 'the crisis.' We had to launch with our best shot. Readers would not give us six · months to get it right. Matthew offered me a new short story by Graham Greene which had come his way. I also half-inched for serialisation a book by V.S. Naipaul which Andreas and I had bought for the newspaper earlier in the year. This ran for several weeks. In the early issues, James Fenton was prevailed upon to write about his prawn farm in the Philippines and the Olympics in South Korea. Andrew Gimson wrote about the SDP. Sebastian Faulks wrote a column for a few weeks. Mark Lawson popped up everywhere.

The first issue carried on its cover a black-and-white picture of Naipaul, taken at the last moment by Brian Harris. In its murkiness, it rivalled the cover of the first dummy. Steve Conaway and Adrian thought that it was unbearably gloomy, but there was generally an air of relief about the entire issue. A couple of days before it appeared, as Andreas, Matthew and myself were being driven to one of our fortnightly lunches, Matthew thanked me emotionally for 'saving the company'. (Andreas remained silent during this undeserved encomium.) Matthew had conceived an extreme view of Alexander's errors, and several times over the coming months suggested that it would be a good idea to sack him. 'People can't change,' he announced. 'Alexander will never change. He just won't.'

Alexander's 'sin' in the eyes of Matthew and others was not only his failure to organise enough memorable articles for the early issues. It was to have disdained collaboration and to have gone it alone. He had not sought the advice of senior colleagues on the daily paper, some of whom now believed that they were touched with genius, and when advice was thrust at him he had seemed evasive or ungrateful. He had not genuflected properly to the tutelary gods of the Independent. The launch of the magazine was a dress rehearsal for the greater drama which was to take place on the Independent on Sunday.

The magazine was not widely appreciated at City Road for several months. Even today there may be some hard-line critics in the recesses of the Home department, that redoubt of true believers in the myth of the Independent. Like those Japanese soldiers who turn up from time to time in the depths of the jungle unable to credit that the second world war is ended, they still maintain that the magazine is dull and boring and, in some mysterious, undefined way, unIndependentish. In the early months such criticisms were very strong, notwithstanding the widespread sense of relief at the first issue. The increase in our Saturday circulation was almost entirely attributed by Matthew, Steve and Adrian to the new second section of the newspaper rather than to the predominantly black-and-white magazine. Assaults on the magazine became a part of the general sport of board meetings, the most persistent critic among the non-executive directors being Bruce Fireman, who dressed up his personal opinions as *ex cathedra* judgments. 'I am afraid that I have to say', he would declare, 'that I do not think that the magazine is very good.' Five-second pause for effect. 'I'm sorry to have to say this, Stephen.' Gracious nod in my direction. 'A number of my friends have remarked to me how they simply cannot read it. They find, and I must say that I share this view, the widespread use of black-and-white photography quite off-putting.' His comments drew sympathetic grunts from one or other of the non-executives. I was left trying to defend Alexander and his magazine.

These critics were confounded when three months after its launch the magazine was awarded the Europa Prize. The in-scrutable figure of Paolo Filo della Torre was mixed up in this. Paolo was a friend of Alexander's and he had recommended the magazine for the prize. Winning it was an undoubted honour which was not to be sneezed at, the more so since it was worth 50 million lire, about £21,000. But because the magazine was classified as a supplement, the awarding committee decided that Alexander would have to share the prize with Andreas, as the newspaper's editor. The two of them travelled to Milan to col-lect the award.

*

Our connection with La Repubblica was growing. During the week after the launch of the magazine, Andreas, Adrian and I went to Rome to discuss 'collaborative ventures' with the founding editor of La Repubblica, Eugenio Scalfari, and his col-leagues, including Paolo Filo della Torre, who had flown over from London a few days before.

Eugenio and Andreas had already met. Though they were very different men, they had fallen in love with each other at first sight – or at any rate Andreas had fallen in love with Eugenio. Under the latter's editorship, La Repubblica had been transformed from a Roman newspaper with a circulation of 50,000 into a national daily with sales approaching a million copies. Eugenio was a walking success – wealthy, intellectual, handsome and attractive to women. With his coiffured white hair, prettily trimmed white beard and fine brow, he did not correspond in appearance to any English notion of what a jour-nalist should look like. Nor did his languid manner suggest that he was the sort of editor who would roll up his sleeves. His mind was more likely to be on his next signed 2,000-word piece on the future of Europe or the nature of *perestroika*.

Unlike though he was to Andreas, he became for him a sort of role model. He reflected back some of Andreas's admiration. At the centre of their love affair was Europe. For Eugenio the nation state was an aberration of history, and he longed for the day when pan-cultural intellectuals such as himself could move between London, Paris or Rome within a unified elite. This too was Andreas's dream, though he was for all practical purposes monoglot. Ever since I had known him he had been a believer in a federal Europe. He had once explained that this was because, as Europeans, Britons could once again be citizens of a super-power. He seemed to admire some European countries more than his own, and was sure that France was a better governed and more efficient nation than Britain.

We arrived in Rome on the evening of September 9th and had a late dinner *al fresco* with Eugenio and his colleagues, and our correspondent, Michael Sheridan. This was the first time I met Prince Carlo Caracciolo, the chief executive and part-owner of La Repubblica, though I scarcely spoke to him. After dinner, returning to the hotel, we dropped off Paolo at his 'club'. He opened a door in a wall, which was otherwise without any apertures, and disappeared inside, like a monk returning into the silent mysteries of his monastery.

The next morning we gathered in the offices of La Repubblica in Piazza dell' Independenza. Eugenio proposed the creation of a group of European-minded newspapers. He also suggested that the Independent and La Repubblica should take shareholdings in each other's companies. Andreas was cagey about this second idea.

Paolo Filo della Torre of course had different ambitions – to acquire an Atex computer in the midst of all this European utopianism. He did not do his cause much good when introducing Adrian.

'I would like to introduce Andreas Witham Smeeth who is one of the most brilliant editors on the world' – here he shot a glance, half conspiratorial, half tremulous, at his own editor, the great Eugenio Scalfari – 'and the founder of Il Independente. You will all 'ave 'eard of 'im, of course. And also we 'ave 'ere Stephen Glover who is the most fantastic foreign editor and 'as just launched a marvellous magazine and I am sure it will be a very great success and he is also one of the original founders. And this is Adrian O'Neill, an assistant director.' Adrian, who happened unbeknown to his hosts to be half Italian, bridled and smouldered at this cursory demotion.

After a few hours' discussion, during which it was finally agreed that Paolo could have his long-dreamt of computer, we adjourned for lunch to the Grand Hotel, which might have been shifted in its entirety from Eastbourne. We sat at a long table in a private room beneath hideous chandeliers. Juan Luis Cebrian, founding editor of the Spanish newspaper El Pais, had flown from Madrid for the occasion. After an endless series of elaborate courses, Eugenio rose to speak. He sketched out his vision of a common European future when the three news-papers might work together in important ventures. He said how honoured he was to have at his right side the great Andreas Whittam Smith whose brilliance was responsible for the creation of the Independent. After Andreas had returned the compliment, and referred to Eugenio as 'a great man', we arose a little unsteadily and returned to the offices of La Repubblica. Later we were driven in Italian fashion to the airport – Eugenio and Andreas in Eugenio's bullet-proof Alfa Romeo, Adrian and myself, less precious, following in a car which had no obvious defences against the depredations of Italian terrorists.

It was a few weeks later that Andreas took delivery of his black Mercedes.

*

None of us could have predicted that within two years La Repubblica and El Pais would become major shareholders in Newspaper Publishing plc. Our worry that autumn was that Robert Maxwell, scenting the success of the Independent, might try to take us over. At the end of October we learnt that Maxwell had been buying shares in the company, increasing his holding to about 8 per cent. At a few hours' notice Andreas summoned our advisers – lawyers from Herbert Smith, merchant bankers from S.G. Warburg, stockbrokers from James Capel – to an emergency meeting in our dungeon-like dining room.

Andreas began dramatically. 'I believe that we have been put on notice by Mr Maxwell' – he always called him Mr Maxwell,

as if the use of a Christian name might imply a degree of chumminess – 'that he intends to take over this company.'

The facts did not at all justify this interpretation – Maxwell
had been picking up relatively few shares – but there was much
nodding of heads and thoughtful sucking of pencils. A young
man from James Capel said that Mr Maxwell might be attempting to gain control of the Independent so that he could throw in
the newspaper to sweeten the forthcoming flotation of Mirror
Group Newspapers. This seemed a reasonable theory. However, it was clear that not much could be done at the moment to
deter Mr Maxwell. The only hope lay in re-writing the Articles
of Association more tightly to limit the size of individual shareholdings.

At the beginning of December Marcus Sieff resigned as
chairman of Newspaper Publishing. The reason, he told me on
the telephone, was the extraordinary behaviour of Charles
Richards, our Jerusalem correspondent. Marcus had gone to
Israel during the general election campaign and had contacted
Charles to suggest that they meet for a drink. Perhaps he
privately hoped that he might still induce Charles to visit the
underpants factory but, in the event, he did not have the chance
even to say hello. He waited for Charles for six hours at his
hotel before retiring to bed at midnight. For a long time he had
put up with what he regarded as anti-Israeli reporting of the
intifada in the Independent, and now the newspaper's correspondent couldn't be bothered to turn up for a drink.

When Marcus told me this story I wondered what horrible
punishment we might devise for Richards. To keep Rupert
Murdoch or Tiny Rowland waiting for six hours might show
commendable independence of spirit in a young reporter, but
Marcus Sieff's good manners, not to mention his advanced age,
demanded special courtesy. In wishing to put Charles immediately on the rack I had however forgotten his chaotic
nature. His story had a terrible plausibility. He had agreed to
meet Marcus at the Hilton Hotel. Finding that he could not get
away from work, he had rung the hotel in Tel Aviv to leave a
message for Marcus saying that he would be late. Marcus meanwhile was spinning the hours away at the Hilton Hotel . . . in

Jerusalem. When Charles finally arrived in Tel Aviv, and discovered his error, he asked for a message to be sent to Marcus in Jerusalem. Marcus never received this.

Andreas said that the resignation must be rescinded. 'We can't afford to lose him now.' He felt the slight on Marcus's behalf, the more so because he believed that Marcus Sieff was 'a great man'. It was also true that Marcus's chairmanship suited Andreas very well. He no longer inspired awe or fear in Andreas. He had become, as a consequence of his relative infirmity, a remarkably easy-going, not to say 'hands-off' chairman, who allowed Andreas to dominate and direct board meetings almost as though Newspaper Publishing were his own private company.

Andreas and I rushed in his new black Mercedes to pay court to Marcus in his office at Marks and Spencer. The two of us explained Charles Richard's version of events, which Marcus seemed to accept. But he did not change his mind about resigning. He was getting old, he said, and quite apart from this matter he felt that he had had enough. Andreas replied that the company needed him as its chairman. He then suggested that the Independent should send a high-minded, objective journalist to Israel to write a long article about the underpants factory and Neve Shalom. The journalist he had in mind was Andrew Gimson. There was no question of compromising our independence. But it would immeasurably help Andrew if Marcus could spare him a few minutes before he left. Marcus said that he would be very pleased to.

So Andrew was despatched to Israel on what Andreas described to him as 'a special mission' – to keep Marcus Sieff as chairman. Not without grave misgivings, Andrew generously agreed to go. He produced an article which showed no obvious signs of Israeli propaganda. More important, he also visited the underpants factory and Neve Shalom. This was good enough for Marcus Sieff, who did not mention resignation again.

★

With the magazine more or less successfully launched, we turned our minds again to the idea of a Sunday newspaper. We had already learnt in April that a group of people were planning to launch a quality Sunday newspaper, which was in due course called the Sunday Correspondent, and we didn't want them to have the market to themselves – if there was a market. Research commissioned in July and presented on August 24th suggested that 'reader dissatisfaction' with the existing quality Sunday papers was a little less than that which had existed in the daily market before our launch.

There was also Andreas's old notion of buying the Observer. One year later this did not seem quite so preposterous. It had erupted again in July, and Christopher Barton had produced some estimated figures for the Observer which suggested that the paper might be making about four million pounds a year, which is to say more than we were. The problem was that there was no indication that Lonrho, which in this context meant its chief executive, Tiny Rowland, wanted to sell it. Andreas took the bull by the horns, and on July 20th he wrote to Rowland suggesting a meeting to discuss the possibility of 'a close association' between the Independent and the Observer. 'The Sunday newspaper market', wrote Andreas, 'is a natural development for us.'

No reply was received from Mr Rowland to Andreas's letter. For a time the Observer was put on one side, and we began to think of launching our own Sunday newspaper. In October editorial heads of department were asked to draw up prospective budgets. But when we started to discuss ideas, we were lacking in inspiration. I felt exhausted after 'the crisis on the magazine'. Moreover, the Saturday paper was not yet established. But the real problem was that we had represented it to ourselves and the outside world as a 'weekend paper' which did away with the need for a Sunday paper.

There was also a more self-interested argument. The Independent appeared to be heading towards permanent profitability. For the financial year beginning October 1st 1988 we were projecting a profit of over £4 million. It seemed likely that the founders' convertible shares would become ordinary shares, and there was already talk of persuading the investors to allow the founders to 'convert early' on the basis of our promising financial performance. The official argument was that conversion would protect the independence of the company because the directors would control more shares. Andreas said to me that he thought it 'a point of honour' for us to achieve conversion.

For all the founders an important matter, conversion was for Christopher Barton an obsession which seemed to dominate all his thinking about the company. The more mundane work of the finance department seemed increasingly to be done by Graham Luff, his ever-smiling number two. More than a year earlier Christopher had skilfully contrived the early repayment of the original loan stock through a bank re-financing, in part because he realised that without such a manoeuvre the internal rate of return would probably be insufficient to convert many of the founders' shares. At a directors' lunch on October 6th he argued – certainly not to deaf ears – that the early launch of a Sunday newspaper 'might put the conversion of founders' shares very much at risk'.

For all these reasons the launch of a Sunday paper was put on ice, and on December 1st Andreas rushed off a dramatic memorandum to all staff, announcing that there would be no Sunday paper in 1989. 'Increased resources' would instead be directed to the Saturday paper.

This statement, which was reported in the press, must have led to celebrations at the offices of the Sunday Correspondent. The planned paper had acquired an editor, Peter Cole, a chief executive, Nick Shott and a chairman – Douglas Long. At the end of November they had produced a business plan which bore a striking resemblance to our own prospectus.

As our plans to launch our own Sunday newspaper ebbed, so the Observer re-entered our calculations in a rather unlikely form. Shortly before Christmas, Andreas met at Mark's Club in London an American publisher called Ralph Ingersoll. Mr Ingersoll's father, also Ralph, had founded a left-wing newspaper called PM in New York before the war. That paper, which had tried to get by without advertising, had eventually failed, but after the war Ralph senior had set up a successful chain of provincial newspapers. At some point he and Ralph junior had fallen out, which is to say that the son had gained control of the little empire which his father had built up. With the help of a friend called Michael Milken, an expert in 'junk bonds', Ralph junior had borrowed a lot of money and was using it to build his father's publishing empire into something really colossal. Ingersoll Publications employed 15,000 people. Mr Ingersoll himself was said to be worth $500 million.

At dinner at Mark's Club this tycoon put a notion to Andreas. Ingersoll Publications was looking to Europe for acquisitions. It was sizing up Lonrho's provincial newspapers, which included the Glasgow Herald. Mr Ingersoll had in mind to make a bid for all Lonrho's newspaper interests and then to sell on the Observer to a third party. Would Newspaper Publishing be interested? You bet it would, said Andreas. The figure of £80 million, as a price for the Observer, seems to have been bandied across the table.

My first account of this exchange came not from Andreas, but from Matthew, a week or two after the event. Matthew came into my office.

'I thought you might like to know that we're going to buy a newspaper,' he said.

'Really?'

'Apparently. I've just seen an extraordinary letter lying on Andreas's desk for him to sign,' he said.

'What did it say?'

'Well, it was to someone called Ralph Ingersoll, and it said something like: "It was very good to meet you at dinner the other day when we discussed the acquisition of the Observer by Newspaper Publishing."'

A day or two after this Andreas told the executive directors about his dealings with Ralph Ingersoll in slightly more subdued tones. He suggested that we build up a more exact picture of the Observer's finances. We had got hold of a copy of the Observer's internal management accounts, which showed that the paper had made a profit of just over £3 million in the year ending 30th September 1988. We discovered exactly how many people the newspaper employed. We also learnt that in September 1987 the Observer had seriously considered launching a quality daily newspaper in order to spread its costs across the week.

Now that we knew the Observer's costs and revenues we could work out what profits we could make out of it. Obviously we could reduce its costs drastically by sharing overheads.

On existing sales of 750,000 we could hope to make an annual profit of about £15 million. On the other hand, it was a newspaper with a gently declining circulation whose sales could be expected to fall sharply if the Sunday Correspondent were launched. Yet even if its sales fell to 580,000 we could still make a reasonable profit of £4 or £5 million a year. Such a circulation seemed a bit pessimistic. Our board agreed that it was worth bidding up to £55 million for 'Andrew', which was our codename for the Observer, named after the street which the paper had until recently inhabited in the City. It seemed quite likely that our shareholders, who at this time tended to think that we could do no wrong, would stump up the money.

There was also the question of who would edit the Observer if we acquired it. Matthew and I were the inevitable candidates, and we settled the matter between us during a two-minute conversation on our car telephones. Matthew said that he did not particularly want to edit a Sunday newspaper because it would mean that he would have to work on a Saturday when he wanted to see his children. He added that my 'reflective mind might be better suited to Sunday newspapers'. But as deputy editor of the Independent he would want 'a bigger editing role' since Andreas would, after all, have his work cut out as chief executive of a much larger company.

He set out his proposals in a memorandum dated January 4th 1989 to Andreas and the other executive directors. He envisaged Andreas continuing 'to chair' the morning conference at which he could 'inject ideas into the system, set and define priorities, draw attention to inadequacies, and generally impose his personality on the paper'. From midday Matthew would assume 'the main burden of editing', busying himself with departmental heads 'in a way which is consistent with the beliefs and preoccupations of AWS'. In normal circumstances Matthew would take the 5.30 front-page conference but 'remain available to AWS to push forward any idea which had occurred to him'. Very thoughtful.

This memorandum, outwardly reverential though it was towards Andreas, was an unabashed bid for power. It reflected Matthew's feelings of frustration since the launch of the Independent, his sense that he had been squeezed out by

Andreas and the departmental heads. Andreas did not immediately accept its suggestions – as things turned out, he had no need to – but the Manichean form of editing which Matthew proposed was eventually adopted. Uncharacteristic though it may seem, Andreas may have given this power away because of the voices of caution which occasionally spoke to him. Do not be seen to hold too much power to yourself, they may have said to him, lest the board or the shareholders or someone else forces you to make a choice between being editor and chief executive. In name, at least, he has remained both.

I did not think that we would buy the Observer. For one thing, Tiny Rowland had shown no interest in selling it, even to so mighty a mogul as Ralph Ingersoll junior. For another, we were a small company which had not yet made a full year of profits and the Observer had been around for nearly two hundred years. Still, it was a nice idea, and the prospect of being an editor was appealing.

At 9.30 am on January 10th the executive directors, except Matthew who was away, met Ralph Ingersoll in a private room at Brown's Hotel which Andreas had booked. The Savoy had been full up. Bruce Fireman joined us about noon, somewhat to the displeasure of Andreas who was itching to do a deal without the assistance of an experienced merchant banker. Mr Ingersoll had brought with him Sir Gordon Brunton, a peppery old relict of the old Times who had hitched himself to the young tycoon, and a couple of lesser sidekicks.

We settled ourselves at a long table, fussed over by flunkies offering us coffee. Mr Ingersoll, with Sir Gordon on his right, sat on one side; Andreas sat opposite him. I was at one end of the table, so close that I could have put my hand on Mr Ingersoll's fluffless dark blue suit. I was trying to work out whether I had ever met someone worth $500 million.

Ralph – we were now on these terms – was a man of about forty, with thin light-coloured hair and the permanent tan of the very rich. He wore gold rimmed spectacles. His shirt was light blue, with one of those large power collars, and his tie, made of a thick silk, looked as though it was double-knotted. He had learnt, or been told, that a man of his standing should be very still. He hardly moved – and that went for his lips too. As a result, I had to lean forward to catch what he was saying. He began with a *tour d'horizon*.

'We have been expanding in the States,' he said, 'but we think that may be a market which is near saturation. We are looking for openings in Europe. We see a market of 350 million people which has many opportunities. We have just been looking at something in Yugoslavia ... We see possible bargains here in the UK too. You know that we already own the Birmingham Post, and we believe that the conurbation of five million or so people has one of the best growth prospects in Europe.' He paused a couple of seconds to let this bombshell sink in. 'Now I have been associated with Michael Milken of Drexel, Burnham Lambert – '

At this point Andreas nodded to indicate that he knew all about this legendary financial wizard and master of the 'junk bond'. These were the roller-coaster years of the Reagan-Thatcher boom and Mr Milken's indictment for fraud was still some way off.

'– and we work on a simple formula, which values companies at a fixed multiple of discounted cash flow.'

It may have seemed simple to him but I could not make head or tail of it. I looked around the room to see whether my colleagues looked any the wiser. Andreas was inscrutably red-faced, inscribing notes in his reporter's notebook like a policeman at the scene of an accident. Christopher Barton had tilted his head and was looking down his nose at Ralph with the smile of an American tourist in Oxford Street just about to be shown the three-card trick. Adrian just sat there as though to move a single face muscle would give the game away. Steve looked as though he had heard this sort of stuff a dozen times before and was wondering when Ralph was going to get on to the meat.

The meat came eventually from Sir Gordon Brunton. He had developed a good double act with Ralph. 'I don't know whether I'm sticking my neck out here. I haven't consulted about this with Ralph, and he may tell me afterwards that I've gone too far.' According to Sir Gordon, their formula for paying for a company was 'ten times operating cash flow'.* On this basis he valued Lonrho's newspaper interests excepting the Observer at between £110 and £130 million. He was a bit vague about the profits that these newspapers were making, but no matter. He accepted our figure of £8.4 million for the operating cash flow of the Observer – our research was more detailed than theirs – and therefore valued the paper at about £80 million. He suggested that a bid for £200 million for all Lonrho's newspapers might clinch the deal. They would then pass on the Observer to us for £80 million. In a phrase which might have fallen more naturally from the lips of Ralph Ingersoll junior, he observed that no one had ever paid too much for a publishing company.

Andreas conducted himself throughout these proceedings as though he had found himself for the first time in an Arab bazaar. This cautious attitude seemed to surprise Ralph, who had apparently formed the view from his conversation at Mark's Club, as well as Andreas's subsequent letter, that £80 million was more or less in the bag. Andreas now came up with the alternative figure of £26 million. The basis for this was five times cash flow, £42 million, minus the estimated costs of reorganisation and acquisition. There was no magic about the five times multiple. It was just half Ralph's figure.

Ralph now looked at Andreas as though he had turned out to be a bad disappointment. 'I don't think that it is a realistic figure for Andrew,' he said. Ralph had tried to enter into the spirit of the occasion by using our codename for the Observer. Tiny Rowland was 'Cecil' (as in Cecil Rhodes, whom he was supposed to resemble in the scope of his African ambitions) and Ralph himself, though he did not know this, was 'Rand'. 'When we met, and subsequently, I had got the impression that you were in for more than that.'

At this point we adjourned. It was clear that we weren't going to get anywhere with £26 million. Steve Conaway and I hinted to Andreas that he was being a little churlish. A little more give

---

* Cash flow is the difference between cash coming in and cash going out of a business in a particular period, and can be either negative or positive. Operating cash flow is cash flow calculated before deducting tax payable or adding any tax repayable, and before deducting any interest paid to any lender.

and there could be a deal. When the meeting re-convened in the same private room over lunch Andreas increased our offer to £42 million. Bruce seemed to qualify the new figure, but Andreas overruled him.

So it was agreed that Rand would bid £42 million to Cecil for Andrew on our behalf. I don't think any of us came away believing that this would ever happen – that Cecil would ever sell or, if he did, that Rand would pass on Andrew to us. As we left the hotel, Andreas turned to me and asked: 'Will you put this in your book, Stephen?' I had never suggested to him that I would write about the Independent, nor did I have any particular intention to do so. 'What book?' I replied.

Three weeks later Andreas received a letter from Rand dated February 20th which confirmed that his ambitions as a deal-maker would have to wait. It was copied by him to the directors and annotated 'No reply.'

Mr Ingersoll wrote that it seemed to him that the straight-forward structure that was discussed before Christmas at Mark's Club was becoming rather too complex and he would prefer to approach Cecil independently.

He said he felt this way because he was confused by their assessment of Andrew's value . . . from £80 million down to £26 million . . . back to £42 million, etc. He was also concerned that the board would not be able to commit irrevocably to the 'put option' which had been discussed, which rendered a joint undertaking dangerous from his point of view.

He also added that 'we've assumed we'd bid for everything except Andrew', and that it was still his intention to attempt to acquire all of those assets and not own Andrew under any conditions. He signed his letter, 'Cordially Ralph Ingersoll II.'

Eighteen months later Ralph Ingersoll II was forced to relinquish his American publishing empire after a 'technical default' on the repayment of a 'junk bond' debt.

★

Alexander was looking for a new deputy editor of the magazine. In December he had parted company with Paul Barker. Now Christina Garrett, the hyper-efficient managing editor, announced that she was leaving, and it was agreed, principally for reasons of economy, that a single replacement be found who could do both jobs.

Since my departure from the magazine my relations with Alexander had been uneasy. For understandable reasons he was disinclined to regard me as in any sense his saviour, and in so far as he consulted with anyone he reverted to his former habit of dealing with Andreas, which was admittedly what he had asked for at the time of his appointment. He discontinued some of the meetings which I had insisted he hold. At the same time, I found myself defending Alexander against the criticisms of executive and non-executive directors, some of whom, such as Matthew, periodically suggested his dismissal. Perhaps I should have told Alexander all this, but, apart from intimating that he still had his detractors, I did not discuss it with him. It is a difficult thing to say to a man – especially when he is running an increasingly successful magazine – that some of his colleagues would like to get rid of him, the more so if he is recovering from a battering.

From early January Alexander began to look for a deputy. Though he may not have applied himself to this task with remarkable vigour, he none the less produced two plausible candidates for Andreas and me to meet. At least in one case we were moderately impressed, but Alexander did not show great enthusiasm for his own choices. This was his natural manner, never to praise too much even what he rather liked, but in these circumstances his hanging back was misinterpreted by Andreas and myself. We saw it as a re-assertion of a non-urgent way of doing business. It seemed to us also that Alexander, despite prodding from both of us, was still reluctant to plan ahead enough ambitious pieces which, in Andreas's words, would be 'memorable' and 'talked about' and would 'make noise'. No doubt this was true, but what we could not fully accept, despite the increasing praise for the magazine, despite the Europa Prize, despite even the judgment of our own eyes, was how good it was, and how close to the original conception.

Time passed, and no further candidates were produced by Alexander. Andreas began to believe that he was being deliberately evasive. Finally another candidate was wheeled out by Alexander. Though the man was what Matthew would call 'a

Andreas Whittam Smith before the launch of the Independent

Matthew Symonds relaxes on the 'brothel sofa'

Foreign staff of the Independent gather in Bunhill Fields before the paper's launch

Adrian O'Neill and Douglas Long admiring the first issue of Today

Andreas chairs an early meeting at City Road

– and makes his own coffee with Linda Tanner looking on

'Missile tube blast sank Soviet sub'

By Mark Urban
Defence Correspondent

SUBMARINE design experts said last night that an explosion in a missile launch tube caused the damage which sank the stricken Soviet Yankee class submarine in the Atlantic Ocean.

According to one, the form of the blast — caused by missile fuel rather than warheads — was such that it would have blown off missile hatches, and may well have split the whole tube.

The Yankee-I class submarine, carrying 16 SS-N-6 ballistic missiles, was crippled by an explosion and fire. The idea in which they are set are extremely strong, being designed to cope with the forces involved at launching missiles

under water. At least one of the liquid-fuelled missiles exploded, following a fire during maintenance.

This allowed water to rush into the rest of the submarine. It is not known whether the explosion happened before or after the submarine surfaced on Saturday night.

After it surfaced the crew were able to assess the damage, which included a gaping hole, where the missile tube hatch had blown off

during yesterday morning. The submarine sank in three miles of water — too deep for the boat's bulkheads to withstand the pressure. They would have "popped" as the boat sank.

The compartment housing the Yankee's two nuclear propulsion reactors is the strongest part of the boat and would have been the last section to collapse — the rest of the hull could have imploded first.

The wreck has so deep that salvage by any current methods would be difficult, if not impossible.

Scientists do not believe that

there is any environmental risk from either the reactors — if they have broken up — or the missiles. According to Professor John Fremlin, a British specialist in radioactivity, it would take 1,000 years for any contamination to reach the surface.

At least three Soviet submarines have been lost at sea in recent years despite a major effort by Soviet designers to make them safer, more efficient and more comfortable to work in.

The Yankees are by no means old by Soviet standards. They are of a similar layout and vintage to Britain's Polaris boats. Nineteen

Liberals signalled, page 9

Baker to set up 10 city colleges

By Colin Hughes
Political Correspondent

PLANS to create between 10 and 15 city technical colleges funded jointly by government, grant and private industrial sponsorship, will be announced today by Kenneth Baker, Secretary of State for Education.

INSIDE

James Fenton gives a goat to the rebels.
Page 10

Unheard victims breast cancer.
Page 14

William Rees-Mo on the BBC's sticky wicket.
Page 16

Theatre seats for you. Available tickets. Page 20

CONTENTS

Conservatives try to halt sterling slide

- Bundesbank chief to see Thatcher
- Pound falls to all-time low

By Sarah Hogg and Andrew Marr

Outlook: Page 19

An armed policeman keeping watch yesterday from the roof of the Bournemouth centre where the Conservative Party Conference opens today. Conference security, Page 2

Terrorist 'helped by Syrian envoy'

By Heather Mills
Crime Correspondent

SYRIAN INTELLIGENCE co-ordinated an alleged Arab terrorist to sacrifice his pregnant girlfriend in a time-bomb blast on an El Al jumbo jet at 39,000 feet, the Old Bailey heard yesterday.

Leader comment, page 16

Heseltine challenges Government over jobs

By Anthony Bevins
Political Editor

A DIRECT challenge to the Government's industrial and unemployment strategies has been launched by Michael Heseltine on the eve of the Conservative Party conference.

Interview, page 17

Summary

Crime wave will engulf Britain

LORD LANE, the Lord Chief Justice, said that "a huge wave of crime" threatens to engulf Britain as a result of a lowering of standards in every range of life.

Report and analysis, Page 3

■ HOME

War on terror: Trade unions in Northern Ireland say to take an important stand against terrorism with a clampdown on intimidation. Report and analysis, Page 2

Earnings cut: The CBI is warning that it earnings do not fall substantially inflation could force the next government to adopt tax incomes policy. Page 1

■ FOREIGN

Treaty violation: A huge early-warning radar system that the United States wants to build on a Yorkshire moor is in violation of a 1972 treaty which nearly brought the US and the Soviet Union. Page 6

Class champion: Kasparov wins world title in Leningrad. Page 9

Visa cost: A new visa scheme which begins in the Indian sub-continent on 15 October will cost Britain £60m a year to issue 120 photographic officers abroad. Page 6

■ CITY

Investors Gas: Subscribers for the British Gas issue are to be allowed to put their shares into a Personal Equity Plan. Page 21

■ BUSINESS

BCW bonus: Over 1,500 members of Lloyd's face further losses from the BCW syndicate Page 18

TSB championate: Government Peat Marwick are writing to those suspected of making illegal multiple applications for TSB shares asking for an explanation. Page 19

Whateve the size of your party

Bournemouth offers a warm welcome to the biggest conference. And the smallest. The spacious and luxurious Bournemouth International Centre with its two highly flexible halls incorporating the latest technology, and the famous Pavilion Theatre, with its revolving stage, combine sophisticated Bournemouth as Europe's most attractive conference and exhibition venue. Can we confer? Ring Gill Price or Maureen Justice on 0202 28841/22123 or write to them at the Bournemouth International Centre, Dept ID, Exeter Road, Bournemouth BH2 5BH. Telex: 418518.

BOURNEMOUTH INTERNATIONAL CENTRE

Pope's homage to obscure saint

From Patrick Marnham
in Cure d'Ars

THE POPE chose to plant the whole of the third day of his pilgrimage to France in one village, devoting his parish of the Curé d'Ars.

While the Pontiff was in Ars it was impossible for almost anyone else to go there. Even the villagers were obliged to display identity cards and were prevented from making freely around their own village. I saw one old lady being forbidden by a rigidist of the Gendarmerie Nationale from entering the house where she had been born.

Ars has been a place of special importance for the Pope since he was a young priest. Indeed, the example of Saint Jean-Marie Vianney, the Curé d'Ars, means more to the Polish pope than it does to some French priests.

The visit was a humble man who was appointed to this particular parish in 1835. His reputation as a confessor spread slowly

throughout France. Pilgrimages to this little village grew, and for the last 40 years of his life the curé was literally a prisoner of his followers. He died in 1859, was canonised in 1925 and declared to be the patron saint of parish priests.

Since the Second World War his cult has dwindled. Ars contains a little village frequented by the pious and a gravely pilgrim curio. When it was first announced that the Pope had decided to visiting, some French priests even grumbled at being reminded of the example of this unfashionable saint, a priest who spent his life either seated in the confessional or on his knees.

Yesterday, in a vast marquee erected in a

meadow outside the village, the Pope reminded all the bishops and many of the 4,000 priests and seminarians of the importance of their forgotten saint.

Like so many of his sermons, it was highly political, but couched in code. He referred to the perils facing the church due to the lack of vocations, but insisted that priestly vocations were unique and could never be delegated to lay people. In saying this he was denying the possibility of such innovations as a married priesthood.

When he referred to the house spent in prayer by the Curé d'Ars, he was admonishing those priests who concentrate their efforts of social work. He prayed the priests of France to return to their parishes and address themselves to the sins of their parishioners, to rescue a certain observance of Sunday, and to insist on more private confessions.

The logo comes alive by Annie Leibovitz

A sense of relief all round with the eagle back in safe hands

Andreas at the launch of the Independent on Sunday

Paper dreams . . .

Enter young mother, with a smile saying what words can't

Griffiths walks into a press conference at St Thomas's Hospital in London yesterday after being reunited with her baby daughter, Alexandra, who was kidnapped more than two weeks ago

By Cal McCrystal and Tim Kelsey

THE YOUNG woman kept smiling. All she could say was: "I cannot describe it in words." The start of her sole kept repeating: "Marvellous, marvellous."

That was it as far as speech was concerned: unless one were a reporter from the *News of the World*, but even the purchase of baby Alexandra's story for a reputed £75,000 could not allow a journalist to prise the meaning through St Thomas's Hospital yesterday.

Alexandra Griffiths, the newborn baby kidnapped from St Thomas's more than two weeks ago, was recovered after a tip-off to police that the kidnapper, a woman aged 25, was in a Crouch-end village.

Dawn Griffiths, 20, and her boyfriend Geoffrey Wardle, greeted Alexandra in a press conference at the hospital, a joyful conclusion to their agonising wait throughout a police search that somehow so contrasts Europe and Australia.

The parents had spent the night in the Lambeth hospital with their daughter. The child, wrapped in a white shawl, gurned with each breath and slept placidly in her mother's arms throughout a press conference but kept replying to reporters and photographers.

She later announced that it was "marvellous" to have her back. Her mother, who must have shared millions of hearts by her tearful television appeals to the unknown kidnapper, smiled delightedly but said very little. The occasion was somehow marred by another press conference and the couple announced that the baby had sold their story to the *News of the World*.

The infant had been reunited from the hospital and has a woman who described herself as a bank visitor. Dawn helped police to draw up an artist's impression of the kidnapper.

It was this sketch which led to the baby being found at The Old Police House in Bedford on Friday night. Alexandra's parents were driven there in a police car.

Mandela sets release terms

Mandela after meeting her husband in Cape Town yesterday

From John Carlin in Johannesburg

Winnie Mandela says her husband would turn back at the prison gate if ANC conditions were not met

DOUBTS grew yesterday over the early release of Nelson Mandela, after it emerged that he is refusing to be freed until conditions set by the African National Congress for political order have been met.

Foremost among these is the unmasking of the ANC, whose leadership is feared to rise or resist, and the lifting of the three-year state of emergency. In an interview given to The Independent on Sunday in Soweto, Winnie Mandela said that neither her husband, Nelson Mandela nor the ANC would accept his release on government terms.

After speaking to him for four hours at his prison house near Cape Town, she said when the emerged has "come prepared" but "cocked up" until the release would take place.

A spokesman for Kobie Coetsee, the Minister of Justice, said, however, that she was not aware of any development that could delay Mr Mandela's release. Mr Coetsee said last week that the release was "just a matter of time".

In her interview with one of her lowest hopes, Mrs Mandela expressed the background to what the anti-apartheid, her husband set in his own difficulties.

"The price of his release is the change of events within reach," she said. "That is the prize of his release and there is no way that Mandela will step out of that prison without that package."

The ANC's other demands are: the release of all political prisoners and detainees, the cancellation of all laws' trials and exile campaigns, the lifting of restrictions on all political organisations, the withdrawal of all troops from the townships and guarantees of the freedom of all opposition forces to organise, pressures on Pretoria would ease substantially.

The suggestion that there might be a last delay in releasing Mr Mandela usually came from the government first. Winnie, under severe pressure from the white exile, best fears in places in the past 10 days to diminish the high expectations of a speech Nwaximi F W de Klerk is due to deliver this Friday at the opening of parliament.

Four lead release of a organisation of the financial "Mandela" speech by F W de Klerk, the first president in 1990, Mr Botha's

Independent on Sunday staff after the announcement of 'integration'

Final party: Stephen Fay speaking, Ian Jack on the far right

serious person', indeed in some respects rather eminent, Andreas immediately took against him, and saw his candidature as a further attempt by Alexander to delay the business of finding a proper deputy. It was at this point that Andreas suggested that we choose one for Alexander ourselves.

He hit on the name of Oliver Gillie. Gillie was the Independent's medical editor, in which role he evinced a healthy interest in sexual ailments. He was part of a populist cell on the home desk which believed that the magazine should be grittier and less elitist,* and he had expressed such views in an unsolicited memorandum to Andreas. Now Andreas was convinced that Gillie was the perfect deputy, and he persuaded me against my better judgment that this was so. Matthew, to his credit, would not come along with the plan. He was perfectly happy for Alexander to suffer the humiliation of having a deputy imposed upon him, but felt that Gillie, who had little magazine experience, was the wrong man.

Gillie had first to accept the job, which unwisely he did. On Andreas's suggestion he wrote a job description for himself. This was short, sharp and brutal, amounting to a declaration that Gillie would be the *de facto* editor of the magazine. Even Andreas, whose blood was up, saw that a more diplomatic approach was desirable, and so he asked me, whom he supposed to have a better grasp than he did of what the deputy editor of the magazine was meant to do, to write out a job description. This was signed by Andreas, given to Gillie, and later copied to Alexander.

A meeting was fixed for the afternoon of Monday March 6th in Andreas's room to tell Alexander what we had done. I arrived a little early to discuss with Andreas how we should proceed. I found him in his manic mood, red-faced and, as on that terrible evening in Greenwich, with a kind of suppressed grin on his face.

---

* The cell had been fortified when John Price, previously number three, was appointed home editor when Jonathan Fenby left in September to become deputy editor of the Guardian. Jonathan's departure was not well managed. When he was still weighing up whether or not to leave, he came to City Road on his day off to see Andreas, and was kept waiting for three hours.

'You do realise that this is it, Stephen. That this is the big one?'

'What do you mean?'

'That he may threaten to resign but we must go through with it.'

It was at this moment that I began to regret our plan.

Alexander was too stunned by what Andreas told him to say very much, other than expressions of wonder and confusion. He sat there like an animal which has been hurt, which cannot comprehend the undeserved pain, and my heart bled for him. Afterwards he came to my office in a more combative mood. He was waving a letter in his hand.

'I shall think about whether or not I am going to resign, but Andreas's behaviour is quite contrary to the terms of my appointment.' It was typical of him to argue the case on legalistic grounds rather than appeal to some higher moral plane. 'It says here that I will enjoy an absolute veto, see there "absolute veto"' – at this point he thrust the letter towards me as if I might doubt his word on the matter – 'on *all* appointments. There.' The letter dropped down in front of me.

'Yes, I see that, I had forgotten that. But I suppose Andreas will merely say that times have changed.'

'Times have changed!' He said this in an incredulous, mocking voice, as though such an argument were unimaginable.

A little later he attacked me for supporting Gillie as his deputy.

'You're surely not telling me that of all the people in the world Oliver Gillie, who plainly doesn't even *like* the magazine as it exists, is the best possible choice, absolutely the *numero uno*, to become deputy editor?'

'I think he will probably be very good,' I said.

'I don't believe you mean it. I simply don't believe you can think that.'

This conversation, and similar ones over the next few days, were not acrimonious. Alexander seemed to blame Andreas more than me, which was perhaps unfair.

After several days of brooding, on March 11th Alexander wrote a long letter to Andreas, three and a bit A5 pages of single-spaced type, a 'blind copy' of which he showed to me.

The attacking office memo is a dangerous weapon to use, since it can be too easily evaded, but Alexander's was a masterpiece – lucid, passionate, dignified. Its general approach was that of the great detective trying to find a reasonable motive for an apparently irrational crime. He began by saying that he could not 'understand the motivation' behind Gillie's appointment when, according to most people's opinion, the magazine was a success. There was no 'organisational disarray' on the magazine which could justify a precipitate choice. The kindest interpretation he could think of was that Andreas was being 'cruel to be kind', ending the alleged dithering by forcing a decision. In fact, he had come to the conclusion that with the magazine's limited resources the salary of a deputy editor could better be spent on 'new junior editors, both permanent and casual'. Whereas there had seemed to be some sense in sending me to edit the magazine for a short time, Oliver Gillie's appointment was purely irrational. 'Given all the circumstances, it is inevitable, despite Stephen's assurances to the contrary, that I should wonder whether the intention is not to ease, freeze or in some other way manipulate me out of my job. But I will endeavour not to believe that . . . ' The final impression of the letter was that he would not, for the time being, resign.

Andreas replied six days later in characteristically brusque fashion. He was 'sorry' that Alexander felt 'so wounded' by the appointment of Oliver Gillie, and fully understood 'how upset' he was. 'In you,' wrote Andreas, 'the Independent magazine has a strong and gifted editor. But it also needs, in my view, a strong and gifted deputy editor, which I believe Oliver to be.' Andreas concluded by saying that he was sure that Alexander would 'take the Magazine much further, and in this enterprise you have my enthusiastic backing.'

Oliver Gillie lasted six months on the magazine. Alexander then got the deputy he wanted. I do not think that he has ever forgiven Andreas. He and I became closer friends, though perhaps in his heart he has not wholly forgiven me.

*

At the beginning of June, I flew to Moscow with Peter Jenkins, the Independent's increasingly esteemed political columnist. We drank champagne throughout the flight, and discussed whether or not we should launch a Sunday newspaper. Peter was in favour of the idea, though he had a very low opinion of Sunday papers in general, which he thought were full of confected articles, and he seemed to favour a seven-day paper on the American model.

We expected to be met at the airport by our correspondent Rupert Cornwell, and to be taken by him to some godforsaken hotel booked via Intourist. But as we made our way towards the long queue at customs a handsome young man came towards us, hand outstretched.

'Hallo,' he said. 'Do I have the pleasure of meeting Mr Glover and Mr Jenkins of the Independent newspaper?'

By a slight grunt and a nod of the head Peter conceded that this was the case.

'My name is Boris,' said Boris, 'and I have been asked to look after you.'

'Ah,' said Peter. He and I looked at each other, trying to weigh up the advantages and disadvantages of being in the hands of a KGB minder.

'Yes, please come this way. I will look after your luggage. And then we go to the car. Please, give me your passports.'

As Peter and I waited for Boris, we debated how it was that Boris or his masters even knew that we were arriving in Moscow.

'Please,' said Boris, returning with stamped passports. 'This way.'

As he swept us towards the car, we spotted Rupert Cornwell, who was waiting for us.

'Hello, Rupert,' I said. 'There seems to have been a strange mix up. Er, this is Boris, and he is taking us to a hotel.'

'But I've booked you into a hotel,' said Rupert.

'Well, Boris here thinks we should go with him.'

'I wish you had told me,' complained Rupert.

Boris took us to a long sleek black car, and invited us to get in. It was, he told us during our journey, called a Chaika, and ranked second to a Zil for the *nomenclature*. Peter, who was already warming to Boris, began almost to purr. He shot me a look which said, 'For God's sake don't say there has been a mistake. Let's go along with this,' and settled back in his seat, fussing with the little curtains on the side windows, which he pulled backwards and forwards, as though this were the kind of thing an important member of the party should do.

Our hotel was surrounded by a huge steel fence and approached via sentries who lifted a barrier after a few words from Boris. Peter and I exchanged glances. Perhaps this was not going to be such fun after all. Leaving the happy security of our party limousine, we walked up vast marble steps which led into a huge empty marble hall full of marble pillars and, although it was still daytime, blazing chandeliers.

'So, this is your hotel,' said Boris. 'Please, the car is at your disposal. Tell me whatever you want, and I will get it for you.'

'Well, a drink would be very nice,' said Peter.

'Ah, there we have a little problem,' confessed Boris. 'This is a party hotel and President Gorbachev has decreed that no one should take alcohol here.' He said this in a tone of voice which implied that he thought the architect of *perestroika* was barking up the wrong tree.

'Never mind,' replied Peter generously. He was forming a plan. As soon as Boris was gone we commandeered the Chaika and drove to the shop for foreigners in the National Hotel in Red Square, which he knew well from a previous visit to Moscow. We loaded up with bottles of Russian 'champagne' which we smuggled back to our rooms.

We were not after all guests of the KGB. A couple of days before we had left London, Andreas had murmured something to me about a conference. 'Pop in if you can.' Since he had seemed so vague, I had thought no more of it. Now it transpired not only that was there a conference but that Peter and I were official delegates.

Inside the hotel was a large debating hall with an enormous round table shaped like a Polo mint. The morning after our arrival, the two of us were ushered into this room and invited to sit down. In front of us was a small Union Jack. All around the table there were other delegates blinking behind their flags. It was then that I spotted the slightly sinister, bearded figure of Eugenio Scalfari. So this was his work.

In the eight months since our meeting in Rome something

called the Group of Six had been born, which was a collection of supposedly independent newspapers. It comprised La Repubblica, El Pais, a German paper called Suddeutcher Zeitung, a French magazine called Le Nouvel Observateur – and the Independent. At this conference Moscow News, a pro-Glasnost official organ, had joined the team. Though a director of the Independent, I knew nothing about this pan-European organisation. I assumed now that Eugenio and Andreas had cooked it up.

Having organised other appointments, we were a little grumpy to be cast in this unexpected role, but Peter rose to the occasion. He had over the years, at other conferences for which he had been able to prepare himself, developed a masterly form of delivery. He spoke slowly but fluently in a gravelly sort of voice, looking almost sad, as though he bore the burdens of the narrow world upon his statesmanlike shoulders.

Effective though this performance was, he had however in point of stamina more than met his match in Eugenio Scalfari. Eugenio spoke for nearly an hour in Italian about the dangers to *perestroika*. After about ten minutes I threw off my headphones, which were offering an incomprehensible translation of Eugenio's pearls of wisdom, and simply watched the master at work. While Peter just pretended to be a statesman, and was in fact a hack with a good reporter's instincts who happened to adore the good things of life, Eugenio had transcended journalism and lived in that delightful make-believe world in which the mere articulation of opinion is an end in itself.

After Eugenio had finished, a grim-looking senior official of Novosti Press gave him a bouquet of red roses and kissed him on both cheeks.

'If there's one thing I do when I get back,' I whispered to Peter, 'it will be to get Moscow News removed from the Group of Six. It's about as independent as the Kremlin.'

'Oh, that would be a bit mean, I think,' said Peter.

The two of us managed to escape from the conference to snatch our interviews. We met Gennady Gerasimov, the Soviet foreign press spokesman, and discussed with him Gorbachev's vision (Eugenio's too, as it happened) of 'a European home' which stretched from the Atlantic to the Urals. Gennady was sent a free copy of the Independent every day, and in an act of solidarity he had covered a long table with the last few weeks' issues. (These free copies were Andreas's idea. Graham Greene was also a recipient – the only other one, I think – and wrote a letter for publication from time to time by way of thanks.) We also saw Sir Rodric Braithwaite, the British ambassador. In Peter's company it was very difficult to get in a question; indeed it was moderately difficult for Sir Rodric to get in an answer. Peter had developed the kind of question which is really a long statement of opinion and ends with a request for confirmation. 'Am I right in believing that?' or 'Do you think that is indeed the case?'

His love of life was unquenchable. If not interviewing, we would be sprinting around some church or art gallery. If not doing that, we would be eating or drinking in the company of old acquaintances press-ganged by Peter. In a city not re-nowned for good restaurants, he would bustle unerringly towards the best tables as though directed by a higher force and, after an exchange of words with a recalcitrant waiter, and the quick passing over of a dollar bill, caviar and Russian 'cham-pagne' would be summoned up.

In his exuberant escapades Peter naturally expected the occa-sional assistance of the local foreign correspondent, in this case Rupert Cornwell. But Rupert was a different sort of journalist, for whom life was all work and little fun, and he did not take kindly to being asked to play Sam Weller to Peter's Mr Pick-wick. The only time that Rupert looked remotely happy was when Peter and I boarded the night train for Leningrad, whose art galleries and restaurants lay waiting to be plucked.

8

Mr Jubb Tells Us Not to Launch the Sunday

The early summer of 1989: still the happy golden days of the Thatcher-Lawson boom. All seemed well with the economy and the Independent. In an editorial the paper declared that Britain probably had the most entrepreneurial culture in Europe. Our circulation had passed 400,000, and we were making money – even a little more than had been budgeted. At an extraordinary general meeting in March the founder directors had converted their shares. Peter Jenkins, for all his journalistic life a believer in the remorseless decline of the British economy, was apparently persuaded that this depressing trend had finally been reversed. He was buying stock in Newspaper Publishing plc.

Occasionally we would visit our shareholders. They were happy too. Their shares were now worth £5 each. On one such visit, a sleek young man with a yellow polka-dot tie and beautiful blue suit said that he believed that the Independent was worth one hundred million pounds. Why exactly a hundred million pounds? 'I'm not sure,' he said. 'It's a nice round number. It just seems the absolute minimum for a newspaper.' We all smiled. A hundred million pounds!

Ah – happy days, and yet still we did not forge ahead with our own Sunday newspaper. The reason was that the company was due to float on the stockmarket in the early part of 1990.*

* In fact on the unlisted securities market, a junior division of the stock exchange.

A new launch, inevitably involving financial uncertainties, would postpone this. Most people were in favour of an early flotation. Newspaper Publishing shares could be sold via Tom Attwood, who had moved to the stockbrokers James Capel, but a stockmarket listing would offer much greater 'fluidity'. The staff who had options, the founder directors with their new shares, above all the institutional shareholders – nearly everyone wanted a market in which they could cash in a few or a lot or even all their chips under the best possible conditions. Andreas, less interested in money than power, had misgivings, since he feared that the flotation might enable someone, Mr Maxwell perhaps, to gain control of the Independent.

I would have liked an early flotation but, like one or two other directors, believed that the company should launch a Sunday newspaper. And I hoped to be its editor. The Sunday Correspondent, it was now certain, would be launched in the autumn. Many good journalists were joining the new paper, and it was a fair bet that it would succeed if left to its own devices, thereby denying Newspaper Publishing the chance to break into the Sunday market in the foreseeable future. If we did not launch a Sunday newspaper, it was difficult to see what our next step would be.

As for wishing to be an editor, let others judge. I felt that I could help launch a good newspaper which the company would be proud of. I felt too the tug of freedom, the desire to pull away from Andreas. What we think about others is so often ambivalent, but my reservations about Andreas had grown so that they were crowding out my old feelings of affection and respect. Oh, I understood that whatever happened he would always be there, but I longed sometimes to breathe different air, to have other colleagues.

Whether we bought the Observer or launched our own newspaper, it was assumed that I would be the editor. Matthew was, as he might put it, 'relaxed' about this. At the board meeting on May 31st I suggested that I might set up a small working party to produce dummies of a Sunday newspaper. Apart from myself, no one was very keen on the idea, though Andreas was supportive. He was always good at keeping his options open.

The board gave its approval.* But I don't think that anyone at the meeting, myself included, could have guessed that within nine months we would have launched the Independent on Sunday.

After giving the matter about three seconds' thought, I asked Sebastian Faulks to help me. I liked his writing and he had been a success as our literary editor. He had also worked on the Sunday Telegraph, and presumably had some 'feel' for Sunday newspapers. More than that, I thought it would be fun to work with him. No prospective deputy editor could have been more different from Matthew.

On June 1st Andreas put up a notice which announced that the board had 'approved the setting up of a working party to produce dummies of a Sunday newspaper'. I was in Russia with Peter Jenkins until June 11th, and until my return Sebastian and I could not do very much. If we had decided to pull stumps, no director would have complained or asked questions, so low was the level of interest in the project.

For the second time in nine months, I left the foreign department in the hands of Nick Ashford. He had been complaining of back pain for a few months, and visiting a physiotherapist without any obvious benefit. I told him that if the Sunday newspaper went ahead he would, I was sure, be appointed foreign editor. He said little in reply, though I knew it was the job he wanted above all others.

That summer the Independent was beginning to expand until it occupied nearly the whole building as other tenants gave up the fight of trying to share premises with a newspaper. Our dining rooms were spirited up from the dingy basement to the ninth floor, from which you could gaze out at the City of London and all its riches. Sebastian and I moved to part of the eighth floor, which had been lately vacated by an oil company. As you got out of the lift you turned right, passed through double-doors on one of which we stuck a notice which

---

* So unmomentous was this decision judged to be, it received no mention in the board minutes. On the other hand, much time was spent discussing, and approving, the launch of the Indy, a weekly newspaper for children, under the editorship of Simon Carr.

clamoured 'This is the Independent on Sunday', and entered a largish abandoned office. To the left there were three small rooms, two of which Sebastian and I occupied. The greater part was an open area, with a dirty yellow ruckled carpet on which stood five old wooden desks and two or three battered grey filing cabinets, stuffed with curling stationery and well-thumbed dockets, evidence of old transactions and forgotten commerce. From this dusty new home, strangely reminiscent of the Telegraph as I had first known it, we watched the world go by. On hot days we could see from our cubicles young men and women who had climbed out on the roofs to lie in the sun.

There was something gently absurd about the two of us sitting there, cut off from our departments, discussing how to create a Sunday newspaper which no one seemed to want very much. Bibi occasionally came up to see us, as would Kirstie Macintosh, soon to become my personal assistant. They would have a look in their eyes, indulgent but suspicious, that one reserves for people who step outside the mainstream for an eccentric whim.

We soon felt that you could not launch a newspaper with two people. We needed a third person – preferably someone with experience of Sunday newspapers. Sebastian suggested Ian Jack, who had worked on the Sunday Times when Harry Evans was its editor and, more recently, for the Observer. At the mention of Ian Jack's name everyone said how nice a chap he was and how good a writer, and that he was writing a book.

Like Sebastian, I had never met Ian. But I remembered a story that Tina Brown had told me in 1975 or 1976. Trying to make her way on the Sunday Times, where she had caught the eye of Harold Evans in more ways than one, she had been given a spell on the 'Look Page' which at that time was edited by Ian Jack. At lunch or dinner one day she gave me an account of her tribulations. I had the impression from what she said that Ian Jack was a gnarled old Fleet Street hand in his fifties, though he must have been in his very early thirties.

The portly, bearded man whom Sebastian and I met at Frederick's restaurant in Islington seemed far from Tina's account. He had spent little time on sartorial matters; his hair, streaked across a balding pate, looked as though it had not seen any shampoo for a while. He spoke softly, with one of those mellifluous Scottish accents so pleasing to an English ear. Though he was a little shy, a few drinks helped to warm him up, and he chuckled agreeably at our jokes.

'What is your book about, Ian?' I asked, not realising that this is the question most authors dread to hear.

'Well, it's a bit difficult to explain, really. I suppose you could say that it's about India . . . and trains.'

'Ah.'

Towards the idea of a new Sunday newspaper he was friendly though a little sceptical. He said he admired the Independent, and that he had once interviewed Andreas. He agreed that quality Sunday papers had deteriorated, particularly the Sunday Times. Perhaps his reservations had to do with the two of us. Later he told me that he had been worried at lunch that Sebastian and I seemed too much alike, though experience had shown him that this was not the case.

He said that he did not want to do anything which might jeopardise his book. He had always wanted to write one, and now he owed it to himself to complete it without being side-tracked by journalism.

'Well, what about helping us out for a day or two a week and seeing how it goes?' I asked. 'You could still spend most of your time writing your book. None of us knows how long this thing is going to last. It could futter out or we could find ourselves launching a national newspaper. How many chances does one get to do that?'

He said that he would think about it. So far as money went, we should talk to his agent, Gill Coleridge.

As we loitered outside the restaurant preparing to take our leave, Ian mentioned that he had been watching the test match on television. England were being hammered by Australia. His interest in cricket surprised me.

'Isn't Pringle hopeless?' said Sebastian, referring to the all-rounder who had not scored any runs or bowled any wickets.

'They should get rid of him,' replied Ian. 'And they must do something about Gower. He's not the right captain.'

'I agree,' said Sebastian.

Later that afternoon he telephoned Gill Coleridge. She asked for a sum of money which I said was too much, and the deal faltered. But we increased the offer and after a couple of days it was agreed that Ian would join us on a part-time basis.

*

Our weekend edition, with its second section and magazine, closely resembled a traditional Sunday newspaper. Our readers on Saturday would not want a paper on Sunday which gave them the same stuff all over again in exactly the same form.

There would be other readers who hadn't read the Saturday Independent but even they would be unlikely to embrace the conventional Sunday package of a two- or three-section newspaper with a colour supplement. The Sunday Times, with even more sections, and the Observer already offered that, and the Sunday Correspondent would do so shortly. The Sunday Telegraph, minus a magazine, was in the same game. We could of course set out to copy the existing formats, and simply try to do it better. But even if the existing Sunday newspapers were worth emulating so slavishly we would end up with a newspaper which looked like our own weekend edition.

So our early discussions in mid-June – between Sebastian and myself, and Ian when he was there – almost entirely concerned the shape of the paper. We imagined broadsheets and tabloids in almost every conceivable configuration. One suggestion of Sebastian's was a single-section broadsheet of forty-eight pages with a books supplement of sixteen pages. The idea here was to get away from the multi-section giganticism of the Sunday Times, which we all wanted to do, but I thought that it was unlikely that so slim an offering could thrive in the Sunday market.

Then there was the question of a colour supplement. Our Saturday magazine had cleverly exploited an old form, but it was not easy to see how we could pull that trick again. Advertisers would not be attracted to a colour supplement unless they believed that it drew different readers from its Saturday sister. But, according to Adrian O'Neill, neither would they welcome a 'niche' publication about fashion or the environment. Without sufficient advertising revenue, a supplement would die.

Nothing we thought of – broadsheet or tabloid, with or without a colour supplement – convinced us. We talked and talked, consulted designers, asked journalists for their opinions, and then talked again. It was as though we were trying to crack a code without having deciphered a single element. But I felt that if we talked enough, and I listened enough, suddenly everything would fall into place, as it had when we were devising a magazine. No single person would have the complete answer, whatever it was. It was floating about, a bit here, a bit there, in our minds and others' minds, mixed up with a lot of nonsense, needing to be put together like a kind of jigsaw if only someone could see the connections.

It was time for another visit to The Swan at Streatley. On Saturday June 24th Sebastian, Ian and myself went off for the weekend with fifteen other Independent journalists. I didn't ask Andreas or Matthew to come, though I had arranged a meeting with them for the following Tuesday. I felt the delicate process of pulling together some ideas and rejecting others would somehow be more difficult if they were there – which is to say that they would want to do it in their own way.

Almost everyone at the meeting felt that quality Sunday newspapers were less good than they had been. Their sternest critic was Peter Jenkins. At dinner on Saturday night he let fly with the authority with which he had held forth in Moscow on the dangers to *perestroika*. He said that Sunday papers were full of 'crap' – of worthless articles written by journalists who often did not know what they were writing about. Ian Jack, who had passed his career on Sunday newspapers, looked unhappy at hearing his life's work dismissed in this way. However, Peter continued, he understood why we needed to launch a Sunday paper since it was the most obvious route by which the company could expand, which it needed to do if it were to remain independent of predators. Expansion was something which our shareholders demanded of us.* If we must launch a Sunday paper – so be it; that was Peter's message. But make it as unlike all other Sunday newspapers as possible, and use as many journalists from the daily paper as you can.

---

* Such was our analysis at the time, though events have made it look a bit silly. A small profitable company should be more attractive to investors than a larger unprofitable one.

After dinner some of us went for a walk along the Thames – Peter Wilby, the Independent's education editor, Lindy Sharp, a sub-editor in the features department, Christopher Gilbert, from the foreign desk, and myself. As we slithered about a little tipsily on the dark riverbank, Lindy said to me, 'What does it feel like for all this to have happened to you when – what? – five years ago you were on the Daily Telegraph?'

'Well . . .' I replied. Peter Wilby chuckled, whether at her question or my discomfiture I did not know.

On Sunday morning we gathered in a house-boat moored by the hotel. Peter Wilby had brought along that morning's newspapers which he waved around in order to illustrate his case. He said that Sunday newspapers were guilty of a con-trick in their approach to news. So-called news stories were more or less pure inventions or they were wildly over-dramatised. 'Look at this story here,' he said. Because he was slightly deaf, he tended to bellow his lines. 'This is an example of the Sunday 'follow-up' which tells the reader absolutely nothing he hasn't read in the daily papers. And this' – more brandishing of papers – 'is the hyped-up story which no one believes. And here is a typical silly Sunday story which is just filling up space.'

It was a striking performance, the more so because Peter, having spent most of his journalistic career on the Observer and the Sunday Times before coming to the Independent, might be expected to know what he was talking about. He maintained that it was not the almost complete absence of proper news on a Saturday which led to these confected or bogus stories. He believed that Sunday papers scratched at the surface of things, that they had 'abandoned the high ground of investigation'. It followed from this that the best way of avoiding these errors was to have a seven-day operation, with daily journalists, a superior breed according to Peter, writing for Sunday.

Nick Garland, veteran of the design controversy and of the magazine meeting at this same hotel, also spoke. He had not worked himself up to quite the passionate intensity he had shown previously, but he was bubbling promisingly. He said that while he had believed before the launch of the Independent that the paper should be classical and part of a tradition, he now believed the opposite about the Independent on Sunday. It should be different, it should be radical, principally because we had already launched our Sunday paper on a Saturday, and couldn't do it again, but also because Sunday newspapers had an identity crisis. Although quality Sunday papers carried little proper news (today, not many days after the massacre in Tiananmen Square, was an exception) they pretended that they did, when they should be facing up to the fact that they were magazines. He conceived of a magazine, which might carry a striking picture on its front with a cover story or occasionally an outstanding news article. This magazine would 'wrap' around a thin section, broadsheet or tabloid, which would contain 'pure news' of a sort unavailable in existing Sunday newspapers. After a few minutes he developed the fancy of a thinner 'wrapper' which would bind the magazine and news section together. Opening your Sunday paper would be a bit like opening a box of chocolates: you would strip away the cellophane, and there would be magazine, a section of 'pure news' and possibly other delights.

Whereas I had left the magazine meeting at Streatley feeling that we had a sort of blueprint, this time I left in a perplexed mood, which Ian and Sebastian seemed to share. Everyone agreed that we had to be radical – but how? I liked Nick's wrapper idea, but in its relegation of news it seemed revolutionary to the point of barminess. We were no wiser by the time of our meeting on Tuesday morning at Brown's hotel.

An hour before this, Andreas and I were having breakfast in the same hotel with Donald Trelford. He had been editor of the Observer since 1975, where he had displayed legendary political skills and a genius for survival. The meeting had been arranged at Andreas's instigation, though Trelford was keen to come. Naturally he had no idea that as soon as we had finished talking to him we would adjourn to a private room where Matthew Symonds, Ian Jack, and Sebastian Faulks would be waiting for us, having had their own breakfast. (Were we mad? What were we doing meeting in a private room in a five-star London hotel?)

Andreas began by saying that we had plans for our own Sunday paper. We could 'go down that route'. However, there might be advantages in some sort of 'relationship' with the Observer. The two newspapers were after all philosophically quite close together. The Sunday Correspondent would inevitably take some circulation away from the Observer, and there was a question as to the future viability of 'stand-alone' Sunday newspapers.*

'Well, of course your Sunday paper would be affected too,' said Trelford, quick as a flash. His eyes darted nervously, as though we had laid a trap for him of which he expected no more than a second's notice.

Andreas half conceded the point. 'Yes, that's true, of course, though our labour and overheads would be very much less than yours.' Trelford cannot have known that we had read a copy of the Observer's management accounts.

'Well, I have always thought that a merger between the two newspapers might make sense,' said Trelford. 'I should say, by the way, that Tiny knows all about this meeting, though of course I can't speak for him.'

'Quite,' we said.

'But I do think', continued Trelford, 'that a marriage of some sort makes sense. I've been editor of the Observer for far too long a time and my only concern now really is to secure the future of the paper. Tiny is seventy-one and, although he's perfectly healthy, he won't last for ever.'

'Quite,' we both said.

'What sort of scheme did you have in mind?'

'What I have in mind', said Andreas, 'is possibly the merger of the two newspapers into a new company in which Tiny Rowland might have fifteen per cent, and we would have eighty-five per cent. We do have a fifteen per cent limit on share ownership.'† Andreas added that he understood that Trelford had no aspirations to continue as editor but there could be some financial role for him in the new company.

---

* i.e. Sunday newspapers with no daily stablemates with which overheads can be shared.
† At an extraordinary general meeting of the company in March 1989, the limitation on the size of a single shareholding had been raised from 10 to 15 per cent.

Trelford did not seem overjoyed by Andreas's proposal of an 85-15 split, but he said that he would tell Tiny what had happened, and be in touch. When he left, Andreas and I remained at our table for a few minutes before joining our colleagues in their private room. We found Matthew engaged in a skirmish with a waiter who was reluctant to produce a cooked breakfast.

Andreas had been excited during our conversation with Trelford, but now that we began to discuss our own Sunday newspaper he became a little distracted and unwilling to concern himself with details. I gave an account of our meeting at Streatley, and told him about Nick Garland's wrapper. Matthew suggested that Nick be summoned to give an account himself, which he was.

'We have to be prepared to think the unthinkable on Sunday,' said Andreas. 'We can be very daring in our look. We must make the existing papers look tired and old-fashioned. When the Independent was launched it became an acceptable badge. We must pull that trick again.'

'Badge values are not so important on a Sunday,' said Matthew.

'The main thing a Sunday paper can do,' continued Andreas, 'is to look forward, to be more daring with ideas. With the resources of the daily paper, we have the ability to manipulate large resources.'

We discussed how much news was available to a Sunday paper. I said that a lot of things happened abroad on Saturday which were badly reported by the existing Sunday papers. Ian spoke about the need to take four or five weeks preparing a major story about, say, water pollution, which might require more resources than would be available on the daily paper. I took this as a small indication that Ian was less enamoured of a seven-day operation than some other people. Then Nick Garland arrived, and delivered his wrapper performance with gusto. Andreas had to leave early.

My impression from these two meetings was that he was much more interested in acquiring the Observer than in developing our own newspaper, so long as the right financial terms could be struck.

On Sunday July 2nd the Sunday Times ran a story about

merger talks between the Observer and the Independent. Terry Robinson, a director of Lonrho, was quoted as saying that the Observer was not for sale. 'We've denied it many times. Why don't we put on the record that the Observer is not for sale.' Donald Trelford admitted that talks were going on but would not be drawn further. 'The Independent has made a formal approach but I can say nothing more.' Andreas was quoted as saying only, 'This is a sensitive matter.'

I interpreted this story as a leak by Donald Trelford. It seemed that Trelford had brilliantly drawn Andreas and me into talks which he had then scuppered by making them public, thereby inviting a denial of sale by Terry Robinson, one of Tiny's closest henchmen. If this was true, Trelford was more than worthy of his reputation. The man was a wonder.

Bruce Fireman, who had had previous dealings with both Trelford and Rowland, then entered the lists. On Monday July 3rd he rang Terry Robinson on his own initiative. Mr Robinson was out. A few hours later Bruce received a telephone call from Tiny Rowland himself, who said that he was sitting by a lake in Abidjan in the Ivory Coast. According to Bruce, Tiny mistook him for someone else, whether out of mischief or vagueness he could not say. Tiny was sure that Bruce was someone called Roland Franklin. He was, said Bruce, a bit 'rambley'. Tiny told him confidentially that he was negotiating to fly Terry Waite out of captivity and into Nigeria. He also banged on about the perfidy of the Al Fayed brothers, whom he accused of having snatched Harrods from under his nose.

Despite all this, Tiny made some sense about the Observer. He expressed surprise that Andreas, having written a letter in July 1988, had not got in touch. His view was that we would do no more than break even if we launched our own Sunday newspaper. This however was not a way of saying that he would sell the Observer to us. The paper was not for sale. On the other hand, he might be interested in taking a share in the Independent – say 25 per cent. Bruce told him that this was not possible, since we had a limit of 15 per cent. Tiny said that the Observer had a plan to bring out a daily paper along the lines of the Wall Street Journal. This might provide some scope for co-operation with the Independent.

The two of them had talked for ages. Bruce was obviously tickled pink to have been on such terms with a tycoon. Tiny promised to ring him again when he returned to London in a few days, but he did not. As if on one of those machines you used to find on sea-side piers, the metal arrow had clanked back to 'Launch your own Sunday paper', and there it stayed.

*

The same Monday that found Bruce talking to Tiny Rowland in Abidjan saw me in Steve Conaway's office, marvelling at his rococo furniture.

'Mr Glover, sir, what can I do for you?'

I told him that I wanted to acquaint him with our editorial thinking, confused though it was. I explained that we wanted to produce a newspaper which looked different from both our Saturday paper and the existing Sundays. Possibly it would have one or more tabloid sections. I mentioned Nick Garland's wrapper idea.

'Yea,' said Steve, when I had finished. 'You may be on to something. What you could do is have two or three tabloid heat-set products which you could print on deadline. Then you could maybe add a news section, Saturday.'

'You mean that you could print a magazine, perhaps two, at the last moment, say on Friday?' This was what he meant by 'heat-set'.

'Thursday, Friday, could even be Saturday morning,' said Steve. 'Here, take a look at this.' He produced a magazine the size of a tabloid newspaper which was a special supplement to Motorcycle News. It was printed on paper which looked like high quality newsprint – more like newspaper than a glossy magazine. 'Some guy dropped this off,' said Steve.

'Could I borrow this?'

'Sure, go ahead.'

Clutching the magazine, I returned to the eighth floor.

Thus was the much emulated Sunday Review section of the Independent on Sunday born out of Motorcycle News. Steve had supplied the indispensable missing clue. For three or four weeks we had been searching for a new form for our Sunday newspaper. From the meeting at Streatley, from our own discussions, from Nick Garland's 'wrapper', came the idea of creating something which would be *central* – Nick's chocolate box, if you like – which would seem of *value*; not a colour supplement, whose very name conveyed that it was something extra which you didn't have to have, nor a familiar broadsheet section full of the familiar articles. We would have such a section, as a vehicle for news, but at the centre of the paper would be this beautiful thing, the essence of the Independent on Sunday. The wonderful discovery was that it was possible to print, late in the week and on magazine presses to colour magazine standard, *a publication which could contain deadline news.* In a new form it would be possible to carry features arising out of the week's news, current theatre and arts reviews, television listings and so on – a news and cultural magazine within a Sunday newspaper.

Of course the thought processes were not so quick, though they were quick enough, since our first dummy was produced only five weeks later. On July 2nd 1989 the Sunday Review did not yet have any form or specific prospective content – nor a name; that came some time later from Ian Jack – but it was about to become a concept which, though since trimmed to practical realities, has endured.

I showed 'Motorcycle News' to Ian and Sebastian, and explained the wonders of producing heat-set colour to deadline, and I asked Adrian O'Neill whether he thought advertisers would like such a publication. He was surprisingly favourable, and became one of the keenest early supporters of what Steve Conaway called 'the heat-set tab'.

On June 14th Sebastian and I had had a cloak-and-dagger meeting at the Waldorf Hotel with Nicholas Thirkell, the unsung designer of the Independent. After his last experience, I thought that he would never want to set foot in City Road again, but Thirkell was surprisingly forgiving, even though he still wore the expression of someone who has been seconded to mine-sweeping duty. Mindful of his former difficulties, he was anxious to secure an agreement to design the entire Independent on Sunday from beginning to end. Even though I believed that he was a sort of genius, I was reluctant to acquiesce, knowing that a time would come when other people, journalists probably, would have to be allowed to have their say. Nick undertook to do some work on a broadsheet section, and twelve days later produced his first dummy and a new masthead, which showed the Independent eagle in a new position, its feathery wings apart, and beak poised to bite your head off.

Now, a little over a week after my meeting with Steve Conaway, Thirkell came to City Road to talk about the Review.* 'It is a kind of hybrid,' I explained. 'Neither a newspaper nor a magazine.' 'When would you like to see a first dummy?' Nick asked. 'What about the end of next week?' I replied. Nine days later, at five o'clock on July 21st, Thirkell returned with two white boards. One was a putative cover. There was a small drawing, with a single 'coverline' in a sea of white – what journalists call 'white space' – and the eagle flapping its wings in the top right hand corner. When Nick Thirkell had gone, Ian Jack compared this cover to a menu in an upmarket brasserie. This was not intended as a particular criticism; perhaps more as a compliment. The second board showed a 'spread' with headlines (Thirkell had chosen a face called Bodoni, very like that used on the magazine) and text. Thirkell had given us the beginnings of a form.

In early July Sebastian went on a lunching expedition. He had declared, and neither Ian nor I had disagreed, that we needed a female features editor to redress the all-male composition of the Independent on Sunday. He drew up a list of some of the leading women journalists in Fleet Street, and began to lunch them one by one. 'Any luck with so-and-so?' I would ask when Sebastian returned to the office. 'Well, she was all right but she may be a bit too downmarket for us.' The next day I would ask again how things had gone. 'Fine, thank you. She was quite interested, but I think she may be more of a writer than an editor.' After the lunching of 'Sebastian's girls' had gone on for a couple of weeks to no great avail, we decided that he and Ian would have to act as features editors for the purposes of the dummy. Ian looked after the first part of the Sunday Review comprising the news related features, and Sebastian was in charge of the second half which carried pieces about education, travel, gardens, health and so forth.

At the end of June it had been announced that the Sunday

---

* Though this name was not yet in use, I shall use it for the sake of convenience.

Correspondent would be launched on September 17th. I had a mad idea in my mind that we might pre-empt its launch. It was mad because the board had not even considered whether we should launch a Sunday paper and it was mad because it was almost inconceivable that, even if we did, we could beat the Sunday Correspondent into the market. Still, however crackers the idea might be, I thought we should produce a dummy as quickly as possible. I fixed on August 13th and went to see Adrian O'Neill to ask whether we could arrange some 'live' market research of copies of the dummy which could be delivered into people's homes. 'What's the hurry?' he asked. 'I just think we should get on with it,' I replied lamely. After some argument he agreed that it would be done.

Among the journalists on the Independent, opinions were divided about a Sunday newspaper. Many were in favour, believing that it was the most natural way for the company to expand, and fearing that the Sunday Correspondent was about to steal our clothes. Others were interested to discover whether an Independent on Sunday might offer them promotion or new opportunities. Every day there was a steady stream of supplicants to the eighth floor. But there were also journalists who were opposed. They had worked incredibly hard and felt that their share options were some sort of recompense. Launching a new paper was, they believed, a risky enterprise which might threaten the value of these hard-won options and involve them in even more strenuous work. The epicentre of such feelings was the home desk, the engine room of any newspaper. Here there was still much grumbling about the magazine, which was regarded as an elitist, loss-making venture which paid too much money to too many journalists. They feared that a Sunday paper might go the same way. There was a touch of arrogance too, a feeling on the part of some of those who had been founder members of the Independent that if there were to be new ventures these would be safest in their hands. Their most loquacious spokesman was the home editor, John Price, who described our activities to Peter Wilby as 'boys' games'.

Among the directors, Christopher Barton was strongly against launching a Sunday newspaper, believing that it would jeopardise an early flotation, which had become for him the sole point of living, the focus of every waking hour. Though Matthew liked the idea of the Review, and was enthusiastic about the work Thirkell had done, he also believed that a launch could not be allowed to interfere with the planned flotation, about which there were now almost daily meetings. He said to me that 'A Sunday paper is just not going to happen before flotation.' Andreas's feelings were more difficult to read. He kept remarkably aloof from the whole enterprise, scarcely ever visiting us on the eighth floor, where we had moved into larger offices. At one of the midday directors' meetings he said to me, after receiving a progress report: 'You must be bold. This is the time to be bold.' 'Well, that's exactly what we are trying to be,' I replied a little huffily. Matthew agreed. 'I've seen what they've done.'

Though he made almost no practical contribution to the dummy, Andreas influenced the shape of the tabloid business section. Earlier in the year he and Matthew had conceived of a business magazine as a supplement to the daily paper on a weekday. Matthew had shot off on the mandatory trip to New York full of optimism but he returned with the verdict that the British market was too small to support such a magazine. When we started to think about our Sunday newspaper dummy, the unreconstructed idea of a business magazine was dusted off and applied to the Independent on Sunday. Here I deferred to Andreas's much greater knowledge of financial journalism. I asked Peter Wilson-Smith, deputy City and business editor, to help us produce a business section which tried to be a magazine.

Sceptics and true believers alike helped to produce the dummy of August 13th. The production of the Review began on Saturday August 6th and ran on to the following Wednesday. The main feature, a piece about London as 'the sick city of Europe', was heroically written by Ian at the last moment after its intended author had submitted another piece. (Ian had been working full-time for several weeks, without giving any long-term commitment.) The broadsheet news section and the tabloid business section were put together on Saturday 13th.

Though we hired one or two people from outside the paper to help, such as John Ryle as acting literary editor (I had last seen him at school but he betrayed no flicker of recognition), nearly everyone who worked for the dummy was seconded from the Independent. Some helped as sub-editors for a couple of days, others for two or three weeks. Christopher Gilbert master-minded the sports coverage. Mike Stent, night editor on the daily paper, brilliantly organised the production of the dummy. Michael McGuinness, Crozier's deputy, became increasingly involved in the design, particularly of the broadsheet and busi-ness sections, as Nicholas Thirkell receded.

The broadsheet section comprised something close to 'pure news'. There were lots of shortish home and foreign news features, a conventional centre spread, including one long leader (written by me at the last minute entitled 'The biggest question is, What exactly is Britain for?') and a political column oblig-ingly knocked off by Matthew Symonds. There were seven pages of sport. With its Bodoni headline face and white space, the broadsheet was intended to be restrained and elegant, some-thing which wrapped *around* the Review which was the softer centre of the newspaper. The front page was meant to proclaim that this was a different sort of Sunday paper. At the top there was a huge arty picture of the Palace of Culture in Warsaw, accompanied by a short 'write-off' by Ed Steen. Beneath this was a 1,200-word 'cover story' about toxic waste which, even after valiant last-minute re-writing by Ian, Sebastian and Mike Stent, was virtually incomprehensible. Below this was one much shorter story from Tim McGirk in Madrid and 'the poster', an idea of Sebastian's, which laid out the more interesting contents of the newspaper as though this were a cattle fair.

Lots of people thought that the broadsheet was beautiful (this was the word which Neal Ascherson later used) but it was the Sunday Review which drew most attention. Actually many of its articles were rather plodding, but the whole thing was a con-ceptual triumph. We used very few colour pictures or graphics, fearing, unnecessarily as it turned out, that they might not re-produce well on the heavy newsprint. The brasserie cover showed a drawing by Claudio Munos of Big Ben slipping into the slime,which was likely to be the fate of London, according to Ian's article. The Review contained features, arts reviews, book reviews, letters, columns, fashion, television listings – it was a magazine in itself which was supposed to say to the reader that it was *current, central, complete*, not, as was the case with many colour supplements, *timeless, superfluous and meretricious.*

On the morning of August 13th a copy of the dummy dropped through my letter box. Our activities had already attracted the notice of several radio and television programmes, hoping for a bloody battle with the Sunday Correspondent. Now we were asked to parade the dummy. That morning Sebastian took part in a radio programme with Brian Macarthur of the Sunday Times and David Blake, one of the founders of the Sunday Correspondent. Macarthur said that in a fight between the two new titles, the Independent on Sunday would prevail. This was also the view of Charles Wintour, former editor of the Evening Standard, with whom I flew up to Glasgow to appear on a television programme. The Independent on Sunday, born in less than two months, was reckoned by most observers to be better than the Sunday Correspondent, which was trudging into the market with two broadsheet sections and a colour supplement.

But still we could not say when or even whether we would launch – not because we were coy but because we did not know. During the last few days before the dummy was finished, Matthew had begun to undergo a miraculous conversion. On about Thursday 10th he spoke on the telephone to Andreas, who had been on holiday since the end of July, and said that he believed that we were 'on to something very exciting'. Andreas was due back in a couple of days and it was agreed that the three of us would have dinner together on Sunday August 13th. A copy of the dummy was delivered to his house that morning.

I beheld a curious scene when I arrived at Brunswick Gardens – my first visit there since before the launch of the Independent. Andreas had opened a bottle of champagne and Valerie, his wife, and Matthew were chatting happily. Andreas, however, looked as though he had just heard that his spice-laden ship had sprung a leak. He tried, as though out of politeness, to be welcoming, and smiled wanly at me as he handed me a glass. Valerie was bubbling with pleasure. 'You must be delighted, Stephen. It is brilliant. Many congratulations.' I cannot remember whether she proposed a toast, but it would not have been out of keeping with her mood.

After about half an hour, Andreas, Matthew and I left to go round the corner to a restaurant called Kensington Place. We arrived about ten minutes after the time of our booking.

'I have a table in the name of Whittam Smith,' said Andreas.

'I am sorry,' said the woman who had greeted us. 'You will have to wait a few minutes.'

'But I ordered a table,' said Andreas, in an affronted voice.

'I know, but you were late, and we had some other people waiting, so I gave it to them.'

'I would like to see the manager,' said Andreas.

'I am the manager,' said the woman.

'How can you run a restaurant like this? I run a company and if I ran it like you do nobody would have any faith in me. I want a table *now*.'

'You'll have to wait a few minutes.'

'I want a table now. *Give me a table.*'

'We don't have one at the moment.'

'This is absurd,' said Andreas. With this he swung round, and Matthew and I embarrassedly followed him out.

As we were passing by the front of the restaurant, he noticed someone whom he knew, and knocked on the window.

'Jacob Rothschild,' he informed me.

'Ah.'

'Did you notice', he continued, 'that at no stage did I say that I was *editor of the Independent*?'

'Very impressive,' I said.

We found an Italian restaurant nearby where we had a gloomy dinner. Matthew and I did not succeed in communicating our enthusiasm about the dummy to Andreas, though he seemed to take on trust that it was good. We discussed when we might launch a Sunday paper. I told Andreas about my crazy idea of pre-empting the Sunday Correspondent, and he brightened up momentarily at the prospect of this absurd challenge. But we decided that November was a more realistic date, or possibly January.

The next day a change had come over Andreas. He seemed to have embraced the notion of a Sunday paper and, in calling a meeting of executive directors to discuss a launch date, to be trying to take control of the enterprise. He was back in the driving seat, or pretending that he was, though in truth he had been presented with a *fait accompli*. Afterwards he was sometimes blamed in the press for launching the Independent on Sunday on the cusp of a recession. I suppose that he could have resisted the tide which he encountered when he returned from holiday, but he decided to turn and swim along with it.

By Tuesday evening it was plain that we would not attempt to launch before the Sunday Correspondent, so I decided to join Celia and our children for the second half of their holiday in France. On Wednesday morning, as my car was on the quayside edging towards the ferry, my car telephone rang.

'Bruce Fireman. I just wanted to say that I thought that your dummy was absolutely stunning.' I was in a line of cars which was being ineluctably drawn into the ferry. Bruce began to expound a theory as to why the Sunday Review was so good. 'The thing about the tabloidy magazine section is . . .' As I drove into the ferry I heard his praises fade away.

*

When I returned to City Road twelve days later I found the executive directors in a state bordering on euphoria. Adrian had taken the dummy around more than twenty advertising agencies and in nearly all of them the Sunday Review had been admired. The company conducting the market research of the dummy had revealed that the results were better than those at an equivalent stage before the launch of the Independent or the Saturday paper.* The tide was now running so strongly in favour of a

---

* The research company Hudson Payne Iddiols told us that it had never had a more favourable response in 'new product' research. Needless to say, none of us wholly understood how the Independent on Sunday dummy achieved its score, though Bruce Fireman attempted a written analysis. We were told that it had scored 4.22 out of five as against 4.1 for the dummy of the Saturday Independent and 3.9 for the dummy of the Independent. The 'sample size' comprised 804 ABC1 readers of quality dailies and Sundays, half of them Independent readers, who received a copy of the paper at 7.30 am on the morning of Sunday August 13th. About half the respondents received one of two colour magazines on the environment and 'life-style' which had been produced by two groups of Independent journalists. According to the research company, neither of these magazines was judged by respondents significantly to improve the attractiveness of 'the package'.

launch that even I, who had set the thing going, could not have stopped it.

Only Christopher Barton, among the executive directors, was opposed, but his voice did not count for very much. Graham Luff was virtually running the finance department, and he had overseen the preparation of figures for the monthly board meeting which was to take place on August 30th. These figures suggested that the costs of entering the Sunday market – pre-launch expenses, promotion, capital expenditure and working capital – were about £8.5 million. As the daily paper was expected to make profits of around £9 million in the next financial year, and more still in subsequent years, we believed that we could raise the necessary finance from banks without needing to go to our shareholders.

The breakeven of a three-section Sunday paper along the lines of the dummy had been estimated by Graham at 385,000 copies. Everyone felt that we could easily surpass this figure. (It was in fact amended to 358,000 in the introduction to Graham's report, though his calculations were done on the basis of the higher figure.) At a circulation of 450,000, profits from the Sunday paper would be a little over £3 million a year, at 500,000 almost £5 million.

Spirits had also been raised by an approach from the Sunday Correspondent, which was due to launch in less than three weeks. Our guess was that they had seen our dummy and panicked. Mick Brown, a senior journalist on the Correspondent, had got in touch with his friend, the multi-millionaire tycoon Richard Branson, about whom he had once written a biography. Branson had telephoned Andreas from his boat somewhere off the West Indies, and suggested a meeting. This approach had put Andreas into a kind of ecstasy. A week or so later Branson rang again and suggested that Andreas and some of his colleagues come to dinner at his house to meet the boys from the Correspondent.

On Tuesday August 29th, the evening before our board meeting, we stood outside Branson's house in Holland Park. It was one of those enormous, white, birthday cake houses, put up towards the end of the last century as part of a development for the *nouveaux riches*. Nearly all the houses were now divided and sub-divided into quite spacious flats, but one or two survived intact, an embassy here, a hotel there, a London residence for Richard Branson here.

Dressed as though he had just stepped off his yacht, he greeted us, mumbling apologies, and led us through his house to a long garden and a swimming pool. Next to this pool was a large table around which were sitting the high command of the Sunday Correspondent: Peter Cole, the grey-haired editor whose lugubrious expression suggested that he was not enjoying himself; David ('Bunter') Blake and David Lipsey, the paper's two deputy editors; Nick Shott, the suave young managing director who had 'come from marketing'; and a lawyer whose name I never caught.

As we were fussed over by girls who looked as if they had spent the day picking up sea-shells on a sun-drenched island paradise, Branson tried to explain why he had brought us together. His manner was that of an entertainer at a children's party which threatens to get out of hand. Any moment a custard pie might whizz in his direction. Smiling this way, that way, he explained that he had been approached by Mick Brown and was trying to do his public duty by seeing whether a last-minute marriage or something might not be arranged between the two papers. 'I know Peter,' he said, putting his hand affectionately on the arm of the stone-cold editor of the Sunday Correspondent, 'and I know Andreas well. I just want to help, really' – a rather lame giggle at this point – 'and see whether you can't come together in some way, whether, perhaps, Andreas, you couldn't go ahead with your paper and let Peter here be its editor. I don't know.'

'He's already got an editor,' said Peter Cole grimly. Branson seemed not to grasp this point, and apparently remained unaware of who I was.

Andreas then mentioned his terms which, though suitably vague, could hardly mask our true intention – to acquire our rival in order to close it down. Rattled though they were, the Correspondent people seemed to be thinking – though this was never made clear – of a merger of more or less equal partners, not of being gobbled up and spat out. David Blake, who did more talking than anyone else on their side, got quite shirty. We left realising that no deal was possible, but also that, for all Blake's bluster, their very presence at such a meeting so close to their launch showed how unsure they were of themselves.

The next morning the board of Newspaper Publishing made the decision to launch a Sunday newspaper. The only opposition came from Lord Sieff, who couldn't believe that Independent readers would want to read a three-section Sunday paper after a three-section Saturday one. Though listened to with respect, his lone voice would not stop the caravan, as well he knew. At that time, at the height of their success, the executive directors, and Andreas in particular, enjoyed more authority on the board than ever before or since. It was agreed that the launch should be on January 28th 1990, a decent period after the annual post-Christmas advertising slump. The executive directors had decided that a November launch would not give us enough time to recruit journalists and other staff or to establish contracts with printers. If we were going into the market after the Sunday Correspondent, we might as well do so when we were ready.

Before we could announce our launch to the staff or the press, we had first to inform shareholders. It was not strictly a question of getting their agreement, since they were not being asked to put up new capital, but plainly they would have to be told, particularly since flotation would be postponed. Even before the board had made its decision, Andreas had arranged a series of presentations to our eleven biggest investors, and a further meeting with a group of smaller shareholders, to begin on Monday September 4th.

Andreas, Adrian, Steve Conaway, Graham Luff and myself did the rounds. Andreas would give 'the company overview', I would describe 'the product', Adrian would speak about advertising and Steve would generally blind everyone with science, his message on these occasions being that everything was 'basically doable'. Graham Luff, though not yet finance director, would talk about money. The reception we got was warm, sometimes enthusiastic; in these comfortable City offices, as in our own minds, the Thatcher-Lawson boom showed no signs of ending. Until we flew up north to see our Scottish shareholders, only the fund managers at T R Technology had expressed any reservations.

In Glasgow our shareholders were all sweetness and light. The trouble started in Edinburgh. After a jolly lunch at the Café Royal, we went around to the offices of Standard Life Assurance Company in George Street. These were, as Andreas pointed out with his City editor's eye as we waited in an anteroom, the soul of probity. There were no Flash Harrys here. Quietness broken only by the ticking of a clock, respectable prints, a neatly folded copy of the Scotsman – almost all could be unchanged since this grey stone building was put up two hundred years ago. 'This is the real thing,' murmured Andreas mystically.

None the less, he made an error when we went into a room with a long polished table. It seemed for a moment that Standard Life was only fielding a rather junior girl to hear our presentation. But she was joined by a stern-looking middle-aged man. He introduced himself as Guy Jubb, an almost frivolous name for so august a personage, sat down and fixed his eye on Andreas. 'I am surprised that you have the time to bother with the likes of us,' said Andreas lightly. 'I haven't got a calculator but we must represent about point zero zero one of your entire portfolio.' 'I take an interest in all our investments.' said Mr Jubb coldly. 'Nothing is too small for me.' And with him spoke the long ages of presbyterian rectitude.

When we had finished our standard spiel, Mr Jubb thanked us and asked a few questions. He then delivered a summing up, as might his forbears from the pulpit of many a kirk.

'Thank you for coming. Our view is that it is too early for you to launch a Sunday newspaper. You have probably underestimated the amount of strain that it will place on your management. We are also worried about the outlook for the economy. We think that you will succeed – in the end – but that it will be a long and gruelling battle for you.'

How we laughed in our taxi on the way to the airport. But it was not laughter at the gloomy prophet who had confronted us. It was the laughter of escape – the little boy from the still master, the waking sleeper from a half-forgotten nightmare, exultant with relief.

*

Recruiting again: hundreds of letters, people waiting outside, that strange sensation of power – never again, I had thought. We were looking for about eighty journalists, from within and outside the Independent. And as before, we tried to attract a few 'names' early on, on the basis that where they went others might follow. One such was Neal Ascherson.

He had been at the Observer since 1960, with a four-year break in the 'seventies, and in 1985 he had become one of its two leading columnists. For many on the left, journalists or not, he was a sort of hero. Equally, for some on the right he had been a kind of satanic figure. The origins of this prejudice are unclear; perhaps it had to do with his being an Old Etonian 'leftie' – and yet you would think that there were enough of those. When I told a right-wing friend that I had met Neal on a 'freebie' in Finland in 1984, he whistled, looked up to the sky and nearly crossed himself. In fact the two of us had got on splendidly, though our politics were not the same: we disagreed amicably about independence for Scotland, which he fervently longed for. It seemed to me from that trip, though, and from reading his column over the years, that Neal was not one of those people who had signed up to a set of beliefs. He was assuredly 'left-wing', but his quixotic and rebellious mind permitted him to follow no party line, and in some of his opposition to 'State power' he could join hands with the libertarian right, where I sometimes dabbled a toe. Above all, I loved his writing – which was for me more important than his politics – and the romantic soul which lay behind it.

When we had lunch at Frederick's in Islington in the middle of July he said that he was 'tempted' to leave the Observer. He thought that his old paper's integrity had been damaged since Tiny Rowland had bought and used it to wage war against his enemies, notably the Al Fayeds. But for all that, Neal had a soft spot for Donald Trelford, whom he described as 'one of the lads', betraying a fondness of his own for high jinks which I had glimpsed on that Finnish trip. When the August 13th dummy appeared, Neal fell in love with its beauty. He already admired the Independent, even if it was a bit right-wing: indeed his wife, Isabel Hilton, was one of its founding journalists, and a colleague of mine on the foreign desk. The Independent on Sunday was in his mind elevated by the presence of Ian Jack, a friend of sorts, and a very respectable figure in left-wing circles. So he joined, though leaving the Observer must have tugged at his heart. Matthew, while conceding our public relations coup, was worried that Neal's politics would repel some of our potential readers.

Sebastian and I were determined that Ian should not yet be allowed to return to his book. He was certainly a 'name' but, much more than that, the best and most creative of colleagues. I loved his unportentous passion for newspapers. Quite often he would leave notes on my desk in which he would offer gentle advice, delicately plead a cause, or simply air a dilemma for which there was yet no resolution. In one of these he referred to 'a famous passage from Adam Smith: if the entire population of China were to be wiped out in an earthquake, the sensitive Englishman might feel genuine sorrow but he would sleep soundly. If the same man lost his little finger he would stay awake with worry for nights.' His point, dramatically made, was that most readers of newspapers, quality or tabloid, want to read about things which concern them, which are close to their pain and their experience and their fears, as much as about 'issues' which may excite their imagination but not their self-interest.*

Ian was actually a very serious man, a gloomy 'Fifer', and he could sometimes forget this excellent adage. But he had been blessed with humour and wit, not intermingling with the seriousness, but acting as a kind of leaven upon it. For me he was a figure of true romance who could have been invented by Thomas Hardy or D.H. Lawrence. The son of a working man, he had grown up on the banks of the Forth, watching the ships go up and down that once great waterway. Upon leaving the local school with few or no academic qualifications, he got a job in a public library, where he brooded over social injustice. But there, in the library, he began to read and to develop a craving for the panoply of knowledge which perhaps only an auto-

---

* One should of course beware of taking Adam Smith's dictum too far. As I write this, I am reminded by a newspaper article of Gladstone's pamphlet *The Bulgarian Horrors and the Question of the East* which sold 200,000 copies.

didact can feel. After a time he got a job on the local newspaper, where his eye for detail stood him in good stead as a sub-editor, and quite soon he moved to the Glasgow Herald. Then he went to London, capital of the kingdom, and took a job on the Sunday Times.

He did not take very long to make his mark. Ian had developed a love for India, and indeed often dressed in a semi-Indian fashion; perhaps as a form of escape, perhaps also a part of a journey to find his Scottishness among the relicts of an empire which his countrymen had done so much to build. A story is told, possibly apocryphal, that once he was on holiday in Delhi when rioting broke out. There was no time for the Sunday Times to send a 'fireman' from London, so the little known sub-editor Ian Jack was called upon to 'file'. And of course he did so brilliantly, and his slumbering gifts burst forth.

Ian badly wanted to write his book. He described it so poorly partly because it was so ambitious. It was about India and her past and the empire and Scotland's lost industrial greatness – a twin-headed monster, this, half-benign, half-diabolical – and also about himself. Yet he also wanted to help found a newspaper, indeed had already half done so, and I think he liked Sebastian and me, and believed that the three of us might do it. By the middle of September we had reached a compromise. He would stay until after the launch, if he were then allowed to take whatever time was necessary for the completion of his book.

To create a bandwagon, every week or so throughout October we carried short pieces on the front of the Independent which listed the 'names' who had been signed up by the Sunday paper. Neal Ascherson has joined as a columnist. Now Ian Jack has agreed to become associate editor. Irving Wardle, the famous theatre critic of The Times, will be the theatre critic of the Independent on Sunday. Blake Morrison, literary editor of the Observer, has come to do the same job on the Independent on Sunday. (This was Sebastian's work.) Richard Williams, who recently resigned as features editor of The Times, has been appointed sports editor. Lynn Barber, of the Sunday Express magazine, will be a features writer

Though she had unobtrusively been winning awards, Lynn was not really much of a name. A female acquaintance of

Sebastian's – perhaps one of those girls whom he had lunched a couple of months before – rang to tell him about this unsung genius. Lynn then sent in her 'cuttings' which Ian read and enjoyed. Even so, she might not have been hired had it not been for the disastrous meeting which Ian and Sebastian had with Vicki Woods, in our minds the stronger candidate for the job of interviewer. Vicki arrived late complaining of a migraine, and somehow everything had fallen apart in a spirit of mild mutual antipathy. This left the way clear for the dark horse, Lynn Barber.

'Have you read Lynn's cuttings yet?' Ian would ask me. 'God, no I'm sorry, I simply haven't had time.' This went on for a couple of weeks, and Lynn sent a plaintive post-card to Sebastian asking whether she had been forgotten. Eventually Ian brow-beat me into asking her to come and see me. She giggled a lot and seemed very ill at ease. I explained that we could not afford such comparatively high salaries as the Sunday Express magazine, and would be unable to give her a car, a perk which she had previously enjoyed. 'Ooh. Are you sure?' she asked. 'I'm afraid so,' I replied. 'Well, the car doesn't matter a lot anyway,' she said. 'I just want to join *so much*.'

Another almost-name to join us was my old friend and Isis colleague Christopher Huhne. He had for several years been economics editor of the Guardian. On leaving Oxford he had had striking successes, first with The Economist and then with his present newspaper, but latterly he had been languishing a little, perhaps partly because his credentials as a journalist had been damaged by his standing twice as a parliamentary candidate for the SDP. I knew him to be formidably intelligent and knowledgeable about economics and politics, though even after fifteen years of acquaintance I could sometimes feel exasperated by his assumption that all the world's problems could be solved if only they were entrusted to his care. But it would, I thought, be a useful thing to have on board this one man think-tank.

Driving home one evening in early October, I rang Christopher on my car telephone, having been unable to get hold of him earlier in the day. I told him that I would like him to join the Independent on Sunday as its economics editor, and also as an assistant editor with wider responsibilities. He said that, subject to the right terms, he was very interested.

'You do realise, Chris, that it's a risky business launching a newspaper? If I were shown the door, as a friend of mine your position might not be very strong.'

'Oh, if that happened, if you went, I don't think I would want to stay in any case.'

A couple of weeks after this, Stephen Fay, who had recently been sacked as editor of Business Magazine, came to see me. I knew him only by his reputation, which was that of a good journalist with a sharp temper. I also half remembered that over a year before he and Henry Porter (then editor of the Illustrated London News) had proposed to Andreas that they should launch a Sunday newspaper on our behalf. Andreas had mentioned this idea to the executive directors who had felt that if there was any launching of Sunday papers to be done then they would do it. Henry had subsequently moved to the Sunday Correspondent to become editor of its colour supplement.

The short, rather fierce, red-faced man who now sat before me looked like a Trollopian squire, though the image was provocatively undermined by a pair of light-blue trainers which seemed to be saying 'I'm not who you think I am'. His manner was businesslike, even a little peremptory. Stephen explained that he would like to return to writing. He had been commissioned to do a biography of Peter Hall and he would like to write occasional long features about business and arts, which was why he had come to see me. He thought a great deal of the Independent on Sunday and had been impressed by the sort of people who were joining us.

It seemed an unbelievably good piece of fortune that the second editor of Business Magazine should have walked into my office. It was the only British magazine devoted wholly to business, loss-making it is true, but regarded as more than creditable. The weakest part of our dummy had been the business section which showed few signs of turning into the business magazine we intended. My thought was that Stephen should help Peter Wilson-Smith, City and business editor, to develop magazine ideas. After that, he could write as much as he pleased. Stephen accepted this, but said that he didn't want a full-time job. We agreed that he should have the title 'associate editor, business' and for the time being left the exact commitment a little vague.

★

Lots of people on the daily had believed that the Independent on Sunday should be a seventh-day paper. Andreas even thought this for a time; after a visit to America in September 1988 he had announced that if ever we launched a Sunday newspaper it must be an extension of the daily. That was the American model, but British Sunday newspapers, being so different from their daily stablemates, had their own editorial staffs. After a while Andreas began to accept my view that our Sunday newspaper should have its own 'separate brain' – a group of editors who planned stories exclusively for the Sunday paper. It followed from this that they would need some of their own writers on whom they could depend.

By June, when Sebastian and I began to tinker about, this structure was broadly accepted by Andreas, Matthew and myself. There would be a Sunday editor and a number of other editors – home, foreign, business, arts, books, sports, features, etc. These would draw on a 'pool' of writers which would only be partly shared with the daily paper. On the home side, there would be some writers who would work only for the Sunday, perhaps spending more time on an article than would be possible if they worked on a daily rhythm. But at the same time Sunday specialist journalists would sit with their daily counterparts, providing a common 'bank of expertise' which would be available to both papers. A similar system would apply on the foreign side. Obviously a Sunday paper could not afford its own foreign correspondents, and would have to share those of the daily, but it could have a few of its own foreign writers who, at home or abroad, could work up specifically 'Sunday stories'.

This was the system which I adopted, with one major exception. We discovered, in talking to prospective Sunday specialists such as Judith Judd of the Observer, that they generally did not much relish the idea of working in harness with their daily colleagues. It became clear that if we wanted to recruit the best specialists we would have to offer them the independence of working by themselves – which meant working exclusively for the Sunday paper. But we also discovered, particularly given our limited resources, that we didn't want too many specialists in any case. A couple of specialist posts were converted by me into writing jobs. These were not shared with the Independent.

I wanted the Sunday paper to be as separate as was financially prudent from the daily paper, partly, as I have said, to be freer from Andreas and Matthew, but also because it seemed to me the best way to set things up. Journalists working in the daily newsroom, writing an article in an afternoon, could not easily spend five days on a 2,000-word piece, nor could their daily editors, equally used to a daily rhythm, easily find the time to edit such a piece properly. We believed that we were re-defining Sunday journalism, but even after its transformation it would remain very different from the daily variety. Ian, believing in the different qualities of Sunday journalism even more strongly than I did, argued that the two newspapers needed to be editorially separate. Even Peter Wilby, the apostle of seventh-day newspapers, recanted, and became our home editor. Such changes as I made, Andreas accepted without demur.

Of the eighty-six editorial staff at the time of launch (eighty journalists and six secretaries) twenty-four came from the Independent and sixty-two came from other newspapers. There might have been a greater number from the daily paper had not Andreas and Matthew warned me against recruiting too many journalists from the Independent. The majority, coming from outside Newspaper Publishing plc, naturally saw itself as belonging to the Independent on Sunday. These people admired the Independent but had no experience of it. Their loyalty was to the Independent on Sunday.

Most journalists who joined us accepted our confidence about the financial prospects of the Independent on Sunday. The Independent had succeeded, and the other quality Sunday papers looked as vulnerable as the dailies had at the time of our first launch. The Sunday Correspondent gave rise to some anxieties. My line was that there might be room for five quality papers in the Sunday quality market. If there were not, then it would be the Independent on Sunday which would survive because it would be the better newspaper. Besides, with its lower overheads shared with its daily sister,* it would enjoy a financial advantage over the Correspondent.

Andreas's confidence was very great, though he said to me at this time: 'When I stand shaving in front of my mirror I sometimes say to myself, "You must be mad".' But such private passages of panic were scarcely ever visible in him at work. And who could blame him? Whoever saw the dummy pronounced it brilliant. Stories, impossible to verify, reached us from Wapping. Rupert Murdoch was supposed to predict a circulation of 600,000 for the Independent on Sunday. He was said to have brandished the Sunday Review threateningly in front of some of his journalists and to have asked them why they bloody well couldn't produce something like that. At City Road, Andreas announced to the executive directors in his just-down-from-Mt-Sinai way that the print-run of the first issue on January 28th should be 1,200,000 – almost double that of the launch issue of the Independent. Even in this mood of euphoria, I had some misgivings. Andreas's justification was that it was the same as the circulation of the Sunday Times, and a launch print-run of this size was a way of saying to the world that we were preparing to take on 'the market leader'.

As the weeks went by, evidence began to gather that the Thatcher-Lawson boom was beginning to run on to the rocks. No one could have predicted the almighty shipwreck which lay ahead in the shape of the worst recession since the early 'thirties, but still there were sightings, that autumn and early winter, of sinister, half-submerged outcrops which might necessitate a more cunning course. In October and November advertising revenue on the Independent was significantly behind budget, though it was still ahead of the previous year. 'It's the first tap companies turn off when the storm clouds gather,' says Andreas. 'Advertising is discretionary spending.' Then in December income from advertising fell behind its level of twelve months before. This was the beginning of a long series of

* Both papers would use the same computer system (though of course more terminals were needed) and share the same administrative, advertising, distribution and financial departments.

monthly declines, of re-budgetings and cost-cutting measures, each made in the false hope that it would be the last, that we had touched the bottom. Later, in the pit of the recession, we would look back to these early re-adjustments as halcyon days, which carried no greater burden than the news of the first Dreadnought in the endless Edwardian summer.

Although Andreas declared that a recession was on the way – he had said the same thing in October 1987, after the stockmarket crash – he apparently kept this knowledge in a separate part of his brain where it could not affect his enthusiasm. Once, in early November, he made an ugly scene when he thought that editorial costs were running out of control. They were, and had to be reined back by Graham Luff and myself. The Independent on Sunday, unlike the Independent, was launched almost within its editorial budget. Yet I did not see in Andreas's outburst so much a fear of the recession as a desire to be seen stamping his authority on a project of which he was, in many ways, a spectator.

Graham Luff was on the point of being made finance director. He had come a long way since being recruited by Christopher Barton as chief accountant in 1986. Before that, he had had a patchy sort of career, joining Kodak as a young man after having decided that he could not make it as a tennis pro, and rising after about twenty years to a job in middle management. In his early days at Newspaper Publishing he was humble. 'From where I sit,' he would say, in a tone of voice which implied that he was in the foothills and we were kissing the clouds on the mountain tops, 'I think we might have a little bit of a problem there.' As time went on, he had begun in private to criticise his boss, on which occasions he usually had an attentive audience, as well he knew. 'It's difficult for me to say this, Stephen, because in previous companies I have worked for it's not, how shall I say, normal to criticise senior people, but to be absolutely frank with you, dear old Christopher is driving me mad.' He would then unleash his latest grouse.

Graham had a way with figures. Some accountants may shroud their arts in mystery, but Graham spoke about figures as though he were running a sweet shop – but a properly ordered one. If a budget looked like being overspent he could be very obliging, naturally if the extra funds were required for a good reason. Then he would refer to one of his 'little pots' – small contingencies which he had 'hidden where no one could find them' – on which he could lay a magic hand. He was generally prepared to meet any problem with good-humoured optimism, having what Matthew would call a 'can do' approach. In this respect he was most unlike Christopher Barton, whose *de haut en bas* style of management, enlivened by a more than usually suspicious nature, might have been imbibed at the feet of the old horrors who used to constitute the 'management' of the Daily Telegraph.

Graham was rising to power as the economy was beginning to sink, and it was going to require a lot of astuteness for him to survive the course. I remember saying in December that perhaps we should postpone the launch of the Independent on Sunday but it was only a joke inviting an amused rebuff from Andreas. To postpone now would be ruinously expensive. We had hired most of our staff and were already incurring costs without producing income. And then there was the Correspondent, launched and undistinguished, but able to make its way in the world if only we would let it. No, it was too late to go back, but in any case there was no point. At the very most the cream was being skimmed off the economy; what remained beneath, the hard reconstructive work of the Thatcher years, would see us through.

*

'The Independent on Sunday will look different from other Sunday papers. When the Independent was launched, it looked as though it had been around for a hundred years. The Independent on Sunday will look as though *it has just been invented*. It will aim to be comprehensive yet concise – without that sense of surfeit and garrulousness which you get from your multi-sectioned Sunday newspaper which thuds depressingly on to your door-mat on a Sunday morning. Think of a small, beautiful, perfectly formed city – Florence, perhaps – which has everything within it, and you have the Independent on Sunday. The Sunday Times is like Birmingham – huge, sprawling, disorganised and not very pretty –'

'Hey, I come from Birmingham!'

' – well, like Manchester, then ... We will take news seriously, restore it to the place which it enjoyed in the Observer and Sunday Times fifteen years ago, when you believed what you read, when stories had a *seriousness of intent*, but we will always retain a ... a ... er – *a lightness of touch*. And we will remain true to Independent values – those things for which the Independent has stood during the week will be transferred to Sunday. We are part of the same culture, a re-interpretation of the same idea ....'

So went my sermon to the ecstatic advertising agencies. Now, in the months and weeks before launch, we were selling the paper, first to advertisers then to television, radio and the press.

The story is a good one. The Independent, flushed with success, is entering the Sunday market. Is this over-crowded? Will the Independent on Sunday prevail over the Sunday Correspondent, or will the Correspondent, which is really not at all bad, and has the mighty Chicago Tribune as one of its backers, beat off the challenge of the newcomer? What is the answer? Oh, the answer is that they may both survive. The Independent expanded the daily quality market by 10 per cent and the Independent on Sunday, if it's good, which it will be, should do the same to the Sunday market. That is what successful new products do. (And yet even as we say these things I wonder: surely some markets are saturated; does a brilliant new chocolate bar always have to expand the market to succeed, or can it do so merely at the expense of a less good, old chocolate bar? But these are private thoughts.)

Here is Neal Ascherson, dear, romantic Neal, on *The World Tonight* on Radio 4, three days before launch, asked by Janet Cohen why the Independent on Sunday appealed to him.

'Intelligence, really. I think taking the readers seriously. No trace of writing down. I think there's one large truth about the British Sunday newspaper market, you see, people say, oh, gosh, you know, the market's saturated, there's no more readership for all these Sunday papers, quality Sunday papers crowding into this already overcrowded market place. And this is pure nonsense, because what people fail to understand is this fundamental law, which is that the British have the habit of reading papers which are extremely stupid, whereas the readers are much more intelligent. And people taking papers like the Sun, you know, used to laugh at them. What it means is that there are probably tens of millions of people in the United Kingdom who are reading papers which are stupider than they are. All you have to do is to wean them off this bad old habit.'

And here is Andreas Whittam Smith on Melvyn Bragg's *Start the Week* on January 15th (his only interview) talking about the Independent on Sunday, at no time saying that he is not its editor or suggesting that it might have an editor of its own, or singling anyone out for credit.

After four dummies comes the night of the launch. Inch by inch the dummies have improved, though still it is not a proper paper, can never be, that I have at last learnt, until it has an audience. But almost everyone says how good the dummies are. Lord Sieff says so. George Duncan does too. So does Bruce Fireman. Richard Branson, to whom we have sent a copy, says that we will overtake the Sunday Times in five years. Others also get copies of the penultimate dummy, in which there is a critical article by Dominic Prince about James Gatward, chairman of TVS Television. Mr Gatward issues a writ; we pay £5,000 in damages and several times as much in costs – the first time in English law that a dummy newspaper has been sued. Strange times.

Hard work, sacrifice, dozens of impromptu meetings in my office, laughter. It is like the launch of the Independent again – though not so difficult; we have learnt a lot; I have learnt a lot. But the memory of those early days shows me suddenly how much with success has been lost. For these journalists on the Independent on Sunday, as once it was for those who started the Independent, it is still before the Fall and they are about to create a paper which will be better and purer and braver than any other, for which they will work without consideration, without counting the cost – *their* newspaper. The journalists on the Independent look on with the eyes of experience, of the happily married who look back to the very early days, half sorry, half amused . . .

On the eve of battle I talk to the staff. One thing, I say: let us be daring. No one is going to pick up a copy of the paper on Sunday and say, 'My God, the Independent on Sunday is too daring.' Practically no one in life is criticised for being too daring. But for not being daring enough . . .

Saturday January 27th. The Sunday Review has been printed. The business section has just been finished. There is not much news around, though there is an interesting story from John Carlin in South Africa about Winnie Mandela setting terms for her husband's release. There are no good pictures for the front page. Then, at about 4 o'clock, Mike Spillard, the picture editor, comes into my office and triumphantly puts down a photograph on my desk. It shows Dawn Griffiths, a mother holding her just-recovered kidnapped baby, her eyes sparkling with love. (When I see this picture my eyes prick with tears. Sebastian afterwards describes the same effect.) A couple of hours later, Ian writes the headline. 'Enter young mother, with a smile saying what words can't.' It's not a bad paper. It'll do.

At 10.30 we had a launch party to which hundreds of people came – journalists from the Independent, wives, husbands, friends. Andreas makes a short speech saying how good the first issue looks, how he is sure that the paper is going to be a great success, how striking the front page picture is. Then I make a speech, standing, like Andreas has, on a desk, so that my head touches the ceiling, and I have to talk with a kind of stoop, throwing my neck forwards. I thank Andreas extravagantly for his support and Steve Conaway for having implanted an idea which has flowered into the Sunday Review. I say that it is always foolish on such occasions to single out any colleagues for special mention when everyone had worked so heroically, but I will none the less ignore common prudence and thank Mike Stent and Mike McGuinness, and also Sebastian and Ian without whom . . .

Then more champagne, and, as at that other launch party which now seems so long ago, the first editions arrive. People ask Andreas and me to sign copies. Andreas writes, 'The first of many.' I write, 'The work of many hands.'

Now people are getting drunk and trampling over sheets of our precious paper which are littered all over the ground, breaking into little pieces. I search for Andreas to say a word to him, and find him perched on the side of a desk, looking down, brooding. There he is, Garrick tie, dark jacket, all alone, lost in his own thoughts. This is no celebration for him. Seeing him then I saw only a man who felt apart from things, as I had done on October 6th 1986. Seeing him now, in the photograph which has immortalised the moment, I find in his estranged look the future foretold.

9

Prince Caracciolo Comes to Town

The day after the launch of the Independent on Sunday, Andreas paid me an unprecedented compliment. 'I've just been speaking to Nick Garland,' he said. 'He thinks the first issue was magnificent. Whatever happens, it is a very great achievement. A very great achievement.'

By that Monday evening we had learnt that out of 1,237,370 copies distributed from nine print centres, only an estimated 760,000 copies of the first issue had been sold – a return rate of 38.6 per cent. It was a respectable sales figure, more than 100,000 greater than for the first issue of the Independent, but short of many predictions and of our hopes. Leo Burnett, the advertising agency, circulated an instant paper predicting a 'settled down' circulation of 500,000, but this seemed difficult to believe.

Though the circulation of all the other quality newspapers was affected, the Sunday Correspondent took the brunt. The previous Sunday its circulation had been a record 309,000 copies. With our first issue, it fell to 230,000, the beginning of a remorseless decline. The paper had seemed poised, if not for success then at least for survival, like some small mammal which has scrambled almost to the top of a shiny pole only to slither downwards, never again, now it has been weakened by the shock, to climb back.

The Independent on Sunday was not greeted as a journalistic triumph. The world had expected that we would launch with the confidence of a batsman who comes to the crease having already made a hundred, and instantly take on the authority of the Independent. But ours was a new paper still trying to create a character, staffed by journalists many of whom were still unsure of what they were doing. The newspaper took as long to find itself as the Independent had done.

Great achievement or not, it did not take Andreas many weeks to show unease, then traces of panic. He relied on word of mouth and the circulation figures. The first was mixed. From his colleagues on the daily paper he picked up adverse criticism, the judgments of old hands who thought they could do better if only they were allowed to, who in some cases believed that the Independent on Sunday should never have been launched. Andreas was also particularly struck by the view of Simon Jenkins, a columnist on the Sunday Times, whom he had been trying to tempt into writing for the Independent and the Independent on Sunday. Mr Jenkins had first pronounced the Sunday Review a work of genius but then, according to Andreas's account to me, began to question whether it was as brilliant as all that. Its arts coverage, for example, was much less comprehensive than that of the Sunday Times and, so Mr Jenkins had noticed, did not include late theatre reviews which, for deadline reasons, had to be shuffled into the broadsheet section. These conversations with Andreas led to Rupert Murdoch offering Simon Jenkins the editorship of The Times. But long after he had departed from the scene his reservations were still swirling around in Andreas's head.*

Circulation followed a similar pattern to that of the Independent after its launch, falling almost every week. Issue One: 760,000. Issue Two: 540,000. (An expensive 7,000-word essay by Salman Rushdie, his first public response to the *fatwa* against him, apparently made little difference.) Issue Three: 480,000. (Thanks *very* much, Leo Burnett.) Issue Four: 425,000. Issue Five: 395,000 (Now it's getting rough.) Issue Six: 383,000. Every week I stand in front of the IoS staff and tell them the figures. We simply have to steel ourselves. One day, for no particular or obvious reason, it will 'bottom out'. One day. Yet still

---

* Mr Jenkins's reservations about the Sunday Review did not prevent The Times under his editorship producing a clone for its Saturday edition a few months later.

we are going down. At 360,000 Andreas announces that the decline has stopped, but it has not. We lurch down again, to 333,000 in April. Our only compensation is that the Sunday Correspondent is going down faster still, a crazy shooting star in front of our more sedate meteorite.

The paper was getting better but the circulation was getting worse. The Sunday Review was much admired. People loved its design and were amazed by the quality of its colour reproduction on newsprint. Though we discovered that its deadlines were not so late that it could accommodate late features – these had to be shifted into the broadsheet – it felt more essential and more comprehensive than any colour supplement. But some people wanted a colour supplement too. They found the Review too austere and highbrow. In the early weeks we ran an impressive number of earnest pieces: André Brink on South Africa, Professor E.J. Hobsbawn reflecting on the demise of communism, and, best of all, Dr Jonathan Miller discoursing on death in a piece whose only wit could be found in Ian's cover-line – 'Last Exit from Camden'. Even our new-found star Lynn Barber, with her entertainingly abrasive interviews of John Aspinall, Sir John Junor and Peter O'Toole, could not wholly dissipate the gloomy pall that hung over the early part of the Review. For a time we had forgotten, Ian included, Adam Smith's reflections about Chinese earthquakes.

Many journalists could not easily write the features which were the staple of the broadsheet section. They had not always grasped the simple precept that a feature must have a beginning, a middle and an end. There were several exceptions, such as Cal McCrystal, a subtle and versatile Sunday Times hand, and James Dalrymple, a dour Scotsman who had come from the Independent where he had won an award for his reporting. Others, out of youth or inexperience, would write pieces which left point A and raced through many of the letters of the alphabet, though not in any ordered sequence, before stopping dead for no very obvious reason. In later months, Peter Wilby proved himself an excellent 're-write' man, and Stephen Fay a surprisingly sensitive teacher of younger writers. Many journalists improved, some enormously so: Rosie Waterhouse, a promising young reporter at launch, became within six months an outstanding investigative writer. But in the early days there would be a mad scramble on a Saturday morning, with Ian, Sebastian, Mike Stent and myself re-writing pieces at the last moment which we had 'picked up' in the computer system. Sebastian, who worked with marvellous facility, had a particular bugbear, which was the 'drop intro' – the piece which begins, 'All was quiet in Little Sodding, and Mrs Snooks was making her usual cup of cocoa,' and goes on in like manner for several hundred words before coming to the point, if there is one. Even after emergency surgery, one or two pieces were published in the early issues which barely made sense.

To begin with, we were not very good at *presentation* in the broadsheet. A few weeks after launch Ian left one of his little notes on my desk. 'It seems to me that in the news pages as a whole,' he wrote, 'but perhaps especially on the foreign pages, a vital ingredient is missing. What we have at the moment are some perfectly good stories mixed with some decent (if dead) photographs. Nobody seems to have sat down and thought: what is the best way to display this story or collection of stories? How shall we engage the attention of the reader? Should the headline speak to the picture? How do we give the headline, picture and story the kind of unity that will give a page clarity and (equally important) interest and excitement?' This was right. The broadsheet, in the early days, was put together too much like a daily quality newspaper, where the news has an impetus of its own, and time is short, so it's not possible or even desirable to spend hours thinking about how a single story should be presented. There *was* news to report for the Independent on Sunday, but most of the articles were background or news features which could not be, or should not be, slapped on the page. They had to receive almost the same care in terms of design as articles in a magazine.

The tabloid business section, with its long features aimed at the general reader was a mixed success. With a picture on the front, it looked like a magazine, albeit one printed on grotty paper. Ladies wrote to me from the Home Counties to say that although they had never read a business section before they had lapped up the 'cover story' in that week's issue. In the City the word was not so favourable. The section was said to be 'weak on news' with 'market sensitive' information. Indeed it was – that was the inevitable consequence of trying to produce a magazine with general appeal. The advertisers, wishing to appeal to City readers rather than ladies in the Home Counties who did not know a rights issue from a share placement, began to grumble. Slowly, without a single decision being made, the business section began to drift towards the conventional, as the broadsheet had already done.

For the first month many of us worked six days a week, and even after I had decreed that we must work a five-day week the hours were long and gruelling for most staff. There were not enough journalists. We were still working with the slowness of inexperience. Ian, who was features editor and a lot more, would spend hours in his little office at the far end of the floor (he and Sebastian had side-by-side cubicles) hunched in front of his terminal, wading through interminable articles. Once when he was subbing a piece, while Stephen Fay was talking to him, he fell asleep. By March he was speaking again of returning to his book. It was still too early for him to go and I asked him to remain until the beginning of June.

*

In January Nick Garland returned to the Daily Telegraph as its cartoonist. Following the publication of his book *Not Many Dead* he had barely been on speaking terms with Andreas and Matthew. When he told them that he had received an offer from the Telegraph they made little effort to dissuade him from going. I tried to convince him that the paper he had joined had not changed, but my lone voice among the founders was not enough.

On February 10th Nick Ashford died. He had learnt at the end of August that he had advanced cancer. He said then that perhaps his career would not be as long as he had hoped. Nick fought as hard as anyone could, but was weakened by a major operation, and got no benefit from various alternative medicines. Even so, he was working at City Road a week before he died.

His wife Giuliana believed that if he had not worked so hard from the moment he joined the Independent he might not have died; that if he had gone off to Australia, as he had proposed, he might still be alive. When I was foreign editor I worked hard and late enough, but on few nights did Nick leave before me. Why did he do it? Not for money or fame or advancement. His belief in the Independent, in its importance, its worth, was as great as Andreas's or Matthew's or mine or anybody's.

In the end he did become foreign editor, but he was slowly dying. The department was in turmoil because of my abrupt departure. Every day he forced himself to come into work to talk with correspondents, attend meetings, sort out budgets, deal with complaining journalists. This was what he had wanted to do, and this he would have been so good at, but every day his disease made the struggle worse until his friends could not bear to watch.

*

Andreas and I normally met for twenty minutes one afternoon a week. In the middle of the third floor, which was a long open-plan area entirely occupied by Independent on Sunday journalists, was my office. It was a pre-fabricated square room in the usual style, obligingly erected with windows so that everyone could glimpse whatever dramas might be taking place inside. Andreas would walk in and sit down on one of the grey bench-seats which ran around three sides of the room. I would get up from my desk in the corner, my back towards the window and the car-park, and go over to sit near him.

Sometimes at these meetings he would produce a good idea from his reporter's notebook. Once, shortly after launch, he offered some rare advice. 'When the Independent was launched, I listened too much to what people said. I was frightened. It took me some time to be sure of myself. You should not be frightened.' 'I won't be,' I assured him.

He was never critical to my face, but about three months after launch, when circulation had still not bottomed out, he began occasionally to leave grumpy memos which I would find on my desk when I came into work after the weekend. These read like schoolmasterly reports. 'I must admit to being disappointed with this week's issue so far as the broadsheet is concerned.' 'I was disappointed to see no coverage of the Liverpool corruption story on Sunday.' But Andreas had no grander suggestions to make. He may have been unaware of it, but the paper was improving because of our own efforts.

The recession was gathering force, though Chris Huhne kept telling me that these were early days, only the intimations of doom. The Independent on Sunday had been launched amid a flurry of cost-cutting measures. Andreas was worried. All the directors were worried. By March we had already revised our profit forecast for the year ending September 30th 1990 from £9.2 million to £4.5 million before the exceptional costs of launching the Independent on Sunday – a profit of £580,000 with those costs taken into account. The reason was that the Independent was falling behind its advertising budget, though its circulation remained strong, while the Independent on Sunday was miles away from its own targets which had been set by Adrian O'Neill. It was not primarily a question of circulation, though advertising yields would have been a little better if we had been selling more. The problem was a diminishing amount of money in the Sunday advertising market, and the two newcomers were bound to suffer more than the three established titles.

I knew Andreas very well and I foresaw an impending crisis. Soon the mounting panic in his mind, engendered by the recession and the still declining circulation, would join forces with his view of himself. Though I had tried to make him feel involved in the Independent on Sunday, I knew that he felt excluded, and that this sense of exclusion was the more painful because he believed in his own journalistic genius which had helped to save the Independent in similar circumstances.

There were no signs of the coming storm, other than Andreas's occasional memos. But I knew that it was coming.

*

On May 4th Andreas exceptionally called the twelve o'clock directors' meeting in the boardroom. He had arrived early and placed himself strategically at the head of the table. I sat down on his left.

'I am very worried,' said Andreas, 'about the circulation of the Independent on Sunday. We thought that it had bottomed out, but it obviously has not. Last Sunday it was 325,000. I don't think that it has reached the bottom yet. I think that it will go below 300,000.'

'I don't agree,' I interrupted. 'The recent declines have been much smaller. I think that we are at the bottom. We won't go below 300,000.'

'What do you think, Adrian?' asked Andreas.

'I think we have a problem,' said Adrian. 'I am very worried.'

'Graham?' asked Andreas.

A few days before Graham Luff had told me how much he had enjoyed the previous issue of the Independent on Sunday.

'To be frank,' said Graham, avoiding my eye. 'I find the paper a little bit too worthy, if that's the right word. I find some articles just a little bit difficult to read.'

Andreas went around each executive director in turn, as though certain of the support he would receive.

It was clear when he had done the rounds that he was not going to ask for my opinion, so I gave it.

'I repeat what I said. I think we are near the bottom, we may have reached the bottom. Of course we are not perfect. There are lots of improvements we can make, some we are making. One of the problems, as you know, is resources . . .'

'I am afraid,' said Andreas, 'that it goes deeper than that. I can't let this go on. As chief executive I have a duty to shareholders and the company. I intend to call a meeting of your senior editorial staff and the senior editorial staff of the daily to discuss what must be done. I can't predict what it will be, but it may be very radical indeed.' With this uncertain threat, the meeting broke up.

Later that day I spoke with Matthew on the telephone. He had been rather unforthcoming in his criticisms at this meeting, and I hoped for some support from him. However, a shadow hung over our relationship. About eight weeks before, completely forgetting the diabolical role which Matthew had attributed to him concerning the 'revelations' in Private Eye, I had hired Francis Wheen as the diarist of the Independent on Sunday in place of Ed Steen, who became a features writer. For me the scandal of Matthew's mistress was part of another world, another time. But not for him. When Matthew heard that I had taken on Francis, he came to see me, and asked me to rescind the appointment. 'I'm terribly sorry,' I said. 'I simply forgot all about it. I would not have done it if I had known. But I can't go to Francis now and say: Sorry Francis, you can't have that job after all.' Whereupon Matthew had replied: 'Well, in that case I shall never be able to read the Independent on Sunday again.'

Notwithstanding this ringing endorsement, Matthew was helpful when I rang him. I told him that I could not put up with Andreas chairing the proposed meeting. So long as I was editor of the Independent on Sunday I should preside. Matthew said that he would talk with Andreas, and a little later he rang me back. 'I've had a word with Andreas,' he replied, 'and I've told him how deeply you feel about this and I've got him to agree that you can chair the meeting. He'll behave himself.'

The meeting was fixed for 3 o'clock on Tuesday May 8th in the boardroom. As I was sending the invitations, I could, within the limits of prudence, choose who would come. Apart from Andreas and Matthew, I asked John Price, the home editor, who could be presumed to be an opponent of the Sunday paper, David Robson, the features editor, who probably was, Charlie Burgess, now managing editor, who might be, and Hamish McRae, business editor, who probably wasn't. I also asked Alexander Chancellor, who could be counted on as an ally, and, from among my own colleagues, Sebastian, Ian, Stephen Fay and Richard Williams. Peter Jenkins asked himself.

The morning of the meeting I received calls from two friends on the Independent. They told me that they had heard Andreas say that he was thinking of taking over the editorship of the Independent on Sunday.

And yet, when the meeting came, he was as mild as a lamb, and scarcely said a word. I sat one end of the long table, making copious notes, and Andreas and Peter Jenkins sat at the other. Friend and foe were otherwise mixed together. Our daily colleagues made polite criticisms of the Sunday paper. The Sunday team, in a tone set by Ian, struck the attitude of hard-pressed journalists eager for helpful advice and keenly aware of the need for further improvements. Peter Jenkins said that there should be more interchange between the two papers, and more opportunity for people on the daily such as himself to write. As he spoke, Andreas whispered into his ear the words (passed on to me later), 'Ask him that. *Ask him that.*' It was easy to agree to Peter's request, and to Matthew's suggestion that we should all have lunch more often.

Andreas's coup had not worked principally because he had not held the meeting or been able to set the agenda and prise out the conclusions he wanted. But although victorious, I felt stung by what he had done. I should not have been, I had seen it all before, but still I was. When I got home I dashed off a letter.

Private and Confidential

May 8th 1990

Dear Andreas,

On Friday I didn't convey my full astonishment at your behaviour. The effect on myself we can for the moment leave aside: I can decide how much to put up with. But these shock tactics have damaged the Independent on Sunday.

The rumour was, may still be, that you would like me gone. If I have heard that you have confided in one or two senior staff of the Independent, you can be sure that almost everyone else on the IoS has heard it,* and many outside. Journalists wildly exaggerate – but they need to have a seed.

Our rivals, who might have thought that we believed that we were doing reasonably well, must be delighted by this account of events. Henry Porter had heard it on Friday. Imagine their joy at the Correspondent.

If your purpose was as you stated [at our directors' meeting] on Friday, I do not understand why you did not simply come and talk to me. I will not be undermined. You must make your views clear to me, and if you want me to continue you must endorse me publicly to try to repair some of the damage that has been done.

Yours ever,
Stephen.

* This appears not to have been the case.

Andreas never referred to this letter. The circulation of the Independent on Sunday had bottomed out after all. Sales in May averaged only 11,000 fewer than in April. In June they rose by 8,000 to 333,000, and after falling back a little in July, rose again in August to 338,000. After that circulation increased for five successive months.

*

A couple of weeks after this botched coup Andreas received a telephone call from Sir John Nott – he who was secretary of state for defence during the Falklands war and once stormed out of a television interview with Robin Day. In his retirement from politics, Sir John had not gone short. He had become chairman of Lazard Brothers and Co. Ltd, the merchant bank, in which guise he regularly appeared on lists in City pages as one of the most highly paid men in Britain. He had now got mixed up with the Sunday Correspondent. Sir John was 'consultant' to the newspaper's owners, Sunday Newspaper Publishing plc, and prospective chairman.

His line, as related by an exultant Andreas who met him a few days later, was that in the Chicago Tribune the Sunday Correspondent had a resolute and a mighty backer. The company already owned 17.5 per cent of the British newspaper and had plenty more money where that came from. In February it had stumped up more cash when the Correspondent, five months after its launch, was re-financed. The Chicago Tribune was ambitious to expand in Europe (shadows of Ralph Ingersoll II here) and it was for that reason that it had invested in the Sunday Correspondent. It had every confidence in the newspaper, and its editor Peter Cole, and had even sent one of its most senior editorial executives, Michael Packenham, to lend a hand. (This was the man who had lectured me about the New York classified market when I was learning about colour magazines.) However, the Chicago Tribune had great respect for Newspaper Publishing plc and would be interested in exploring a deal with us which would in some way preserve the existence of the Sunday Correspondent.

Andreas was attracted to the proposal of some sort of merger, with the Independent on Sunday as the senior partner. I was less euphoric. As the weeks passed, it became clear that the Sunday

Correspondent was weakening, and that the circulation of our paper had at the very least stabilised. On the four Sundays from May 20th the Correspondent sold 173,000, 176,000, 195,000, and 179,000. On the same dates, we sold 323,000, 318,000, 356,000 and 329,000. Our rival was a wasting asset. During this period Andreas had meetings with Sir John Nott (whom I never saw), Nick Shott, the chief executive of Sunday Newspaper Publishing, and finally with Scott Smith, senior vice president and chief financial officer of Tribune Company (the definite article is omitted, perhaps in deference to the organisation's grandeur).

From these different conversations a plan emerged which was approved by our board on June 19th. We would pay the closure costs of the Correspondent (codename 'Granny') which could be as much as £6 or £7 million. We would incorporate the defunct newspaper's title on our masthead and offer employment to ten or so of its journalists. New shares in Newspaper Publishing plc would be issued to existing shareholders of Sunday Newspaper Publishing plc in proportions to be fixed according to the number of Correspondent readers who could be deemed to have switched to the Independent on Sunday. And who would pay for all this? The answer was Tribune Company, which would be invited to take up 2.47 million shares in our company at £7.50 each, which would give it 15 per cent of the enlarged equity. Existing shares had been changing hands at around £6 each, and it was reckoned that Tribune should be expected to pay a premium for so large a holding, especially as we were being asked to pay to close down a newspaper which was looking increasingly battered. Our hope was that when all monies had been paid to finish off the Correspondent there would be some cash left to help us weather the recession.*

---

* One possibly rather spurious justification for offering Tribune Company so large a shareholding was that it would balance Robert Maxwell's stake, which was creeping up towards 10 per cent. In May Maxwell rang me to complain about a light-hearted profile of him written by Sebastian. In fact, he was extravagantly courteous. 'Just thought I'd mention it,' he said, when I had offered a defence of Sebastian's teasing piece. He said he admired the paper. 'Could you tell me', I asked, 'why you continue to buy shares in Newspaper Publishing?' 'Because', he replied, 'I think that you chaps are doing such a good job down there. But if you wish me to desist, you only have to tell me, and the show will move on from the Palace to the Alhambra.' I related this conversation to our board; no one believed him.

Scott Smith was reluctant to pay so much, or at any rate his bosses in Chicago were. Though he could have been mistaken for the kid brother of Ralph Ingersoll II, Scott was not one whose thoughts tended naturally towards high multiples. He had not thrown away his time at business school. Steve Conaway, whose roots in the snowy wastes of Minnesota were perhaps not so far from Scott's, was of the view that Chicago types would feel flattered to have a stake in a Fleet Street newspaper. This was a judgment which possibly said more about Steve than Scott. Scott spent a day 'looking at the books' and afterwards Andreas and the executive directors took him out to the Savoy Grill. (Andreas now had an account there.) The object of the dinner was to persuade him that we were all good chaps and that, as an executive of a rich American company, he should not mind about paying over the odds. It was a dinner which had taken place on thousands of occasions since 1941. You've got the money, we've got the brains. Scott did not seem to be wholly taken in.

He returned to Chicago. He spoke at least once on the telephone with Andreas about the price per share which Tribune would pay. When Andreas floated the idea of not bothering to pay any money to close down or incorporate the Correspondent, but letting it instead sink under the weight of its own failure, Scott said that would not be possible. Tribune Company's proposed investment in Newspaper Publishing could not be 'decoupled' from our payment to the Correspondent.

After another special board meeting on July 20th, Andreas faxed a letter to Scott on July 25th. Having said that 'finding the right relationship with Tribune Company was more important than a possible deal with the Sunday Correspondent,' he asked again for £7.50 a share for 2.47 million shares, which would amount to 15 per cent of the enlarged share capital. More significantly, he undertook to 'enter in good faith' talks 'designed to find an acceptable method of taking your holding to 29.9 per cent'. Beyond this point a takeover might be triggered. For some weeks Scott had said that Tribune was interested in a larger holding. 'We on our side,' wrote Andreas in a burst of eloquence, 'are prepared to contemplate a shareholding which would change the nature of this company for ever. And we who say this are the same group of people who four years ago left secure jobs and re-mortgaged our homes to found this company.'

The next day, while Scott and his colleagues were chewing on this letter in Chicago, there was an interlude. Andreas, Matthew and I posed for a 'group photograph' in Bunhill Fields. Tina Brown, ever loyal, had dreamt up the idea of including her old friend and his colleagues in the annual 'Hall of Fame' in Vanity Fair, of which she was editor. The photographer Annie Liebovitz and about a dozen assistants were despatched via Concorde. By the time she and her troupe arrived in Bunhill Fields they had acquired a golden eagle, symbol of the Independent. 'He won't hurt a fly,' his owner assured us. As the three founders sat on a bench, overlooked by half-waving, half-jeering journalists poking their heads out of the rear windows of our building, I felt the beak of the eagle brush along the top of my head. 'Damn Tina,' I murmured.

'Now, Andréarse – can I call you that? – I want you over here,' said Ms Liebovitz. I love this place. Blake, Defoe . . . incredible.' She then took pictures of the three of us before coming to the point of the whole exercise.

'Andréarse, I hate to ask you this, but how would you feel if *he* [this was the eagle] were to kind of perch on your arm for a couple of seconds.'

Andreas looked at the eagle. The eagle looked at Andreas.

'All right,' said Andreas, with an attempt at a laugh – the laugh of a boy who has been dared to climb a tree with very few low-down branches.

And so he did it – held the eagle. The weight was very great, and he could scarcely hold up his arm. But his courage was perhaps greater.

'Anything for the Independent,' he said.

Back came Scott's fax on July 27th. After some introductory flannel, in which Scott re-iterated Tribune's interest in becoming 'the leading shareholder in Newspaper Publishing, and its continuing active support for the Sunday Correspondent', he offered £6 a share for 2.47 million shares on the understanding that the founding directors would vote their shares in favour of amending the Articles of Association to assist Tribune

Company in increasing its holding to 29.9 per cent of the company. 'Andreas,' concluded Scott, laying an epistolary hand on the shoulder of the chief executive of Newspaper Publishing plc, 'please convey to your board that this very attractive offer is also our best offer.' In fact, Andreas wheedled an extra ten pence per share out of Scott over the telephone.

A draft letter to Tribune Company was prepared accepting these terms, though the number of shares was slightly reduced to 2.25 million. Our lawyers had already prepared a draft contract for our purchase of the Sunday Correspondent. Most of the Correspondent's shareholders had said that they would go along with the Tribune plan, which would at least give them something back on their investment. Discussions had gone on with Nick Shott though his staff remained in the dark. It seemed that the closure costs might be less than £6 million. We agreed with Shott that we would take on twenty-five people from the Correspondent, most of them journalists. The last issue of the newspaper was pencilled in for August 5th.

One day, being driven into work by my driver Alan Kelly, looking up from the newspaper I was reading, I noticed Peter Cole sitting at the wheel of his Volvo estate in the next lane. He was staring ahead and did not see me. I thought, I may know things about this man's future which he does not know himself. And there, but for the grace of God, go I.

There was a last-minute hitch. We were becoming less and less inclined to pay good money to close down a newspaper which was evidently going bust. While the circulation of the Independent on Sunday was strengthening, the Correspondent, ever weaker, sold 165,000 copies on July 1st even with the benefit of television promotion, and by the end of the month was scraping against 150,000. Nick Shott talked of transforming it into a tabloid if a deal could not be agreed with us, but it was difficult to believe that they could raise the money to do this, or, even if they did, that it would survive very long. We estimated that the paper was losing over a million pounds a month and that its existing funds would run out at the end of September.

The reason we found for scuppering the deal was certainly not bogus. One of the Correspondent's shareholders was the Guardian which, as a result of an investment of nearly

£2 million at the time of the re-financing in February, now owned seventeen and a half per cent of the newspaper. We had assumed at the time that the Guardian's investment was calculated to injure its main competitor, the Independent, which is to say that by prolonging the life of the Correspondent it intended to make life uncomfortable for us. By late July, however, it had apparently accepted the Tribune plan. Our worry now was that once we had incorporated the Correspondent into the Independent on Sunday there was nothing to stop the Guardian launching its own Sunday paper in a further show of playfulness. We therefore asked the Guardian for an undertaking that it would not do so within twelve months. This it would not give.

It was the rock on which the deal formally foundered, though the deeper reason was our feeling that the Correspondent was doomed to die. In the two and a half months since Sir John Nott had approached Andreas, our position had strengthened greatly in relation to the Correspondent. I had always been sceptical about a deal, perhaps because I thought more highly of the Independent on Sunday than my fellow directors. Now Andreas had grasped how much stronger our own paper was. At a meeting of executive directors in early August, to which Bruce Fireman came along, it was agreed not to proceed. 'They're dead in the water,' said Steve Conaway. 'It's not worth *one cent.*'

Almost in a mood of truculence, some of the Correspondent's shareholders gave it a final lease of life. The Guardian and Tribune Company put in a little more money, and Robert Maxwell offered printing facilities. Even the Observer, according to Andreas, considered popping in a bit of cash in order to weaken us. The Sunday Correspondent became a tabloid and lost whatever dignity it still had. Peter Cole was replaced by John Bryant, once non-practising features editor of the Independent. Our own deal with Tribune Company automatically fell through, though we told ourselves that one day, when the Correspondent had finally died, Scott would be in touch. He was, but by that time it was too late for him.

We had had a narrow escape, though we did not know it. If Tribune Company had gained 29.9 per cent of our company, it is almost certain that they would now own it.

★

On July 9th, more exhausted than I had ever been, I had suddenly taken a week's holiday, leaving Stephen Fay in charge. Since April, he had been playing a bigger role, first as associate editor, and then, with Ian's departure in early June, as joint deputy editor with Sebastian. For his part, Sebastian was becoming increasingly disenchanted with his job. He shrank from the occasional confrontations which are part of executive life. Some of his holiday coincided with my week off, and before he departed we discussed the possibility of his spending all his time writing from the beginning of September.

While I was away the paper had a singular scoop. Mrs Thatcher had asked a group of British and German academics to Chequers to discuss whether a re-united Germany presented any threat to Europe. The view on the whole was that she didn't, but one or two comments were made which suggested that the Germans were not always utterly lovable. All this was recorded by Charles Powell, Mrs Thatcher's main foreign policy adviser, in a minute which found its way to the Independent on Sunday. In fact its recipient had sat on it for a few days, and only showed it to Stephen when Nicholas Ridley resigned having made some fairly stiff remarks about the Germans in an interview for the Spectator. Stephen decided to re-print the minute in full. For some people it carried the suggestion that the government was more preoccupied than it should have been with the possible defects of the German character. The story made headline news. On that Sunday, July 15th, circulation went up sharply.

My only involvement with the scoop came after my return when two gentlemen, one of them faintly sinister, came to see me muttering about the Official Secrets Act. They naturally wanted to know who had leaked the minute and I naturally refused to tell them.

On Ian's departure I had appointed Richard Williams as editor of the Sunday Review. This was a new position which consisted chiefly of looking after the features in the first half of the Review. Richard had distinguished himself as our sports editor, though his background was more in general features. At The Times he had been features editor. Before that he had been in charge of a 'new paper' planned by Rupert Murdoch in Wapping which turned out to be a front for the removal of all News International's newspapers to Docklands. This deception had reportedly been a great shock to Richard, and had perhaps contributed to his later defection from the Murdoch camp.

Richard's great tragedy, according to his friend David Robson, was that he was not born Italian. He was a man for whom style seemed to be almost everything, and he wore a permanently tragic mien. Quite often he dressed entirely in black. He would stride around the third floor, head down, lost in contemplation, like Prince Hamlet on the battlements, but a very handsome and elegant version. I could not work out what he felt about anything. Was he right-wing or left-wing? Did he believe in God? Did he love his country? It was impossible to say. Indeed he was so unforthcoming at the time of his original interview that had it not been for his high reputation I would not have hired him. He was one of those journalists who is fascinated by the new and knows about new schools of thought or movements almost before they know about themselves. He had a particular obsession with youthful cults, being himself a kind of adolescent Peter Pan whose never-never land was forever the 1960s. Several bright young journalists came to the paper through his good offices, one of whom, Zoe Heller, then almost wholly without experience, is destined to be a star.

I did half detect two things in Richard, aside from his high competence as a journalist. One was a love, a passion almost, for the enterprise on which he had embarked. The other was a desire to be thought well of, in a moral sense, by his colleagues.

I had agreed with Ian that he would not return until the following spring. During his absence he would be paid a small retainer and I had secured a largish number of share options for him. There had been an emotional party when he left, almost as though he were going for ever, at which I described him as 'the Imran Khan of journalism' in praise of his many talents.

Six weeks later, on July 25th, Ian wrote a long letter to Celia about a remote Scottish ancestor of hers called James Macalister

Hall. They had discussed this character at a dinner the previous evening. Macalister Hall had founded the British India line in the mid-nineteenth century which he had built up into the largest merchant fleet in the world. With part of his vast fortune he had built a country house at Killean on the west coast of Scotland, where Celia's mother had spent much of her childhood. 'You should go and visit Killean,' wrote Ian. 'It lies in a fold of the Kintyre peninsula facing the Atlantic, protected from the gales by a surprisingly thick little forest and up a steep track from the main road. There are many farm buildings . . .' Ian had discovered this place while doing research for his book on India. 'Last night in a Chinese restaurant you met probably the only man on earth who is interested in J.M. Hall. Why am I interested? That's a long story, but, briefly, because men such as Hall . . . had a large and so far under-investigated impact on the world, flooding Britain with tea and India with Lancashire cotton and Glasgow steam engines.'

On August 13th I left for a three-week holiday – the first time that I had been away for so long since the launch of the Independent. I felt that I had earned it. The Sunday paper was now on an upward swing. Though newspaper sales usually go down in the summer, circulation seemed likely to be better in August than July.

Before I left, Andreas asked: 'Should you be away for three weeks? I never take three-week holidays.' 'Surely that is not true,' I replied. I had admired him for taking long holidays during which he steadfastly refused, so he said, to read the Independent or any other newspaper.

Shortly after getting back, I received a hand-written card from Peter Jenkins, that bell-wether of fashionable opinion. He wrote that on returning from his holiday in Tuscany he had picked up the Independent on Sunday and been amazed by the number of fascinating and well-written articles which had confronted him. The Review had always been praised, but he had found the broadsheet equally good. He wondered whether the two of us might have lunch together. It was with this formal bestowing of hands that I realised we had made it.

What makes a good newspaper, what mysterious alchemy

transforms a jumble of perfectly readable articles into something which has authority and presence and conviction? We are most of us, journalists more than any, so faddish in our judgment of newspapers. 'The Telegraph is very good at the moment,' a journalist might say to another in El Vino as though this is an original insight rather than the received opinion of the moment. And what is 'very good?' The Telegraph which is so praised today is hardly different from the Telegraph of a year ago which was pronounced by the same journalists to have grown rather stale. And yet perhaps it is better in some little ways which together amount to quite a lot.

That autumn the Independent on Sunday was a much better paper than it had been a few months previously. There were several scoops, such as the Chequers piece. Our presentation of stories had improved, particularly of the double-page spread, sometimes three- or four-page spreads which we ran, week after week, on the Gulf crisis, and then, in November, on the struggle for the leadership of the Conservative party. These features were more clearly and entertainingly written. They looked good and made some sort of sense of the world for readers.

And yet these improvements, which can be pinpointed here and there, do not alone explain what happened. The paper was lighter, wittier, less portentous, more daring without being foolhardy – those qualities which come with confidence and praise. There is a mysterious bond between journalists and their audience of other journalists and 'media people' and, beyond them, the mostly silent army of readers whose true opinions are only to be guessed at, unless some letter or piece of market research should provide a sudden flash of understanding. Journalists are like actors save that they can scarcely see or know their audience; no less than actors, they depend upon that encouragement or approval which is necessary to give of one's best. And what does the audience want for that approval to be given? The great journalist or editor does not steer by the lights of market research, though he will nod at them as he passes by, but follows the guidance of his own past, that shared experience and common knowledge which unite him with his unknown reader.

I wanted to love the Independent on Sunday in all its parts, to be proud of every single thing in the paper. Yet a good editor must not want a paper to be like him (or her), a mere reflection of his own interests. A paper is too great and diverse a thing, too variegated to be encompassed by a single mind, however curious that mind may be. But he should understand everything. How will the readers, if he does not? The editor is the generalist, insisting on clarity and even simplification, representing at every turn the interests of the reader, the final mediator between the bewildering complex world and the people who buy his newspaper.

*

During the negotiations with Tribune Company and the Sunday Correspondent we had largely lost sight of the deteriorating finances of the company. In the twelve months ending September 30th 1990 we made a loss of £7.86 million, after charging £3.98 million of exceptional costs incurred in launching the Independent on Sunday. A year earlier we had budgeted for a profit of £9.2 million before exceptional costs. The disparity of £9.1 million between plans and results was almost entirely attributable to a shortfall in advertising revenues. These were getting worse. In October 1990 advertising revenue on the Independent (excluding the magazine) was £857,012, or 23.1 per cent, down on the previous October, though the circulation decline over the same twelve months was tiny – 415,000 from 421,000. Even with constant trimming of costs, of which there had just been a further bout, these huge variances were bad news. The Independent was no longer making anything like enough money to cover the losses of the Independent on Sunday, for which breakeven, as a consequence of the slump in the advertising revenue, was now stratespherically higher than the projected figure of 358,000 copies which Graham Luff had worked out before the launch of the paper.

Around October Andreas seemed to wake up fully to our predicament. 'It's a good thing we've got two strong titles,' he said to me one day, 'otherwise we would be in the knacker's yard.' Since no bank would go on covering losses of this sort during a recession, it was clear that we would need an injection of capital. Tribune Company was still nursing the Sunday Correspondent towards its grave and was therefore out of the reckoning. A list of possible trade investors was drawn up with the assistance of our merchant bank, S.G. Warburg. Two names on this list were those of La Repubblica and El Pais.

None the less we did not go cap-in-hand to these newspapers. During September we had been working on a three-year plan. It was an exceedingly optimistic document. The decline in advertising revenue was seen as temporary. On the back of higher projected circulation for both newspapers, income from advertising was supposed to rise steadily during the next three financial years. At the end of the period, September 1993, the Independent would be selling 461,000 copies and the Independent on Sunday 470,800.* This latter figure was relatively modest in view of the aim, stated in the plan, for the Independent on Sunday to overtake the Observer and the Sunday Telegraph, each of which was selling more than 550,000. This would only be done, it was conceded, by 'adding value' to the paper. Value would also be added to the Independent. The implication here was that money from new investors would not be used so much to pay off debt as to improve 'the products'.

If you believed the advertising and circulation projections, post-tax profits were mouth-watering – £543,000 in the first sticky year of the plan, then £8.6 million as the economy revved up and £15 million in the final year as it took off heavenwards.

Andreas began to sound out the Italians and the Spanish – the 'southern Europeans' as they were not very flatteringly known. He was soon convinced that La Repubblica and El Pais would be ideal investors. He knew the leading characters at both newspapers and liked them – love would be more apt a word so far as Eugenio Scalfari was concerned. The European dimension of such a deal was also very attractive to him. Not every director

---

* The 'eight hundred' in this figure is a stroke of genius. These circulation projections were prepared with the help of the Henley Centre for Forecasting which produced many other projections for us, most of them more short-term. These were often over-optimistic, largely for the reason that Henley had not allowed for the depressing effect of a severe recession on circulation. A 'model' is only as reliable as the information which is put into it.

was so enamoured of the idea. Matthew spoke disparagingly of Italian business practices. But, with Tribune Company out of the running, alternative investors were not exactly lining up.

And so Prince Caracciolo came to town. He came to look at the books, though there were lesser mortals who could do that, such as Corrado Passera, rumoured to be something of a hard man. The Prince – Carlo – was not a hard man. He came to City Road with his friend and fellow member of the 'black nobility', Count Paolo Filo della Torre. Whereas Paolo was rounded and beaming, a kind of stage Italian brimming with extravagant compliments, Carlo was thin, distinguished-looking, and reserved. But the two men, chief executive and foreign correspondent, were evidently close. To Andreas, Paolo was just a journalist, and he grumbled about his presence during the negotiations but, to Carlo, 'Filo' was a friend, someone to be relied upon and trusted in all weathers.

Almost everything I knew about Prince Caracciolo, Paolo had told me. He was a crazy Anglophile, notwithstanding the fact that one of his ancestors, the illustrious Commodore Francesco Caracciolo, had been hung in the bay of Naples on the judgment of a court set up by Nelson. The Caracciolos were a Neapolitan family of almost unfathomable antiquity but they seemed to have adapted nimbly to the modern age. Carlo had made a large fortune, first as the owner of the magazine Espresso and then with La Repubblica. His sister had married Gianni Agnelli. Carlo was rich, as well connected as it was possible to be in Italy and indisputably grand, and yet he had this strange wish (this was my interpretation, not Paolo's) to be associated with something in London, capital of a country which perhaps still loomed in his mind as it had done when he was a young man. It was this, rather than the utopian Europeanism of his friend Eugenio, which drew him to the Independent.

He obviously cannot have had the faintest idea of what he was letting himself in for. A few years before retirement, the great battles of his business life behind him, he must have looked forward to a monthly visit to London where, after an uncontentious board meeting, he could move smoothly between his suite at the Berkeley Hotel and the houses of friends;

visit the Chelsea flower show in May and, come gentle September, venture to a country garden to make modest comparison with his own estates.

The three-year plan was shown to Carlo and to our other friends from La Repubblica and El Pais. Graham Luff prepared a plan for the executive directors which was printed on white paper contained in a red plastic file. The 'southern Europeans' had a similar file, though their paper was green.

Talks did not go entirely smoothly. Corrado Passera gave Andreas and Graham quite a hard time. He was said to be the right-hand man of Carlo de Benedetti, the multi-millionaire media tycoon, whose shareholding in La Repubblica, by far the largest, was about three times as big as that of Carlo, behind whose more respectable skirts he was sheltered so far as this deal was concerned. The Spanish were also more businesslike than either Carlo or Eugenio, and less inclined to European rhetoric than the latter. Juan Luis Cebrian, the founding editor of El Pais, now its chief executive, was a small, dark, intense man who apparently belied the theory that journalists do not make good businessmen. Javier Diez de Polanco, as bald and smooth-faced as Juan Luis was hairy, was a nephew of the founder and major shareholder of Grupo Prisa, which owned El Pais. Javier could speak almost no English, but this oversight did not deter him in the slightest. His general demeanour, then and later, was that of a Victorian governess who has wandered into a Chinese flea market and expects to be fleeced at any moment.

The grand signing took place in the boardroom on November 16th. La Repubblica and El Pais had each agreed to subscribe for 2,145,592 new ordinary shares in the company at a price of £5 each, which would raise £21.5 million before expenses.* (The share price, less than Tribune Company had offered four and a half months before, reflected our weaker financial position which no three-year plan could disguise.) This new subscription gave each newspaper a holding of 12.49 per cent in Newspaper

---

* In fact the money was not paid over until February 1991, partly because El Pais had to seek permission from the Bank of Spain to transfer funds out of the country, and partly because the Office of Fair Trading had to satisfy itself that El Pais and La Repubblica, which seemed to know each other's every move, did not constitute a 'concert party'.

Publishing plc. It was also agreed that each could raise its holding to 14.99 per cent of the enlarged share capital by making a 'tender offer' to existing shareholders (excluding the founders) for 5 per cent of their shares. This was partly intended to sweeten our investors who, whatever gloss was put on the affair, were being diluted.

After the signing there was a celebratory lunch in our two dining rooms and the boardroom, to which senior editorial and non-editorial staff were invited. Champagne was drunk. Neal Ascherson fell in with Carlo Caracciolo. It turned out that many years before Neal and some other journalists had rescued Carlo's journalist brother from some nasty Italian right-wingers in Algiers. 'What a very jolly lunch that was,' said Neal afterwards.

We had come a long way since Paolo first set out to acquire his Atex computer. But you wouldn't have known that the company had been changed by this investment. Why, perhaps it had not been. At a staff briefing that afternoon Andreas said that neither La Repubblica nor El Pais had any designs on the company. Rather, they were represented by Andreas as being part of the team, 'us' versus 'them'. They and the founding directors and the staff shareholders would now own 45 per cent of the company and could ward off any predators. Things would go on as before. And so, for a time, they did.

★

These months were halcyon days for the Independent on Sunday. In the teeth of promotion from all its competitors – we could not afford to spend a penny ourselves – its circulation rose from an average of 348,000 in September to 355,000 in October and 365,000 in November. Its market share was also edging up. The re-launched tabloid Sunday Correspondent enjoyed half an Indian summer and, helped by the old trick of giving away motor cars, sold an average of 242,000 copies in October. But this was not enough. On the evening of Wednesday November 27th I was listening to the radio at home. It was announced that the Sunday Correspondent had closed. Rather than a sense of exultation, I felt that chill which any journalist will feel on hearing that a newspaper has died.

Two journalists had joined us from the Correspondent before its final hours. One was Henry Porter, editor of its colour magazine, which was thought by many to be the best part of the paper. Henry had practically been one of the founding fathers of the Correspondent, and when it had seemed possible that the newspaper would not raise its initial finance he had led a raid on the august portals of Tribune Company. At one point, several months after the launch of the Correspondent, he was spoken of as a possible editor. The fount of such speculation may well have been Henry himself. When I had come across him at Alexander Chancellor's fiftieth birthday party in January 1990, Henry had said that he should be appointed in place of Peter Cole who was in his view a terrible editor. This had shocked me, since I did not think you should criticise your editor in public, least of all in front of another editor.

None the less, I had tried to hire Henry in April. In part this was a straightforward attempt to demoralise the Sunday Correspondent by poaching their best man but, more than that, I felt that Ian would have to be replaced when he left. Though Henry flirted a little over lunch at Rules restaurant, he would not come. Whatever his feelings about Peter Cole, he was still emotionally embroiled with the Correspondent, and perhaps still hoped to be its editor. But when the paper's management decided to turn the paper into a tabloid off he stomped.

One of Henry Porter's oldest friends was Stephen Fay. Almost two years before, the two of them tried to persuade Andreas that they held the key to a successful Sunday newspaper. Now Stephen began a campaign to get his friend a job on the Independent on Sunday. 'I do think you should talk to Henry,' he would say to me. 'He's got such good ideas about features.' I felt a little ambivalent. Henry was no longer a trophy which we could hang above the fire-place to defy the Correspondent, since the paper was past defying. Moreover, we had done better than could have been expected without re-placing Ian. I also remembered Henry's remarks about Peter Cole. On the other hand, he was an imaginative journalist with admirably irreverent tendencies. The long feature in the broad-sheet ('Inside Story') needed more thought than anyone had had time to give.

I explained some of my worries to Henry when he came to see me in my office. He was a large man who found it impossible to keep still. A leg would shoot out in one direction, and he would place a restraining hand on it as though frightened that it might do someone some damage, and while he was doing this the other leg would make its own separate bid for freedom. In this respect he had better self-control than Ian Hay Davison, another restless man, whose feet at many a board meeting had unconsciously lashed out at my shins under the table. Hay Davison had another interesting habit of not quite getting your name right.

I told Henry that one or two of the staff would regard his joining us as tantamount to having Genghis Khan to tea. 'I don't know why people are so frightened of me,' he complained. 'You obviously think that I am a bit of a bull in a china shop, but I am really very easy to get on with.' 'I'm sure you are,' I replied, and, I am glad to say, hired him as associate editor (features).

As well as superintending the Inside Story feature, Henry took over the light column on the centre pages which had bounced around from one unsatisfactory writer to another. In this column he managed to offend many people, most memorably when he gave his readers the benefit of his opinions about the German race. As an editor and a journalist he was a member of the one-last-phone-call school of journalism. (One suspected that it was sometimes the only call.) He needed to speak to someone to check a theory or rumour he had heard, and if that someone, who was probably rather grand or well-placed, should come through, then all would be well. If not, not.

The other refugee from the Sunday Correspondent was Don Macintyre. He was not one of those who goes to the station to buy a first-class ticket at the first pit-pat of gunfire. Don would only leave when his paper was in ruins, and even then he had to be yanked out of the rubble. This loyalty to the Correspondent was odd, since Don had won the reputation of changing jobs often. As labour editor he had been a founding journalist of the Independent (bringing with him from The Times the rest of the labour team, Dave Felton and Barrie Clement) before going to the Sunday Telegraph as political editor. He then went to do the same job at the Correspondent. After we had parted company with our own political editor earlier in the year, we laid siege to Don. There were lunches, letters, late-night drinks – every device known to wooing was used, with Stephen Fay and Peter Wilby stepping into the breach when my own exertions faltered. During this period of several months, Stephen Castle, our political correspondent, heroically ran the political coverage single-handed. Don finally succumbed only when he had virtually been deprived of a paper to write for.

If Henry Porter approached an article with a jaunty air, like a man who has suddenly taken it into his head to snatch a day's fishing, Don confronted every piece as though he had been asked to climb Everest without proper boots. In this he was the more typical journalist, though his *angst* was unusually extreme. For him there would probably be no last-minute call. Throughout every Thursday and Friday he would practically live on the telephone, curling a lock of hair around a pencil or forefinger in nervous agony as he listened patiently to the views of politician after politician. Then, after amassing enough information for a short treatise, he would inevitably declare that he had not got much of a story, even if he had a small scoop.

They were good days those, good for all the journalists on the Independent on Sunday, and nothing which happened later could change that. For all the little squabbles and petty jealousies and political manoeuvrings inherent in any human organisation, it was an exceptionally happy newspaper. After the battle with the Correspondent it was the morning after Agincourt. In December our circulation averaged 379,000, in January 406,000, a monthly average not to be exceeded for twenty months. Our market share had risen from 12.2 per cent in September to 14.4 per cent in January.* In part the high sales were driven by an interest in the Gulf crisis – on the Sunday after war broke out we sold 424,000 copies – but that seemed to show that we were covering it well.

January comes. Andreas returns from a three and a half week holiday. The same Gulf war which brings a higher circulation tightens the recession one more notch, and advertising revenues

---

* Defined as the percentage of sales in a market consisting of the Sunday Times, Observer, Sunday Telegraph and Independent on Sunday.

fall further. But we do not notice the worsening finances, have not grasped that the £21.5 million from the 'southern Europeans' will not be enough to see us through. Neither do we know that the recession which has so far affected only advertising will soon damage the circulation of both newspapers.

On Saturday January 26th we have our first anniversary party. There is an air of mild euphoria which seems even to have touched Andreas.

'I don't think you will ever go below 400,000 again,' he pronounces, as the two of us stand in a huddle with Chris Huhne and his wife.

'Really?' I reply.

'My feeling', says Chris, who, annoyingly, is correct more often than such a person has a right to be, 'is that our real circulation is about 385,000, and the rest is the Gulf war.'

'I don't believe you're right,' says Andreas.

10

The Visit of the Chelsea Men

Though it was good for newspaper circulation, the Gulf war depressed advertising revenues still further. This setback, like every previous one, hurt the young Sunday paper more than its established daily sister. By early March the Independent on Sunday was making losses of about £150,000 a week, and the Independent was tipping into the red. In the first five months of its financial year Newspaper Publishing had lost £4.2 million. The apportionment of profit and losses to each title was a vexed question, according to how overheads were distributed in the management accounts, but even by the most favourable interpretation the Independent had made a profit of only £315,000 over this period.*

The management of Newspaper Publishing reacted remarkably slowly. The strong circulation of both titles was diverting our attention. As late as the February 27th board meeting the executive directors gave a very upbeat account of the Sunday newspaper's performance. A couple of non-executive directors made unhappy noises about the Independent on Sunday's financial position, and Bruce Fireman went so far as to suggest that we should consider closure. Andreas got quite steamed up.

---

* Sometimes it suited the executive directors to load as many losses as possible on to the Sunday paper, on other occasions it did not. The company's financial year began on October 1st 1990. Advertising revenue is normally much stronger in the first half of the year.

'Management has absolutely no plans whatsoever to alter our course.' He said this in his Old Testament prophet sort of way as though he would brook no opposition on the matter, and his face flushed purple.

During March I started to worry more and more about the losses that the Independent on Sunday was making. I discussed matters with Graham Luff, and he told me that he was working on some figures which suggested that at the present rate of losses the new capital produced by the Italians and Spanish would tide us over only until July or August. At the same time, the circulation of both papers began to decline. The Independent fell from 419,000 in January to 405,000 in February to 402,000 in March. Over the same three months the Independent on Sunday went from 406,000 to 402,000 to 386,000. It looked as though the recession was now biting into newspaper sales.

Then on March 20th came the John Major lunch. Though there was no immediate reaction, the jealousies which it unleashed seemed to swirl around the building for many days. At the time, I did not notice any change in my relations with Andreas, but my conversation with Matthew less than a week after the Prime Minister's visit suggested that Andreas's feelings towards the Independent on Sunday, and to me, had changed for the worse again. It was pretty clear from what Matthew had said that Andreas was thinking of trying to seize some degree of control. That lunch was a kind of turning point after which everything got steadily worse.

By the end of the month I was sure that losses were so great that there was bound to be a crisis. I confided my fears to Christopher Huhne at lunch on March 27th. Sooner or later, I said, Andreas and the other executive directors would wake up to the enormous losses. I knew that Andreas would exploit our predicament by proposing the integration of the two newspapers and the independence of the Sunday newspaper would be destroyed. I would be offered some reduced role which I would refuse on the grounds that I was the author of the *status quo* and could not honourably associate myself with new arrangements.

'Don't be silly,' said Chris. 'Circumstances change. All you've got to do is say, I'm sorry. Circumstances have changed. '

I shook my head. 'I don't think so,' I said.

★

On April 10th Andreas asked me whether I would come and see him in the afternoon. This was unusual. Normally when he wanted to see me he simply popped up to my room on the third floor. When I arrived in his office I found Matthew there as well. He looked uneasy and would not meet my eye. Andreas's mood was jocular in a forced sort of way. He dug around in a perspex file which was lying on his desk and produced a sheet of paper.

'I've been looking at this,' he said, brandishing the sheet. 'What it shows is the market share of the Independent on Sunday is pretty flat. If you look you will see that its market share was 14.2 per cent in December, which was after the closure of the Sunday Correspondent, and then in January, with the Gulf war, it went up to 14.4, then in February it was down a bit at 14.3 and last month it was down a bit again at 14.1.' He pushed the sheet in my direction as though I might wish to verify the figures independently, and continued.

'We have to face the fact that we're on a plateau and the question is what we need to do to get off it.'

I agreed.

'Matthew and I think,' he went on, 'that the Independent on Sunday is a very competent newspaper, *very* competent. It's 95 per cent there but it just needs that little x-factor.'

'Well, of course it can be improved,' I said. 'Everything can. But I don't think were going to get up to 450,000 or 500,000 copies unless we add something to what we've got – some sort of magazine, probably – and probably promote as well.'

'Mmm,' said Andreas. 'I'm not sure that is the case. What I think is that you could make a lot more *noise*. What do you think, Matthew?'

Matthew delivered a little prepared speech which I had heard before from Andreas's lips about how the Independent on Sunday did not always seem to *care* enough.

'What I would like', said Andreas, now leaning forward on his chair, 'is for you to allow me to come up to the third floor and take some meetings. I need to know what your colleagues are thinking, and I can't do that unless you let me come up.'

There was a pause. They both looked at me.

'You know what my reply to that will be,' I said after a while.

'No, I don't,' replied Andreas with a nervous laugh.

I managed to keep my composure, and spoke slowly. 'If you come up ... my staff will wonder what the hell is going on. They think they're doing OK. They think they are producing a perfectly good newspaper ...'

'It is very competent,' said Andreas.

'And if you come up they will be confused. Some of them don't know you very well, and it is natural that they should look to me as their editor.'

' I don't think that's strange,' said Andreas.

'I don't see why you can't let him come up,' broke in Matthew in an exasperated tone. 'I just don't see the problem.' He emphasised each of these six words as though he were addressing a backward child.

'Look,' I said. 'Of course if Andreas wants to come up to the odd meeting he can do that. He's been up to meetings before. You came to that meeting with the business staff, Andreas. But don't you see the effect on the morale of the paper of presiding over meetings when I am present? What would they think?'

The meeting ended inconclusively. I agreed to think about Andreas's request. I knew that it would not go away. The next day I had breakfast with Stephen Fay, my deputy, and told him what had passed. He was astonished.

*

On April 16th I received a memorandum from Andreas dated the previous day, and headed 'Meeting with senior IoS editors.' Andreas wrote that he 'would welcome the chance tomorrow (Tuesday, 16th April) to meet with you and your senior editors.' The purpose was twofold. He wanted to explain why the target circulation of the Independent on Sunday had to be 'level-pegging' with the Observer and the Sunday Telegraph. And he wanted to 'comment upon the editorial formula in what I hope will be a helpful way.' He concluded: 'I trust you agree that this would be worthwhile and can arrange a suitable time.'

I understood, of course, that this request was part of a continuing campaign against me, but since it had to do with the general development of the newspaper, rather than its day to day editing, it could not be reasonably opposed. I told Andreas that it might be difficult to fix such a meeting on that day and suggested lunch later in the week. I rang Ian Jack at home and suggested that he might like to come. I also asked Stephen, Sebastian, Christopher Huhne, Richard Williams and Henry Porter. A date was set for April 19th.

It was a constructive lunch, and it did not presage any of the dramatic events of the next few weeks. Andreas began by saying that the Independent on Sunday was a 'very accomplished' newspaper, but that we had severe financial problems. Long-term survival lay in increasing the circulation of the Sunday newspaper to that of the Observer and Sunday Telegraph, both of which stood at a little over 550,000. Christopher Huhne suggested that the company should consider cutting costs through a programme of redundancies.

'I can well see the attraction of that,' said Andreas, 'but I don't *think* that I am in favour. It is something which I have always wanted to avoid. I have made it a point of honour to come through this recession without making a single person redundant.' Discussion turned to the newspaper.

'As I say,' said Andreas, 'I do think that it is a very accomplished paper, but – and Stephen will have heard me say this a number of times – I don't think it creates enough *noise*.'

Some of my colleagues complained that we hadn't had any money to invest in serialisations or expensive and time-consuming blockbusters of the sort that distinguish Sunday newspapers. Ian described these as 'properties'. Henry volunteered to draw up a list of ideas for properties for Andreas. The cost was instantly put at half a million pounds a year. It was agreed that Richard would continue working on a dummy for a new fourth supplement devoted to beauty and fashion.

Three days after this lunch, on the following Monday, Andreas called a meeting of the six executive directors to discuss the future of the Independent on Sunday. I sensed, notwithstanding the upbeat tone of Friday's lunch, that some directors might be putting forward panic measures, so that morning I circulated a thousand-word memorandum to the directors.

I wrote that 'a cool, confident company' would regard the challenge facing us as less awesome than launching the Sunday newspaper. We had 14 per cent of the market. The challenge was to increase 14 per cent to 18 per cent within twelve months, and 'thereby to create an asset which will be of value to the company for the foreseeable future'. The choice lay between investing further in the Independent on Sunday and altering the cost base of the paper, which meant seven-day publishing – integration. I had always been sceptical about that, and my scepticism had grown. Even if the Sunday Review were preserved with its own independent staff, the danger was that seven-day publishing would destroy the character of the Independent on Sunday. I was also sceptical about the size of potential economies. 'It is very likely that in absorbing the Sunday paper the daily, which has its own circulation difficulties, would be weakened.'

I arrived a little late at the meeting: Monday was my day off, and I had come in from home. The mood was unbelievably different from that at lunch three days before.

'Stephen,' said Andreas, as I sat down. 'I've had an idea. Tell me whether you think I am mad.'

'OK.'

'My idea is that we suspend the publication of the Independent on Sunday until advertising has recovered – maybe a year. Then we come back with a big re-launch and a new fourth section.'

'Well . . .'

We spent about an hour discussing this extraordinary proposal. Apart from Andreas, it did not have any strong supporters. Steve Conaway argued that once we had suspended publication we would probably never start up again. My view was that it was too dire a solution, if thus it could be dignified, to our problems. The contrast with our discussion on Friday was shocking. So far as integration was concerned, Andreas referred only briefly to my memorandum. He said: 'I agree with Stephen that integration probably isn't the right solution.'

Two days later, on Wednesday 24th, we had a monthly board meeting. The future of the Independent on Sunday was the main topic of discussion. If anything, the mood of panic of Monday's meeting was surpassed. Andreas outlined the different options: investment in 'the Sunday product'; suspension; closure or – possibly – integration. Nobody thought much of Andreas's idea of suspension, and closure drew little support. But neither did anyone, apart from myself, speak in favour of the kind investment which Andreas had himself proposed at lunch five days earlier. Javier Diez de Polanco* said that this was the time to cut costs. His words seemed to make an impression on many of those present.

After the board meeting was over, Andreas, Matthew and myself took Javier to the Savoy for lunch. Even at this moment of financial reckoning it was thought appropriate to visit Andreas's favourite watering-hole. At lunch Javier repeated his imprecations about economy. His message was 'Batten down the hatches.'

'Steve,' Javier favoured this intimate form of address, though we had exchanged no more than a dozen words before. 'It would be ... *mejor*, yes it would be better, to save costs now. Then after the recession ...'

On Friday afternoon, two days later, Andreas's secretary rang up to ask whether I could pop down to Andreas's office. It was a week since our expansionist lunch. I arrived to find Matthew also there, sitting in very much the posture he had assumed at that meeting a little over two weeks before, only on this occasion he looked more guilty, indeed almost anguished. His face was white.

'Come in, Stephen,' said Andreas. 'Sit down.' I came in and I sat down. So there we were: the three founders of the Independent.

'Matthew and I have been discussing what we should do about the Independent on Sunday. The more I think about it, the more I am sure that integration is the best solution. You see, it's the only way of reducing costs at a stroke.' As he spoke

---

* Javier was Juan Luis Cebrian's 'alternate' which meant that he could attend when Juan Luis was not present. Much to Bruce's annoyance, he came in either event, so there were often two Spaniards. By contrast, I never saw Corrado Passera, Carlo Caracciolo's alternate, at a board meeting.

he made little jabbing movements with his fingers.

'I see,' I said, too taken aback to say anything else.

'As you know, I am going away to Colombia tomorrow.' I did know this. Andreas and his wife Valerie had been invited to a conference organised by El Pais in Bogota, and were being flown there first-class. 'And I shall be away for a week. While I am away, I shall ask Matthew to conduct a study into integration to see whether it will work.'

'And under your plans what do you wish to happen to me?'

'Well, once you put the newspapers together', replied Andreas, placing his fingertips together to emphasise this new relationship, 'you would have no need for an editor on the Sunday paper because power, if you like, would have been devolved to the departments, and there wouldn't be any centre left.' More jabbing of fingers in the air.

'I see.' I was too stunned by the betrayal to say anything else.

'But,' Andreas went on, 'you would remain an executive director and sooner or later something would come up. I don't know what it would be. It might take six months but something would come up.'

' I think in that case I would resign,' I said. 'I would not want to stay.'

'I implore you not to,' said Andreas.

'Yes,' spoke up Matthew from the corner.

There was silence. I had predicted what was now happening and yet when it came it was none the less a shock. Deeper down a voice was beginning to stir which said, you need not accept all this, they are trying to shock you into compliance. Yet on the surface I was compliant.

'This is terrible.' said Matthew, shaking his head in disbelief as though at the unforeseen vagaries of fortune. 'Terrible.' And then he said: 'I feel sick.'

'Well,' said Andreas, in a summing-up tone of voice. 'So Matthew will conduct his investigation.'

'I think it would be a good idea, Andreas,' said Matthew, who seemed to have recovered from his nausea, 'if I were to invite daily heads of department to my house on Monday so that there is not a lot of gossip here.'

'Yes. Should you be there?' Andreas asked me.

'No, I don't think so,' I replied, perhaps unwisely. My immediate thought was that I did not wish to be publicly identified with a plan to integrate both newspapers. I was going to fight it.

' Well I think that's it, then,' concluded Andreas. 'Integration is' – he searched for the right word – 'probable.'

★

On the morning of Tuesday April 30th a story went around the offices of the Independent and the Independent on Sunday. The previous afternoon Matthew Symonds was said to have invited heads of department on the daily newspaper to his house in Twickenham. He had told them that there was a stark choice facing the Independent on Sunday. Either the paper would be integrated with its sister daily or it would be closed. He was reported as saying that forty journalists would have to be made redundant, nearly all of them on the IoS.

Everyone on the Sunday paper was shocked by this news. Most were unaware that any crisis was brewing. Some knew about the lunch eleven days previously at which Andreas Whittam Smith had spoken bullishly about the paper's future and discussed plans for expansion. Only a few knew what had happened since that lunch. I had told Stephen of all subsequent developments. Ian, who had abruptly ended his sabbatical, was also fully in the picture. So was Henry Porter.

My own reaction to the news of the meeting in Matthew's house was also one of astonishment. Matthew was not acting *ultra vires* in holding the meeting during Andreas's absence in Bogota, as was generally believed. But he had gone far beyond what had been agreed with Andreas in my presence, which was that he and his colleagues should merely investigate the practicalities of integration. Certainly no one on the board of Newspaper Publishing had spoken with any conviction about closure, the brutal, sole alternative now presented by Matthew.

I thought integration a bad idea. Though in western Europe and the United States many daily and Sunday papers are integrated, the tradition in Britain has been to run them separately. This reflects the different qualities of daily and

Sunday journalism in this country. It is asking a lot of journalists to do both jobs and produce good results. Integration had been attempted on the Daily Telegraph and Sunday Telegraph two years previously, but by most accounts it had not worked, and the process had been largely reversed. I thought that the Independent on Sunday was a good paper which would improve under its existing arrangements, and I wanted to continue as its editor.

Over the next two weeks I put the case against integration to the executive and then to the non-executive directors. For at least a month I had foreseen that there would be pressure to cut costs and I had prepared alternative plans. But there was another strategy proposed by Stephen and Henry which I had not thought of. This was that a stake in the Independent on Sunday, at least 51 per cent, should be sold to a third party to raise money to pay off debts and make editorial improvements.

Unbeknown to me, Stephen and Henry had discussed the idea with Stephen's friend Alistair McAlpine at the end of the previous week. Lord McAlpine had mentioned the matter to Sir Gordon Reece who for some reason had consulted Sir Tim Bell, Mrs Thatcher's friend and publicity adviser. Sir Tim, as it happened, was no friend or admirer of the Independent and Newspaper Publishing. Within a day or two the word was out in the City that the Independent on Sunday was up for sale. On Saturday April 27th I was telephoned by Brian Macarthur of the Sunday Times who had heard the story. Though by this time Stephen had told told me that he and Henry were up to something, I told Macarthur correctly that neither I nor the board of Newspaper Publishing was trying to sell the paper.

When I learnt that Matthew was offering the crude choice of integration versus closure, I was convinced that sale of the title should become an official rather than a freelance alternative. By Tuesday April 30th, the day on which rumours of Matthew's meeting began to circulate around City Road, Stephen and Henry had told me what they had done. It was not very much. Alistair McAlpine had put out a line to the Barclay brothers, mysterious and fabulously rich twins residing in

Monte Carlo. Stephen admitted that progress was not very promising. The plan needed time if it were to have any chance of success.

I introduced the notion of a possible sale to the executive directors in a long memorandum that Tuesday. It began with a critique of integration or 'seven-day working'.

> I believe that our present assumptions about seven-day working are flawed and unrealistic. A good Sunday newspaper and a good daily newspaper cannot be produced with the number of people now being contemplated.
>
> A target of 40 redundancies, most of them on the Independent on Sunday, has been arbitrarily chosen. As editor of the Independent on Sunday, and knowing well the way the Independent works, I do not see how these reductions can be achieved ...
>
> It is not simply a question of numbers. Over the past year I have learnt how big is the gulf in the British quality newspaper market between daily and Sunday journalism. I suspect that most people on the daily have not fully grasped this. Sunday newspapers depend on specials, or dozens of little properties, to coin a phrase. In a Sunday newspaper there is no momentum of news. I do not see how an integrated paper, which inevitably works on a daily rhythm, can adapt itself sufficiently to a weekly one. The experience on the Sunday Telegraph was that it could not, and that paper has expensively and painfully reversed the process of integration.

The memorandum proposed the compromise figure of fifteen redundancies while retaining the two newspapers as they were, and then mentioned the possibility of a sale.

> We must therefore think more carefully about the idea of selling a share in the IoS. There are problems. How could one define profits and costs if the two titles were to continue to share overheads? What if the purchaser of a major stake in the IoS wished at some future date either to change or sell the newspaper? But there are advantages too.

1. The losses from the Sunday operation would be dramatically reduced, at a stroke.

2. Since closure is an option, it would remove the prospect of our having to meet closure costs. Newspaper Publishing plc would also be able to make a charge for shared services, many of which, in the event of closure, it would have to continue to make by itself.

3. The company, proportionate to its shareholding, would be able to make a return on its investment.

4. The stigma of closure would be avoided.

This memorandum was faxed to Andreas in Bogota. It drew no immediate response from him or the other executive directors. Two days later I had a testy lunch with Matthew and he bitterly attacked the idea of selling a share in the IoS.

'Our trademark is our most precious asset,' he said. 'You can't sell a piece of it.'

'Well, I see the point, and maybe it is difficult, but if integration is not possible, surely sale would be better than closure.'

'I would rather close the Independent on Sunday than sell it,' he said.

'I think you are mad,' I replied.

Many of the journalists on the Sunday paper were enthusiastic about the idea of a sale. They were very angry with the management not excluding me for, as was widely thought, having spirited up a crisis. They believed, and had been told many times, that they were producing an excellent newspaper and were incredulous to hear that, at least in the view of Matthew Symonds, it suddenly faced closure or integration – and, in either event, the loss of many jobs. When I addressed them on the afternoon of Thursday May 2nd I emphasised that there were other options. One was to cut costs by different means, which was the choice I favoured. The other was to sell a share in the title.

Stephen and Henry were meanwhile barely containable. Henry wanted to fly off to New York where he had arranged meetings with several financiers. Even at this stage I was reluctant to let him go, at company expense and in company time, without the knowledge of the chief executive.

On Wednesday I had encouraged Stephen Fay and his editorial colleagues to send Andreas a fax requesting time to explore the idea of a sale or buyout. On Thursday afternoon Andreas rang me from Bogota. I explained that feelings were running very high as the result of Matthew's meeting. I told him that I believed that the question of a sale should be looked at. He replied that 'We should be prepared to look at any alternative.' He then asked me to put Stephen Fay on the line. While they spoke I left my office. After three minutes Stephen emerged. 'He's given us the go-ahead,' he said.

Other colleagues were as keen to look for a buyer as Stephen and Henry, the latter of whom now took to the skies for New York. Ian was enthusiastic. So was Richard Williams. He knew Richard Branson and suggested that he and I should pay a visit to the tycoon.

Richard and I went to Branson's house in Holland Park, where twenty months previously negotiations had taken place with the Sunday Correspondent. I gave an account of the Independent on Sunday's financial position. Losses were running at well over £5 million a year. On the other hand, breakeven at the time of launch had been calculated at around 350,000, and in January 1991 we had sold an average of 406,000 copies. The losses were entirely due to the advertising recession. If circulation could be raised to nearer 500,000 through a combination of editorial improvements and promotion (of which there had been none since launch), the Independent on Sunday could be very profitable when advertising recovered.

Branson wrote down everything I said in a school notebook. He was polite but a little wary. He said he would get in touch shortly. The next morning he telephoned.

'Hi, Richard here. Just to say that the Sunday Times have been trying to dig up some information. We didn't tell them anything. Talk to you soon.'

He never did, though that evening, Thursday, I met one of his most senior lieutenants at a party to celebrate the launch of Lynn Barber's new book.

'Won't you buy the Independent on Sunday?' Lynn asked the senior lieutenant as though she were requesting an interview. He seemed to like the idea. 'We must persuade Richard to buy it,' he agreed.

At the same party I met Clement Freud.

'I have it on the highest authority', he told me, 'that if you look at the news stands the Sunday after next the Independent on Sunday *will not be there*. It's going to be closed.'

'How interesting.'

'Yup. I've been told by an unimpeachable source.'

We spoke for about five minutes in a meandering sort of way before he asked:

'And, what do you do?'

'Oh, I'm the editor of the Independent on Sunday . . .'

Mr Freud shuffled away.

The next day, Friday May 3rd, Richard Williams put his head around my door.

'Any news?' he asked.

'Not yet,' I replied.

'We must find a buyer,' he said. 'I'm sure we will. We must find one.'

Among the executive directors there was no enthusiasm for exploring the possibility of a sale. I spoke with Graham Luff and faxed a letter to Adrian, who was away on holiday. Their reaction was similar to Matthew's. I gathered that Matthew had been persuading Andreas, who was still in Bogota, that selling a stake in the Independent on Sunday was unthinkable. His argument about preserving the sacred franchise intact and unsullied was, I had to concede to myself, not unreasonable. So far as I was concerned, a sale was worth considering if the only other alternatives were integration and closure. My preference was still for making editorial improvements to the Independent on Sunday combined with judicious cost-cutting. I was sure that the Italians and Spanish would be eager to make a further investment if a convincing programme were put before them. I said this to Matthew when he came into my office on the afternoon of Friday 3rd. 'I don't want to be diluted again,' he replied, referring to the effect on his shareholding of another refinancing.

'I have something to tell you,' he went on, ' and I wanted you to know it first.' This was said in an almost friendly way.

'Uh-huh.'

'We've done a study of the possibility of integration and we've concluded that it's not possible. It would harm the daily too much.

'Have you told Andreas?'

'No, not yet. He's back on Sunday.'

'So what do you think we should do?'

'I don't think we have any alternative to closure.' The architect of integration no longer believed in his handiwork. His spirit seemed crushed.

I did not in my heart think that the board would favour closure, so it looked as though other options, ruled out by Matthew, would now have to be considered. But by that weekend it was becoming clear that it would take a long time to find a buyer, if one could be found at all. It was difficult to describe to prospective investors how the newspaper's finances could be disentangled from those of the Independent, with Newspaper Publishing plc remaining as a large minority shareholder. I had had breakfast with Alistair McAlpine and Stephen Fay, and there had been some far-fetched talk of French water companies wanting to invest. Henry's news from New York was not promising. Stephen had had initially encouraging talks with an 'investment boutique' which, in the end, had come to nothing. Richard Branson's senior lieutenant seemed to have gone awol.

On the morning of Monday May 6th, Andreas having returned from Bogota, Stephen and Henry and their senior colleagues arranged to meet him in the boardroom at City Road to discuss their proposal for selling a majority stake in the Independent on Sunday. Apart from Stephen and Henry, the delegation consisted of Ian Jack, Sebastian Faulks, Richard Williams, Christopher Huhne, Neal Ascherson, Brian Cathcart, Blake Morrison and Peter Wilby. I learnt later that Andreas told them that the original investors in the Independent had invested in *him*, implying that they would have their work cut out to find backers. He also said that new investors would want a new editor. The executive directors, including him, had arranged to

meet at midday at the Hotel Conrad in Chelsea Harbour to discuss the future of the Independent on Sunday, and Andreas
agreed that the delegation could come to the hotel in the afternoon to put its case.

We had been talking in the small windowless room for about
an hour when the delegation – shortly to be named the Chelsea
Ten – shambled in. It was a Bank Holiday, and most of them
seemed dressed for the beach or the golf course rather than a
business meeting. Neal Ascherson was unaccountably wearing a
pair of dark glasses, which made him look like a sinister tycoon.
Watching this gaggle enter the room, I felt like a parent at his
child's speech day: secretly proud but forced to concede that
appearances were not frightfully promising.

Stephen, however, made a powerful statement which
betrayed little of the belligerence I knew him to feel. He said
that there was common ground among all those present that the
Independent on Sunday was a fine newspaper. (Andreas nodded
vigorously.) It would only flourish if it continued to be separate. He believed, and the delegation believed, that there were
strong commercial and journalistic reasons for seeking an outside investor either to take a stake in Newspaper Publishing or
to form a new company which would publish the Sunday newspaper. In this latter case, Newspaper Publishing might retain a
20 per cent interest in the company. The losses would stop at
once, there would be no redundancies and, unencumbered by
the Sunday newspaper, the daily would soon move into profit.
There were many dangers in the alternative plan of integration.
It might place insupportable burdens on the Independent which
was having circulation problems.* The savings in editorial costs
on the Sunday paper would almost inevitably lead to a decline in
quality. And there would be no prospect of increasing the circulation of the Independent on Sunday, which should be the
overriding aim. Less than 40 per cent of the daily's readers read
the IoS which reflected the tendency of British newspaper
readers to take a different sort of paper on Sunday. Making the
two newspapers more alike would not increase, and might

---

* In April the Independent had sold an average of 385,000 copies and the
Independent on Sunday an average of 377,000.

diminish, the circulation of the Independent on Sunday. What was needed now was *time*. Conversations in Paris, London and New York had suggested that there was keen interest in an established national newspaper, but it was impossible to take such complicated matters very far, let alone conclude them, in a matter of days.

When he had finished, Andreas looked for support to Matthew who, it quickly became apparent, had changed his mind again about integration. (The explanation was this: on learning of Matthew's conclusions when he returned to London, Andreas had told him to think again.) Now Matthew was again a supporter of integration, albeit a more cautious one, while retaining all his former antagonism towards the idea of a sale. He had a spat with Henry.

'Can you tell us', he asked Henry, 'what the internal rate of return of your new Sunday newspaper will be?'

'Don't answer that question, Henry,' advised Stephen wisely.

After Graham Luff had asked a couple of suitably aggressive questions, and Steve Conaway had made some sympathetic noises, Andreas delivered his judgment.

'I think my view is this. The Independent is our most important asset and I do not see how part of that precious asset can be sold to an outside party. What if they changed the newspaper in a way we did not approve of? The more I think about it the more I see the very real advantages in integration. The Independent on Sunday is a very ... *accomplished* newspaper but I think that the Independent has certain strengths which could be of a positive benefit to the Sunday newspaper. I've always believed in integration, so has Matthew, and I didn't agree with Stephen's way of setting up the newspaper at the beginning. Now because of the economic climate we are having to look at it again and I must say that I think there will be very real benefits to both titles in sharing resources in this way.'

He was asked what had happened to the grandiose plans for expansion which had been discussed with him just over two weeks before. He replied that he still believed in the beneficial effects of promotion and of 'properties', and hoped to see these go ahead if the two papers were integrated.

On this note, the Chelsea Ten were dismissed, though without being specifically told that they must desist from trying to find a buyer. It was clear to them that Andreas was now wholly opposed to a sale, as were Matthew, Graham Luff and Adrian, who was still sunning himself in the West Indies. Steve Conaway evidently believed that a sale was impractical, but he appeared unconvinced by the arguments in favour of integration. After the Chelsea Ten had gone, he argued that the savings from integration – a little more than £1 million a year – were very slight and could probably be achieved in a different manner. He said that he had always been the keenest supporter of cost-cutting but he could not see that it was worth running the sort of risks which had been described for the kind of savings they offered.

As the afternoon wore on I repeated the arguments which I had used before. There was now a further point, which was that Matthew and his team had looked at integration and decided it would not work. As I mentioned this, Matthew started to shake his head. 'I'm not keen on it but it's the best alternative,' he said. 'Otherwise we will have to close the newspaper.' Andreas ignored the fact that Matthew had changed, or been made to change, his mind about the impracticalities of integration. Nor did he attempt to meet my arguments.

At about six o'clock Andreas asked two senior managers who had joined us to leave. This left the five directors: Andreas, Matthew, Graham, Steve and myself. Andreas announced that he had something very important to say.

'I have been thinking about my own position,' he said, 'and I have been wondering whether the time has not come for me to separate the two roles of chief executive and editor, and concentrate on editing. The two newspapers will need all the time I can give them now. Matthew, what do you think?'

Matthew replied that he did not think the time had come to split the jobs. He believed, I knew, that Andreas was inadequate both as a chief executive and as an editor, but he felt that his own powers would be diminished if Andreas devoted all his energies to editing. Steve, somewhat to my surprise, gave a similar reply, as did Graham. The time might come, they all said, but it was not now.

'Stephen, what do you think?' asked Andreas.

The answer was that I thought that it would be an excellent

idea for Andreas to give up being chief executive because he did not do the job very well. But it seemed to me that this was not the proximate issue, not the drama of the moment, and I simply said that it was worth considering sooner rather than later.

'I have an ambition,' said Andreas, 'that as this company progresses I will gradually demote myself bit by bit so that when the time comes for me to go I will simply slip away unnoticed.'

I suspected that Andreas was preoccupied with his own role as a result of Juan Luis Cebrian of El Pais raising the matter in Bogota. So far as my own position was concerned, Andreas made no reference to the fact that ten days previously he had told me that my job was to disappear. It was that meeting, I now see, which had made us for ever irreconcilable.

*

The visit of the Chelsea Ten was a watershed. Faced with such opposition, not to mention the absence of a palpable buyer, some of the Chelsea Ten began to have second thoughts. This was not immediately obvious. The next day, Tuesday 7th, they sent a letter by fax to all non-executive directors asking for time to explore the possibility of a sale. Ian went with Stephen to see a high-powered merchant banker at Lazards. But the life of the Chelsea Ten was not a long one.

They had already attracted one enemy in the shape of Lynn Barber. Before setting off for Chelsea, they had met in my office, observed by Lynn who was writing up an interview. For some reason they did not ask her to join them. They were not going to be the Chelsea Eleven. Lynn bitterly resented this exclusion, and went around the building mocking the pretensions of 'the Chelsea Men'.

On Tuesday I tried to soothe her in my office. Of course they should have asked her. Of course they were male chauvinist pigs. But this was a time for looking at the bigger cause, which was the preservation of the Independent on Sunday.

'Oh, I don't know,' said Lynn. 'I've had enough, I really have. I'm so fed up. I don't think I care what happens to the paper.'

'But Lynn! Look what has happened to you since you joined it. You are a star! Whatever you may feel about some of your colleagues, surely you feel something for the paper?'

'I just hate Stephen Fay so much. I don't mind Henry so much . . . And I think you have made lots of mistakes.' By this I took her principally to mean my friendship with Stephen.

The following day, Wednesday, Ian came into my office. This was perfectly normal. We had been speaking once or twice a day in our usual friendly way since he had come back from his sabbatical. On this occasion he looked more worried even than was customary. He spoke a little deprecatingly of Stephen and Henry, and said that they were in danger of alienating some of their colleagues by their sell-or-bust approach. Then he said out of the blue: 'Stephen, you haven't by any chance thought of falling on your sword?' I hooted with laughter at this, thinking that he was joking. His appearance told me that he was not. I replied that I would gladly fall on my sword if it would do any good, but I couldn't see that it would.

Blake Morrison came to see me the same afternoon. He said that he was very worried about the way things were going. He asked me what I was going to do. I said that I would continue to oppose integration, but that a sale seemed increasingly unlikely, especially given the lack of time. I would argue for a combination of cuts and expansion. There was a special board meeting in one week's time and Andreas would try to make the directors come to some conclusion. Blake asked me what I would do if the board voted in favour of integration. I said that if that happened I would resign and anyway there would not be a job for me. Blake said that in such a case Ian would be someone around whom he and others could rally.

The next day, Thursday, seemed strangely normal. As the weekend approached, we naturally spent most of our time trying to produce the best possible issue for Sunday. That evening there was a meeting of some of the executive directors to discuss how redundancies might be handled. I was a spectator at these proceedings, for I didn't accept the premise, i.e. integration, on which the redundancies would be based. At the end of the meeting, Andreas asked me in an almost cheery way whether I could spare him a minute. We walked together from the boardroom to the lift, descended from the ninth to the first floor, went together into his office and sat down.

Andreas was not cheery now. He had gone a kind of chalky

white which, to an expert in the changing hues of his face, indicated great trepidation. He would not look me in the eye. Something strange seemed to have happened to his face. It had lost all mobility.

'I have come to a decision,' he said, speaking with great difficulty. 'I have decided that next week, next Monday, I am going to take over the editing of the Independent on Sunday.' Still he would not look at me. His face was a kind of mask. It was as though it were set in mud and he dared not move a muscle for fear of cracking the cast.

'Some of your colleagues have been to see me,' he went on, 'and they have asked me to come up and to take over – maybe just for a while. I must have a look at how the Independent on Sunday operates. I would like you to take a holiday for three weeks. You may come back to edit the Sunday paper again or you may come back to do something else.' He then repeated what he had said a few days previously about expecting to be demoted himself the longer he remained in the company.

'I find it very difficult to believe,' I said, 'that any of my colleagues have asked you to replace me. Can I ask you who they are?'

'I am afraid I cannot tell you that, for obvious reasons.'

'I see. Well, you are the chief executive and I suppose that if you want to take over the editorship of the Independent on Sunday I cannot stop you. But if that is what you do, of course I will not return.' I felt momentarily borne down and weakened by the suggestion of betrayal by my colleagues on the IoS. I could not believe that any of them would have gone to Andreas in the manner he described, yet here he was asserting it with total confidence.

The next morning, Friday, I told Stephen, Henry and Alexander Chancellor what had happened. They did not know who had spoken to Andreas, though Stephen seemed to think that Ian and maybe Richard Williams had been to see him. They also thought that I should refuse to stand down. Henry was especially adamant.

This line of thinking was developed over a jolly lunch. Alexander, who had threatened in a memorandum to Andreas that he would resign as editor of the Independent Magazine if I left the company, took Andreas's behaviour as a sign that he was no longer wanted. 'Now, Alexander,' said Henry sternly. 'This is not your drama.' Alexander then appointed himself as my 'campaign manager'.

The theory we produced ran as follows. Andreas could not dismiss or replace me because I had been appointed by the board. (This was not strictly true. I had been foisted on the board by Andreas and Matthew and the other executive directors, but on the other hand the board would like the idea that it had appointed me.) We all believed that in trying to get rid of me before the special board meeting on the following Wednesday, Andreas was trying to pre-empt the argument about integration. If I had already been removed as editor, my *locus standi* in arguing against integration would be weakened. If the board meeting were to be the occasion for an onslaught on the notion of integration, I would have to call Andreas's bluff now. On my return to City Road I arranged a meeting with Andreas for that evening.

During the afternoon, Ian came into my office, and sat down. There seemed no particular purpose to his visit. He seemed merely to want to chat, or perhaps just to be there.

'Ian, can I ask you a question . . . I had a strange session with Andreas last night. He said that he was going to come up and take over the editorship of the Independent on Sunday. He told me that some of my colleagues had asked him to do that. I know that you and Richard may have seen Andreas yesterday, but I can't believe you could have said what he reported. Perhaps it was someone else.'

Ian had turned a chalky white which would have done credit to Andreas Whittam Smith's complexion. He told me that he and Richard and Blake Morrison had indeed been to see Andreas because they had felt that the attempt to sell the Independent on Sunday had got out of hand and they wanted to tell him that they admired the Independent and that they hoped that the rift between the two papers would not last for ever. Then, as they were about to leave, Andreas had asked whether it would help at all were he to be seen more on the Independent on Sunday's floor, and they had replied, yes, naturally it would.

'I see,' I said.

'You think that I've betrayed you, don't you Stephen?'

'No, I don't think that. But I don't think that going to see him was very wise.' I could not believe that Ian or his colleagues had told Andreas what he had reported to me.

'God, I feel sick,' said Ian, and I did think for a crazy moment that he was going to be sick. He got up and almost ran out of my room. He seemed nearly to be crying.

A couple of hours later Andreas came up to my office. I asked him to postpone his takeover of the Sunday newspaper until after the board meeting. He wanted to know why. I said merely that this seemed to be the constitutionally correct thing to do. His face had the look of a man trying to remember the capital of Outer Mongolia. He sensed that there was more to my resistance than met the eye but could not quite fathom what it was. 'I *think* I agree,' he said, 'but I will have to think a little bit about it, if I may.'

My approach had been mild and enigmatic. Now, my ends almost achieved, I could not hide my true feelings.

'Just one more thing, Andreas. I remain perplexed by your account of my colleagues visiting you. I have spoken with Ian Jack, and he tells me that he and Richard Williams and Blake Morrison went to see you yesterday afternoon merely to say that they hoped that present difficulties would not leave an unbridgeable rift. They say that when they were leaving, you asked whether it would help if you were seen up here on the third floor and they naturally said yes. And I believe them.'

'I see no profit in talking about this,' said Andreas, his face turning a dangerous shade of purple.

'You may see no profit in it, but for me this is the most incredibly important thing. The betrayal of friends is the most incredibly important thing.'

Andreas rose from his seat. He glided across my office. When he got to the door he turned and said, 'We had better continue this some other time.'

*

The next morning when I came into my office I saw an envelope lying in the middle of my desk. Inside was a hand-written letter from Andreas.

To Stephen Glover Esq.,

Friday 10 May 1991

Dear Stephen,

I write to say that I intend to take over the editing of the Independent on Sunday with effect from 10.30 am on Tuesday next, 14 May. The non-executive directors have been informed. May I suggest that you tell your staff about this change tomorrow (Saturday).

As you know, I hope you will remain as a director of the company and find a new role.

Yours sincerely

Andreas Whittam Smith.

The fact that the letter was hand-written suggested that it was composed in a rush, after Andreas's secretaries had gone home. As he mused about our row, the blood must have rushed to his head.

During the morning, while trying to edit the newspaper, I telephoned Bruce Fireman, Ian Hay Davison and George Duncan. They all confirmed that they had spoken with Andreas, but it appeared that he had given each of them the impression that he was merely coming up to take temporary charge of a newspaper which was getting out of hand. I told the non-executives that we were about to produce a creditable issue, but if there were a sense of confusion on the paper it was entirely the consequence of onslaughts made by Andreas and Matthew. Moreover, Andreas's letter did not propose a temporary takeover. He was in effect trying to sack me, which was something only the board could do. On hearing my version of events, Bruce announced that he had changed his mind and would tell Andreas that he should not attempt to take over before the board meeting. The other two were more circumspect, but I got the impression that they would advise Andreas against his planned coup.

There was an oddly sweet moment as I said goodbye to Ian Hay Davison. Here was a man who over the years could have won a diploma in getting people's names wrong. He had decided that my name was Simon. He had re-christened Adrian

O'Neill as Andrew. Some demon within me must have felt that there was an old score to settle, for as I put down the receiver I found myself saying, 'Goodbye, George.'

Later on in the day a director called to see me. I showed him Andreas's letter. He grinned as though he were a detective presented with an utterly predictable piece of evidence. He told me that some weeks previously Andreas and Matthew had had the idea that Matthew should take over as editor of the Independent on Sunday. Believing this would be a calamity, he had tactfully managed to oppose this idea by suggesting that Matthew was needed too much on the daily. Only then had Andreas and Matthew embraced the idea of integration which they had previously rejected. He said that he was astonished that I was 'still there' after several weeks of sustained assault. My memoranda had simply disappeared into the ether.

'This has got nothing to do with the pros and cons of integration,' he said. 'Integration has nothing really to do with saving costs.'

'I know,' I replied.

He said that he believed that the company was heading for certain disaster. Andreas lacked twenty years' experience as a chief executive.

I asked him whether I could rely on his support at Wednesday's board meeting.

'I'm only a hired hand in this company,' he replied. 'I don't mind pointing out that integration will produce few savings and carries many risks, but I can't go much further than that. Otherwise my head will be on the block the next day.'

I did not hide Andreas's letter from my colleagues. Every time someone came into my office to ask a question – did I prefer this or that photograph; had I read such-and-such an article? – I produced this wondrous letter. Most were as cross as they were amazed. Mike Stent and Henry suggested that I address the staff after the first edition was finished and tell them what had happened. At about seven o'clock we gathered at one end of the newsroom.

I told them that Andreas Whittam Smith had left me a letter saying that he proposed to take over on Tuesday morning at 10 o'clock.

'You can imagine my feelings of shock and bewilderment on receiving this letter from a man with whom I helped found the Independent five years ago. In the first place, no one has suggested that the Independent on Sunday is anything else but an editorial success. Even Andreas Whittam Smith said when he was up here earlier in the week that we were '95 per cent there'.*
In the second place, I do not believe that he has the authority to dismiss me in this manner. I was appointed by the board of Newspaper Publishing and only the board can get rid of me. There is a board meeting on Wednesday and I want to use that occasion to set out the arguments against integration. My fear is that he is trying to pre-empt that meeting, and I do not propose to let him. Whatever happens then, I am sure that there will *not* be a decision to close this newspaper. That is a threat whose purpose is to shock us into accepting integration and redundancies. On Tuesday morning I will be here at 10 o'clock in my editor's chair and I will not vacate it if Andreas Whittam Smith comes up. But I would find it difficult to behave in such a way if I did not believe that I had the support of all my colleagues.'
Whereupon several people said that I had their support. There were various expressions of astonishment at Andreas's behaviour. The meeting then broke up.

Someone suggested that a petition be delivered to Andreas's house, and Henry and others set about organising it. According to a subsequent account by Henry, he and Ian and Peter Wilby went into Ian's office to agree a text. Ian sat by the keyboard and did the typing. Richard Williams kept on popping into the room. He said he would be unable to sign the letter without certain amendments. These were all agreed. They had the effect, says Henry, of slightly watering down the force of the letter.

Andreas Whittam Smith, Esq
31, Brunswick Gardens
London W8

12 May 1991
Dear Mr Whittam Smith

    We do urge you to withdraw your proposal to replace

* Andreas had paid a rare visit to address the IoS staff on the afternoon of Tuesday 7th to explain his opposition to a sale. He had heaped praise on the paper.

Stephen Glover as editor of this newspaper on Tuesday. Stephen says he intends to edit the paper on that day and, unless the board decides otherwise, he has our support.

Stephen deserves this courtesy and loyalty from us and you.

Yours sincerely
(Signatures attached)

By the following morning, Sunday 12th, ninety-one Independent on Sunday staff had signed this letter, including Richard. Four journalists declined to sign. Just before Henry took the letter around to Andreas's house he received a telephone call from Richard who, to Henry's fury, announced that he wanted his signature to be removed.

On Tuesday morning it was difficult to find room even to perch in my office. Anyone who had the remotest cause to attend the weekly 'post-mortem' meeting squeezed in for a ringside seat. Alexander was present in his role as my campaign manager. We all half hoped that Andreas would come along, though I did not greatly look forward to tussling with him over the editorial chair. He did not show up.

Later that day Richard came into my office.

'I just wanted to explain', he said, 'why I did not sign the letter to Andreas. I felt that I had sent him a signal last week and that it would be inconsistent of me then to sign the letter.'

'Thank you for telling me,' I replied.

11

Tears and Farewell

The board meeting was twenty-four hours away. The last few days had been so much a fight for survival that I had spent little time thinking of what I should say. I had not spoken to the non-executive directors save to secure their support against Andreas's proposed coup.

On the morning of Tuesday 14th I had breakfast with Bruce Fireman. He agreed that integration was a bad idea, principally because of the strain it would place on the daily newspaper, but he perversely favoured a new alternative. This was the merging of the Independent on Sunday with the Saturday edition of the Independent to create a kind of bumper weekend newspaper. Alexander Chancellor – my campaign manager – had introduced this notion in a letter which he had sent to all non-executive directors. He wrote that he would prefer the continuation of the status quo but, if that were not possible, he could imagine a weekend edition with me as editor. This idea had caught Bruce's fancy.

I had lunch with my old friend Christopher Huhne and we discussed the wildly varying figures which were being produced by Graham Luff. Between May 3rd and May 13th the envisaged losses under integration had improved by about £8 million in a full year. This was a consequence of more optimistic assumptions about advertising. Christopher remarked that it was one of the most fruitful ten days which Newspaper Publishing had ever spent.

Integration, which had formerly been presented as the least loss-making alternative other than closure, but loss-making none the less, now offered the possibility of future profits. But if integration offered rosier financial prospects, so did the other alternatives which benefited equally from more hopeful advertising projections.

After lunch I went to see George Duncan. I had decided that a visit to Ian Hay Davison would be a waste of each other's time. As I drove drove along the Euston Road, my car telephone rang. It was Bruce.

'What's all this about a letter being sent by your staff to Andreas?'

I explained what had happened. I had not told him at breakfast, fearing exactly this sort of outburst.

'What the Hell do they think they're doing,' he exclaimed. 'It's our paper, not theirs.'

'Come on, Bruce, they have been feeling very upset at what they see as an assault on their newspaper and it was natural that they should want to jump to the defence of their editor. Anyway, you were against Andreas taking over, so why should you mind that the Independent on Sunday journalists agree with you?'

'Well, I think that it's quite out of order for them. We can't have journalists behaving in this way. It threatens the company. I shall have a word with Andreas.'

' I don't think that would be wise, Bruce. You see, the letter had its desired effect, and it might be rather embarrassing for Andreas if you went over it with him.'

'I still think it was out of order,' said Bruce. He seemed half-pacified.

George Duncan was chairman of an industrial company called ASW Holdings plc which has its head office in Sloane Street. Somewhere in the remaining industrial heartlands of the country the workers of ASW Holdings plc were toiling away amid noise and dirt, but inside the company's headquarters you could hear only the gentle rumble of the traffic outside. There was a large boardroom and several offices, all deserted, and there was George Duncan and a secretary who answered the telephone and interrogated you as you came in.

George listened with a kind of doctorly sympathy to my account of what had happened during the last four weeks. He expressed no outrage when I described how Andreas had tried to dismiss me. I explained that everyone who had investigated the practicalities of integration had concluded that it could not be made to work.

'Would you be prepared to work as Andreas's deputy?' he asked.

'No,' I replied, feeling that he was not really taking the point. He was due to chair the board meeting the next day in the absence of Marcus Sieff through illness, and I told him that I would want to speak for some time. I added that I would appreciate it if this could happen early in the proceedings and not, as some might intend, as a sort of coda. He said that this would not be a problem, and I left.

During the morning I had sent a 2,000-word letter to all executive and non-executive directors. I had dropped the notion that the paper might be sold. Particularly for the sake of our foreign directors, I dwelt on the peculiarities of the British Sunday newspaper market, and the failure of the Daily and the Sunday Telegraph to integrate successfully.

The difference between the British Sunday and the daily market is mirrored in the difference in readership between Newspaper Publishing's two titles. The Independent on Sunday has a total readership of 1,274,000 according to the last national readership survey. This compares with a readership of 1,101,000 for the daily newspaper, Monday to Saturday. Despite the apparently similar totals, there is surprisingly little overlap. Only 42 per cent of the daily's readership reads the Sunday, and only 36 per cent of the Sunday's readership reads the daily. Only 458,000 read both.

Clearly there is scope for the company if cross-over can be improved through careful internal promotions such as three-part properties running in the Saturday, Sunday and Monday editions. This could easily be done while continuing to run the newspapers as at present. But there are immense dangers in an integrated operation which might alienate the two thirds of Sunday readers who have chosen not to read the daily. We have to accept that we have two newspapers which have a different character, a different appeal. They are two different interpretations of the same great idea of independence.

That evening Matthew Symonds drifted into my room. I had seen nothing of him for several days. I assumed that he supported Andreas's activities and we seemed to have nothing more to say to each other. A week before we had had an oddly convivial though purposeless drink at Corney and Barrow's in Moorgate. Matthew had been in a wild mood, and at one stage had said with a burst of laughter: 'Why don't we have a coup and get rid of Andreas'? 'Good idea,' I had replied. It had been a joke, hopeless yet touched by secret longing. He had repeated it as we walked back to City Road.

Now Matthew sat himself in my chair, put his legs on my desk and picked up a ruler which he periodically hit against his side. I mentioned an idea which I had discussed with Christopher Huhne, and suddenly it seemed that there might be an alternative to integration acceptable to everyone. Matthew became excited and picked up the telephone. 'Graham, have you got a moment? I'm with Stephen. We may be on to something.' After a few minutes Graham Luff came down. I asked Christopher to join us.

The executive directors, except myself and possibly Steve Conaway, were proposing to get rid of sixty jobs, thirty-five of them of journalists. (The figure had been reduced from forty.) Most of the editorial redundancies would be on the Independent on Sunday. All sixty redundancies would carry one-off costs but, once these had been incurred, there would be savings of nearly £2 million a year.* Andreas was going to propose at the board meeting that £2 million be spent in each of the next two years on promotion of the Sunday newspaper and some £500,000 a year on properties.

---

* In fact the annual savings of integration were estimated by Graham Luff in his report to the board the next day at £1.8 million a year. But twenty-five of the proposed sixty redundancies were non-editorial and therefore had nothing to do with the integration of the two papers. Taking £1.8 million rather than £2 million as the overall reduction in costs, integration offered savings of about £1.25 million in a year. Because of relatively high journalistic salaries, non-editorial redundancies offered fewer savings than editorial ones.

One could get to the same bottom line by a different route. If there were only 17 journalistic redundancies as opposed to 35, and other non-editorial redundancies were kept as planned, the saving would be £1.25 million rather than £2 million. The difference could be funded by reducing the spending on promotion to £1.25 million. That would still buy a lot of promotion. The original £2 million figure was arbitrary and uncosted.

There were two advantages in such a plan. In the first place, there would be fewer journalistic redundancies. The remaining ones could probably be carried out on a voluntary basis. In the second place, with seventeen redundancies – five on the daily and twelve on the Sunday – it would be possible to maintain the separateness of the two newspapers. There might however be a degree of 'co-operation' rather than integration. Matthew had ready a shopping list, to which I gave my agreement. There would be some 'exchange of writing resources' – i.e. Peter Jenkins and others would be encouraged to write for the Sunday paper. (Actually they already had been.) Andreas would be given the title of editor-in-chief and attend a weekly meeting on the Independent on Sunday. There would be joint planning of 'properties'. The sports departments of the two newspapers would be integrated. And the salaries of journalists on both papers would be 'aligned'. This was an old grouse of Matthew's and others on the daily paper.

Graham Luff gave the impression that he might support such a compromise. 'Yes, Stephen, I think it might very well work. I'm warming to it. Definitely warming.' Matthew left, followed by Graham, and I chatted on with Christopher. After about twenty minutes my telephone rang. It was Matthew, speaking from his car.

'I'm prepared to support the compromise we discussed, and recommend it to Andreas, on one condition.'

'And what is that?'

'That you sack Francis Wheen.'

Sack Francis Wheen . . . I had no intention of sacking Francis, but I did not want to ruin the deal by expressing amazement and outrage to Matthew now.

'Well, why don't we leave that, Matthew, until this is all sorted out.'

'All right, then.'

I left City Road to go to the Hilton Hotel in Park Lane, where I was supposed to meet Juan Luis Cebrian who was flying in from Madrid. He was not there, and after waiting half an hour I returned home. About 11 o'clock he rang me. His 'plane had been delayed and there had been no room at the Park Lane Hilton, so he had fetched up at the newly opened Langham Hilton in Portland Place instead.

It was midnight when I got there. Cebrian was eating a sandwich and drinking an orange juice. He looked as though he had walked all the way between the two Hiltons and possibly been mugged a couple of times along the way. I judged that he had not read my letter, so I covered old territory before referring to the new compromise. He wrote down everything I said in a small notebook without giving me the impression that he really knew what I was talking about.

I had arranged to meet Carlo Caracciolo early the following morning, Wednesday, at the Berkeley Hotel. Before I left home Matthew telephoned.

'I've spent half an hour speaking with Andreas,' he said, 'and he's keen to talk to you. I've arranged for you to meet him in his office at 10.30.' The board meeting was due to begin at 12 o'clock.

After a session with Carlo, at which he was polite and non-committal, I arrived at City Road and went up to Andreas's office. It was the first time I had seen him since he had walked out of my office the previous Friday. He had the look of a man trying to make friends with a dog who has not long since bitten him.

I went through the list of proposals I had agreed with Matthew, reflecting that they offered Andreas much more than he could have dreamt of having a month before. For once, he showed a detailed interest in what I was saying. 'I see, a meeting once a week. Would that take place in your room?' Or: 'Yes, the difference in salaries has always been a worry.' I got the sense after a while that he was speaking as though he were in a kind of daze. His mind was not with me but he seemed strangely reluctant, now that he had got me there, to let me go. At about half past eleven I began to feel an inner panic. It was not that I had anything specific to do before the board meeting, but I felt that if Andreas wanted me so badly to stay I should probably be elsewhere. At a quarter to twelve I managed to get away. He had not said that he agreed or disagreed with the compromise which I had put forward. I felt that in some curious way I had weakened myself by spending so much time with my opponent on the eve of battle.

Before going up to the boardroom, I went into my office. Lying on my desk was an envelope. Inside was a note from Alexander.

To: Stephen Glover

From: Your campaign manager

Date: 15 May 1991

Do not under any circumstances resign today.

This was perhaps not *exactly* the letter which one would have ideally hoped to receive from one's campaign manager at this moment, carrying as it did the fairly strong suggestion that the impending battle might be lost. Alexander had provided me more usefully the previous day with 'Notes for Boardroom Speech'. Its main themes were that the Independent on Sunday was an editorial success and that the crisis, which resembled that which had hit the Independent after its launch, was purely a financial one.

The atmosphere in the boardroom was that of the early stages of a rather sticky cocktail party. Everyone was standing around trying to think of something to say. Carlo and Cebrian were shaking the hands of their English colleagues. George Duncan was looking at his watch. By 12 o'clock we were all sitting down.

Andreas had taken his usual position at one end of the long table. Graham Luff sat on his left. Halfway along, on the same side, sat George Duncan with his back to the City, which view John Major had found so unappealing eight weeks before. I sat opposite George, with Matthew several places to my right.

'We find ourselves in a position', said Graham Luff, who had been put in to bat first by Andreas, 'when we are faced with a financial problem on the Independent on Sunday. The executive directors have met and they have come up with a number of different alternatives which are set out in the board papers which you will have received. I'll just run over the alternatives. Firstly, maintaining the status quo of two titles, as at present. Second, integration of the two newspapers into a seven-day operation with redundancies and investment in both titles. Third, closure of the Sunday paper and investment in the daily. Since the board papers went out there has been a further evaluation of three more options.'

Sheaves of papers covered with financial figures were now circulated around the table. They showed the profit and loss for Alexander's bumper weekend newspaper; for a crazed programme of investment on both newspapers without any reductions in costs; and for something close to the compromise which we had discussed the previous evening in my room, only financially less favourable.

The figures for integration were the most promising, apart from those for closure. But there the one-off costs were formidable. Even under integration, the company would have to seek further finance to pay for redundancy costs and short-term operating losses. Graham told the board that he had been in discussion with the banks for a further £9 million medium-term debt and a £6 million overdraft.

'These figures are cooked,' said Steve Conaway in my ear. He was right. The bottom line for the compromise we had discussed should have been the same as that for integration. That was the whole point of it.

Andreas then spoke in his low-key way. He said that he was thoroughly in favour of integration for more than financial reasons. He believed that it would offer a positive improvement to both newspapers. The strength of the daily title would buoy up the Sunday. Whereupon he passed around a little diagram which purported to show how the two integrated newspapers might work together. At the top of a sort of family tree was a little box in which were the initials AWS, MS, SG. This was connected by dotted lines with lots of other little boxes. I had already seen this piece of paper. Several days before, a version of it had been discovered by an Independent on Sunday journalist and stuck up on our coffee machine (with my initials thoughtfully crossed out); Andreas had produced a copy during our meeting that morning. Though the diagram shed absolutely no light on whether integration could or could not work, its boxes and dotted lines offered a bogus plausibility. The board now studied it in the kind of hushed silence that is reserved for obscure texts of sacred importance.

I had my own piece of paper which showed how the compromise gave the same savings as integration, and when my time came to speak I passed this around. I said that I completely accepted the need for cost reductions and redundancies, but by a different route. I argued against full-scale integration, citing again the precedent of the Telegraph, and said that as planned, with 35 journalistic redundancies, it would place an insupportable strain on resources. I then put forward the compromise, the essence of which was that by spending less money on promotion it would be possible to halve the number of journalistic redundancies. I paid an extravagant compliment to Andreas, and said that he would be able to help the Independent on Sunday greatly. I added that the compromise would allow my senior colleagues on the Independent on Sunday, the people who had made the newspaper into what it was, to build it into a bigger success. I felt, as I spoke, that my voice had risen as though I were addressing a large crowd of people rather than eleven men sitting within a few feet of me around a table.

When I stopped I looked over to Matthew. We had agreed that when I had finished speaking he would make clear his support for the compromise. This was the moment I needed him. He said nothing but stared down at his board papers.

Andreas had had several advantages in his battle with me. He had, within the board, the prestige of the chief executive and all the influence that flowed from being the progenitor of the Independent. And he had also enjoyed for many weeks the connivance of Matthew. He could not have achieved his ends alone, and if at this last hour Matthew had cried out in favour of the compromise which we had agreed then compromise there would have been. But Matthew said nothing. It was over.

Bruce broke the silence. 'I'm sorry, Stephen, but I have to say that I can't support your proposal. I believe that the Sunday paper needs the money which has been earmarked for promotion.'

'But that would still be over a million pounds a'year under my plan.'

'I don't believe that is enough in present circumstances.'

'I must say', said Ian Hay Davison, 'that I think that Stephen's idea is an absolute non-starter. But I'm not so sure that integration is the right idea either. I don't think we can afford it. I hate to say it, but I think that the option which is staring us in the face is to close the paper.'

The argument then swung around to closure, which I opposed with as much vigour as Andreas or Matthew. Hay Davison was the only director who positively favoured it, though Bruce seemed to be leaning in that direction. I was the only director to come out against integration, though Steve Conaway popped his head above the parapet for a moment. 'I'm not sure', he said, 'whether the risks of integration justify the savings.'

'I should make clear', I said, 'that if integration goes ahead I do not see how there will be a role for me in the company.'

'Well, I'm sorry,' said Hay Davison, 'but I was on a board once where one of the directors threatened to leave and he was listened to, wrongly, and the whole thing turned out a mess. It's sad if you go but if we can't alter our policy, and if that's what you want to do, well, so be it.'

Bruce was more reasonable. 'I very much hope that Stephen does not go. He has done an excellent job on the Independent on Sunday and I think the company needs him. But senior executives must expect to be re-assigned from time to time.'

George Duncan then asked whether it was the mood of the board that integration of the two newspapers should go ahead. By nods and grunts everyone gave his assent except Hay Davison and me.

'In that case,' I said, 'and I would like every word of this minuted, I want to set down my fear, my expectation, that integration will not succeed, that it will probably lead to closure of the Independent on Sunday and more financial problems for the company and it will harm the daily paper a great deal.'

George looked pained. This sort of thing was not supposed to be said at board meetings. 'Well, if that is what you want to be said ... I'm sure you can have a word with Keith later if you would like the minute to be withdrawn ... I would just like to say, and I am sure that I am speaking for the whole board, that we all very much hope that in the cool light of day Stephen will decide to stay on. I'm sure that there is still an important role for him to play.'

'Hear, hear,' said Bruce.

I left the boardroom and walked down the six flights of stairs to my office. It was lunchtime but there were quite a lot of people on the Independent on Sunday floor. Some of them rushed up to me. 'What happened, what happened?' they asked. 'No good, I am afraid. We lost.' 'Oh, God, oh no.'

Journalists gathered around the door of my office and I made a short speech. I told them what had happened and how desperately sorry I was. A couple of people were crying, and I could have gladly wept myself. As I was speaking, a telephone rang nearby which Kirstie answered.

'It's Matthew,' she said. People tittered.

'Tell him I'm addressing my staff and I will ring him later.'

She told him. 'Matthew says it's incredibly important and he only wants to speak to you for a moment.'

'Tell him that I will speak to him later.'

I finished my speech by saying that we had now to do our best to secure the best possible terms for the Independent on Sunday. That meant ensuring that redundancies were spread as evenly as possible between the two newspapers. Well over half the journalists on the Sunday newspaper would find themselves working under the new arrangements and we had better try to make them work.

Barbara Gunnell, a sub-editor, asked what I would do. I replied that I found it difficult to imagine how I could stay on. 'Don't do anything too hasty,' she advised.

Andreas had arranged a meeting for 3.30 at which he would address heads of department or their deputies. A press statement was released, a copy of which soon found its way to me.

PRESS STATEMENT

The Independent and the Independent on Sunday are to

integrate their main news departments. The exact structure and extent of integration will be worked out by the department heads of both newspapers in the coming weeks.

The board of Newspaper Publishing plc believes that there will be positive advantages for both newspapers above and beyond necessary cost-cutting in the face of continuing deep recession in advertising. There will be some job losses, but it is not possible to estimate the number until the precise formula for integration is settled.

Stephen Glover, the editor of the Independent on Sunday, will continue to edit during the transitional period and the board has asked him to play a key editorial role within the company.

A forward development programme for both newspapers has been approved, beginning with a significant increase in the editorial paging of the daily newspaper.

Andreas Whittam Smith
Editor

As statements to the press go, this was not one of the most accurate. The number of job losses had in fact been pretty accurately estimated at sixty. No one had asked me whether I wished to continue 'to edit during the transitional period'.* And the significant increase in editorial paging of the daily newspaper was to wait many months.

Throughout the afternoon many friends visited me. Alexander came and we discussed whether I would resign and whether he would. Andrew Gimson told me that he had decided to go. I urged him to hang on so that he could collect some money from redundancy. He said that he could not be bothered with that. A little later Francis Wheen pushed something into my hand. 'This is a copy of a letter which I have sent to Andreas,' he said.

---

* Matthew told me later that he had telephoned while I was speaking to my staff to tell me that he had persuaded Andreas that I should remain as editor during 'the transitional period'.

May 15th 1991

Dear Andreas

I am writing to let you know that I am resigning as diarist of the Independent on Sunday. I think that the treatment of Stephen over the last few weeks has been shabby, devious and dishonourable.

Yours ever
Francis (Wheen)

It was evening now and we were drinking champagne. Alexander took Francis's letter from me and told him not to be silly. Lynn Barber then tore it up. Francis merely wrote another one and sent it down to Andreas's office. Then Alexander, Francis, Andrew and myself squeezed into my car and went to our house and drank a lot more champagne. Alexander played the piano and Francis and Andrew sang hymns in a hearty way. 'Abide with Me', 'Oh God our help in ages past', 'Guide me O Thou Great Redeemer'.

After dinner, Francis would not stay the night. He needed to rise at 5 o'clock to get an early train to Oxford, near to which he lived. He knew, he said, a nice little Salvation Army Hostel near Paddington where he could lay his head.

*

During the next two weeks the cracks which were visible between IoS executives before the board meeting opened further. In some cases old friendships were broken, never to be repaired. Everyone was caught between loyalty to the old regime and adherence to the new one as represented by Andreas and Matthew. I encouraged no one to resign.

For most journalists staying on simply meant having a job, and implied no love for the new arrangements. They are the foot soldiers of journalism, the silent majority whose unsung labours create every newspaper, the ordinary hacks who regard every management, every editor even, with rightful suspicion. They had learnt, or they were in the process of learning, that a company founded by three journalists did not operate by different God-given laws, that like everything else it was part of the fallen world.

For a few executives it was a little different. If they stayed on they would have to co-operate and work hand-in-glove with their new masters. Richard Williams, it was clear, would stay and prosper. Even before his 'signal' to Andreas he had accepted an invitation to dinner at Matthew's house to discuss integration. After he had asked that his name be scratched out from the list of signatories there was no question where his heart lay. Michael Church, the arts editor, would remain if he could. Blake Morrison and Sue Matthias, a commissioning editor on the Review, would also stay. So, I guessed, would Neal Ascherson, though not an 'executive' in any formal sense. Neal had followed the events of the past few weeks with fluctuating interest. Occasionally he was overcome with bursts of passionate enthusiasm. When interviewing Prince Sadruddin Aga Khan, the United Nations High Commissioner for refugees, in Geneva, he was supposed to have asked the prince whether he would like to make a little investment in a Sunday newspaper.

Other heads of department were in a quandary. They had fought against what had happened but, now they had lost, they wondered with reason whether it made sense to give up their positions and their salaries in return for the quick fix of voluntary redundancy. In this camp were Peter Wilby, Brian Cathcart, who was foreign editor, Michael Spillard, picture editor, Simon O'Hagan, sports editor, and Christopher Huhne. To a great extent their decision depended on what they would be offered by the new regime. Lynn Barber was also undecided. She seemed still to wish a plague on everyone's house. Alexander could not resist trying to lure her to the magazine, while still threatening to resign himself.

Finally there were the diehards who did not want to work for the new regime. Francis Wheen did not return to the office after leaving his letter of resignation. He did not get any money for redundancy. Nor did Andrew Gimson, who, on the day after the board meeting, gave me a copy of a letter which he had sent to Andreas on Independent on Sunday writing paper.

Thursday 16 May 1991

Dear Andreas,

Because I have no faith in the plan you announced yesterday, and because I think that Stephen Glover has been very badly treated, I wish to resign from both the daily and the Sunday papers. Stephen has asked me to go on writing my column while he is still editing the Sunday, so I would propose to leave when he stops doing so. Perhaps you could let me know whether that would also be an acceptable time for me to stop writing leaders.

Thank you very much for the kindness you have shown me during my four years at the Independent, including two months' unpaid leave to write my first novel. I hope that my lack of faith in your plan will prove unjustified, and that the paper will go from strength to strength.

Yours sincerely,

Andrew

Andrew Gimson.

Mike Stent regarded everything that had happened over the past few weeks as a betrayal of the company he had joined as a sports sub-editor five years before. Michael McGuinness could not bear the thought of being put back in harness with Michael Crozier. Stephen Fay and Henry Porter, who had put themselves almost beyond the pale by attempting to sell the Independent on Sunday, even though they had initially received Andreas's approval, did not want to stay. Stephen had sunk into a gloom, and kept muttering 'What a waste, what a waste, what a bloody *cock-up!*' He had given a lot to the newspaper, and it owed much to him. He had hoped to devote the rest of his journalistic life to helping make it into a great newspaper, and he could scarcely credit that this was to be taken away from him for reasons which he regarded as venal or trivial. I guessed that he sometimes felt anger against me, that he partly saw (and he was not alone) the events of the past weeks as a meaningless struggle for power between three men, with the Independent on Sunday as the sacrificial lamb.

Sebastian Faulks also wanted to leave, but for him this was not a tragedy. I sensed in him something not far from relief, though touched by regret. The days of the Independent on Sunday's first dummy were long past. Since that creative outburst Sebastian had been very slowly withdrawing from the newspaper, occasionally nudged along the way, never resentful, always good-humoured, sometimes slightly bemused. His column was good, his jokes were good, his interviews were good, but in all that he did something was held back that would only be put into play when he came to do what he did best and loved most – the writing of novels.

Ian Jack waited. He had to wait because until I resigned he could not be offered my job, or at any rate what remained of it. Matthew had in fact asked him a couple of weeks earlier whether he would like to be executive editor but the offer was then suspended. During the week following the May 15th board meeting, Ian would sometimes come into my room and sit there disconsolately, as though waiting for some sign. 'He wants your benediction,' said Christopher Huhne. I could not give it.

I had decided to resign, though for a few days I found it difficult to write the letter. I wanted to go because you cannot embrace a thing which you have so opposed. I knew of course that if I stayed it would be possible over the months and years gradually to reverse the decision that had been taken. It would become clear even to the most zealous supporters of integration that not every aspect of their master plan worked. And when the economy recovered I could use my power as a director to recover more and more things which had been lost. Christopher Huhne urged me to adopt this course. So did Simon Carr who telephoned me from New Zealand. 'Hang on in there, Stevie,' he said. 'You can't give up everything you have done.'

But I could and I would. Nothing would have persuaded me to work again with Andreas Whittam Smith or Matthew Symonds. For a long time I had had little love for either of them. The last few weeks had been like a horrifying expedition during which all one's worst fears about former friends are confirmed. Notwithstanding my general unhappiness, and my regret that I had not successfully defended my colleagues' interests, I felt the liberating sense of relief that I would not have to spend any more of my life working with these two men. This feeling would be a boon in the months ahead.

I wanted the last couple of weeks of the old Independent on Sunday to be as much fun as possible. A group photograph of the editorial staff was arranged and a party at the Foreign Press Club was fixed for May 29th. On the morning of Saturday May 18th I wrote a 1,000-word leader for the following day's issue which, though it came from my heart, was at odds with the notion of political independence as it had been interpreted since the foundation of the company. It appeared under the headline 'A Nation Tired of Tories'.

Parties are stronger than governments. The Conservative party and the Labour party are great organisations which will survive the errors or short-comings of individual leaders. They draw their power from the people and they change only as the people change. Governments, by contrast, are merely collections of fallible human beings. They can suddenly fall apart, like other smaller institutions,* because their leaders lose their vision or their energy or their common sense. It is sometimes difficult for us to remember this, so high and mighty seems the edifice of the state behind which any government operates. But a government can be gone in a day ...

In many ways [the final paragraph read] Mr Major is not to blame. He assumed office after Thatcherism had degenerated into hubris and vanity. But the new model Tories seem to have no good ideas, and spend their time digging themselves out of the rubble of the past. It now seems likely that Mr Major will defer the general election for as long as possible in the hope that by this time next year the economy may have recovered enough to remind voters that the Tories are supposed to be the party of sounder economics. There may be last-minute tax cuts and pledges of extra government spend-

* such as Newspaper Publishing plc ...

ing, particularly on the health service. The end of it all may none the less be the same – that the nation has grown tired of these Tories and will, and should, vote Labour.

This leader was admittedly mischievous but it did reflect my idea of true independence. It was not Andreas's or Matthew's. For them independence means never saying that one political party is better than another, even if they believe that it is. I had committed a grave sin.

When I arrived at City Road on Tuesday 21st the directors were in a state of mourning. So was Peter Jenkins who seemed incapable of believing that such a leader could have been written, and written moreover by me. Adrian O'Neill had been moved to address his entire advertising staff. This was an aberration, he told them. Independence did not mean freedom of thought. It meant, as it always had and always would, that the Independent *and* the Independent on Sunday would never express any preference at any time for any political party.

On the afternoon of May 22nd I went to see Andreas in his office to inform him that I had decided to resign. When I told him a look of shock and pain passed over his face – the kind of look that expresses the soul's anguish at the unexpected news of a close friend's death. But he did not try to dissuade me.

'I am sorry. I suppose you may, not now, but some time, in six months' time, wonder whether you made the right decision. I know I would. Not now, but on some future occasion.'

'I don't think that I will ever regret it.'

'Maybe you won't. I know that I would . . . I wonder if there is some way of keeping up a relationship.'

'There is one way that I could keep half a foot in the company, which would be by becoming a non-executive director.' This was an idea that Alexander had raised over the past few days. 'I am not sure that I would want to be one, so this is not a proposal, it's just an idea.'

'Yes,' replied Andreas cautiously. 'I'll certainly think about it, Stephen.' He ran his forefinger over his lips. 'The other way would be a consultancy. We'll have to see what the non-execs think.'

'We can both think about it,' I said.

I got up to go. Andreas got up too.

'I have pinned your prophecy of doom above my desk and I shall look at it every day to remind myself,' he said.

'Well, it may not come true. It may not happen like that. I obviously hope that it doesn't.'

'I'm told that some people have been comparing me to Maxwell and to Northcliffe,' he said. 'I don't like the comparison with Maxwell, of course, but I don't mind being compared to Northcliffe. He was *by far* the greatest proprietor of all, I think. Don't you agree?'

'I'm not sure,' I replied, not wishing to bruise the delicacy of the occasion by pointing out that Northcliffe went mad.

★

Now Ian was free to accept the executive editorship. And yet when it came he seemed not to be sure that he wanted it after all. Even before I resigned he had been showing signs of indecision. He didn't think that integration was a good idea – indeed he profoundly believed that Sunday papers were a different species from daily ones. In so far as they could be made sense of, he did not like the proposals of Matthew and his colleagues, since they seemed bound to make the Independent on Sunday a mere seventh-day Independent, uncompetitive against its rivals. He asked me what I thought he should do. I replied that I could not advise him, but that if he took the job it would be a bed of nails.

'What will you do now?' Ian asked me.

'Oh, I don't know. Go on holiday. After that I'm not sure. Perhaps I'll write a book about the Independent.'

'You can buy yourself a country house. You could buy Killean.' He did not seem to be joking.

The next day I received a long letter from Richard Williams. It was an eloquent outpouring, an attempt to make sense of his recent behaviour and a kind of testament of broken love for the old Independent on Sunday. He wanted to 'put on record my gratitude for the opportunities you've offered me' both on the sports pages and the Sunday Review. The launch of the paper had been 'every bit as exhilarating' as he had hoped, and he had never for a moment regretted leaving The Times. However, 'you may feel, though, that in the past few weeks I haven't shown you as much personal support as you might feel you deserved. That's true, and it has occupied my thoughts constantly.' He wrote that he had always admired 'my quiet manner of leadership' but felt that the paper needed 'a change of – quite literally – direction'. He felt that the gap between the daily and the Sunday was too wide and it was for this reason – 'to rebuild the bridges' – that he had been to see Andreas and it was for this reason he felt unable to sign the letter. He also pointed out that he could not support the efforts of the Chelsea Ten because 'I came here to work for the company set up by you, Andreas and Matthew rather than some spatchcocked variant.'

In his estimation the two of us hadn't 'exactly been close, thanks to our differing temperaments and interests' nor, perhaps, had we seen the best of each other. But he believed that the paper had been a good one, given its inadequate resources which 'had been rendered almost farcical' by the worsening recession. He was 'desperately sorry' about the way the adventure looked like ending up. 'Last Thursday, when you concluded your (final?) weekly address, there was a moment of numb silence and stillness before the staff began to disperse back to their desks. People's minds were very full at that moment. I'll never forget it; I felt like weeping.'

On Friday May 24th I agreed with Andreas that I would remain until Saturday June 1st. I wanted to leave before then, but Peter Wilby persuaded me that I should stay until the chaotic negotiations concerning the exact form of integration had achieved some resolution. The same day I received a letter from Bruce Fireman. Two days previously I had written to all the non-executive directors explaining my decision to resign.

Fireman Rose Limited
39 Botolph Lane
London EC3R 8DE

23rd May 1991

Dear Stephen

I am not surprised but I am disappointed by your letter of yesterday. There is no good reason for you to resign. You have a future with Newspaper Publishing plc and as one of its most senior people, you must expect to be reassigned from time-to-time.

I know that your feelings about the job of being editor of the Independent on Sunday are different from mine. It is clearly in a different category from being foreign editor or home editor or editor of the magazine. Andreas has proposed a plan which kept you at the core of the company and would ensure that your talents were still deployed to the company's advantage.

Let me emphasise that no one wants you to leave the company. The situation is different from the situation of Chris Barton. You must therefore know my response to your suggestion.

Yours,

Bruce
(Bruce A. Fireman)

I replied to this four days later.

Dear Bruce,

Thank you for your letter. I am sure that I should be flattered by your remarks, but I fear that you ignore fundamental human realities.

I would still like to remain as a non-executive director, if that is what the board wishes, and I hope I can still look for your support in this matter.

Yours ever,
Stephen

*

A lot of people wanted to leave the Independent on Sunday, and a few the Independent, under the voluntary redundancy scheme now on offer. This was partly because they wanted nothing to do with the new arrangements, and partly because terms for redundancy were quite appealing. The minimum, for someone who had joined the Independent on Sunday at launch, was four and a half months' salary. For those who had worked previously on the Independent there was an entitlement of a further month's pay for every year of employment. A person who had joined the Independent before its launch and then transferred to the IoS could expect nine months' pay. One or two executives with six-month contracts did even better.

Others, though attracted by these terms, decided to stay. Peter Wilby was persuaded by Ian Jack to be his deputy. Christopher Huhne decided to remain as deputy business editor of both newspapers only to be promoted to business editor when the new appointee, Ian Griffiths, suddenly left for the Evening Standard. Brian Cathcart became assistant foreign editor (Sunday) and Michael Spillard deputy picture editor of the combined newspapers. Several other executives found bolt-holes in the new regime. Some of them may have thought, like me, that integration might not be for ever, and that one day they might be able to win back their autonomy.

So great was the voluntary exodus that only two or three people were asked to leave. One was Michael Church, who was savagely treated. Michael had heard that he was going to be removed as arts editor, and he came to me on the afternoon of Thursday May 30th to ask whether this was true. I replied that I did not know since I was not privy to the new arrangements. I suggested that he ask Andreas, who was. A couple of hours later Michael returned to my office with a beaming face. Andreas had said that there would be no major changes in the arts department, though in his view the arts pages could be improved in two or three respects. 'Well done,' I told Michael. 'I'm delighted.' But the next morning Michael saw Ian Jack and Richard Williams interviewing a candidate whom he guessed was intended to be his successor. He sought a meeting with Richard Williams that afternoon. It was suggested that he apply for voluntary redundancy.

Ed Steen was called in to see Andreas. Matthew was also there. They did not sack him. They said that everything he had done on the newspaper since he had joined the Independent five years previously had turned out in one way or another to be a *démarche*. He had survived so long only because of my protection. Perhaps they did not know or had simply forgotten that this man in long past days had helped me to set up the foreign desk on the Independent. Now they told him that he could stay if he wished, in a humble writing capacity, but if he did so he would, in Andreas's words, 'have to improve by 2,000 per cent' and 'would be starting from zero'. Ed took this as a hint that he was no longer wanted and left.

There was a lot of drinking that last week. On Wednesday 29th there was a party in the Foreign Press Club where, five years before, I had sat while Andreas answered questions about the Independent's planned foreign coverage. Now there were several speeches. James Fenton spoke in a way baffling to most people but touching to me about the old days of the Independent foreign desk and the division of the Far East into zones of influence. Stephen Fay said it was a pity we had not understood Andreas better. Henry Porter had written a long poem in rhyming couplets which, after apologies to the two real poets present, James and Blake Morrison, he declaimed:

> This paper then is one of seven heavens
> No Price, no Felton and please, no Bevins.
> But Beware
> Below stairs
> There are Men with drooping moustaches
> who want to kick our Sunday asses
> Men in the daily features areas
> certain of their powers superior . . .
> Men who under the seven-day banner
> have shown no style and an absence of manner
> Men (and women) who, in short, display
> Such total ignorance of our Sabbath day.

Then I said a few words. I wished the integrated Independent on Sunday well, and I hoped it would have the loyalty and dedication of its journalists as had the Independent on Sunday which I had edited. And I hoped too that the people who ran the company understood this loyalty and would return it.

'The Independent was originally a success because the people who started it – Andreas, Matthew and myself – believed in the journalists who joined them and trusted them. We knew who, under our direction, made the paper, but somewhere, with success, with whatever it was, that knowledge was lost. If it can be recovered then I believe in the future of our newspaper and this company.'

The May board meeting was due to take place on Friday 31st. I had decided that I would tell the board that I would like to remain associated with the company as a non-executive director. It is difficult to tear yourself away from something which you have helped to found, though the prospect of attending a monthly board meeting as little more than a spectator, forced to assume a degree of chumminess with Andreas and Matthew, was not enticing. I also knew that the office of a non-executive director did not carry much power or influence. But there was another argument.

Andreas and Matthew were not the company. People who run businesses are generally very adept at pretending that their interests and those of the company they serve are in every way the same. If they are attacked or criticised, that is represented as an assault on the company. But of course they are not the company, any more than the members of a government are the state, and I felt that there was something to which I could cling and remain loyal which was quite separate from them.

Andreas, having said that he hoped for some sort of continuing 'relationship', had come to the view that he did not want me to be a non-executive director. The day before the board meeting he told me that he felt 'neutral'. He said: 'I can see arguments either way and I can't honestly say that I feel strongly in favour.' I was beginning to feel that this was something worth having.

Matthew was very keen that I should become a non-executive director. I didn't believe that this feeling was motivated by guilt, since he plainly did not think that he had done anything to feel guilty about. He simply could not bear the idea of my leaving the company which I had founded with him. Because he still liked me, he wanted me sometimes to be there, and he even hoped that some day, though in not too elevated a capacity, I might work for the company again.

On the morning of the board meeting I received the following letter from Andreas Whittam Smith on Independent writing paper.

<u>Private & Confidential</u>

31 May 1991

Stephen Glover
The Independent on Sunday

Dear Stephen

I write to confirm our agreement concerning your terms for leaving the company.

We agreed that the company would pay you one year's salary and any pension rights, and that your car would be given to you.

In addition, I will recommend to the board that you should be released from any limitations on the disposal of our shares which were put in place at the time of conversion. We assumed that you would still be subject to the pre-emption agreement with La Repubblica and El Pais.

This is a sad moment. It is painful to discuss your severance terms but, however harsh your judgement may be of me and others who remain, you do have the satisfaction of knowing you were <u>a</u> founder of The Independent and <u>the</u> founder of The Independent on Sunday. When you read the two newspapers you will always see something you partly created.

Thank you for your wonderful contribution.
Best wishes.

Yours sincerely
Andreas
Andreas Whittam Smith

Andreas was late for the board meeting. So was Carlo Caracciolo. When Carlo arrived he moved with a grand flourish towards Andreas's usual chair at the head of the table and sat down in a proprietorial manner. Was this a vision of future things? Andreas arrived a minute later and was forced to sit on the right of Marcus Sieff. As he did so, he smiled shyly at me and, quite against my inclination, I felt for a moment something of my old affection for him streaming back.

The meeting was principally concerned with the re-financing

of the company. The dilution which Matthew had said he did not want was of course going to happen. Shareholders would be asked to subscribe £8 million of further capital; it was expected that La Repubblica and El Pais would stump up most, if not all, of this. In any event, they would each increase their shareholding above the 15 per cent limitation whose purpose had been to keep out dominant shareholders.* This limitation would have to be formally removed at an extraordinary general meeting of shareholders. A medium-term loan of £9 million would also be sought from three banks.

At the end of the board meeting I was asked to leave so that the directors could discuss whether or not I should be a non-executive director. I went down to my office. After about ten minutes Matthew tore in.

'It's all right, I've done it,' he exclaimed. 'They want you to be a non-executive director.'

'Good,' I replied. 'Thank you for your help.' And then I added: 'There are, I assume, no conditions.' The previous day I had told Matthew that although I wished to remain on the board I would not accept any conditions.

'Well, there are a couple of conditions,' he replied, 'but don't you dare pull out now after all I've done. I spent half an hour before the board meeting trying to persuade Marcus Sieff that you should stay on the board and I made a long speech when you left, saying that I wanted you to stay because I believed that you might one day play some executive role again in the company.'

'What did Andreas say?'

'Andreas didn't say anything. George Duncan thought that a clean break would be best. But I argued them round.'

'And what are the conditions?'

'Well, they won't release you from your undertaking not to sell shares ... But, look, Andreas and Marcus are waiting for you upstairs.'

* La Repubblica and El Pais acted as underwriters – i.e. guarantors – of this second rights issue, but, surprisingly, they were able to take up only 38 per cent of the new shares, with existing institutional shareholders taking the rest. Even so, La Repubblica and El Pais each increased its stake to 18.04 per cent of Newspaper Publishing plc. The new shares were issued at £2.50 each – half what the southern Europeans had paid less than a year earlier.

I arrived back in the boardroom and sat down. Marcus had the air of a man brought in to settle a dispute which he did not really want to understand. He said that there had been a consensus that I should be asked to stay as a director, but there were conditions. In the first place, the arrangement would last for a year, and would be renewed only if the board and I wished it to be. I would get no emoluments (the annual fee for a non-executive director was £12,000) since I had received a year's salary on termination of my contract. So long as I remained as a non-executive director I could not write for any other newspapers, but if I wrote for the Independent or the Independent on Sunday I would not be paid. Finally, I would not be released from my undertaking not to sell any shares before March 31st 1992. That was it.

I was getting the impression that some members of the board were not desperately keen that I should become a non-executive director. Andreas was sitting to Marcus's right looking red-faced and ruminative. I imagined him at the board meeting, allowing its sillier members to build up this list of conditions, saying nothing when a word from him would have brought an end to all this foolishness.

'Well, thank you Marcus,' I said. 'Can I think about it for a day or two? I hadn't expected any conditions and I will need to think about them. Some of them don't matter, but I might want to write for other newspapers, and if Christopher Barton was allowed to sell his shares when he ceased being an executive director I don't see why I shouldn't be. Andreas, you said that you would recommend that I should be able to sell my shares.'

'Yes,' said Andreas, 'but the mood of the meeting was that in the circumstances it would be better not to alter that undertaking.'

'I see. Well, I would like a few days, if I may.'

'Of course. Take as long as you want,' said Marcus generously. 'I hope it will all work out.'

As I walked down the stairs it occurred to me that there was one condition which they had not thought of. They had not said I could not write a book.

*

So the last day came. The last time on that newspaper that I would be asked the hundred questions to which an editor is expected to give an instant answer.

After the first edition had gone, we had another party. Most of the Independent on Sunday staff were present. Celia came with our sons Edmund and Alexander. Presentations were made and gifts exchanged. Peter Wilby spoke in praise of Stephen Fay, whom he had first met over twenty years before. Stephen Fay spoke in praise of me. He said how much he had enjoyed working on the Independent on Sunday. When he had first met me he had thought that I was a disciple of Machiavelli of the Florentine school. He had learnt recently that this was not the case at all, but he didn't think any the worse of me because of it. I then spoke for a few minutes, thanking everyone for their hard work and praising their achievement.

We were all gathered around my office. Shortly after I had finished speaking someone came out of it with a familiar cry. 'Matthew is on the telephone.' 'Oh, God,' I replied, 'I don't want to talk to him now.' Celia volunteered to speak to him. 'Don't be rude to him,' I said. 'Just say I am tied up.'

A little later Sebastian arrived. He had been playing cricket. I asked him whether he would make an impromptu speech, and he agreed to. He recalled the days when he and I and Ian Jack had together planned the Independent on Sunday. Nicholas Thirkell had produced a design for the cover of the Sunday Review which, because of its vague likeness to a certain sort of trendy menu, had been nicknamed the brasserie. Now Glover's brasserie was giving way to Jack's Bistro. Some of the menu would be changed but other elements would remain the same. Neal Ascherson, in his role as sommelier, would continue to recommend and urge the merits of the revolutionary 1968 vintage . . .

When Sebastian had exhausted his image, Neal made a short, passionate speech. He recalled how much he had loved the original dummy. It had been *beautiful*. That, above all else, had persuaded him that this was a newspaper which he wished to work for. He had felt in the last months that we had begun to fulfil our promise, that something exceptional was beginning to be born. He quoted a German writer who had written of

Dresden after its carpet bombing, 'A brilliant star has been extinguished.' He was staying on, but he felt like a person who clings on to a bad marriage.

During Neal's speech I observed Ian Jack, hovering on the edge of the crowd, looking unhappy. Afterwards he sat down next to Celia on the bench-seat outside my office. A little later I saw Celia get up, and Ian retreat to his office at the end of the newsroom. Evidently there had been an exchange of words.

Celia told me later what had happened. Ian had asked her how she was. She had replied that she was all right. 'What is Stephen going to do?' Ian had asked. Celia said there were a number of possibilities but she thought that I would write a book about the Independent and the Independent on Sunday. Ian then said, 'He shouldn't do that.' Celia asked him what he meant. 'Because he would have to be very honest about himself, and that could be very painful,' he replied. Whereupon Celia had told him that he needn't worry about what I should, or should not do, and had then got up and walked away.

At the time I simply saw Ian going back to his office and my heart went out to him. A few minutes later I followed. He was standing by his desk, his back to the window, facing in my direction. He was crying.

'Oh God, I feel so awful,' he said. 'I feel so awful. I wish I'd never had that lunch with you and Sebastian.'

As he spoke, he paced around the room, as though these jerky movements might distract him from his pain. Now he was weeping as I had never seen a man weep. 'I feel so awful.' He kept repeating this phrase, sometimes substituting terrible for awful, and then he said: 'The trouble is that you're so damned likeable.'

I just stood there. I said nothing. There was nothing I could say. An age seemed to pass as Ian moaned and dug into his pocket for a handkerchief.

'I'm sorry about this display. . . The stupid thing is that I don't even think the newspaper has a future. I don't think Andreas and Matthew understand Sunday newspapers. I don't like Matthew, nobody does, I suppose, and Andreas is . . . interesting to me in a way, but I don't think he begins to understand what it takes to produce a Sunday newspaper.

Now there was something I could say. 'Well, you know what I think of them.'

'What are you going to do, Stephen?'

'I'm not sure. Maybe write a book . . .'

'I said to Celia that I didn't think you should write a book because it would cost you a great deal. '

'I see.'

'I can see how launching and editing the Independent on Sunday must have cost you a lot. You are incredibly impressive on a Saturday, Stephen, but you're not so good on a Tuesday. Sunday journalism is about tricks. It's not proper journalism at all, really. You should have been an editor of a daily newspaper.'

'Maybe you're right.'

'Perhaps you could become foreign editor of the Daily Telegraph?'

'Oh, well, I'm sure I'll find something to do.'

'You'll be all right, Stephen. You'll be fine.'

And so I left my old friend and returned to the party. There were kisses and there were tears. After a while we left – Celia, Edmund, Alexander and myself – and Alan Kelly drove us away from City Road to a restaurant, where the five of us had dinner.

12

The Final Act

I became a non-executive director and once a month drove to City Road to attend board meetings. To begin with, my presence unsettled Andreas. I would place myself next to him and watch his hands shaking slightly. But I was now no more than a spectator of the affairs of the company which I had helped to found. After a year, in June 1992, I resigned from the board.

The departure of my colleagues and myself from the Independent on Sunday, following weeks of internecine warfare, had attracted a certain amount of adverse publicity for Newspaper Publishing. But these stories were soon largely forgotten, or discounted as aberrational. Few people who had not been involved in these events said that Andreas or Matthew or anyone else had behaved in a particularly bad way. It was a little local difficulty and life would go on.

And so, for a time, it did. Once it had absorbed the shocks of integration, and suffered a small dip in sales, the Independent on Sunday settled down. In a surprising number of ways it seemed to be the same paper. Ian Jack successfully resisted attempts to make it into a mere seven-day version of the Independent. Although the main news departments were largely integrated, the Sunday Review remained wholly separate from the daily paper. Many of the more extreme integrationist notions were shown to be impracticable. Quietly, subtly, cautiously, Ian made sure that more and more decisions concerning the Independent on Sunday should be made by him and those directly answerable to him.

In September 1992 he was formally appointed editor of the Independent on Sunday; according to the theology of integration he had been executive editor and Andreas had been editor. The word integration has since dropped out of use.

The paper did not enjoy the improvement in circulation which Andreas and Matthew had spoken of, nor, I am glad to say, did it suffer the cataclysm which in a moment of anger and dismay I had feared. There was no more talk of having to sell 600,000 copies. By October 1991 circulation, which from May 1991 included foreign sales of about 10,000 copies, had risen slightly to an average of 390,000, or 14.5 per cent of the market. It drifted down in November and December, and remained low at 372,000 or 13.9 per cent of the market in January 1992, before rising a little in February and March. The general election boosted the April figure to 402,000. Circulation then fell back, but rose strongly in August, and again in September and October, when it reached 426,000, the paper's best ever figure, before slipping back. In January 1993 sales stood at 396,000 – a little less than two years earlier.

The Independent did not fare so well. The high-water mark of its circulation had been in March 1990 when it sold 423,000 copies. The decline in sales, which had begun in the early months of 1991 continued throughout the year. By January 1992 it was selling 368,000 copies. The paper, about to be overtaken by the Independent on Sunday at the time of integration, was now selling fewer copies than its stablemate. It had become duller and its sense of daring was less apparent: the foreign pages once full of delightful innovations were, if anything, less imaginative than those of its rivals. The paper ran more sex-related stories in its news columns, and sometimes salivated over them on its feature pages. These transparent attempts to win more readers by pepping up coverage fell curiously flat. Stories which seemed appropriate to other papers seemed like impostors in the Independent.

Newspaper circulation depends on people's spending power, and as the Independent had benefited from a rise in real disposable incomes in the mid 1980s, so it was now suffering from their decline. For a time the fall in sales could be attributed largely to these effects from which the Independent on Sunday, as a recently launched paper, was partly exempt. The fact that The Times, the

Daily Telegraph and the Guardian were also losing sales in proportions similar to the Independent seemed to support this theory. But from the second half of 1992 the Independent began to lose ground more quickly than its rivals.

At first Andreas did not seem very worried. In April 1992 the Independent briefly outsold The Times by about three thousand copies. Andreas threw a party at 40 City Road to celebrate the fact that for the first time the Independent had overtaken The Times. The next month The Times was back in front, and has remained so ever since.

The Independent continued to shed some of its best journalists. Godfrey Hodgson, a good writer who had been miscast as Nicholas Ashford's successor as foreign editor, was sacked. The columnist Germaine Greer was allowed to slip away. Patrick Marnham, who having given up reporting was writing a weekly column from Paris, did not have his contract renewed. Andreas did not try to keep on the two creators of the Alex cartoon after the Daily Telegraph had made them a lucrative offer. When, in August, Alexander Chancellor announced that he was leaving the magazine to go and work for the New Yorker, Andreas made only a cursory attempt to persuade him to stay. In December 1992 William Rees-Mogg resigned to write a twice-weekly column on The Times. Though he was regarded by some as a fogey who was misplaced in the pages of the Independent, his loss was another blow. At the paper's launch he had served the same role as a transplanted Norman castle might in the virgin wilderness of Nebraska, helping the young paper to build a bridge to the past. If the Independent immediately seemed to its readers to be about a hundred years old, some of that effect could be attributed to Lord Rees-Mogg.

All newspapers lose good journalists from time to time. What was extraordinary was Andreas's imperturbability in the face of this continuing exodus. He had always made it a point of principle never to try to persuade someone against going to another newspaper. It was as if he believed that the flame of the Independent burnt so strongly in him that the comings and goings of lesser mortals were immaterial. He seemed to have forgotten his precept at the time of launch, which was that one should always ask oneself before making any appointment, 'Is this person the best available?' The principle of 'Buggins' turn' now operated whenever any senior journalist left. By the beginning of 1993 all the 'barons' who had launched the paper had gone and, save in one or two cases, they had been replaced by departmental heads who were less inspired, less daring and less aware than their predecessors of what the paper had originally been about.

There was one loss about which Andreas could have done nothing. In May 1992 Peter Jenkins died of a rare lung complaint. His memorial service at St Margaret's, Westminster, was packed with journalists and Cabinet ministers, one of whom, Michael Heseltine, delivered a short address about his old friend. Peter had seemed to some people to take himself very seriously, and with young and insignificant journalists he could be aloof or even offhand. His manner was sometimes absurdly grand. But beneath this outer shell his friends discovered a man of boundless curiosity and fun. His long study of politics had given him an instinctive understanding of the way in which politicians' minds operated. With his death the Independent lost its most respected voice.

As chief executive Andreas continued to have many other responsibilities. Even so, he deferred to Matthew more than was necessary or desirable. Matthew, for example, usually took the important evening front-page conference; sometimes Andreas sat humbly in attendance. The origins of this bizarre division of powers lay in the memorandum which Matthew had written to Andreas in January 1989 proposing that he should undertake 'the main burden of editing'.* It seems odd that Andreas, who has such a high view of his own journalistic abilities, should have allowed Matthew so much scope. But with me gone he needed Matthew's continuing support more than ever in the boardroom and other struggles that lay ahead.

Despite the gradual weakening of circulation, Newspaper Publishing weathered the continuing storms of the recession surprisingly well. In the financial year ending October 1st 1991 it lost £10,313,000, chiefly as a result of the losses of the Independent on Sunday and the one-off costs of redundancies and integration.

* See page 177 and passim.

In the next financial year it managed to make a profit of £28,000. This was achieved through a further round of cuts in labour and overheads amounting to over £3 million. In all, since June 1991, £5 million of costs had been taken out, less than a third of which related directly to integration. Plans for expenditure on promotion and 'properties' on the Independent on Sunday, which had been presented as the very cornerstone of integration and the reason for opposing my last-minute compromise, were scrapped. At the same time there was an increase in advertising revenues on the Sunday paper, reflecting advertisers' belief that the title was here to stay.

By January 1993 the Independent was selling 353,000 copies – significantly fewer than the Independent on Sunday. In February, usually a slightly stronger month, sales slipped to 349,000. There was talk of a March re-launch. But Andreas's mind was not totally on the newspaper. As so often before, he was bewitched by the idea of a takeover. This time there seemed to be a strong chance that he would succeed.

*

At the end of 1992 a mysterious German financier called Dieter Bock bought half of the shares of Tiny Rowland, chief executive of Lonrho. He also agreed to underwrite half of a rights issue. As a consequence of both transactions he became by far the company's largest shareholder. Lonrho had been battered by the recession, and the Observer's losses, which it had previously absorbed fairly cheerfully, were becoming painful. It was obvious that Mr Bock, now co-chief executive with Tiny Rowland, would put pressure on his new partner to sell the title.

Andreas knew this, and in December 1992 new overtures were made to Lonrho. Talks took place about which Mr Rowland, for a time, knew nothing. They were conducted on Newspaper Publishing's behalf by Graham Luff, who was now managing director. It was plain even to Andreas that without enormous investment the Independent on Sunday could never be 'level-pegging' – the word he had used back in April 1991 – with the Observer. Though that paper had mislaid a lot of circulation, thereby increasing its losses, it was none the less still easily outselling the Independent on Sunday, with sales of 523,000 in

January 1993. Andreas believed that if the two competing Sunday papers were merged the combined newspaper might sell 700,000 or 800,000 copies, generating profits which would transform the fortunes of Newspaper Publishing.

The only problem was that Newspaper Publishing had a rival in the form of the Guardian, still smarting from its botched investment in the Sunday Correspondent. As a paper unashamedly of the liberal-left, the Guardian had more in common with the Observer than did the Independent. Moreover, it could promise to keep the Observer alive whereas Newspaper Publishing would close it. Andreas later denied this, implying that the spirit, if not the title, of the Observer would live on. But he could not hide the fact that under his plan there would have been three broadsheet Sunday newspapers against four in the event of the Guardian succeeding.

On the other hand, as a public company Newspaper Publishing could offer something which seemed more likely to induce Tiny Rowland to part with his beloved newspaper – equity. Mr Rowland had long coveted a stake in the Independent. As a part of the Scott Trust, the Guardian could not offer shares even if it were minded to. By early April protracted negotiations had produced the outlines of a deal which seemed very likely to succeed. Lonrho would take a 20 per cent stake in Newspaper Publishing and be paid up to £15 million, dependent on the 'settle down' circulation of the merged Sunday newspaper. Tiny Rowland would have a seat on the board of Newspaper Publishing.

Andreas believed he was home and dry. But Lonrho, for a time unbeknown to Andreas or his colleagues, was negotiating with the Guardian in the hope of securing a better price. On the evening of Saturday April 24th three Newspaper Publishing executives went to watch the Observer being printed at the Financial Times plant in dockland. This visit, which Lonrho certainly knew about in advance, caused an uproar. It was seen as a piece of confounded arrogance on the part of Newspaper Publishing, an impression which Lonrho did nothing to dispel.

The previous day, Friday April 23rd, the Evening Standard had 'splashed' with a story about the imminent demise of the Observer (such would be its fate if Newspaper Publishing bought it) under the headline 'Observer On Its Deathbed'. This article galvanised a group of Observer journalists into writing a letter to Tiny Rowland, pleading with him to do everything within his power to ensure that their paper was sold to the Guardian rather than the Independent. Some of the great and the good also began to stir. The leader of the Liberal Democrats, Paddy Ashdown, fired a warning shot over the bows of any newspaper which might close the Observer. In the view of the writer and broadcaster Melvyn Bragg, the Independent would be damaged if it bought the Observer merely to close it. David Astor, who had edited the paper from 1948 to 1975, said that a bid by the Independent would have to be referred to the Monopolies and Mergers Commission if another newspaper were interested in keeping the Observer alive. Something of a campaign got going in which the Independent, previously seen as a beacon of enlightenment, was portrayed as a voracious predator which was prepared, in pursuit of its short-term commercial interests, to force the closure of a famous, once-great newspaper which had been in publication since 1791.

Andreas kept his counsel and it was impossible to tell whether he understood the enormity of what he was trying to do. Still confident that he was about to do a deal with Lonrho, he made a short statement, schoolmasterly in tone and somewhat opaque in meaning: 'If people thought clearly about the commercial realities, they would see there are certain things which would be sensible to do and certain things which would be foolish to do.' These were not sentiments calculated to win over sceptics.

In the real world, Andreas seemed to be saying, people like him recognised what had to be done, even if that meant closing a newspaper. But the real world turned out to have different values. On Thursday April 29th it was announced that the Guardian was to buy the Observer for £27 million, subject only to the say-so of the President of the Board of Trade, Michael Heseltine. Tiny Rowland may have been influenced by the persuasive powers of Observer journalists, and possibly he was genuinely irritated by the undercover visit made by Independent executives to watch the Observer being printed. And in the end the Guardian had offered more money 'up front'.

After so much work, not to mention other previous abortive

attempts to buy the Observer, this defeat was an incalculable blow for Andreas. The attempted acquisition had been the last roll of the dice. One moment the Independent looked like a predator, ready to gobble up a venerable newspaper. The next it was a small company which was not making any profits and had just squandered some £350,000 in an abortive takeover which had seriously damaged its wider reputation. With this setback, the entire house of cards collapsed with a speed that even I found astonishing.

Throughout the negotiations with Lonrho, Andreas had had the support of most of the executive and non-executive directors. The southern Europeans, however, had become increasingly un-enthusiastic, and when the proposed takeover of the Observer encountered a growing amount of flak their scepticism began to turn to alarm. They were influenced by the views of Sir Ralf Dahrendorf, Warden of St Antony's College, Oxford, who had succeeded Marcus Sieff as chairman of Newspaper Publishing in February 1992, in effect as their appointee. Sir Ralf is a man of the liberal-left, and as events progressed the conviction grew in him that it would be wrong for a newspaper such as the Independ-ent to be instrumental in closing down the Observer. He also believed that the proposed takeover of the newspaper had so preoccupied management that insufficient attention was being paid to the two Independent titles.

Matters came to a head on Wednesday April 28th. Andreas knew that the Guardian was on the verge of striking a deal with Lonrho. So far as Carlo Caracciolo, Juan Luis Cebrian and Sir Ralf Dahrendorf were concerned, this was a matter for rejoicing rather than otherwise. Andreas appears to have suspected the southern Europeans of conveying their opposition to Lonrho, and of helping to deliver the Observer into the hands of the Guardian.

Relations between Andreas and Sir Ralf had been deteriorating for many months. He now accused Sir Ralf of betraying him. This was the last straw for Sir Ralf. On May 3rd he sent a letter to Andreas, copied to all directors, resigning as chairman of Newspaper Publishing. He wrote that Andreas could not have failed to notice how far apart their conceptions were 'with respect to the substantive requirements of a liberal newspaper'.

He found himself 'pleased rather than upset by the outcome of the Observer negotiations'. The relationship of confidence which must exist between a chairman and a chief executive had broken down, and it was in the interests of the company that he should resign with immediate effect.

On the same day he wrote in similar but even franker vein to his friends, the southern Europeans. His relationship of confidence with Andreas, always tenuous, had been irreparably damaged. He believed Andreas to be a 'man of the political right' whose underlying political attitudes were evident in his approach to the company and in his style of management. Andreas set people against one another and 'as a consequence instils more fear than loyalty. It is no accident that during the recent splurge of comment on the Observer deal, the Independent had no friends anywhere, not even among its editorial staff.' All the same, he did not believe that Andreas should go – creating the Independent had been a remarkable achievement – and he was not prepared to preside over his removal.

This was by any standards an unusually bitter falling out between a chairman and a chief executive, but no mention was made of it in the Independent. When some weeks previously the Financial Times had lost its chief executive after a disagreement, the paper had carried a balanced story of the affair. By contrast the readers of the Independent were now offered only a five-line paragraph on page three which baldly reported the fact that Sir Ralf had resigned. During the newspaper's attempt to buy the Observer they had been denied any account of what was going on, though the Guardian had carried occasional reports notwithstanding its own involvement. The only public acknowledgement of the row between chief executive and chairman was a story in the Financial Times on May 8th and a piece in the Guardian on May 12th, which quoted liberally from Sir Ralf's letter to Andreas.

The failure to buy the Observer, with all its attendant bad publicity, concentrated the resentment felt by the southern Europeans towards Andreas, which had been bubbling below the surface for many months. An unnamed representative of El Pais could not restrain himself from describing the Independent to a Times reporter as a 'bloody arrogant bunch of people'. In private they went a good deal further. 'The problem is Andreas,' said one very senior executive from La Repubblica. The same man criticised the recent redesign of the Independent which had been met with general horror when it was launched upon the world on March 18th. Under the direction of Michael Crozier, the self-proclaimed designer of the Independent, much of the newspaper's original design was unceremoniously thrown out in what seemed almost a deliberate act of self-destruction. A seven-column grid had been introduced along with a new Plantin typeface and ubiquitous rules. Headlines were set left. The centre pages – what Nicholas Garland had described as 'the West End' of a newspaper – were a particular mess.

In the days and weeks following the Observer *démarche* the southern Europeans were apparently girding themselves for action. In private they said that Andreas would have to step down as chief executive. One or two of them even wondered whether he was the right editor. When they had announced publicly that they wished to increase their joint stake of 37.2 to just over 50 per cent, and to find a British partner to take a large shareholding, it was widely assumed that a takeover was in play. This was apparently confirmed when on May 11th the board of Newspaper Publishing (now without a chairman) announced that it was seeking to raise fresh capital from new and existing shareholders. It emerged that Officia Meccanica Cerruti, an Italian printing group which supplied La Repubblica, had bought a 2.4 per cent stake from the administrator of Robert Maxwell's private interests.

And yet weeks and then months passed without anything happening. Andreas and the executive directors had embarked on another three-year plan – always a useful device for slowing things down – and the southern Europeans seemed ready to await the outcome. La Repubblica and El Pais had asked Schroders merchant bank to find out whether the Takeover Panel would consider that the two papers were acting in concert if they jointly acquired more than 50 per cent of Newspaper Publishing. It was expected that there would be no reply for several weeks.* The southern Europeans appeared to have calmed down. Whereas in May they had privately questioned Andreas's editorial abilities, now they merely said that he should not continue as chief executive. If only he would devote himself full-time to editing, all might be well again.

Andreas was finally brought to accept that he should not continue in both jobs. After a Newspaper Publishing board meeting on 29th July it was announced that he was stepping down as chief executive. He would, however, become deputy chairman, and of course remain as editor of the Independent. Andreas reacted to these changes in an upbeat way. In an article in the Independent, written in the tones of a Soviet official organ reporting the latest Politburo promotions, he was reported to be 'very happy' to return to full-time editing. 'There's absolutely no doubt in my mind that editing, as opposed to being chief executive, wins by about one thousand to one,' he said. The search for a new chief executive began, spearheaded by Ian Hay Davison, who after seven years as a non-executive director had been appointed chairman of Newspaper Publishing with Andreas's full approval.†

*

Towards the end of August Andreas took it into his head to visit the former Yugoslavia. That month's board meeting was cancelled. Although sales of both papers were slipping, and the question of the company's refinancing was far from resolved, the board of Newspaper Publishing did not meet for eight weeks. Work was allegedly continuing on the three-year business plan, though this version was never formally presented. Less ephemeral plans were afoot on both newspapers for an autumn re-launch. The southern Europeans, meanwhile, seemed to be conducting a leisurely beauty contest for a suitable British investment partner. Two leading candidates were Associated Newspapers (publishers

---

* When it finally came, the answer was that the two newspapers were not deemed to constitute a concert party as matters stood, but they would be if together they advanced to take more than 50 per cent of the company. This ruling must have played a big part in the development of the notion of a Consortium in which the Italians and Spanish, along with others, would be open and legitimate partners.
† George Duncan resigned from the board in June 1993 and Bruce Fireman in September. They had both harboured not unreasonable hopes of becoming chairman.

of the Daily Mail and the Evening Standard) and Mirror Group Newspapers.

On September 6th News International reduced the price of The Times from 45 to 30 pence. This bolt from the blue drew forth a querulous front-page leader in the Independent which suggested that in some countries Rupert Murdoch's cross-subsidy of a loss-making title, i.e. The Times, would be illegal. But although his move was undoubtedly calculated to damage the Independent, not to mention the Daily Telegraph, it did not immediately have that effect. Sales of The Times rose sharply but the Independent, far from sinking back, actually sold more copies in September than August – 332,000 as against 326,000.

At the beginning of October a new chief executive called Patrick Morrissey arrived at City Road. He was a former Beechams marketing executive who had worked as the managing director of Mirror Group Newspapers during Robert Maxwell's reign. In 1990 he had left after a disagreement to found his own consultancy. Not everyone thought that Mr Morrissey was the catch of the century, but he managed none the less to negotiate for himself a very handsome package from a company which was now losing money. His salary in the first year would be a minimum of £187,500 and he was guaranteed, in addition, one per cent of the pre-tax profits of the company until September 30th 1998, subject to a maximum of £500,000.

Patrick Morrissey embarked on a three-year plan of his own. According to the testimony of the public relations company which was soon appointed to represent him and his patron Ian Hay Davison, the incoming chief executive found the books in disarray. The Independent was due to be re-launched on October 12th, the Independent on Sunday two days earlier. Television advertising had been lined up. A great deal of money had been committed, and Morrissey believed that revenue had to be increased. He proposed that the price of the re-launched Independent should rise from 45 pence to 50 pence, while the Independent on Sunday should go up from 90 pence to one pound. Andreas and Matthew went along with the plan.

To combine a cover price increase with a re-launch would have been unwise in any circumstances. Coming so soon after The Times' reduction, it was a disaster. The sales of both the

Independent and its Sunday sister began to plummet. In the case of the daily, the effect of the re-launch was no less damaging than the price rise. It suddenly looked like a different sort of newspaper. Far from constituting an improvement, the re-launched version threw out more bits of the past that had not already been jettisoned in the March redesign. The 'puffs' above its masthead gave it the appearance of a much more popular paper. Some long-suffering readers objected to the substitution of colour photographs for the black and white ones which had so distinguished the Independent; others did not like two sections. Where stately Oxford rules had once held sway, there were now mauve lines, and others in a ghastly orange. It was as though Michael Crozier, who oversaw the changes, had re-established, at least in part, the newspaper which Nicholas Thirkell, Alexander Chancellor and Nicholas Garland had triumphantly smothered some seven years before.

The circulation of the Independent fell from 329,000 in October to 314,000 in November to 302,000 in December. Over the same months the Independent on Sunday declined from 371,000 to 357,000 to 335,000. In effect the several million pounds spent on re-launching and promoting the two titles could as well have been burnt in City Road. The daily paper had now lost 14 per cent of its circulation over the previous twelve months; the Sunday paper 15 per cent. Despite the increase in their cover price, by mid-December the papers were producing less revenue than they had before the re-launch. What had looked like crisis suddenly threatened to be a catastrophe.

As things went from bad to worse, a split began to develop among the directors. Patrick Morrissey, who was generally supported by Ian Hay Davison, was labouring away at his three-year plan, the final version of which he was due to present to the board on December 21st. It would propose yet another round of cuts in the editorial budgets. Morrissey believed that Newspaper Publishing should seek a trade investor on the basis of his plan, which promised very healthy, and to some not wholly credible, profits after three years.

Andreas and Matthew thought that there had been enough cuts. As sales fell, they blamed Morrissey for forcing through the price increase. Relations between the two founders and the chairman and the new chief executive were becoming acrimonious. Morrissey seems to have devised a plot to remove Matthew from the board. He actually sacked Suzanna Taverne who had succeeded Graham Luff as finance director. But she refused to be budged until satisfactory arrangements were made regarding compensation, and continued to come to work.

Like Morrissey, Andreas and Matthew believed that Newspaper Publishing needed a trade partner, but they wanted it to be one of their own choosing, not his or Ian Hay Davison's. The idea grew, shared by the Italians and Spanish, that if this partner could print, distribute and manage the Independent there could be very considerable savings. Though the southern Europeans continued to harbour reservations about Andreas and more particularly about 'the stammering one', as they described Matthew, they increasingly found themselves in the same camp, at odds with Morrissey and Hay Davison.

Talks had been held with Associated Newspapers and with United Newspapers, publishers of the Daily and Sunday Express. Michael Green, chief executive of Carlton Communications, had been contacted. But by mid-December all but two companies had ruled themselves out or been ruled out. Of those left, one was the Telegraph group, whose chairman and largest shareholder was Conrad Black. The other was Mirror Group Newspapers, whose chief executive since October 1992 had been David Montgomery.

Montgomery is a thin, bleak Ulsterman, a journalist by calling, who edited the News of the World and later Today newspaper, where he was also managing director. After a time he fell out with News International, publishers of Today, and departed. To almost everyone's surprise, he popped up after a while as chief executive of Mirror Group Newspapers, though his management experience was slight and apparently undistinguished. When he took over he gave assurances about retaining editors which he broke within a few weeks by sacking Richard Stott, editor of the Daily Mirror, and Bill Hagerty, editor of the People, both of whom he later accused of presiding over anarchy. He dismissed a hundred non-staff journalists and about fifty staff ones. Several of the Daily Mirror's best columnists and writers decided to leg it off to other newspapers. Under his stewardship the circulation of the Daily Mirror declined, though this was partly attributable to the Sun's price cut in July 1993. But because costs were hacked back, profitability was restored to the group which Robert Maxwell had plundered.

It was not very surprising that such a man should become friends with Matthew Symonds. In some ways the two had much in common. Less predictable was the liaison which developed between David Montgomery and Prince Carlo Caracciolo. Whereas Montgomery was 'driven' and abrasive and short on charm, Carlo was relaxed and easygoing and could have run a charm school single-handedly. However, La Repubblica was in a fix as an investor in Newspaper Publishing. With El Pais, the paper had invested over £32 million in the company since November 1990. The southern Europeans feared they would be asked to throw good money after bad, or else accept their losses and withdraw from Newspaper Publishing in an embarrassing way.

Carlo knew very few people in senior management positions on British newspapers. Introduced to David Montgomery by a mutual acquaintance at Hambros, Mirror Group Newspaper's merchant bank, he fell into the habit of visiting him whenever he came to London. He began to see the point of the dour Ulsterman, whom he recognised as a tough and efficient manager, qualities in short supply at City Road. In January 1994 Carlo told me that he must have had a hundred meetings with Montgomery over the previous twelve months. The Italian aristocrat admired the way in which his new friend had 'fought his way up' from modest beginnings. He believed him to be a loyal and straightforward man.

By no means everyone who knew Mr Montgomery shared this view of him, particularly those Mirror journalists who thought that he had broken his word to them. Carlo, who after all usually spent no more than a couple of days a month in London, may not have been fully aware of David Montgomery's reputation. But in his own way he was as loyal as he believed the chief executive of Mirror Group Newspapers to be, and when he discovered what much of the world thought about his new partner he was not inclined to alter his own opinions. The bond between the two men has consistently been underestimated by their opponents.

In the end, of course, it was a business relationship. Montgomery produced a plan for the Independent which Carlo described as brilliant. Mirror Group would print and distribute the Independent and the Independent on Sunday, sell advertising for the newspapers and promote them – in fact, generally manage all the non-editorial affairs of the company. By this means, savings of over £10 million a year could be achieved, which might be enough to return the two newspapers to profitability.

There was an alternative to Mirror Group Newspapers in the shape of the Daily Telegraph. Andreas, who had several meetings with Conrad Black, for a time favoured this approach. There was talk of him having a seat on the Telegraph board. But the southern Europeans, particularly the Spanish, could not easily stomach the prospect of a link-up with a right-wing group. They had convinced themselves that Mirror Group Newspapers was respectably left-wing. No less important was the fact that alone among the suitors the Mirror had agreed to buy the southern Europeans' shares in Newspaper Publishing at an agreed price if profit targets were not reached. El Pais and La Repubblica had found a way out without losing their money.

By the board meeting of December 21st, at which Patrick Morrissey unveiled his long-awaited three-year plan, Andreas had come around to the southern Europeans' way of thinking, as perhaps he had to. He may have been influenced by the thought that at the Telegraph there were a number of people who believed that they might be able to edit the Independent better than him, whereas there was no one at the Mirror who could plausibly hold this view.

At this meeting the boardroom split widened into open disagreement. Andreas, Matthew, Adrian O'Neill, Carlo and Juan Luis Cebrian informed the board of their intention to form a Consortium with an unnamed third party, subsequently declared to be Mirror Group Newspapers, to make a bid for Newspaper Publishing. Ian Hay Davison, Patrick Morrissey and the other directors formed themselves into a committee of independent directors 'for the purposes of considering and recommending upon the various options open to the company for its future recapitalisation, restructuring and ownership'. War had begun.

*

On the same day that the board of Newspaper Publishing split into two, a meeting took place at the Dorchester Hotel in London. Among those present were: Dr Tony O'Reilly, chairman of Independent Newspapers plc of Ireland, and also chairman of H. J. Heinz & Co; Roy Greenslade, a former editor of the Daily Mirror who kept the enormously wealthy Dr O'Reilly informed about the British press, and may have brought the plight of the Independent to his notice; and Michael Gatenby, a senior director of Charterhouse Bank which, all those years ago, had helped us to raise the money to launch the Independent.

Dr O'Reilly, a former Irish rugby international, had left his run perilously late. The question was whether Independent Newspapers, in which he held a 28 per cent share, should try to involve itself in Newspaper Publishing. There was no answer that evening. It was not until the early part of January, by which time some sums and calculations had been done, that a decision was made to go ahead. But rather than make a full bid, which might be prohibitively expensive, the intention was to tempt the southern Europeans away from Mirror Group Newspapers.

With this in mind, a lunch was arranged in a private dining room of the Crillon Hotel in Paris on Friday January 14th. The guests, Carlo Caracciolo and Juan Luis Cebrian, could not have been more lovingly courted had they been two young starlets. The food had been arranged by Tony O'Reilly's wife, Chryssie Goulandris, a Greek shipping heiress reputed to be even richer than her husband. Apart from the two hosts, also present were Liam Healy, chief executive of Independent Newspapers; Brendan Hopkins, head of international operations; Victor Blank, chairman of Charterhouse Bank; and his colleague, Michael Gatenby.

The lunch, which lasted over three hours, was by all accounts most enjoyable. Dr O'Reilly presented himself as someone who understood the character of the Independent, though he could not hide the fact that he had made little study of its finances and had few specific proposals. Carlo later said that he had found him most charming, as much of the world seems to do. However, the Irish did not succeed in peeling the southern Europeans away from David Montgomery. They had not realised, at any rate until this lunch, how very far advanced the Consortium was in its plans, nor how close were the ties that bound it, and in particular Carlo and David Montgomery, together. This insight did not prevent them coming away from the lunch in the hope that they might nevertheless be able to prise the Consortium apart.

What was now described as the Mirror Group Consortium had hoped to make a bid in early January. But it had been delayed, in part by the complex legal framework that was needed to define relations between its different parties. Then there was the question of how much money should be offered for Newspaper Publishing. Clearly it was not in the Consortium's interest to pay more than was necessary, and Schroders, which was acting for La Repubblica and El Pais, went so far as to suggest unattributably to several journalists that £35 million might be a fair price for the company. Since there were just over 21 million shares, this implied a share price of £1.70, considerably more than had been obtainable in recent months but less than some investors had been hoping for in the event of a takeover. Andreas said to one close colleague that he wanted 'a number with a two in front', which seemed to imply £2 a share.

Neither the Consortium nor the Irish had yet made a bid for all or part of Newspaper Publishing, but it was widely assumed that both would do so soon. Most of the journalists on the Independent titles were bitterly opposed to Montgomery, partly on account of his management record at the Mirror, and partly because of his reputation as a purveyor of 'yellow journalism'. It would in truth have been difficult to find anyone further removed from the original ideals of the Independent. Journalists were at first incredulous and then embittered that Andreas should be leading their newspapers down such a path. He seemed surprised by their response. Cosy fireside chats, which had been arranged by him for the purpose of explaining to little groups of journalists the inestimable advantages of the Consortium, had to be abandoned. The journalists' union chapel passed an almost unanimous motion critical of the Consortium. An editorial council, a leading light of which was Neal Ascherson, was established to draw up an editorial charter. Two union executives were flown to Madrid so that Juan Luis Cebrian, a man of respectable left-wing credentials, could put his case to them. Alas, to no avail. The only journalists who spoke in favour of the proposed arrangements were close associates of Andreas and Matthew.

For the first time since the founding of the Independent, Andreas found himself opposed by most of his staff, many of whom had hitherto revered him in spite of every setback. Though two warring camps had slogged it out before my colleagues and I left the Independent on Sunday, some journalists on the daily paper had been unaware of the nature of the disagreement, and had given Andreas the benefit of the doubt. Others were happy to see the rebellious and costly Sunday paper – this was how Andreas and others had represented it to them – being brought to heel. This time all the facts were beyond dispute. Andreas and Matthew were prepared to put the newspaper which they had helped to found in the hands of David Montgomery, or at any rate of the Mirror Group Consortium, though there was another seemingly more respectable suitor waiting in the wings.

A group of Independent journalists had a friendly meeting with representatives of Dr O'Reilly. He was their preferred candidate, in part simply because he was not Mr Montgomery. It was perhaps natural that they should romanticise him a little. Though Mr Montgomery's sins had been carefully charted, Dr O'Reilly had had few business deals in this country, and he could not be condemned for what was not known. He also gained much from being Irish (but from the Catholic south, rather than the Protestant north where Mr Montgomery hailed from). He was in fact a capitalist red in tooth and claw who during the 1970s had been criticised by the Left in Ireland for his rapacious acquisition of companies, some of which foundered in mid-decade when the recession came and the banks called in their loans. One of the businesses which he bought into at that time had been Independent Newspapers. This had prospered, though the centre-right titles which the group publishes do not appear to have very much in common with the Independent and Independent on Sunday.

On January 24th the Consortium finally announced that it was considering making a bid for all the shares in Newspaper Publishing which it did not own.* Three days later Independent Newspapers made a proposal. It would invest £21 million in

* i.e. the 37.2 per cent owned by La Repubblica and El Pais, and the 10 per cent accounted for by Andreas, Matthew and Adrian O'Neill.

Newspaper Publishing by means of a new non-voting convertible unsecured loan stock at £3 per share. On full conversion, this would give the Irish 24.99 per cent of the enlarged ordinary share capital. They would later make a separate cash offer for 20 per cent of Newspaper Publishing's existing shares at a price of £2.50 per share, which would represent a further investment of about £11 million. Irish Newspapers would then own some 40 per cent of Newspaper Publishing.

This complex offer was welcomed by Ian Hay Davison, chairman of the board committee. His priority was to get the best price for shareholders, and the way to achieve this was to have two horses in the race, which he now had. For reasons which had to do with principle and personal antipathy he was not keen to see the Consortium triumph. On the other hand, the Irish offer had a defect, which was that it provided an 'exit' only for some Newspaper Publishing shareholders. A number of investors had held their shares since before the launch of the Independent. Now they all wanted to get out.

On February 4th the Consortium launched its own bid for Newspaper Publishing at £2.50 a share in cash, or slightly more in the form of a combination of Mirror Group shares and cash. Had it not been for the activities of the Irish, the offer would undoubtedly have been less. David Montgomery and Andreas Whittam Smith took to the airwaves to justify and extol what they seemed to regard as a 'done deal'. But even as they were speaking, Hoare Govett, stockbroker to Independent Newspapers, was preparing to buy 24.99 per cent of Newspaper Publishing in the market at £3.50 a share. This mid-morning, rather than dawn, raid was accomplished in about twenty minutes. At Charterhouse Bank the Irish drank champagne in celebration.

Dr O'Reilly's apparent coup threw the Consortium into disarray. The journalists' union chapel at City Road welcomed it, apparently unoffended by this display of raw capitalism. Ian Hay Davison and his board committee also recorded their approval. The following morning some newspaper City pages took the view that the Consortium had been blown apart by Dr O'Reilly's acquisition of a quarter of the company. Its bid had envisaged Mirror Group Newspapers owning 40 per cent of Newspaper Publishing and the southern Europeans 50.1 per cent. That was impossible now that the Irish owned 24.99 per cent of the company. Perhaps David Montgomery would walk away from the mess.

But he did not. To the surprise of many people, the members of the Consortium dusted themselves off and got down to working out a new offer. The Irish were as taken aback as anybody. Their hope had been that they would detach the southern Europeans from David Montgomery, but they did not. During the next couple of weeks Liam Healy and Brendan Hopkins met Carlo more than once without persuading him that they would make better partners than Mirror Group. As ever, Carlo was polite, promised to consider what they had said, and did precisely nothing.

The Irish also tried to woo Andreas. Privately, they had a low opinion of him, and joked that in the event of their running the company they would offer him the title of 'Editor Emeritus'. But they were none the less wary of him, believing that he was so mixed up in the image and reputation of the Independent that it would be foolish at this stage to speak ill of the man in public. On the evening of Friday February 18th Tony O'Reilly had a 45-minute meeting with Andreas during which the Irish tycoon reiterated his commitment to the founding principles of the Independent. According to a subsequent Irish account, Andreas took copious notes. It does not seem to have been a very cordial meeting.

During these fevered weeks no one produced a single journalistic idea about how the Independent and its Sunday sister might be saved. David Montgomery did not even try. Andreas had nothing to say: he had had his best shot with the botched October re-launch. Tony O'Reilly genuflected towards the shrine of independence, and informed his prospective biographer, the journalist Ivan Fallon, that 'the Independent's philosophy and ideals are akin to ours'. Beyond this he had nothing to add. No one did. What had begun as a great journalistic enterprise was now the battleground for dozens of lawyers, merchant bankers and public relations consultants, each of them earning fabulous fees. What they fought over they did not understand. It had become a poor, frail thing, our Independent, losing money hand-over-fist, its circulation down again to 291,000 in January, but for all that *still a newspaper*, and therefore something which men like David Montgomery and Tony O'Reilly would fight over as though it were a priceless pearl.

On February 21st the Consortium improved its offer to £3.50 a share, in the form of cash and Mirror Group shares, valuing Newspaper Publishing at £73.7 million. The next day Independent Newspapers bought a further 5 per cent of the company, also at £3.50 a share, increasing its holding to 29.99 per cent. This was subject to clearance by the Monopolies and Mergers Commission, since the acquisition of 25 per cent or more triggers an automatic reference. On the assumption that approval would be forthcoming, the Irish shareholding of 29.99 per cent would represent the maximum allowable without their having to make a full bid for the company. This they were reluctant to do, believing that it might be ruinously expensive to achieve control. Here was their Achilles heel. They would advance to 29.99 per cent but no further.

Several days of negotiations now took place on various fronts between the board committee, the Consortium, assorted merchant banks and officials of the Department of Trade and Industry. A recommendation by Ian Hay Davison was thought necessary if an automatic referral to the Monopolies and Mergers Commission by Michael Heseltine, President of the Board of Trade, was to be avoided. This gave him a lever in his talks with the Consortium, which was anxious not to undergo such a process for the reason that it could take many weeks during which Newspaper Publishing, already gravely ill, might simply expire. But Mr Heseltine might in any event refer the bid were he so minded. The Consortium therefore insisted that its bid was conditional upon his not referring it. Newspaper Publishing might be worth much less in six weeks' time, and it was unreasonable to expect an offer to lie on the table.

Hay Davison could not budge the Consortium on this point, but he did manage to extract slightly better terms. On March 2nd it was announced that the board committee had given its backing to a £74.4 million cash offer for Newspaper Publishing. This was roughly double the figure the Consortium had originally had in mind. Its holding would be split so that Mirror Group would hold a minimum of 30 per cent and the southern Europeans a minimum of 37 per cent. If Irish Newspapers sold its shares, both parties would have considerably more. If they did not, Andreas, Matthew and Adrian O'Neill would sell their shares to the point where the three of them might hold only 3 per cent of the equity. In either event, the southern Europeans would have voting control over 50.1 per cent of the shares. Newspaper Publishing's non-editorial operations, ranging from printing to accounting, would be subsumed into the Mirror, threatening the jobs of at least 260 of the company's staff. So far as the editorial content of the two newspapers was concerned, Mirror Group gave solemn assurances that it would not interfere in the smallest degree.

The Irish apart, there was little doubt that the remaining investors would accept this bid. Taking a leaf out of Tony O'Reilly's book, the Consortium quickly went into the market to secure acceptances from some 15 per cent of the shareholders, subject only to Mr Heseltine not referring the bid. It was now up to him.

Journalists at the Independent mounted a last-ditch attempt to thwart the Consortium. 'We simply do not believe the promises of editorial independence given David Montgomery's appalling track record at the Daily Mirror,' said a union representative. The chapel wrote to all MPs, urging them to put pressure on Mr Heseltine to impose conditions which would preserve the editorial independence of the two titles. Ninety-nine of them signed an early day motion asking the Minister to attach safeguards. But there was hardly a full-scale campaign against the Consortium. It was not a great issue. Because the Irish themselves had not made a bid, there was no clear alternative.

This must have weighed on Mr Heseltine's mind. He knew that Newspaper Publishing in its existing incarnation was almost bankrupt. There wasn't much time left. And perhaps – who can say? – he remembered how the Independent and his friend Peter Jenkins had given him enthusiastic support when he challenged Margaret Thatcher for the leadership of the Conservative Party in November 1990. Perhaps also he did not want to pick a fight with the people who ran the mass circulation Daily Mirror; when all was said and done, the Irish were foreigners who held little sway here. As a condition of his approval he could have insisted that they were given board seats, which the Consortium had refused, but he did not. On Friday March 18th he waved through the bid without a referral. Independent Newspapers plc was allowed to keep its stake at 29.99 per cent. The Independent as we had conceived it was no more.

*

What went wrong? This book was an attempt to answer this question. It is about what went right and what went wrong.

The Independent was in part a casualty of external factors. When it was launched the paper commanded the centre ground of British politics, the quiet part where reasonable people of all political persuasions could come together. In the Indian summer of Thatcherism the Independent thrived. Independence was a banner which no other paper could raise so high. But when the divisive leader went, the political landscape changed. The centre which had been all ours became full of hubbub and bustle again.

Then the recession came. The Independent, which commercially was the child of Thatcherism, became its victim. Having benefited from the biggest boom ever in advertising revenue, the young company now suffered from the sharpest decline. If we had not mistimed the launch of the Independent on Sunday, we would have been in a stronger position to weather these storms. However distasteful some of us may have found Thatcherism in a political sense, we shared the triumphalism of the age, the feeling that anything could be achieved if only you wanted it badly enough.

And yet it was not the recession which undid our paper dreams, nor even the shifting ground of British politics. In a narrow financial sense the Independent, and its Sunday sister, survived the recession. What harmed them most was principally in ourselves and in our relations with one another. Perhaps I should not have left the company, but the truth is that I could no longer bear working with Andreas Whittam Smith. I have never regretted going.

Andreas believed that he could do almost anything. This enormous success, relatively late in his life, long dreamt of but unexpected, seems to have constituted a deep psychological shock for him. He really believed that it was done by him, not the hundreds of journalists and staff and advisers who had made it possible. People could come and go, but so long as he stayed everything would be all right. In the end we were all of us dispensable – the journalists who had started the paper, the shareholders whose interests he abrogated when he formed the Consortium. He was the Independent, the incarnation of its spirit. In a curious way he is right. He is like a man who sets off on a great expedition surrounded by friends and supporters. One by one he deserts them, or they fall away for reasons of their own, but he keeps on, no longer heading in the direction that was originally intended, all that is left of the expedition.

His journey is finished, though he does not realise it. The question is whether others can still take over before it is too late. Though it is certainly very possible that he will get rid of Andreas, at any rate as editor, Mr Montgomery is not the man to revive the dream. Dr O'Reilly has decided to retain his shareholding, at least for the time being, in the hope that if there is an editorial crisis in six or nine months, as there may well be, the southern Europeans will finally turn to him. I hope they do: they are civilised people and they have a sort of vision. They still hold the key, but they do not know enough about the British newspaper market to rescue the Independent and the Independent on Sunday single-handedly. They need a partner. David Montgomery is the wrong one. Dr O'Reilly may be the right one.*

The nightmare is that the southern Europeans will simply withdraw. There is a 50-page document which sets out the various agreements between the parties of the Consortium. One of these provides for the southern Europeans to compel Mirror Group Newspapers to buy their shares at up to £4 each if after three years the profits of the Consortium are less than 8 per cent of turnover. Assuming that turnover will at that time be about

---

* The Irish have not yet got the board seats for which they are negotiating. Since their 29.99 per cent shareholding gives them certain blocking powers outside the board, it may make sense for the Consortium to have them on the inside. On March 24th the old board of Newspaper Publishing resigned. Andreas became chairman. Carlo Caracciolo and Marco de Benedetto are directors on behalf of La Repubblica; Juan Luis Cebrian and Javier Diez de Polanco for El Pais; and David Montgomery and Cornel Riklin for Mirror Group Newspapers.

£100 million, this implies a profit of £8 million a year. At present Newspaper Publishing is losing money at the rate of about £10 million a year. For the Mirror Group to turn around the company so dramatically within so short a time would be an incredible achievement. In fact it will be impossible without an increase in circulation, and that will not happen unless there is some sort of editorial renaissance, particularly on the daily paper.

Will there be? Can there be? Mr Montgomery disclaims any editorial role. But so long as he remains in charge, the danger is that the Independent will drift down market and may become a tabloid. (Of itself, this physical transformation might not be a bad thing. After all, La Repubblica and El Pais are both tabloids.) If the sales of the Independent on Sunday do not rise (in March 1994 it sold an average of 332,000 copies, 12.5 per cent of its market) it may be bought by, or merged with, the Observer. Its owners, the Guardian, have recently made an approach to Newspaper Publishing which was rebuffed.

My hope is that the Independent is an institution strong enough to survive the depredations of any man, be he Andreas Whittam Smith or David Montgomery. This is what I wrote at the end of the hardback edition of this book: 'For the moment, the Independent – I use the word now to describe the company which I helped to found – is a great ship becalmed on a windless ocean. One day, I hope, I trust, the sweet winds will rise up again, our sails will open and the ship will be carried forward, whatever its crew, to new adventures.'

I still hope.

April 1994

Index

The following abbreviations appear in the index:

IoS – the Independent on Sunday
SG – Stephen Glover
AWS – Andreas Whittam Smith
MS – Matthew Symonds

Discover more about our forthcoming books through Penguin's FREE newspaper...

Penguin
Quarterly

It's packed with:

- exciting features
- author interviews
- previews & reviews
- books from your favourite films & TV series
- exclusive competitions & much, much more...

Write off for your free copy today to:
Dept JC
Penguin Books Ltd
FREEPOST
West Drayton
Middlesex
UB7 0BR
NO STAMP REQUIRED

READ MORE IN PENGUIN

In every corner of the world, on every subject under the sun, Penguin represents quality and variety – the very best in publishing today.

For complete information about books available from Penguin – including Puffins, Penguin Classics and Arkana – and how to order them, write to us at the appropriate address below. Please note that for copyright reasons the selection of books varies from country to country.

In the United Kingdom: Please write to *Dept. JC, Penguin Books Ltd, FREEPOST, West Drayton, Middlesex UB7 0BR*

If you have any difficulty in obtaining a title, please send your order with the correct money, plus ten per cent for postage and packaging, to *PO Box No. 11, West Drayton, Middlesex UB7 0BR*

In the United States: Please write to *Penguin USA Inc., 375 Hudson Street, New York, NY 10014*

In Canada: Please write to *Penguin Books Canada Ltd, 10 Alcorn Avenue, Suite 300, Toronto, Ontario M4V 3B2*

In Australia: Please write to *Penguin Books Australia Ltd, 487 Maroondah Highway, Ringwood, Victoria 3134*

In New Zealand: Please write to *Penguin Books (NZ) Ltd, 182–190 Wairau Road, Private Bag, Takapuna, Auckland 9*

In India: Please write to *Penguin Books India Pvt Ltd, 706 Eros Apartments, 56 Nehru Place, New Delhi 110 019*

In the Netherlands: Please write to *Penguin Books Netherlands B.V., Keizersgracht 231 NL–1016 DV Amsterdam*

In Germany: Please write to *Penguin Books Deutschland GmbH, Friedrichstrasse 10–12, W–6000 Frankfurt/Main 1*

In Spain: Please write to *Penguin Books S. A., C. San Bernardo 117–6° E–28015 Madrid*

In Italy: Please write to *Penguin Italia s.r.l., Via Felice Casati 20, I–20124 Milano*

In France: Please write to *Penguin France S. A., 17 rue Lejeune, F–31000 Toulouse*

In Japan: Please write to *Penguin Books Japan, Ishikiribashi Building, 2–5–4, Suido, Bunkyo-ku, Tokyo 112*

In Greece: Please write to *Penguin Hellas Ltd, Dimocritou 3, GR–106 71 Athens*

In South Africa: Please write to *Longman Penguin Southern Africa (Pty) Ltd, Private Bag X08, Bertsham 2013*

READ MORE IN PENGUIN

A CHOICE OF NON-FICTION

The Time Out Film Guide   Edited by Tom Milne

The definitive, up-to-the minute directory of over 9,500 films – world cinema from classics and silent epics to reissues and the latest releases – assessed by two decades of *Time Out* reviewers. 'In my opinion the best and most comprehensive' – Barry Norman

The Remarkable Expedition   Olivia Manning

The events of an extraordinary attempt in 1887 to rescue Emin Pasha, Governor of Equatoria, are recounted here by the author of *The Balkan Trilogy* and *The Levant Trilogy* and vividly reveal unprecedented heights of magnificent folly in the perennial human search for glorious conquest.

Berlin: Coming in From the Cold   Ken Smith

'He covers everything from the fate of the ferocious-looking dogs that formerly helped to guard East Germany's borders to the vast Orwellian apparatus that maintained security in the now-defunct German Democratic Republic … a pithy style and an eye for the telling detail' – *Independent*

Cider with Rosie/As I Walked Out one Midsummer Morning
Laurie Lee

Now together in one volume, Laurie Lee's two classic autobiographical works, *Cider with Rosie* and *As I Walked Out One Midsummer Morning*. Together they illustrate Laurie Lee's superb descriptive powers as he conveys the poignancy of a boy's transformation into adulthood.

In the Land of Oz   Howard Jacobson

'A wildly funny account of his travels; abounding in sharp characterization, crunching dialogue and self-parody, it actually is a book which makes you laugh out loud on almost every page … sharp, skilful and brilliantly funny' – *Literary Review*

READ MORE IN PENGUIN

A CHOICE OF NON-FICTION

Bernard Shaw Michael Holroyd
Volume 2 1898–1918 The Pursuit of Power

'A man whose art rested so much upon the exercise of intelligence could not have chosen a more intelligent biographer ... The pursuit of Bernard Shaw has grown, and turned into a pursuit of the whole twentieth century' – Peter Ackroyd in *The Times*

Shots from the Hip Charles Shaar Murray

His classic encapsulation of the moment when rock stars turned junkies as the sixties died; his dissection of rock 'n' roll violence as citizens assaulted the Sex Pistols; superstar encounters from the decline of Paul McCartney to Mick Jagger's request that the author should leave – Charles Shaar Murray's *Shots From the Hip* is also rock history in the making.

Managing on the Edge Richard Pascale

The co-author of the bestselling *The Art of Japanese Management* has once again turned conventional thinking upside down. Conflict and contention in organizations are not just unavoidable – they are positively to be welcomed. The successes and failures of large corporations can help us understand the need to maintain a creative tension between fitting companies together and splitting them apart.

Just Looking John Updike

'Mr Updike can be a very good art critic, and some of these essays are marvellous examples of critical explanation ... a deep understanding of the art emerges ... His reviews of some recent and widely attended shows ... quite surpass the modest disclaimer of the title' – *The New York Times Book Review*

Shelley: The Pursuit Richard Holmes

'Surely the best biography of Shelley ever written ... He makes Shelley's character entirely convincing by showing us the poet at every stage of his development acting upon, and reacting to, people and events' – Stephen Spender

READ MORE IN PENGUIN

A CHOICE OF NON-FICTION

Riding the Iron Rooster Paul Theroux

Travels in old and new China with the author of *The Great Railway Bazaar*. 'Mr Theroux cannot write badly … he is endlessly curious about places and people … and in the course of a year there was almost no train in the whole vast Chinese rail network in which he did not travel' – Ludovic Kennedy

Ninety-two Days Evelyn Waugh

In this fascinating chronicle of a South American journey, Waugh describes the isolated cattle country of Guiana, sparsely populated by an odd collection of visionaries, rogues and ranchers, and records the nightmarish experiences travelling on foot, by horse and by boat through the jungle in Brazil.

The Life of Graham Greene Norman Sherry
Volume One 1904–1939

'Probably the best biography ever of a living author' – Philip French in the *Listener*. Graham Greene has always maintained a discreet distance from his reading public.This volume reconstructs his first thirty-five years to create one of the most revealing literary biographies of the decade.

The Day Gone By Richard Adams

In this enchanting memoir the bestselling author of *Watership Down* tells his life story from his idyllic 1920s childhood spent in Newbury, Berkshire, through public school, Oxford and service in World War Two to his return home and his courtship of the girl he was to marry.

A Turn in the South V. S. Naipaul

'A supremely interesting, even poetic glimpse of a part of America foreigners either neglect or patronize' – *Guardian*. 'An extraordinary panorama' – *Daily Telegraph*. 'A fine book by a fine man, and one to be read with great enjoyment: a book of style, sagacity and wit' – *Sunday Times*

READ MORE IN PENGUIN

A CHOICE OF NON-FICTION

When Shrimps Learn to Whistle   Denis Healey

Taking up the most powerful political themes that emerged from his hugely successful *The Time of My Life,* Denis Healey now gives us this stimulating companion volume. 'Forty-three years of ruminations ... by the greatest foreign secretary (as the author quietly and reasonably implies) we never had' – Ben Pimlott in the *New Statesman & Society*

Eastern Approaches   Fitzroy Maclean

'The author's record of personal achievement is remarkable. The canvas which he covers is immense. The graphic writing reveals the ruthless man of action ... He emerges from [his book] as an extrovert Lawrence' – *The Times Literary Supplement*

This Time Next Week   Leslie Thomas

'Mr Thomas's book is all humanity, to which is added a Welshman's mastery of words ... Some of his episodes are hilarious, some unbearably touching, but everyone, staff and children, is looked upon with compassion' – *Observer*. 'Admirably written, with clarity, realism, poignancy and humour' – *Daily Telegraph*

Reports from the Holocaust   Larry Kramer

'A powerful book ... more than a political autobiography, *Reports* is an indictment of a world that allows AIDS to continue ... he is eloquent and convincing when he swings from the general to the specific. His recommendations on the release of drugs to AIDS patients are practical and humane' – *New York Newsday*

City on the Rocks   Kevin Rafferty

'Rafferty has filled a glaring gap on the Asian bookshelf, offering the only comprehensive picture of Hong Kong right up to the impact of the Tiananmen Square massacre' – *Business Week*. 'A story of astonishing achievement, but its purpose is warning rather than celebration' – *Sunday Times*

READ MORE IN PENGUIN

A CHOICE OF NON-FICTION

Ginsberg: A Biography   Barry Miles

The definitive life of one of this century's most colourful poets. 'A life so dramatic, so dangerous, so committed to hard-volume truth, that his survival is a miracle, his kindness, wisdom and modesty a blessing' – *The Times*. 'Read it to the end' – Michael Horovitz

Coleridge: Early Visions   Richard Holmes

'Dazzling … Holmes has not merely reinterpreted Coleridge; he has re-created him, and his biography has the aura of fiction, the shimmer of an authentic portrait … a biography like few I have ever read' – *Guardian*. 'Coleridge lives, and talks and loves … in these pages as never before' – *Independent*

The Speeches of Winston Churchill   David Cannadine (ed.)

The most eloquent statesman of his time, Winston Churchill used language as his most powerful weapon. These orations, spanning fifty years, show him gradually honing his rhetoric until, with spectacular effect, 'he mobilized the English language, and sent it into battle'.

Higher than Hope   Fatima Meer

A dramatic, personal and intimate biography drawing on letters and reminiscences from Nelson Mandela himself and his close family, *Higher Than Hope* is an important tribute to one of the greatest living figures of our time. It is also a perceptive commentary on the situation in South Africa. No one concerned with politics or humanity can afford to miss it.

Among the Russians   Colin Thubron

'The Thubron approach to travelling has an integrity that belongs to another age. And this author's way with words gives his books a value far transcending their topical interest; it is safe to predict that they will be read a century hence' – Dervla Murphy in the *Irish Times*